W9-AYW-674

HARLEY'S LITTLE BLACK BOOK

WRITERS | AMANDA CONNER • JIMMY PALMIOTTI

ARTISTS | JOSEPH MICHAEL LINSNER • NEAL ADAMS • SIMON BISLEY • BILLY TUCCI • AMANDA CONNER
JOHN TIMMS • MAURICET • FLAVIANO • DAVE JOHNSON

Harley's Bla

LETTERERS | DAVE SHARPE • MARILYN PATRIZIO

COLORISTS | PAUL MOUNTS • HI-FI

COLLECTION COVER ARTISTS | AMANDA CONNER AND PAUL MOUNTS

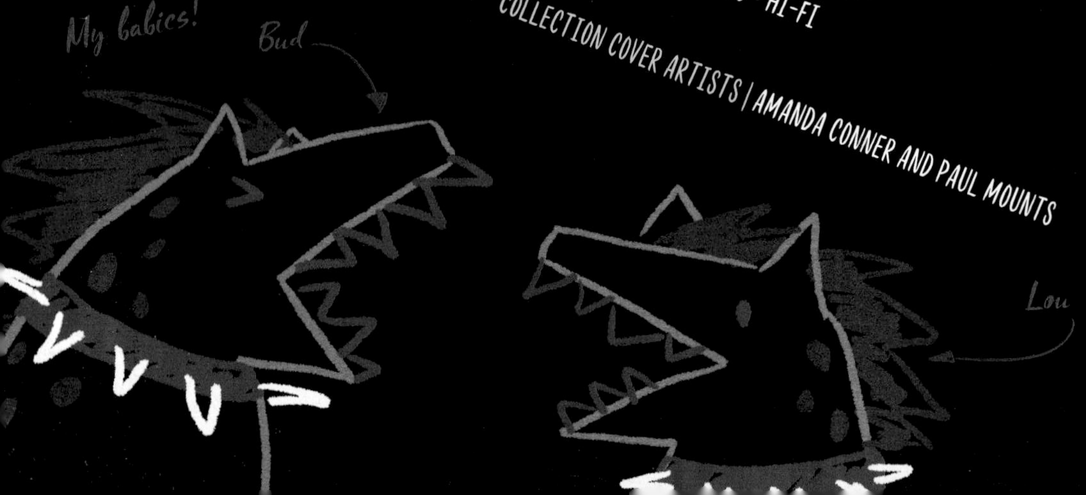
My babies!
Bud
Lou

Little

ck Book

Love ya both!

HARLEY QUINN CREATED BY PAUL DINI & BRUCE TIMM

WONDER WOMAN CREATED BY WILLIAM MOULTON MARSTON

ZATANNA CREATED BY GARDNER FOX AND MURPHY ANDERSON

LOBO CREATED BY KEITH GIFFEN AND ROGER SLIFER

SUPERMAN CREATED BY JERRY SIEGEL AND JOE SHUSTER
BY SPECIAL ARRANGEMENT WITH THE JERRY SIEGEL FAMILY

CHRIS CONROY Editor – Original Series
DAVE WIELGOSZ Assistant Editor – Original Series
JEB WOODARD Group Editor – Collected Editions
ROBIN WILDMAN Editor – Collected Edition
STEVE COOK Design Director – Books
MONIQUE GRUSPE Publication Design

BOB HARRAS Senior VP – Editor-in-Chief, DC Comics

DIANE NELSON President
DAN DiDIO Publisher
JIM LEE Publisher
GEOFF JOHNS President & Chief Creative Officer
AMIT DESAI Executive VP – Business & Marketing Strategy, Direct to Consumer & Global Franchise Management
SAM ADES Senior VP – Direct to Consumer
BOBBIE CHASE VP – Talent Development
MARK CHIARELLO Senior VP – Art, Design & Collected Editions
JOHN CUNNINGHAM Senior VP – Sales & Trade Marketing
ANNE DePIES Senior VP – Business Strategy, Finance & Administration
DON FALLETTI VP – Manufacturing Operations
LAWRENCE GANEM VP – Editorial Administration & Talent Relations
ALISON GILL Senior VP – Manufacturing & Operations
HANK KANALZ Senior VP – Editorial Strategy & Administration
JAY KOGAN VP – Legal Affairs
THOMAS LOFTUS VP – Business Affairs
JACK MAHAN VP – Business Affairs
NICK J. NAPOLITANO VP – Manufacturing Administration
EDDIE SCANNELL VP – Consumer Marketing
COURTNEY SIMMONS Senior VP – Publicity & Communications
JIM (SKI) SOKOLOWSKI VP – Comic Book Specialty Sales & Trade Marketing
NANCY SPEARS VP – Mass, Book, Digital Sales & Trade Marketing

HARLEY'S LITTLE BLACK BOOK

DC Comics, 2900 West Alameda Ave., Burbank, CA 91505
Printed LSC Communications, Salem, VA. 6/30/17. First Printing.
ISBN: 978-1-4012-6976-0

Library of Congress Cataloging-in-Publication Data is available.

PEFC Certified
Printed on paper from sustainably managed forests, controlled sources
PEFC
PEFC/29-31-337
www.pefc.org

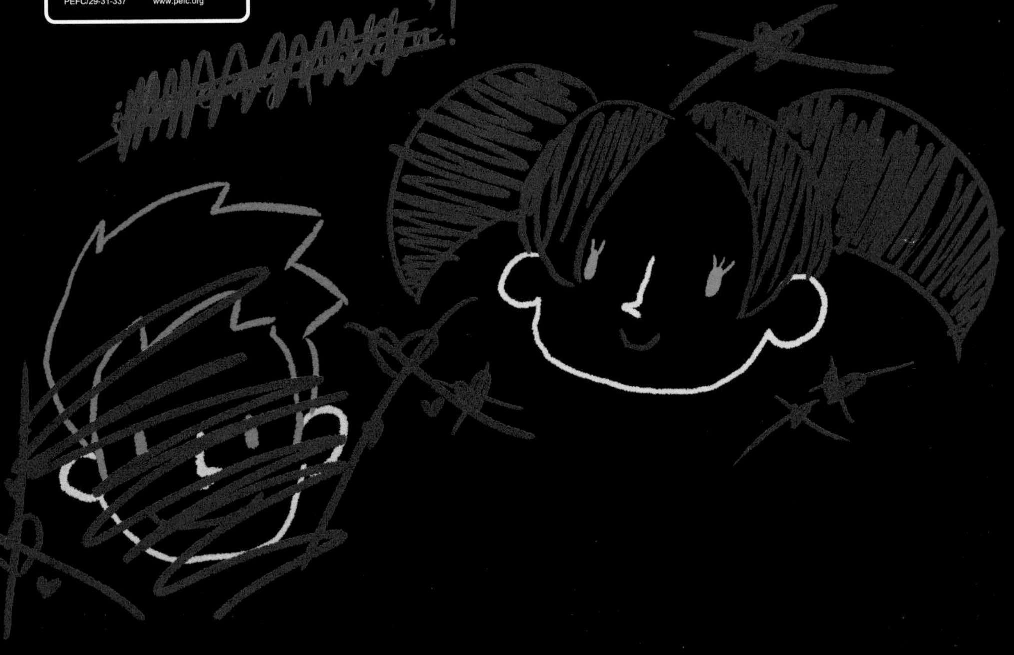

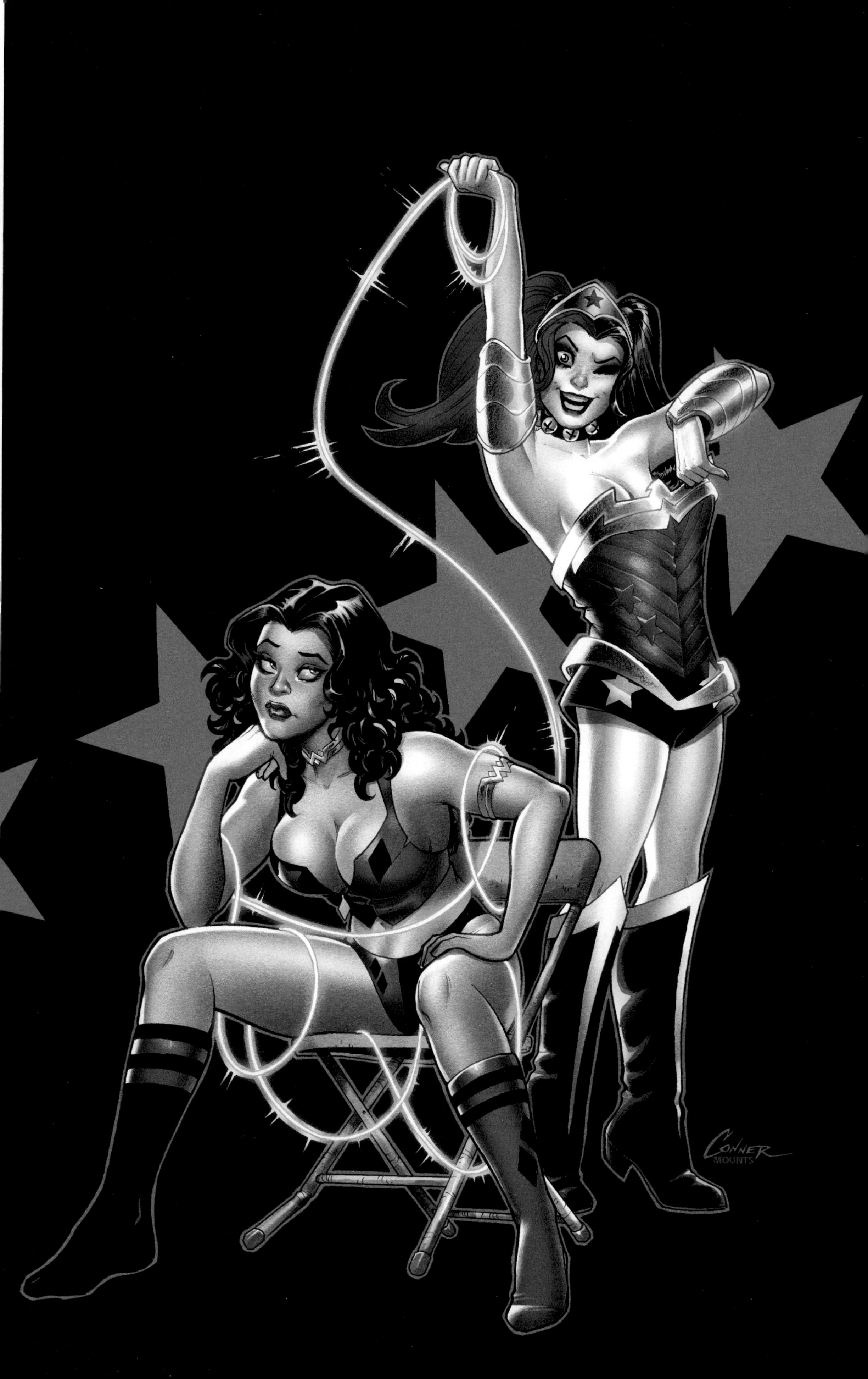
CONNER
MOUNTS

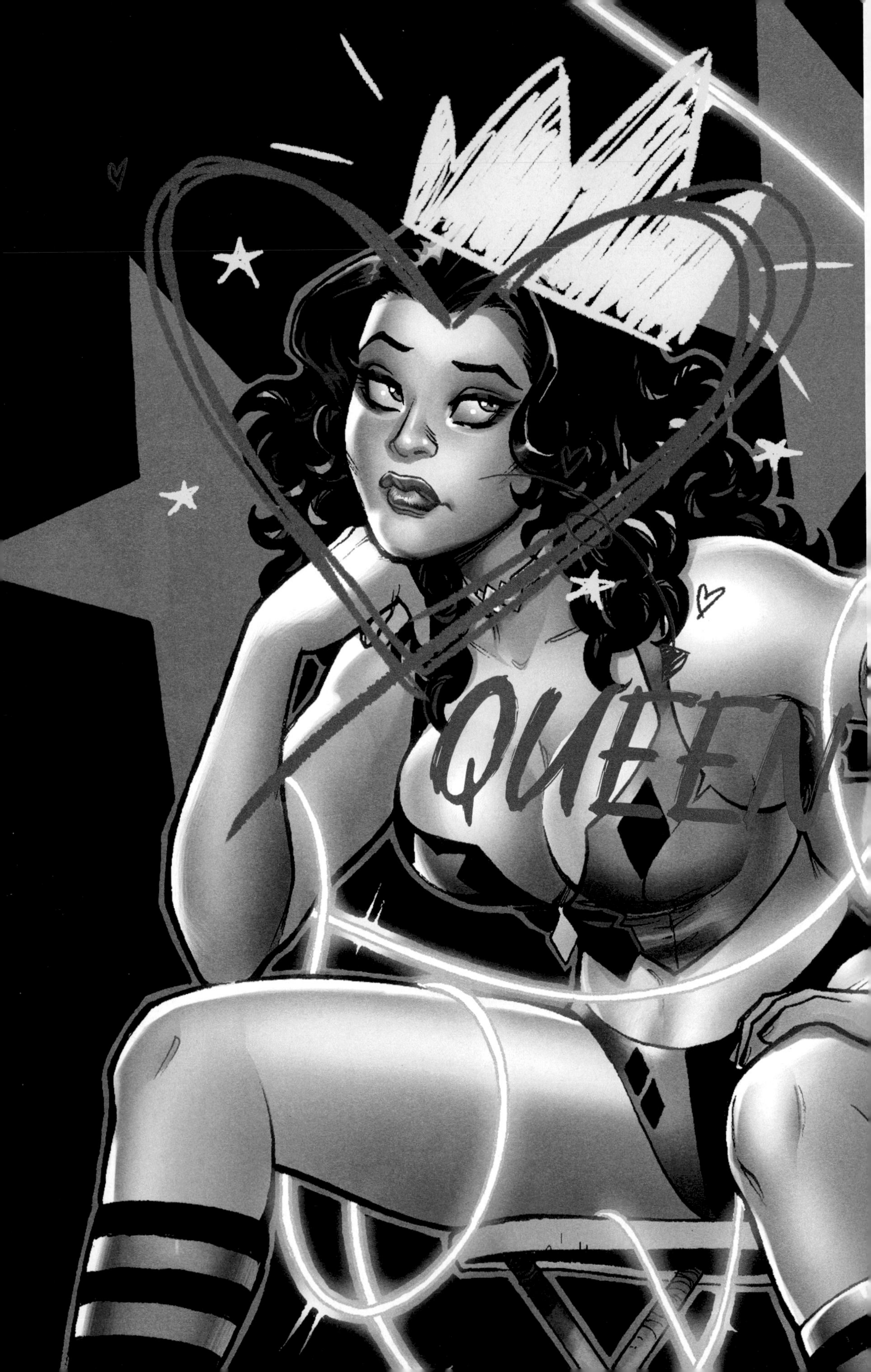
QUEE

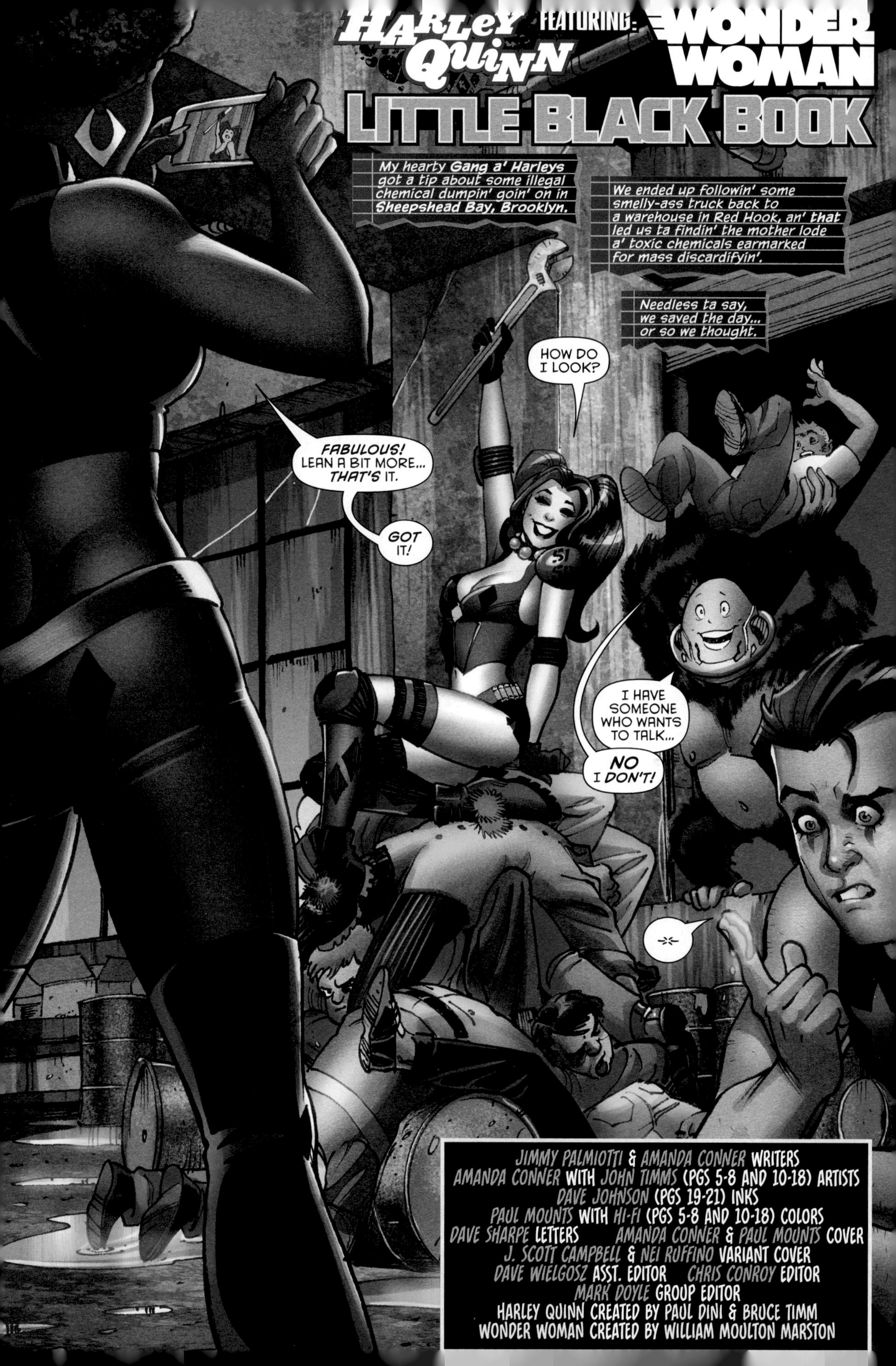
HARLEY QUINN FEATURING: WONDER WOMAN
LITTLE BLACK BOOK
My hearty Gang a' Harleys got a tip about some illegal chemical dumpin' goin' on in Sheepshead Bay, Brooklyn.
We ended up followin' some smelly-ass truck back to a warehouse in Red Hook, an' that led us ta findin' the mother lode a' toxic chemicals earmarked for mass discardifyin'.
Needless ta say, we saved the day... or so we thought.
HOW DO I LOOK?
FABULOUS! LEAN A BIT MORE... THAT'S IT.
GOT IT!
I HAVE SOMEONE WHO WANTS TO TALK...
NO I DON'T!
JIMMY PALMIOTTI & AMANDA CONNER WRITERS
AMANDA CONNER WITH JOHN TIMMS (PGS 5-8 AND 10-18) ARTISTS
DAVE JOHNSON (PGS 19-21) INKS
PAUL MOUNTS WITH HI-FI (PGS 5-8 AND 10-18) COLORS
DAVE SHARPE LETTERS AMANDA CONNER & PAUL MOUNTS COVER
J. SCOTT CAMPBELL & NEI RUFFINO VARIANT COVER
DAVE WIELGOSZ ASST. EDITOR CHRIS CONROY EDITOR
MARK DOYLE GROUP EDITOR
HARLEY QUINN CREATED BY PAUL DINI & BRUCE TIMM
WONDER WOMAN CREATED BY WILLIAM MOULTON MARSTON

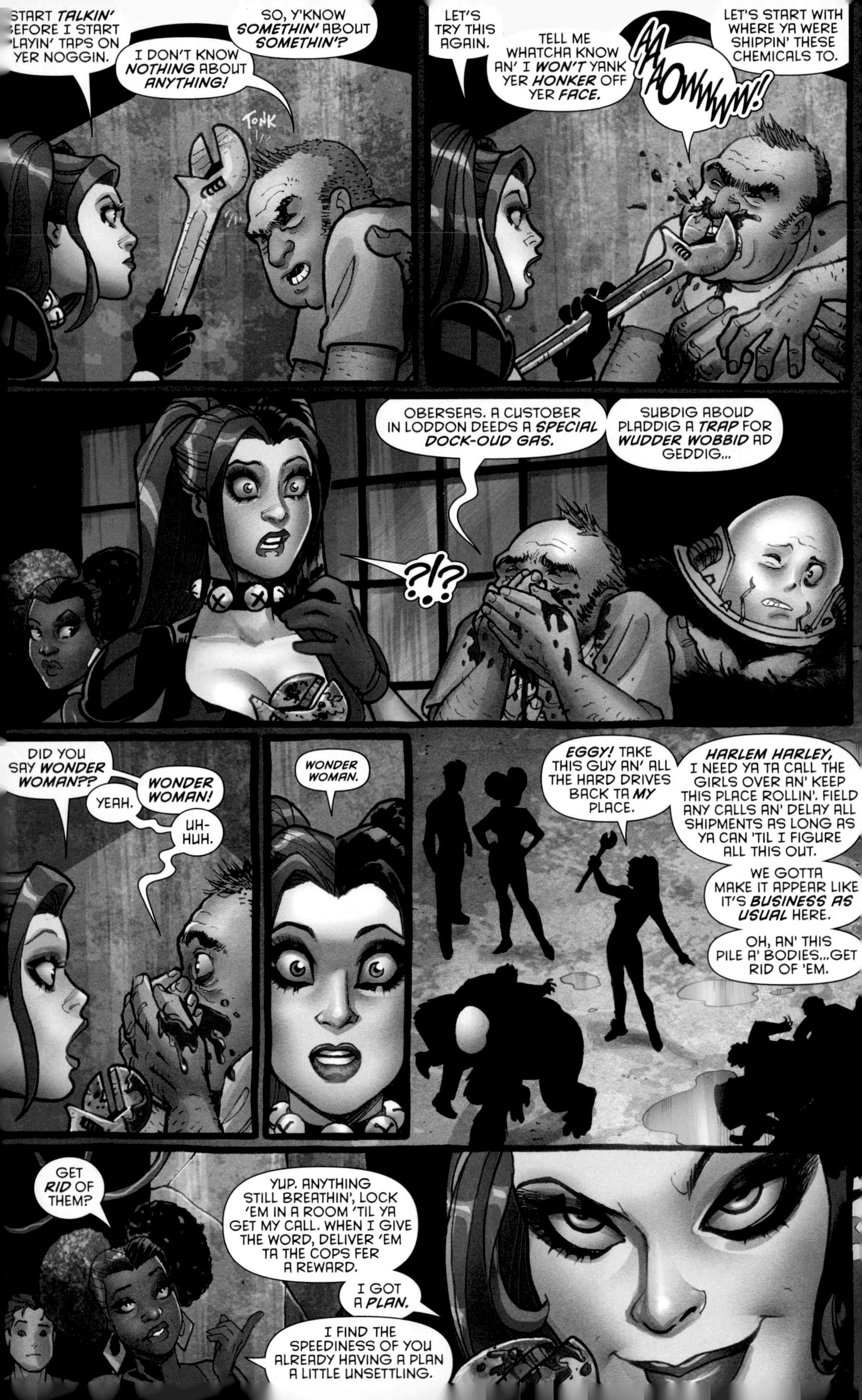

START TALKIN' BEFORE I START PLAYIN' TAPS ON YER NOGGIN.
SO, Y'KNOW SOMETHIN' ABOUT SOMETHIN'?
I DON'T KNOW NOTHING ABOUT ANYTHING!
TONK
LET'S TRY THIS AGAIN.
TELL ME WHATCHA KNOW AN' I WON'T YANK YER HONKER OFF YER FACE.
AAAOWWWW!
LET'S START WITH WHERE YA WERE SHIPPIN' THESE CHEMICALS TO.
OBERSEAS. A CUSTOBER IN LODDON DEEDS A SPECIAL DOCK-OUD GAS.
SUBDIG ABOUD PLADDIG A TRAP FOR WUDDER WOBBID AD GEDDIG...
?!?
DID YOU SAY WONDER WOMAN??
YEAH.
WONDER WOMAN!
UH-HUH.
WONDER WOMAN.
EGGY! TAKE THIS GUY AN' ALL THE HARD DRIVES BACK TA MY PLACE.
HARLEM HARLEY, I NEED YA TA CALL THE GIRLS OVER AN' KEEP THIS PLACE ROLLIN'. FIELD ANY CALLS AN' DELAY ALL SHIPMENTS AS LONG AS YA CAN 'TIL I FIGURE ALL THIS OUT.
WE GOTTA MAKE IT APPEAR LIKE IT'S BUSINESS AS USUAL HERE.
OH, AN' THIS PILE A' BODIES...GET RID OF 'EM.
GET RID OF THEM?
YUP. ANYTHING STILL BREATHIN', LOCK 'EM IN A ROOM 'TIL YA GET MY CALL. WHEN I GIVE THE WORD, DELIVER 'EM TA THE COPS FER A REWARD.
I GOT A PLAN.
I FIND THE SPEEDINESS OF YOU ALREADY HAVING A PLAN A LITTLE UNSETTLING.

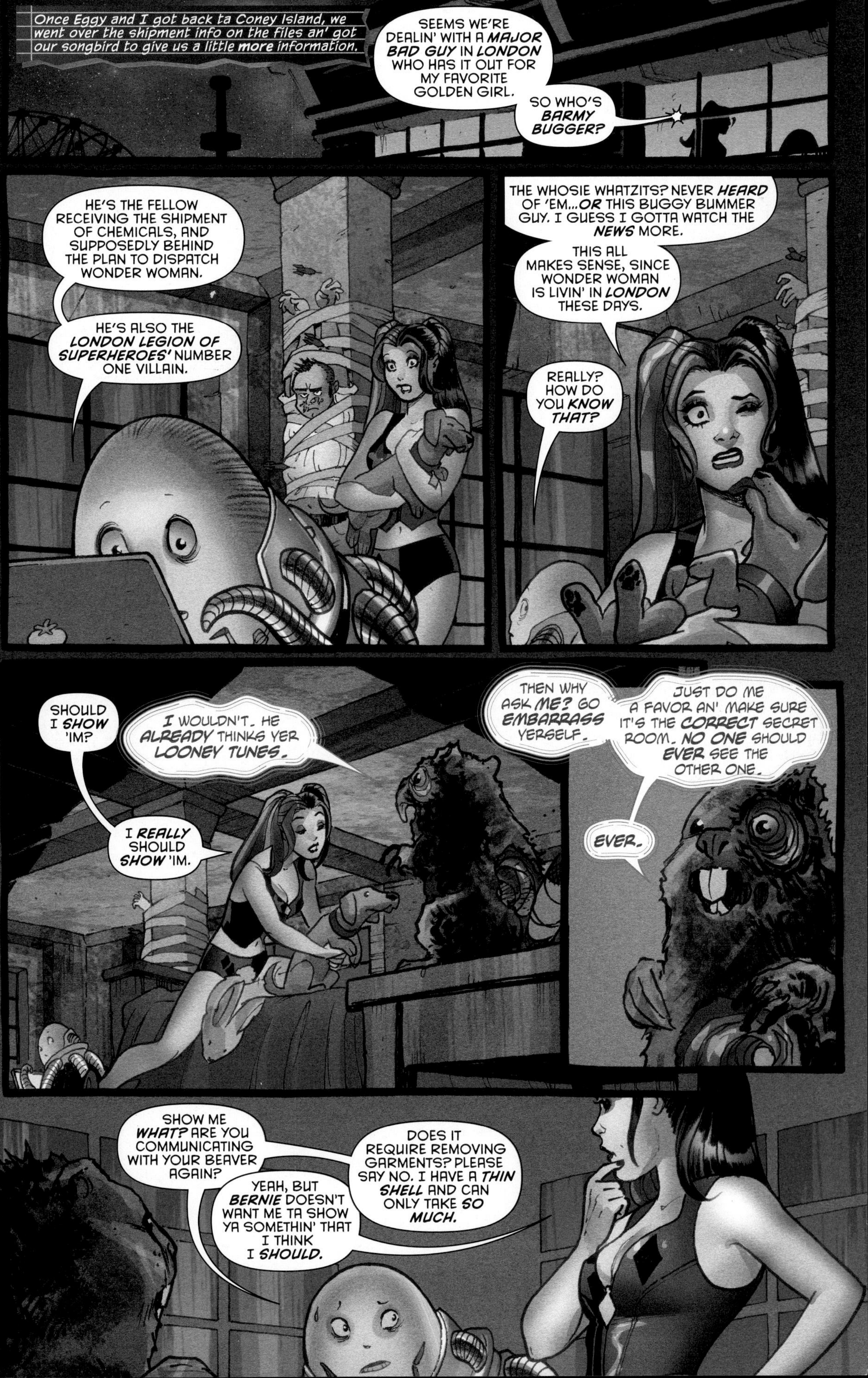
Once Eggy and I got back ta Coney Island, we went over the shipment info on the files an' got our songbird to give us a little more information.
SEEMS WE'RE DEALIN' WITH A MAJOR BAD GUY IN LONDON WHO HAS IT OUT FOR MY FAVORITE GOLDEN GIRL.
SO WHO'S BARMY BUGGER?
HE'S THE FELLOW RECEIVING THE SHIPMENT OF CHEMICALS, AND SUPPOSEDLY BEHIND THE PLAN TO DISPATCH WONDER WOMAN.
HE'S ALSO THE LONDON LEGION OF SUPERHEROES' NUMBER ONE VILLAIN.
THE WHOSIE WHATZITS? NEVER HEARD OF 'EM...OR THIS BUGGY BUMMER GUY. I GUESS I GOTTA WATCH THE NEWS MORE.
THIS ALL MAKES SENSE, SINCE WONDER WOMAN IS LIVIN' IN LONDON THESE DAYS.
REALLY? HOW DO YOU KNOW THAT?
SHOULD I SHOW 'IM?
I WOULDN'T. HE ALREADY THINKS YER LOONEY TUNES.
I REALLY SHOULD SHOW 'IM.
THEN WHY ASK ME? GO EMBARRASS YERSELF.
JUST DO ME A FAVOR AN' MAKE SURE IT'S THE CORRECT SECRET ROOM. NO ONE SHOULD EVER SEE THE OTHER ONE.
EVER.
SHOW ME WHAT? ARE YOU COMMUNICATING WITH YOUR BEAVER AGAIN?
YEAH, BUT BERNIE DOESN'T WANT ME TA SHOW YA SOMETHIN' THAT I THINK I SHOULD.
DOES IT REQUIRE REMOVING GARMENTS? PLEASE SAY NO. I HAVE A THIN SHELL AND CAN ONLY TAKE SO MUCH.

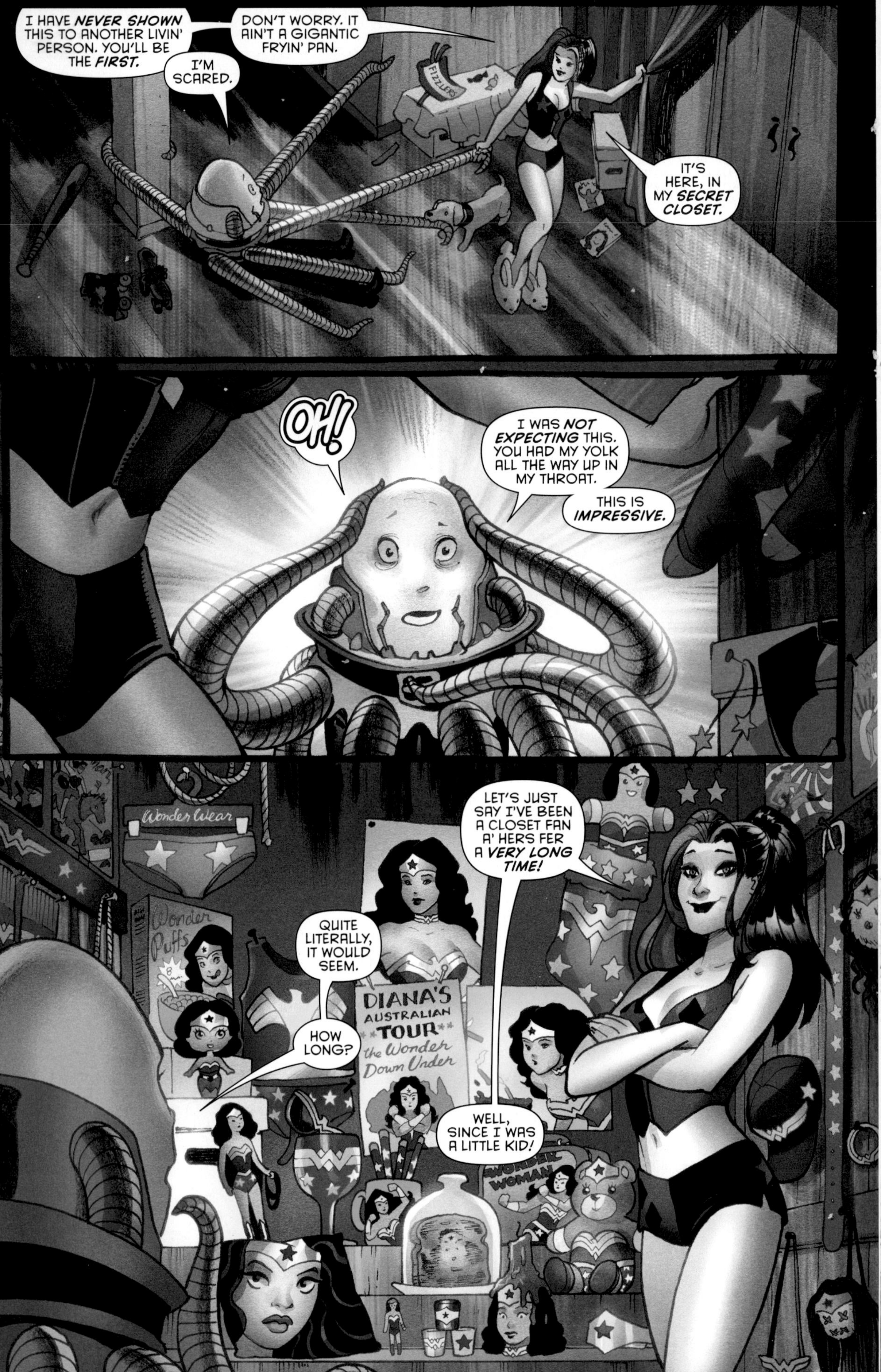
I HAVE NEVER SHOWN THIS TO ANOTHER LIVIN' PERSON. YOU'LL BE THE FIRST.
I'M SCARED.
DON'T WORRY. IT AIN'T A GIGANTIC FRYIN' PAN.
FIZZLERS
IT'S HERE, IN MY SECRET CLOSET.
OH!
I WAS NOT EXPECTING THIS. YOU HAD MY YOLK ALL THE WAY UP IN MY THROAT.
THIS IS IMPRESSIVE.
Wonder Wear
Wonder Puffs
LET'S JUST SAY I'VE BEEN A CLOSET FAN A' HERS FER A VERY LONG TIME!
QUITE LITERALLY, IT WOULD SEEM.
DIANA'S AUSTRALIAN TOUR the Wonder Down Under
HOW LONG?
WELL, SINCE I WAS A LITTLE KID!
WONDER WOMAN

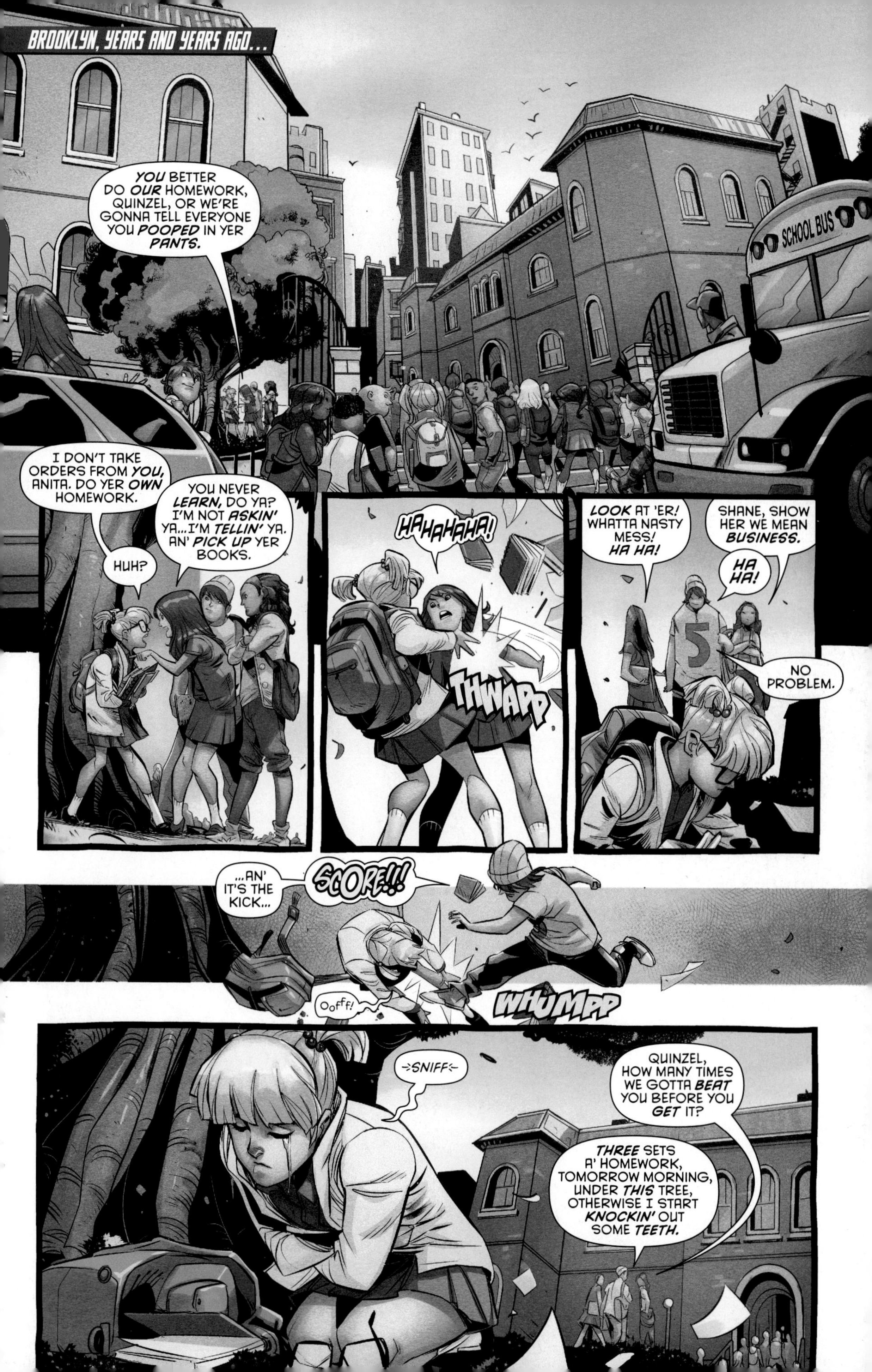
BROOKLYN, YEARS AND YEARS AGO...
YOU BETTER DO OUR HOMEWORK, QUINZEL, OR WE'RE GONNA TELL EVERYONE YOU POOPED IN YER PANTS.
SCHOOL BUS
I DON'T TAKE ORDERS FROM YOU, ANITA. DO YER OWN HOMEWORK.
HUH?
YOU NEVER LEARN, DO YA? I'M NOT ASKIN' YA...I'M TELLIN' YA. AN' PICK UP YER BOOKS.
HAHAHAHA!
THWAPP
LOOK AT 'ER! WHATTA NASTY MESS! HA HA!
SHANE, SHOW HER WE MEAN BUSINESS.
HA HA!
NO PROBLEM.
...AN' IT'S THE KICK...
SCORE!!!
OOFFF!
WHUMPP
-SNIFF-
QUINZEL, HOW MANY TIMES WE GOTTA BEAT YOU BEFORE YOU GET IT?
THREE SETS A' HOMEWORK, TOMORROW MORNING, UNDER THIS TREE, OTHERWISE I START KNOCKIN' OUT SOME TEETH.

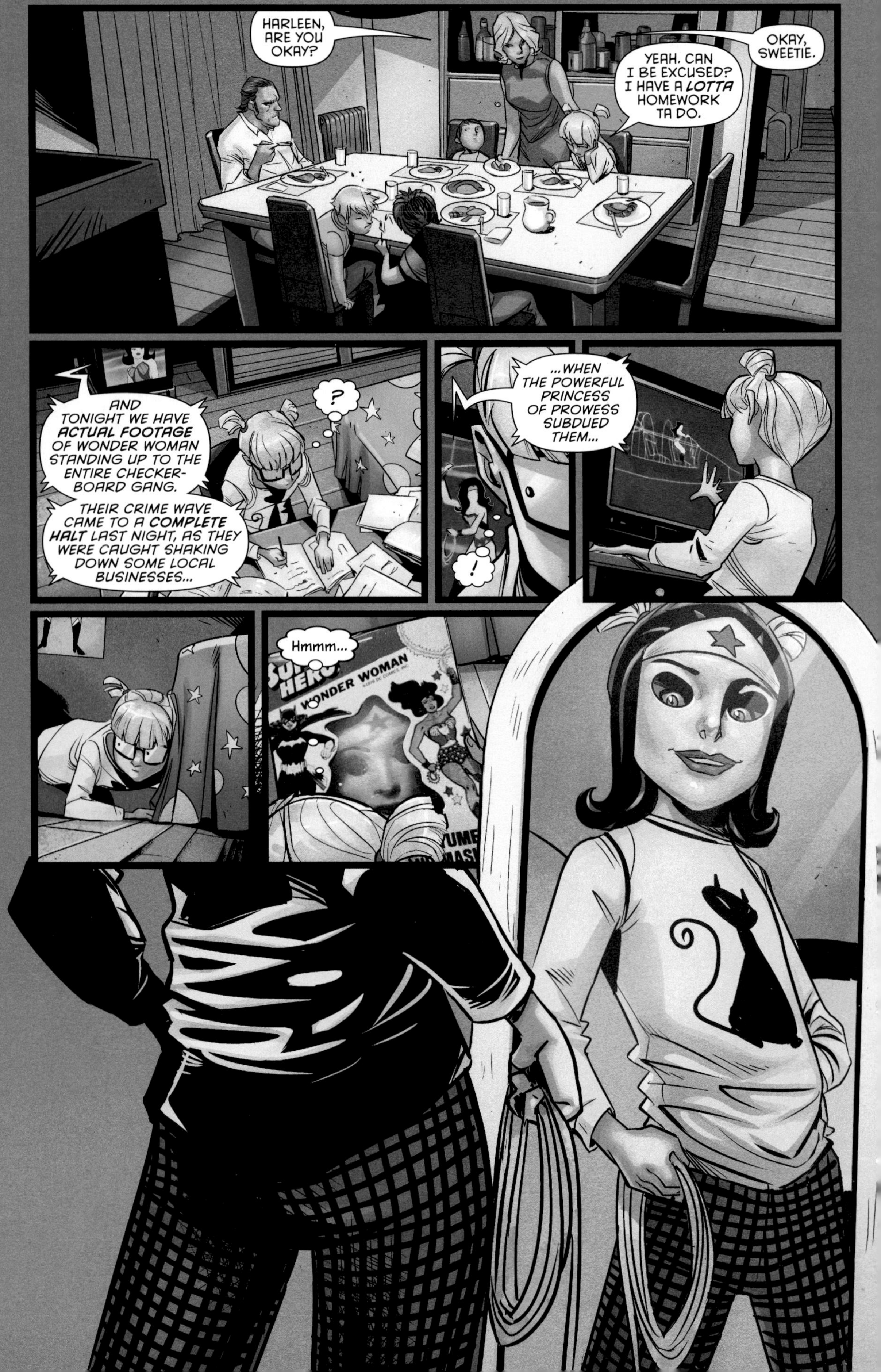
HARLEEN, ARE YOU OKAY?
YEAH. CAN I BE EXCUSED? I HAVE A LOTTA HOMEWORK TA DO.
OKAY, SWEETIE.
AND TONIGHT WE HAVE ACTUAL FOOTAGE OF WONDER WOMAN STANDING UP TO THE ENTIRE CHECKER-BOARD GANG.
THEIR CRIME WAVE CAME TO A COMPLETE HALT LAST NIGHT, AS THEY WERE CAUGHT SHAKING DOWN SOME LOCAL BUSINESSES...
?
...WHEN THE POWERFUL PRINCESS OF PROWESS SUBDUED THEM...
!
Hmmm...
WONDER WOMAN

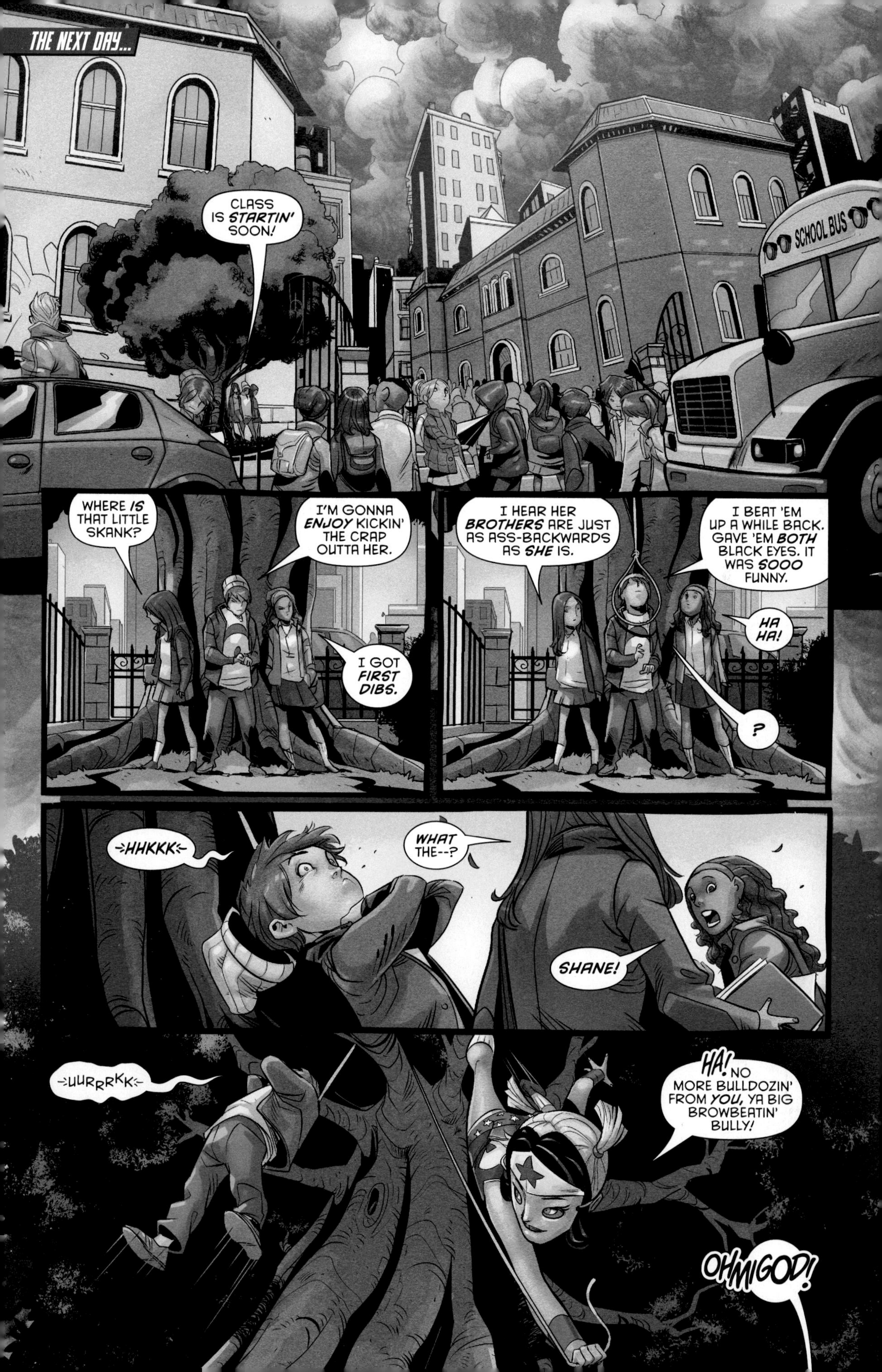
THE NEXT DAY...
CLASS IS STARTIN' SOON!
SCHOOL BUS
WHERE IS THAT LITTLE SKANK?
I'M GONNA ENJOY KICKIN' THE CRAP OUTTA HER.
I GOT FIRST DIBS.
I HEAR HER BROTHERS ARE JUST AS ASS-BACKWARDS AS SHE IS.
I BEAT 'EM UP A WHILE BACK. GAVE 'EM BOTH BLACK EYES. IT WAS SOOO FUNNY.
HA HA!
?
-HHKKK-
WHAT THE--?
SHANE!
-UURRRKK-
HA! NO MORE BULLDOZIN' FROM YOU, YA BIG BROWBEATIN' BULLY!
OHMIGOD!

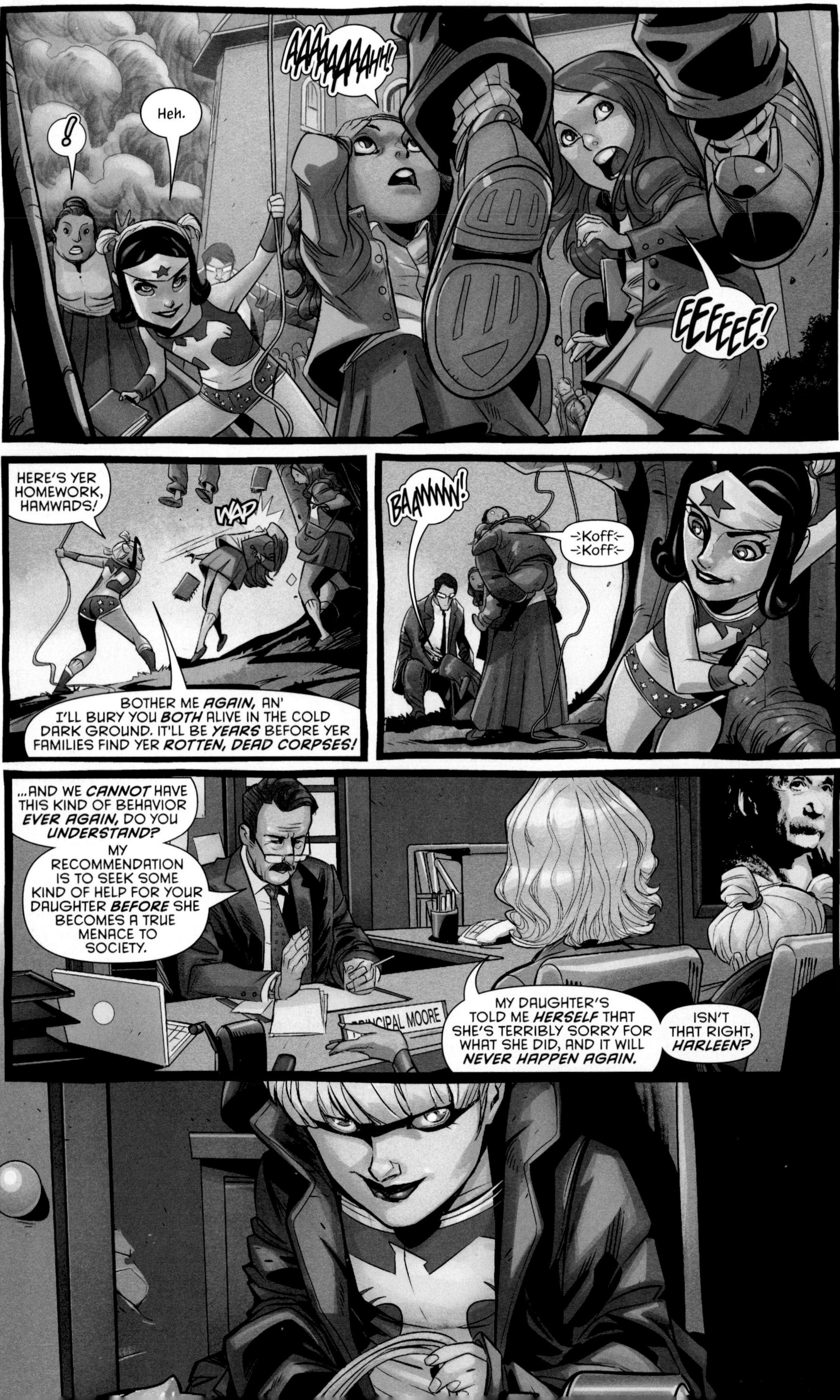
AAAAAAAAAHH!
!
Heh.
EEEEEE!
HERE'S YER HOMEWORK, HAMWADS!
WAP
BOTHER ME AGAIN, AN' I'LL BURY YOU BOTH ALIVE IN THE COLD DARK GROUND. IT'LL BE YEARS BEFORE YER FAMILIES FIND YER ROTTEN, DEAD CORPSES!
BAAWWW!
Koff Koff
...AND WE CANNOT HAVE THIS KIND OF BEHAVIOR EVER AGAIN, DO YOU UNDERSTAND?
MY RECOMMENDATION IS TO SEEK SOME KIND OF HELP FOR YOUR DAUGHTER BEFORE SHE BECOMES A TRUE MENACE TO SOCIETY.
PRINCIPAL MOORE
MY DAUGHTER'S TOLD ME HERSELF THAT SHE'S TERRIBLY SORRY FOR WHAT SHE DID, AND IT WILL NEVER HAPPEN AGAIN.
ISN'T THAT RIGHT, HARLEEN?

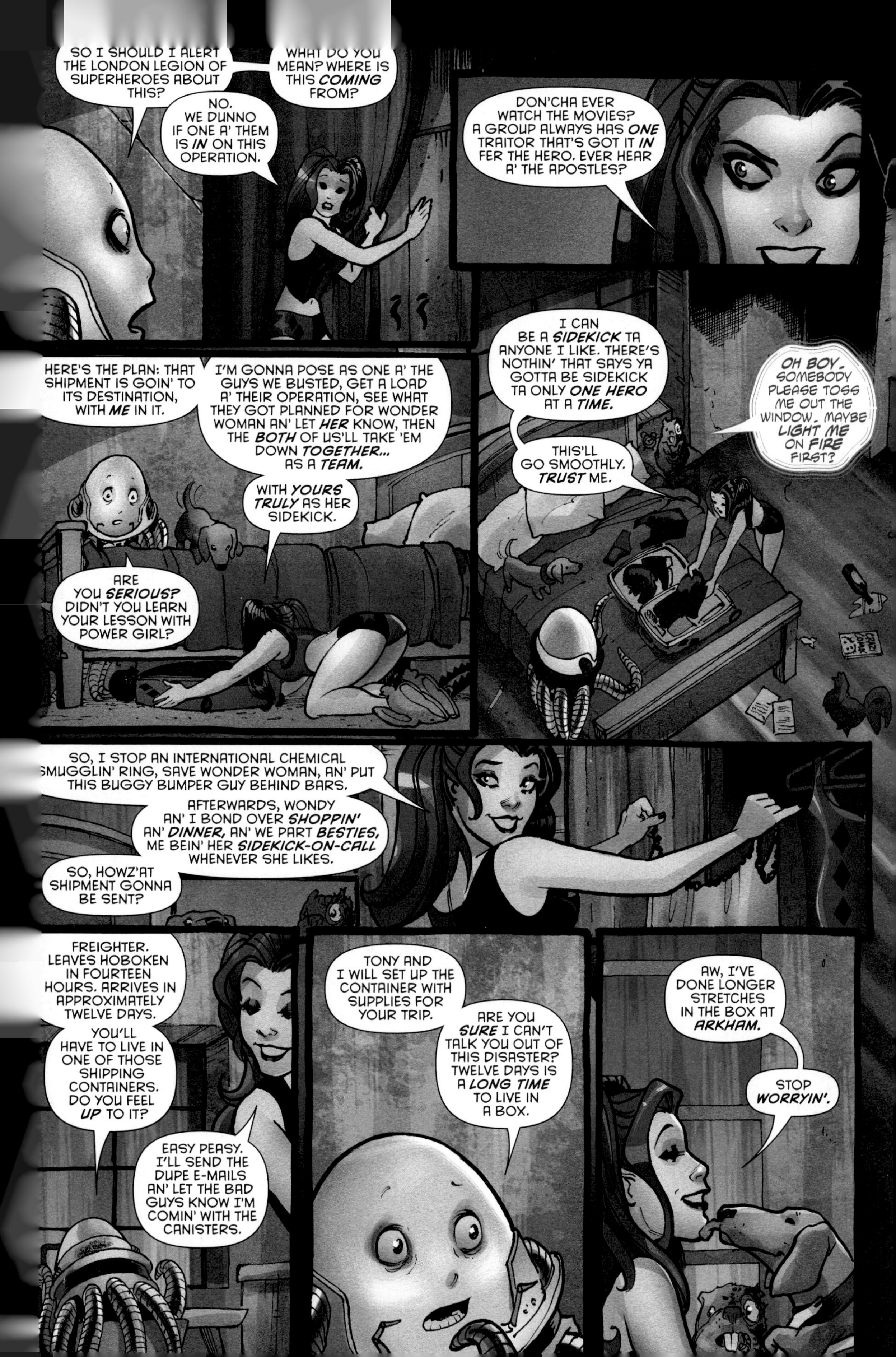
SO I SHOULD I ALERT THE LONDON LEGION OF SUPERHEROES ABOUT THIS?
WHAT DO YOU MEAN? WHERE IS THIS COMING FROM?
NO. WE DUNNO IF ONE A' THEM IS IN ON THIS OPERATION.
DON'CHA EVER WATCH THE MOVIES? A GROUP ALWAYS HAS ONE TRAITOR THAT'S GOT IT IN FER THE HERO. EVER HEAR A' THE APOSTLES?
HERE'S THE PLAN: THAT SHIPMENT IS GOIN' TO ITS DESTINATION, WITH ME IN IT.
I'M GONNA POSE AS ONE A' THE GUYS WE BUSTED, GET A LOAD A' THEIR OPERATION, SEE WHAT THEY GOT PLANNED FOR WONDER WOMAN AN' LET HER KNOW, THEN THE BOTH OF US'LL TAKE 'EM DOWN TOGETHER... AS A TEAM.
WITH YOURS TRULY AS HER SIDEKICK.
ARE YOU SERIOUS? DIDN'T YOU LEARN YOUR LESSON WITH POWER GIRL?
I CAN BE A SIDEKICK TA ANYONE I LIKE. THERE'S NOTHIN' THAT SAYS YA GOTTA BE SIDEKICK TA ONLY ONE HERO AT A TIME.
THIS'LL GO SMOOTHLY. TRUST ME.
OH BOY. SOMEBODY PLEASE TOSS ME OUT THE WINDOW. MAYBE LIGHT ME ON FIRE FIRST?
SO, I STOP AN INTERNATIONAL CHEMICAL SMUGGLIN' RING, SAVE WONDER WOMAN, AN' PUT THIS BUGGY BUMPER GUY BEHIND BARS.
AFTERWARDS, WONDY AN' I BOND OVER SHOPPIN' AN' DINNER, AN' WE PART BESTIES, ME BEIN' HER SIDEKICK-ON-CALL WHENEVER SHE LIKES.
SO, HOWZ'AT SHIPMENT GONNA BE SENT?
FREIGHTER. LEAVES HOBOKEN IN FOURTEEN HOURS. ARRIVES IN APPROXIMATELY TWELVE DAYS.
YOU'LL HAVE TO LIVE IN ONE OF THOSE SHIPPING CONTAINERS. DO YOU FEEL UP TO IT?
EASY PEASY. I'LL SEND THE DUPE E-MAILS AN' LET THE BAD GUYS KNOW I'M COMIN' WITH THE CANISTERS.
TONY AND I WILL SET UP THE CONTAINER WITH SUPPLIES FOR YOUR TRIP.
ARE YOU SURE I CAN'T TALK YOU OUT OF THIS DISASTER? TWELVE DAYS IS A LONG TIME TO LIVE IN A BOX.
AW, I'VE DONE LONGER STRETCHES IN THE BOX AT ARKHAM.
STOP WORRYIN'.

LONDON'S NOT CALLING

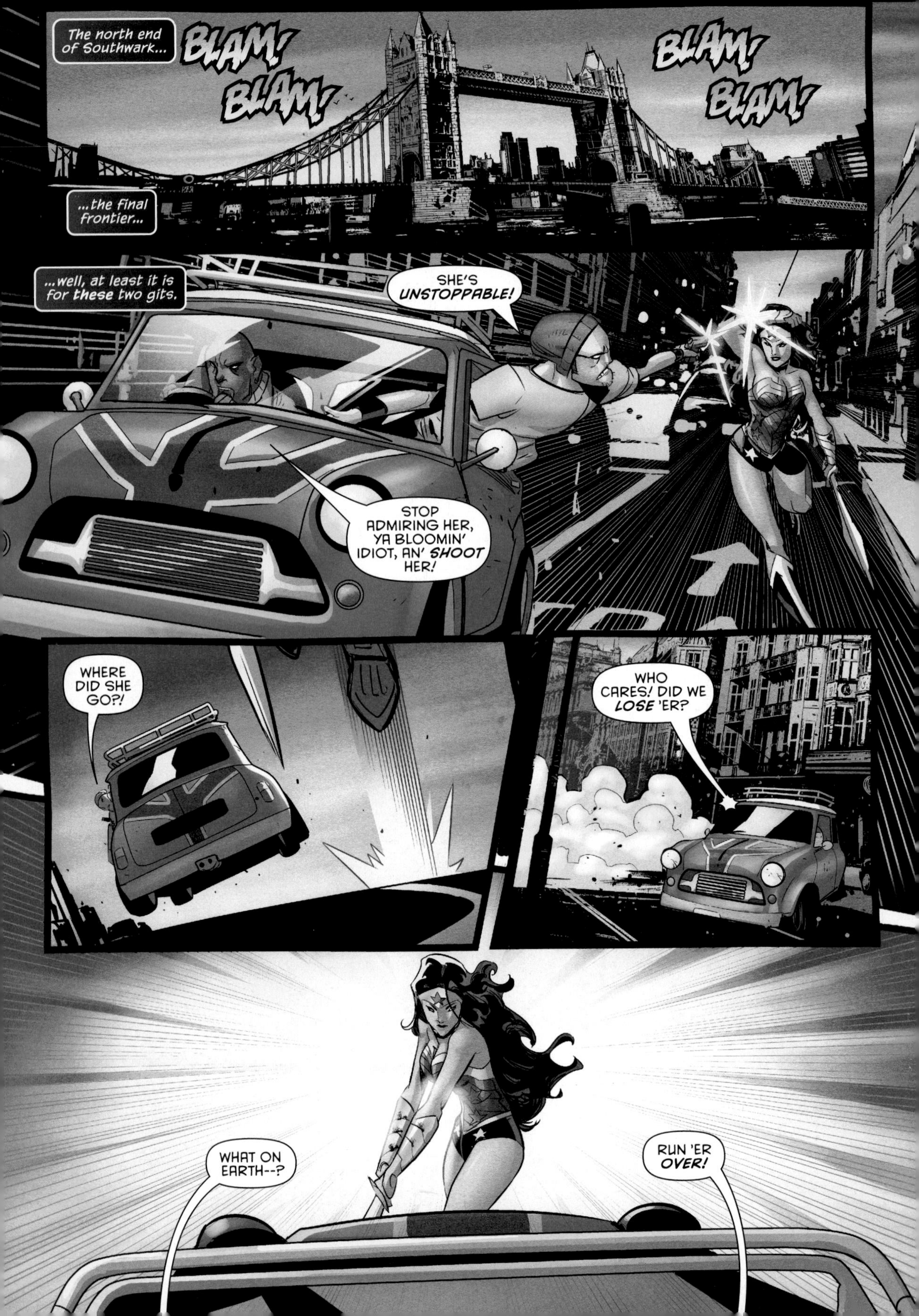

The north end of Southwark...
BLAM! BLAM!
BLAM! BLAM!
...the final frontier...
...well, at least it is for these two gits.
SHE'S UNSTOPPABLE!
STOP ADMIRING HER, YA BLOOMIN' IDIOT, AN' SHOOT HER!
WHERE DID SHE GO?!
WHO CARES! DID WE LOSE 'ER?
WHAT ON EARTH--?
RUN 'ER OVER!

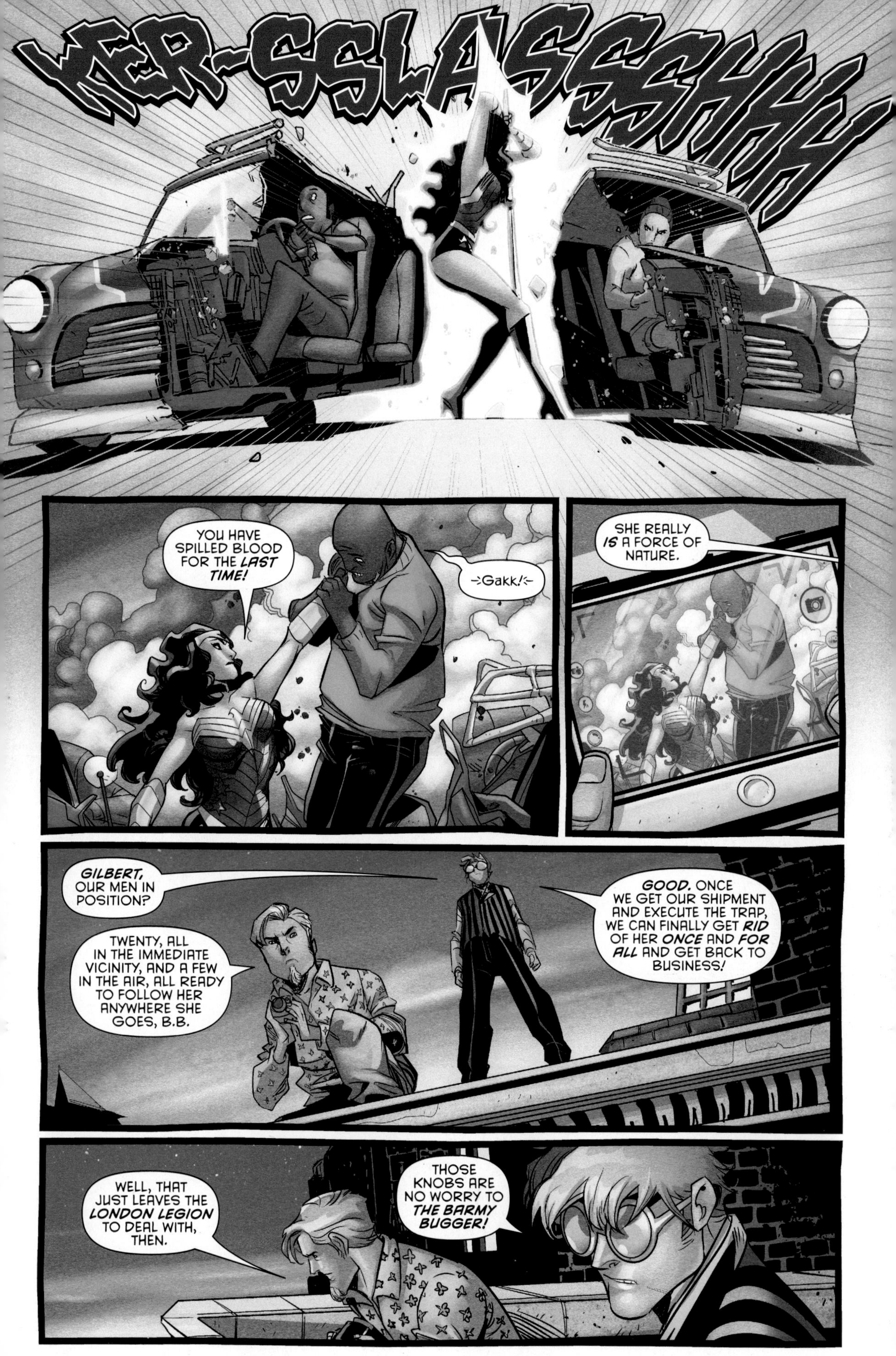

KER-SSLASSSHHH
YOU HAVE SPILLED BLOOD FOR THE *LAST TIME!*
-Gakk!-
SHE REALLY *IS* A FORCE OF NATURE.
GILBERT, OUR MEN IN POSITION?
TWENTY, ALL IN THE IMMEDIATE VICINITY, AND A FEW IN THE AIR, ALL READY TO FOLLOW HER ANYWHERE SHE GOES, B.B.
GOOD. ONCE WE GET OUR SHIPMENT AND EXECUTE THE TRAP, WE CAN FINALLY GET *RID* OF HER *ONCE* AND *FOR ALL* AND GET BACK TO BUSINESS!
WELL, THAT JUST LEAVES THE *LONDON LEGION* TO DEAL WITH, THEN.
THOSE KNOBS ARE NO WORRY TO *THE BARMY BUGGER!*

KNOBS OF WORRY

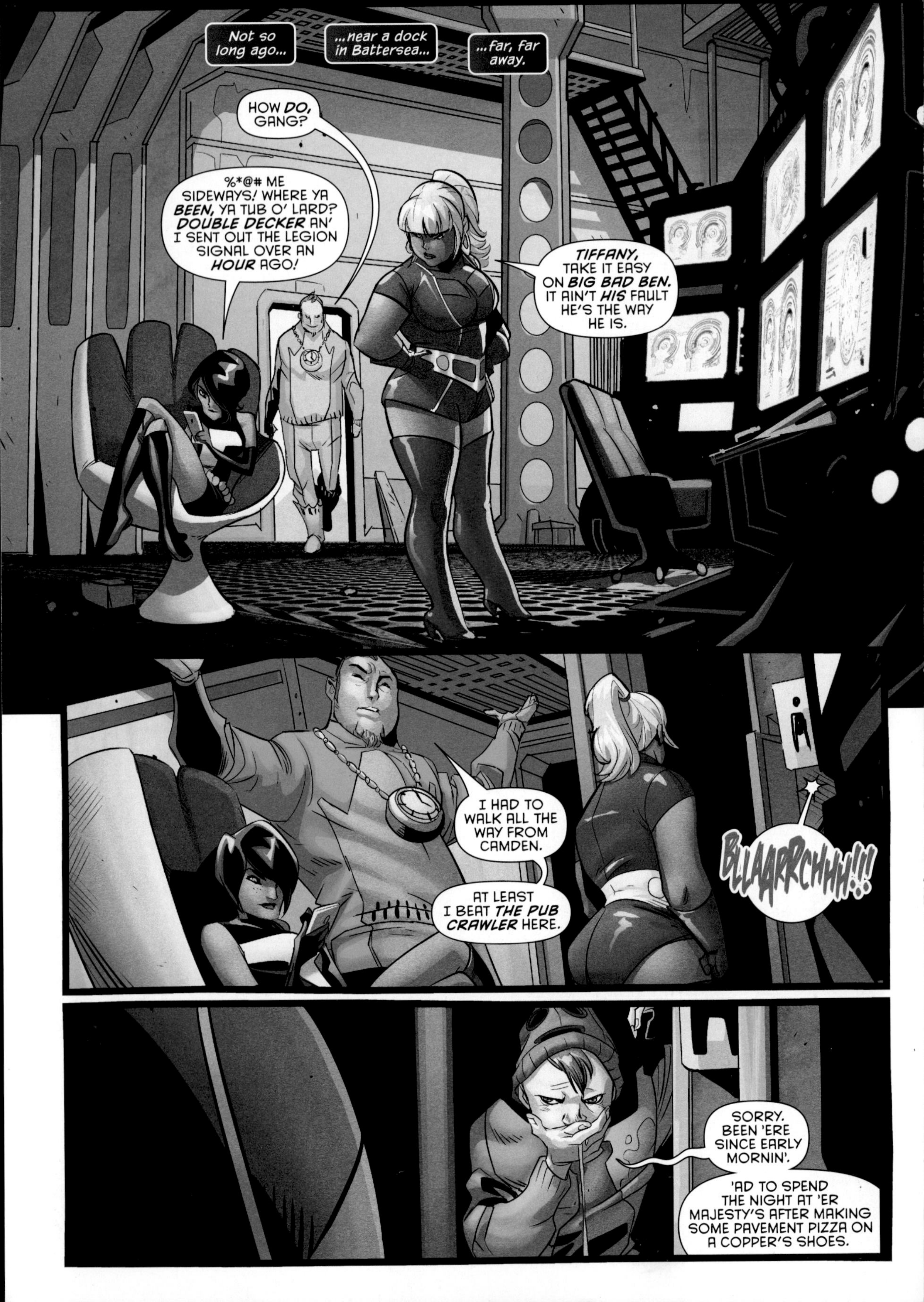

Not so long ago...
...near a dock in Battersea...
...far, far away.
HOW DO, GANG?
%*@# ME SIDEWAYS! WHERE YA BEEN, YA TUB O' LARD? DOUBLE DECKER AN' I SENT OUT THE LEGION SIGNAL OVER AN HOUR AGO!
TIFFANY, TAKE IT EASY ON BIG BAD BEN. IT AIN'T HIS FAULT HE'S THE WAY HE IS.
I HAD TO WALK ALL THE WAY FROM CAMDEN.
AT LEAST I BEAT THE PUB CRAWLER HERE.
BLLAARRCHHH!!!
SORRY. BEEN 'ERE SINCE EARLY MORNIN'.
'AD TO SPEND THE NIGHT AT 'ER MAJESTY'S AFTER MAKING SOME PAVEMENT PIZZA ON A COPPER'S SHOES.

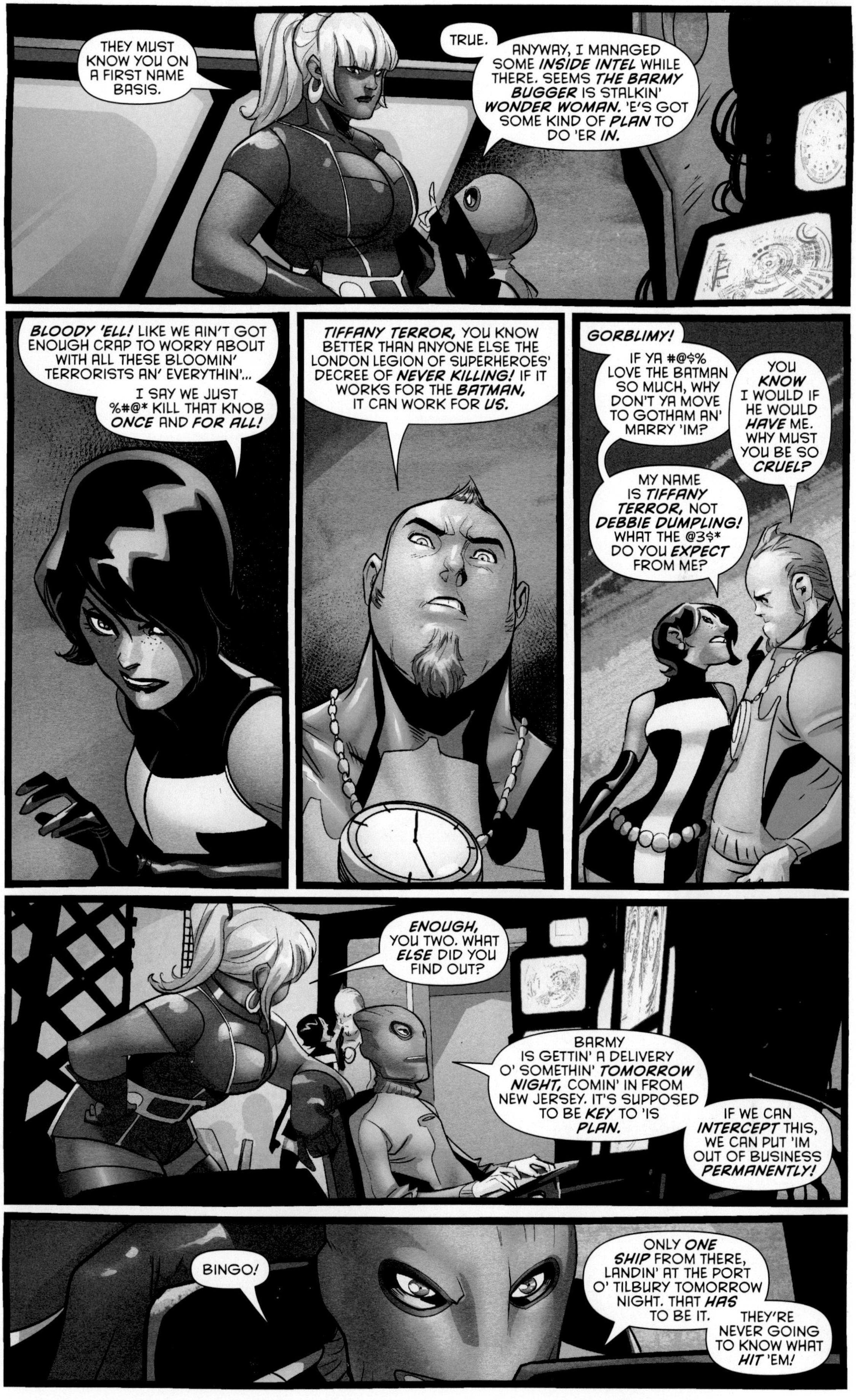

THEY MUST KNOW YOU ON A FIRST NAME BASIS.
TRUE.
ANYWAY, I MANAGED SOME INSIDE INTEL WHILE THERE. SEEMS THE BARMY BUGGER IS STALKIN' WONDER WOMAN. 'E'S GOT SOME KIND OF PLAN TO DO 'ER IN.
BLOODY 'ELL! LIKE WE AIN'T GOT ENOUGH CRAP TO WORRY ABOUT WITH ALL THESE BLOOMIN' TERRORISTS AN' EVERYTHIN'...
I SAY WE JUST %#@* KILL THAT KNOB ONCE AND FOR ALL!
TIFFANY TERROR, YOU KNOW BETTER THAN ANYONE ELSE THE LONDON LEGION OF SUPERHEROES' DECREE OF NEVER KILLING! IF IT WORKS FOR THE BATMAN, IT CAN WORK FOR US.
GORBLIMY!
IF YA #@$% LOVE THE BATMAN SO MUCH, WHY DON'T YA MOVE TO GOTHAM AN' MARRY 'IM?
YOU KNOW I WOULD IF HE WOULD HAVE ME. WHY MUST YOU BE SO CRUEL?
MY NAME IS TIFFANY TERROR, NOT DEBBIE DUMPLING! WHAT THE @3$* DO YOU EXPECT FROM ME?
ENOUGH, YOU TWO. WHAT ELSE DID YOU FIND OUT?
BARMY IS GETTIN' A DELIVERY O' SOMETHIN' TOMORROW NIGHT, COMIN' IN FROM NEW JERSEY. IT'S SUPPOSED TO BE KEY TO 'IS PLAN.
IF WE CAN INTERCEPT THIS, WE CAN PUT 'IM OUT OF BUSINESS PERMANENTLY!
BINGO!
ONLY ONE SHIP FROM THERE, LANDIN' AT THE PORT O' TILBURY TOMORROW NIGHT. THAT HAS TO BE IT.
THEY'RE NEVER GOING TO KNOW WHAT HIT 'EM!

BOX LUNCH

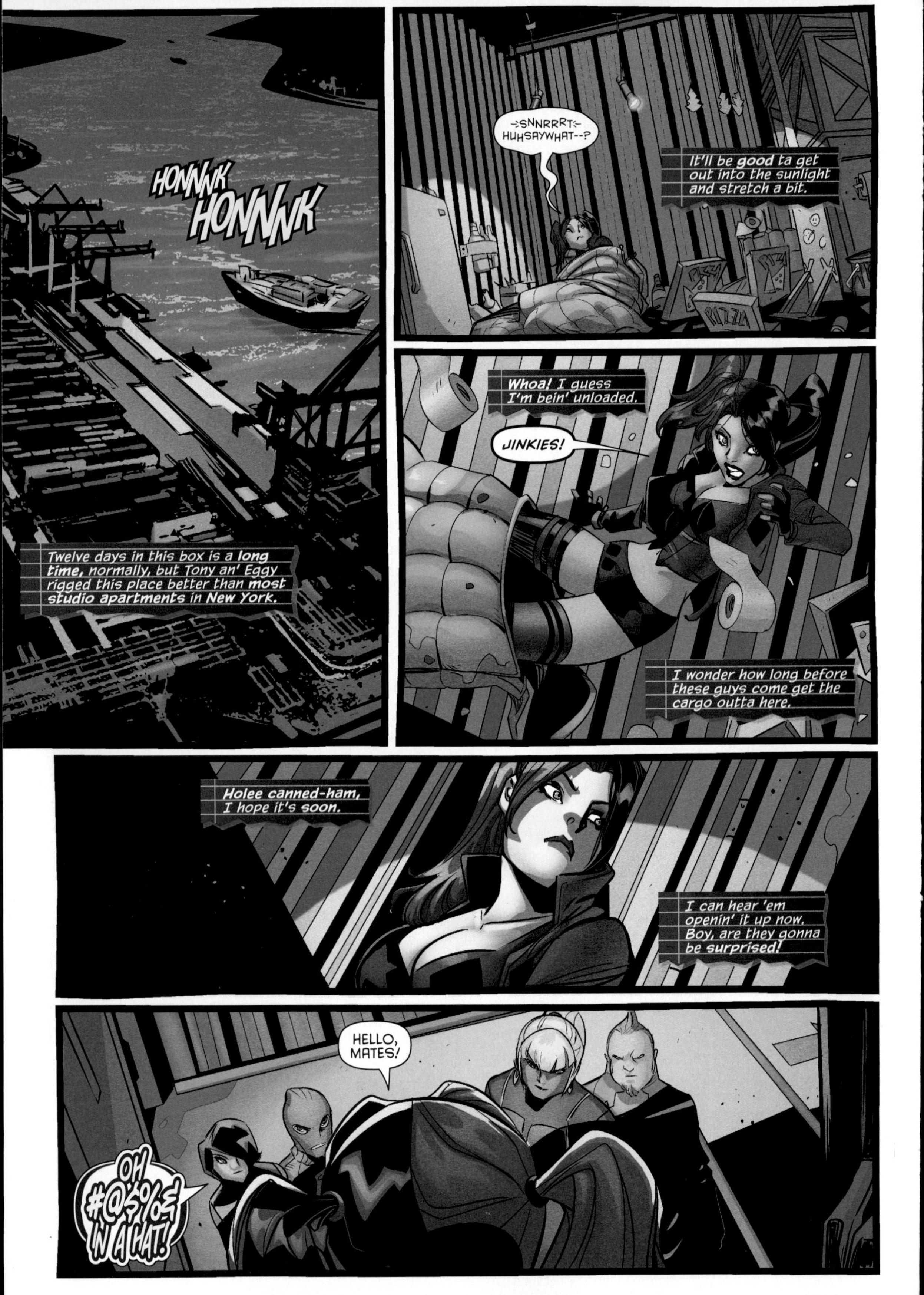

HONNNK
HONNNK
Twelve days in this box is a long time, normally, but Tony an' Eggy rigged this place better than most studio apartments in New York.
-SNNRRRT- HUHSAYWHAT--?
It'll be good ta get out into the sunlight and stretch a bit.
PIZZA
Whoa! I guess I'm bein' unloaded.
JINKIES!
I wonder how long before these guys come get the cargo outta here.
Holee canned-ham, I hope it's soon.
I can hear 'em openin' it up now. Boy, are they gonna be surprised!
HELLO, MATES!
OH #@$%& IN A HAT!

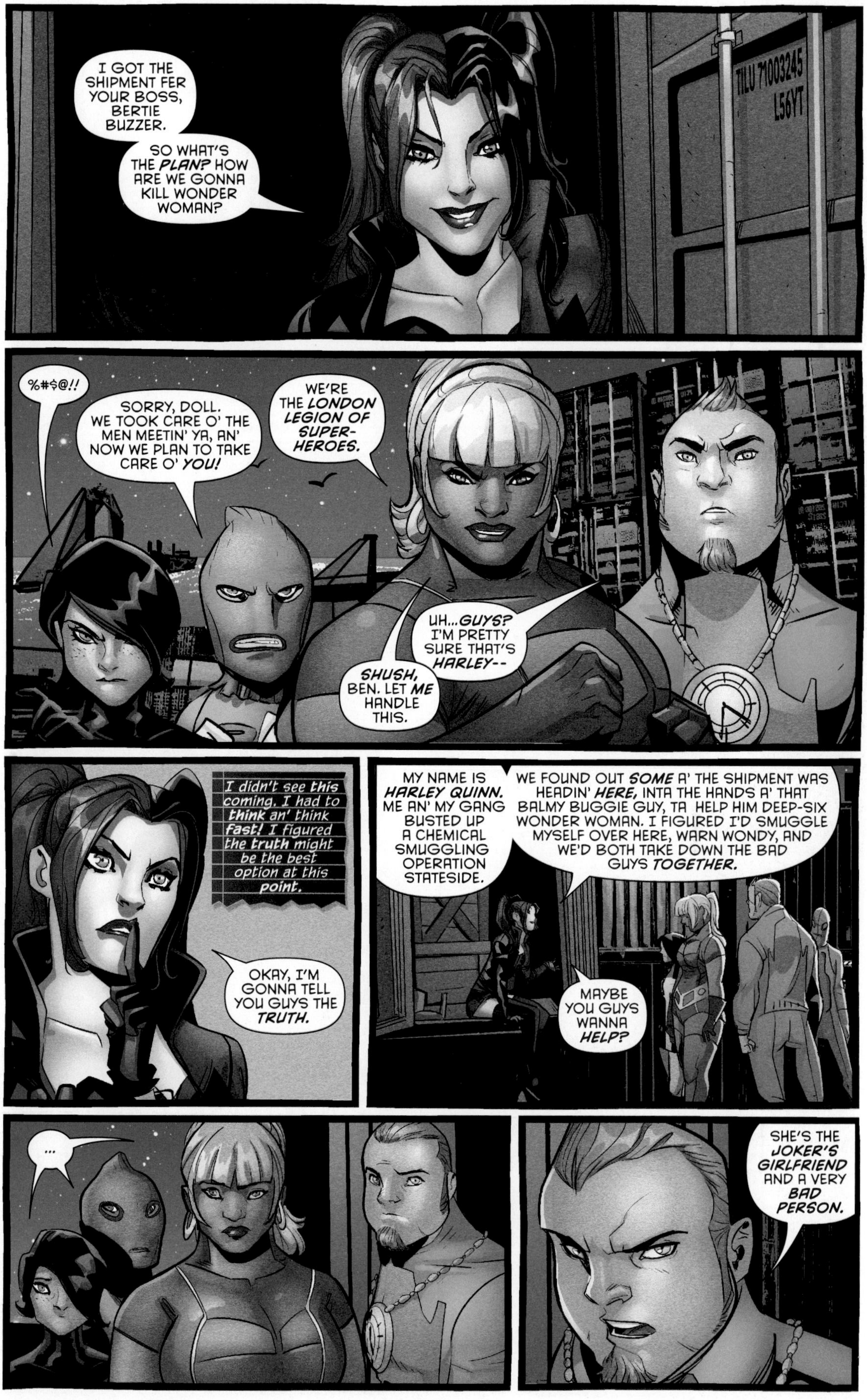
I GOT THE SHIPMENT FER YOUR BOSS, BERTIE BUZZER.
SO WHAT'S THE PLAN? HOW ARE WE GONNA KILL WONDER WOMAN?
TILU 71003245 L56YT
%#$@!!
SORRY, DOLL. WE TOOK CARE O' THE MEN MEETIN' YA, AN' NOW WE PLAN TO TAKE CARE O' YOU!
WE'RE THE LONDON LEGION OF SUPER-HEROES.
UH...GUYS? I'M PRETTY SURE THAT'S HARLEY--
SHUSH, BEN. LET ME HANDLE THIS.
I didn't see this coming. I had to think an' think fast! I figured the truth might be the best option at this point.
OKAY, I'M GONNA TELL YOU GUYS THE TRUTH.
MY NAME IS HARLEY QUINN. ME AN' MY GANG BUSTED UP A CHEMICAL SMUGGLING OPERATION STATESIDE.
WE FOUND OUT SOME A' THE SHIPMENT WAS HEADIN' HERE, INTA THE HANDS A' THAT BALMY BUGGIE GUY, TA HELP HIM DEEP-SIX WONDER WOMAN. I FIGURED I'D SMUGGLE MYSELF OVER HERE, WARN WONDY, AND WE'D BOTH TAKE DOWN THE BAD GUYS TOGETHER.
MAYBE YOU GUYS WANNA HELP?
...
SHE'S THE JOKER'S GIRLFRIEND AND A VERY BAD PERSON.

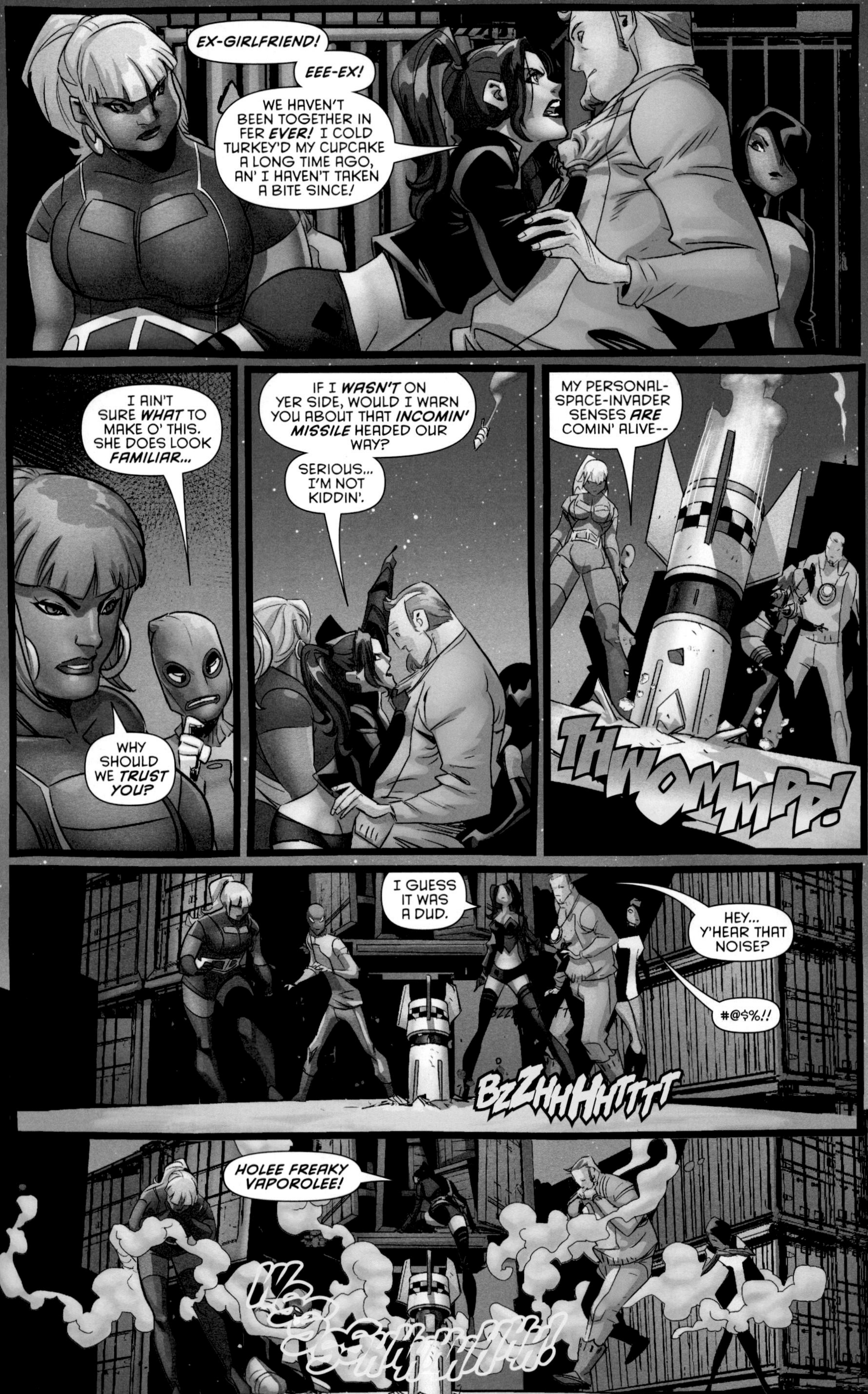
EX-GIRLFRIEND!
EEE-EX!
WE HAVEN'T BEEN TOGETHER IN FER EVER! I COLD TURKEY'D MY CUPCAKE A LONG TIME AGO, AN' I HAVEN'T TAKEN A BITE SINCE!
I AIN'T SURE WHAT TO MAKE O' THIS. SHE DOES LOOK FAMILIAR...
WHY SHOULD WE TRUST YOU?
IF I WASN'T ON YER SIDE, WOULD I WARN YOU ABOUT THAT INCOMIN' MISSILE HEADED OUR WAY?
SERIOUS... I'M NOT KIDDIN'.
MY PERSONAL-SPACE-INVADER SENSES ARE COMIN' ALIVE--
THWOMMPP!
I GUESS IT WAS A DUD.
HEY... Y'HEAR THAT NOISE?
#@$%!!
BZZHHHHTTTT
HOLEE FREAKY VAPOROLEE!

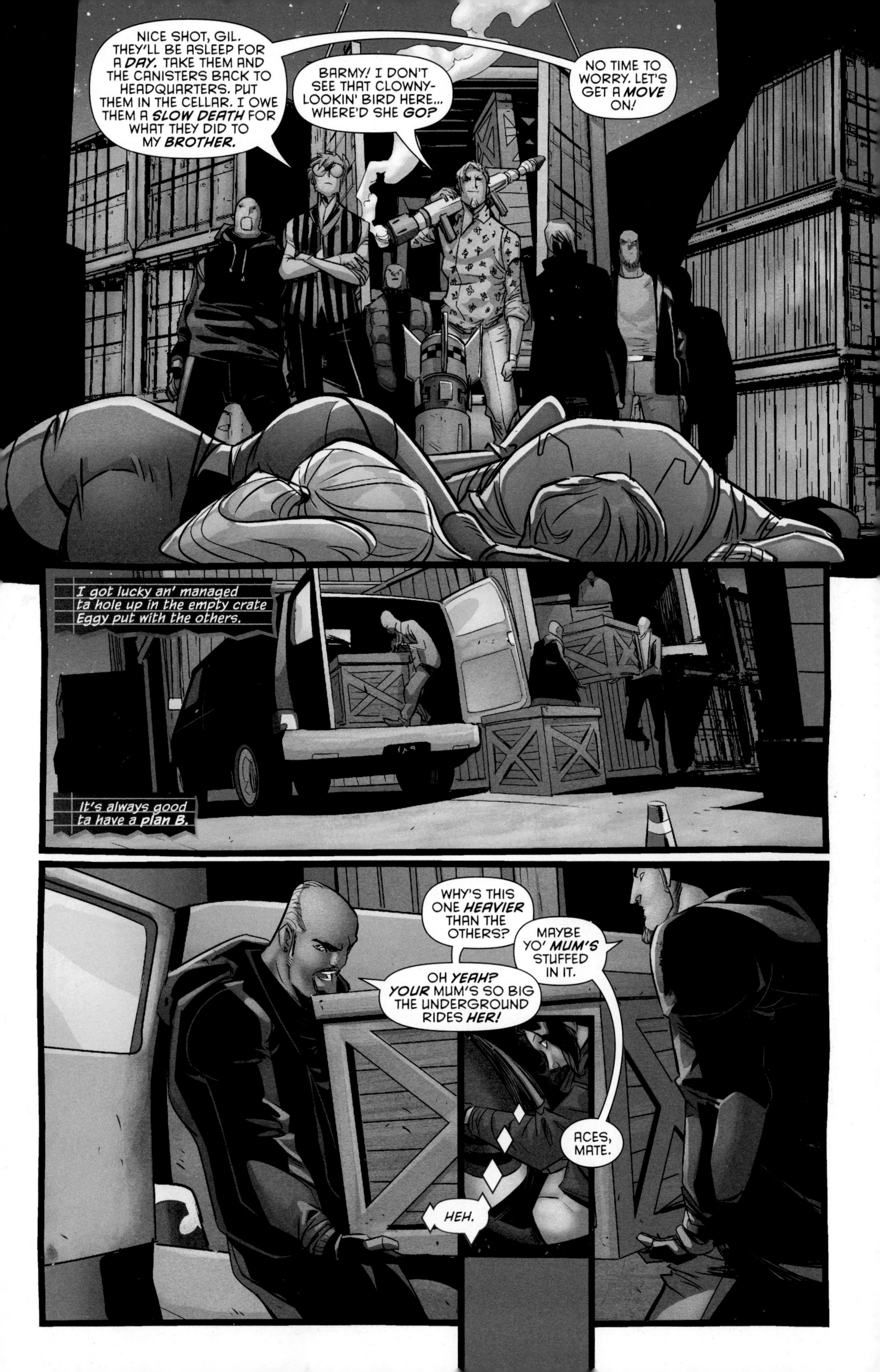
NICE SHOT, GIL. THEY'LL BE ASLEEP FOR A DAY. TAKE THEM AND THE CANISTERS BACK TO HEADQUARTERS. PUT THEM IN THE CELLAR. I OWE THEM A SLOW DEATH FOR WHAT THEY DID TO MY BROTHER.
NO TIME TO WORRY. LET'S GET A MOVE ON!
BARMY! I DON'T SEE THAT CLOWNY-LOOKIN' BIRD HERE... WHERE'D SHE GO?
I got lucky an' managed ta hole up in the empty crate Eggy put with the others.
It's always good ta have a plan B.
WHY'S THIS ONE HEAVIER THAN THE OTHERS?
MAYBE YO' MUM'S STUFFED IN IT.
OH YEAH? YOUR MUM'S SO BIG THE UNDERGROUND RIDES HER!
ACES, MATE.
HEH.

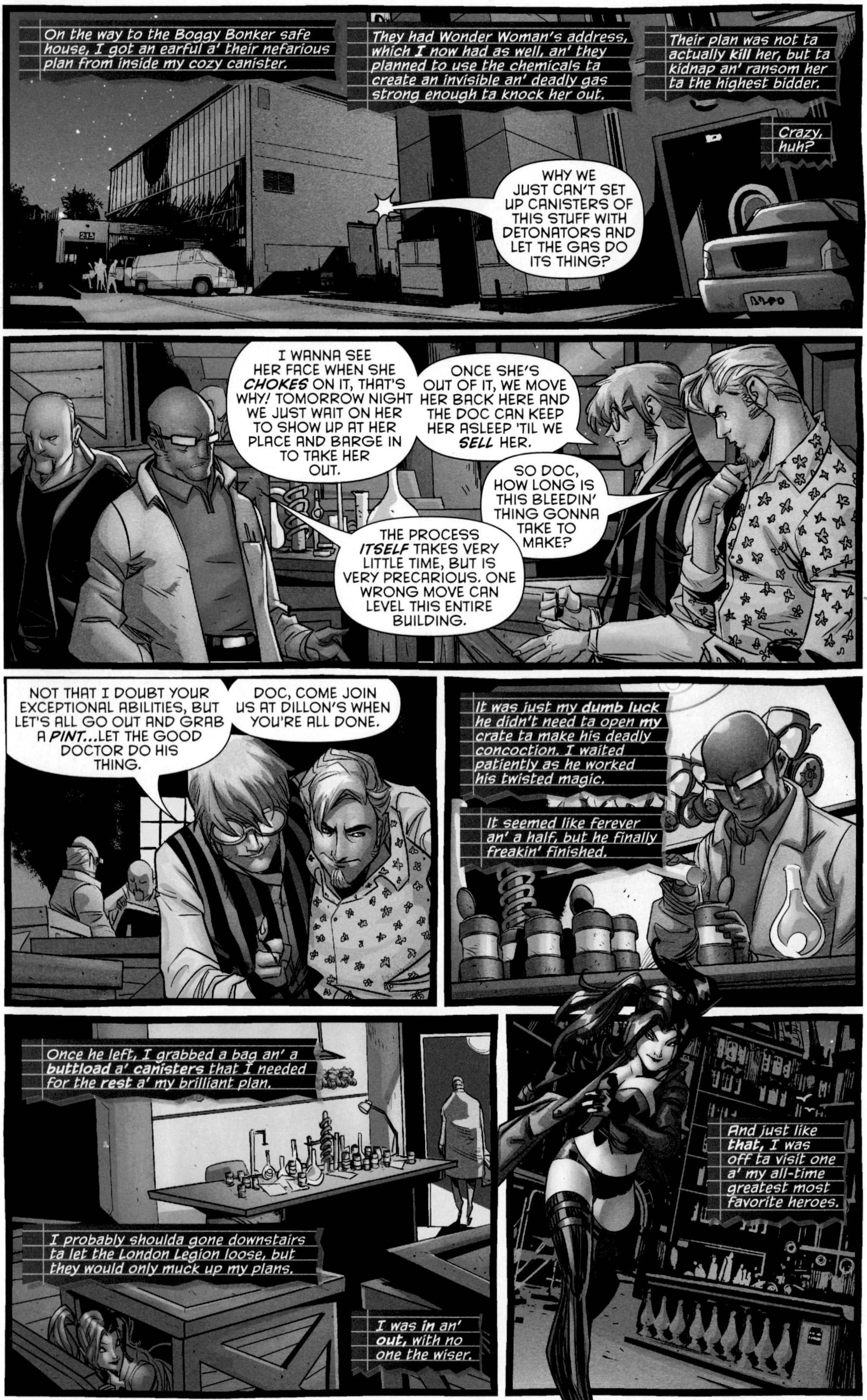

On the way to the Boggy Bonker safe house, I got an earful a' their nefarious plan from inside my cozy canister.
They had Wonder Woman's address, which I now had as well, an' they planned to use the chemicals ta create an invisible an' deadly gas strong enough ta knock her out.
Their plan was not ta actually kill her, but ta kidnap an' ransom her ta the highest bidder.
Crazy, huh?
WHY WE JUST CAN'T SET UP CANISTERS OF THIS STUFF WITH DETONATORS AND LET THE GAS DO ITS THING?
I WANNA SEE HER FACE WHEN SHE CHOKES ON IT, THAT'S WHY! TOMORROW NIGHT WE JUST WAIT ON HER TO SHOW UP AT HER PLACE AND BARGE IN TO TAKE HER OUT.
ONCE SHE'S OUT OF IT, WE MOVE HER BACK HERE AND THE DOC CAN KEEP HER ASLEEP 'TIL WE SELL HER.
SO DOC, HOW LONG IS THIS BLEEDIN' THING GONNA TAKE TO MAKE?
THE PROCESS ITSELF TAKES VERY LITTLE TIME, BUT IS VERY PRECARIOUS. ONE WRONG MOVE CAN LEVEL THIS ENTIRE BUILDING.
NOT THAT I DOUBT YOUR EXCEPTIONAL ABILITIES, BUT LET'S ALL GO OUT AND GRAB A PINT...LET THE GOOD DOCTOR DO HIS THING.
DOC, COME JOIN US AT DILLON'S WHEN YOU'RE ALL DONE.
It was just my dumb luck he didn't need ta open my crate ta make his deadly concoction. I waited patiently as he worked his twisted magic.
It seemed like forever an' a half, but he finally freakin' finished.
Once he left, I grabbed a bag an' a buttload a' canisters that I needed for the rest a' my brilliant plan.
I probably shoulda gone downstairs ta let the London Legion loose, but they would only muck up my plans.
I was in an' out, with no one the wiser.
And just like that, I was off ta visit one a' my all-time greatest most favorite heroes.

HOME INVASION

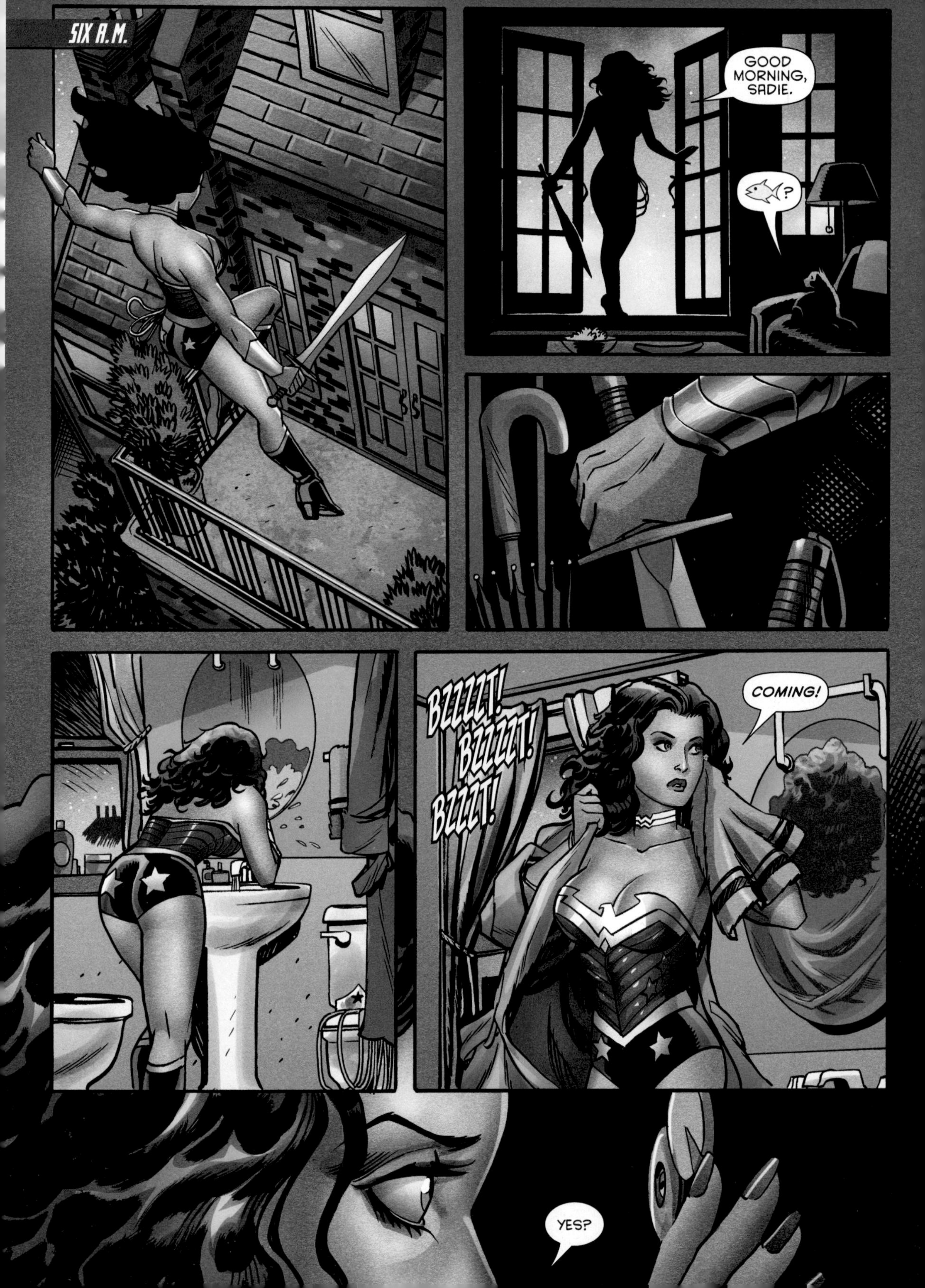
SIX A.M.
GOOD MORNING, SADIE.
?
BZZZZT!
BZZZZT!
BZZZT!
COMING!
YES?

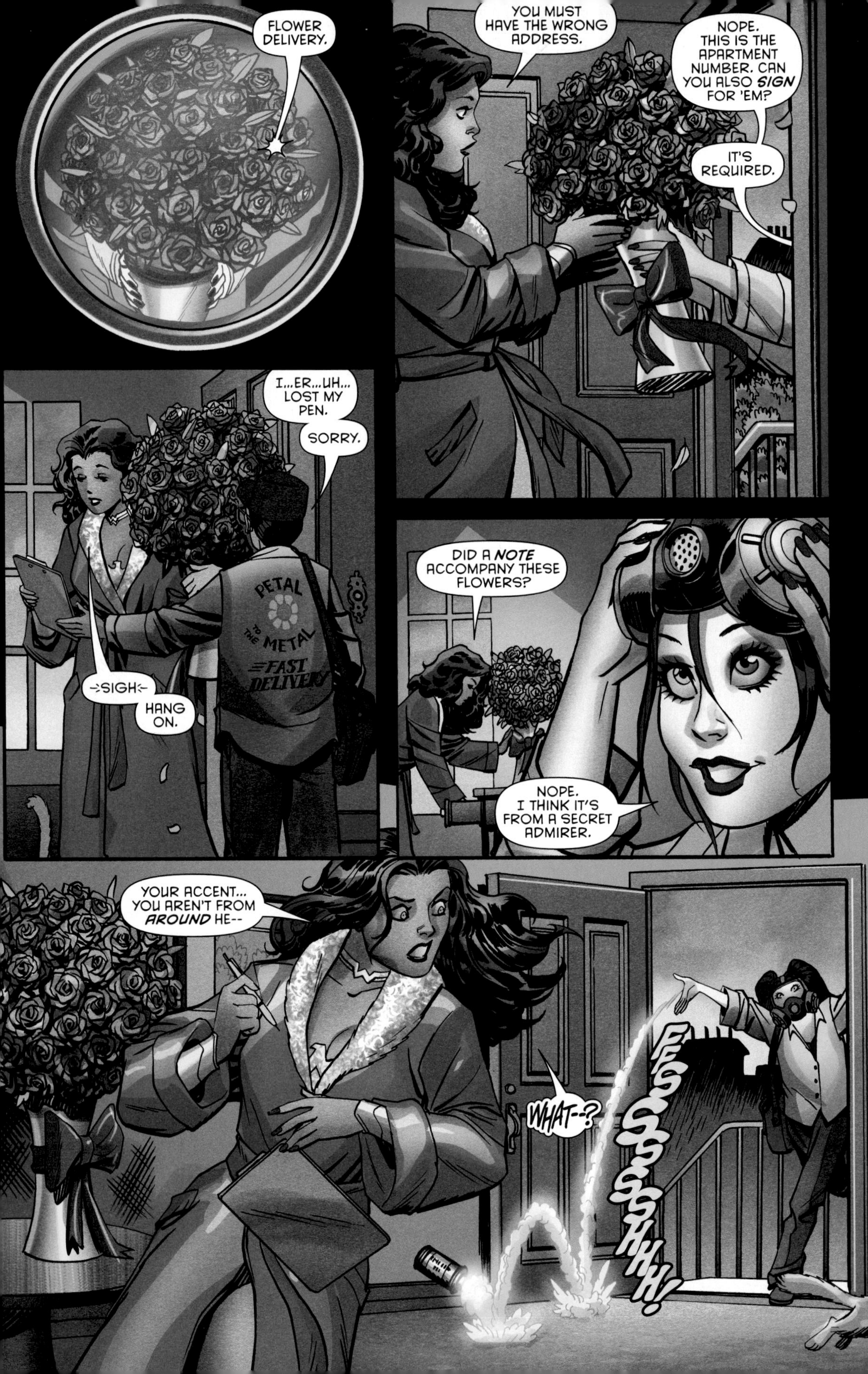
FLOWER DELIVERY.
YOU MUST HAVE THE WRONG ADDRESS.
NOPE. THIS IS THE APARTMENT NUMBER. CAN YOU ALSO SIGN FOR 'EM?
IT'S REQUIRED.
I...ER...UH... LOST MY PEN.
SORRY.
PETAL TO THE METAL
FAST DELIVERY
-SIGH-
HANG ON.
DID A NOTE ACCOMPANY THESE FLOWERS?
NOPE. I THINK IT'S FROM A SECRET ADMIRER.
YOUR ACCENT... YOU AREN'T FROM AROUND HE--
WHAT--?
FFSSSSSSHHH!

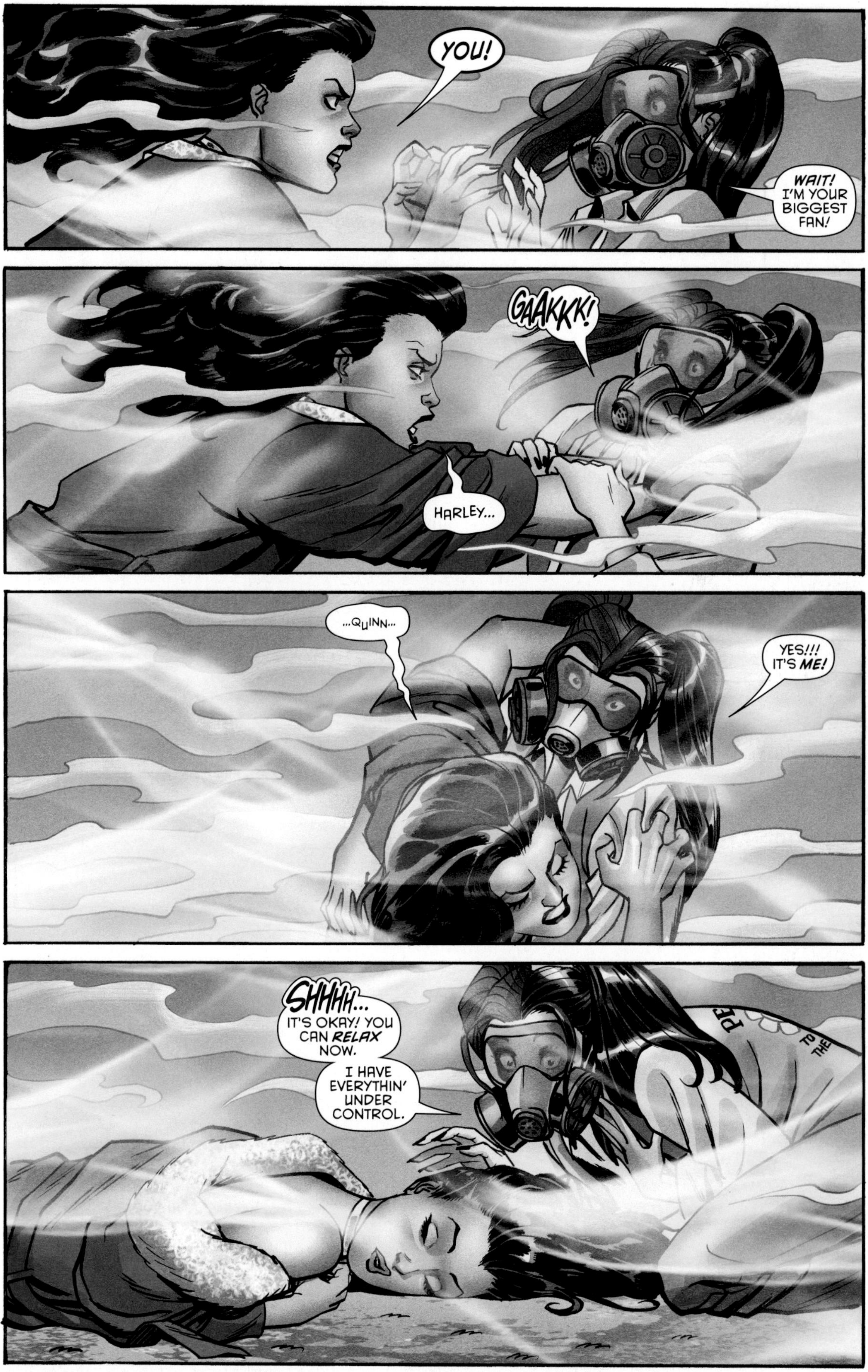
YOU!
WAIT! I'M YOUR BIGGEST FAN!
GAAKKK!
HARLEY...
...QUINN...
YES!!! IT'S ME!
SHHHH... IT'S OKAY! YOU CAN RELAX NOW.
I HAVE EVERYTHIN' UNDER CONTROL.

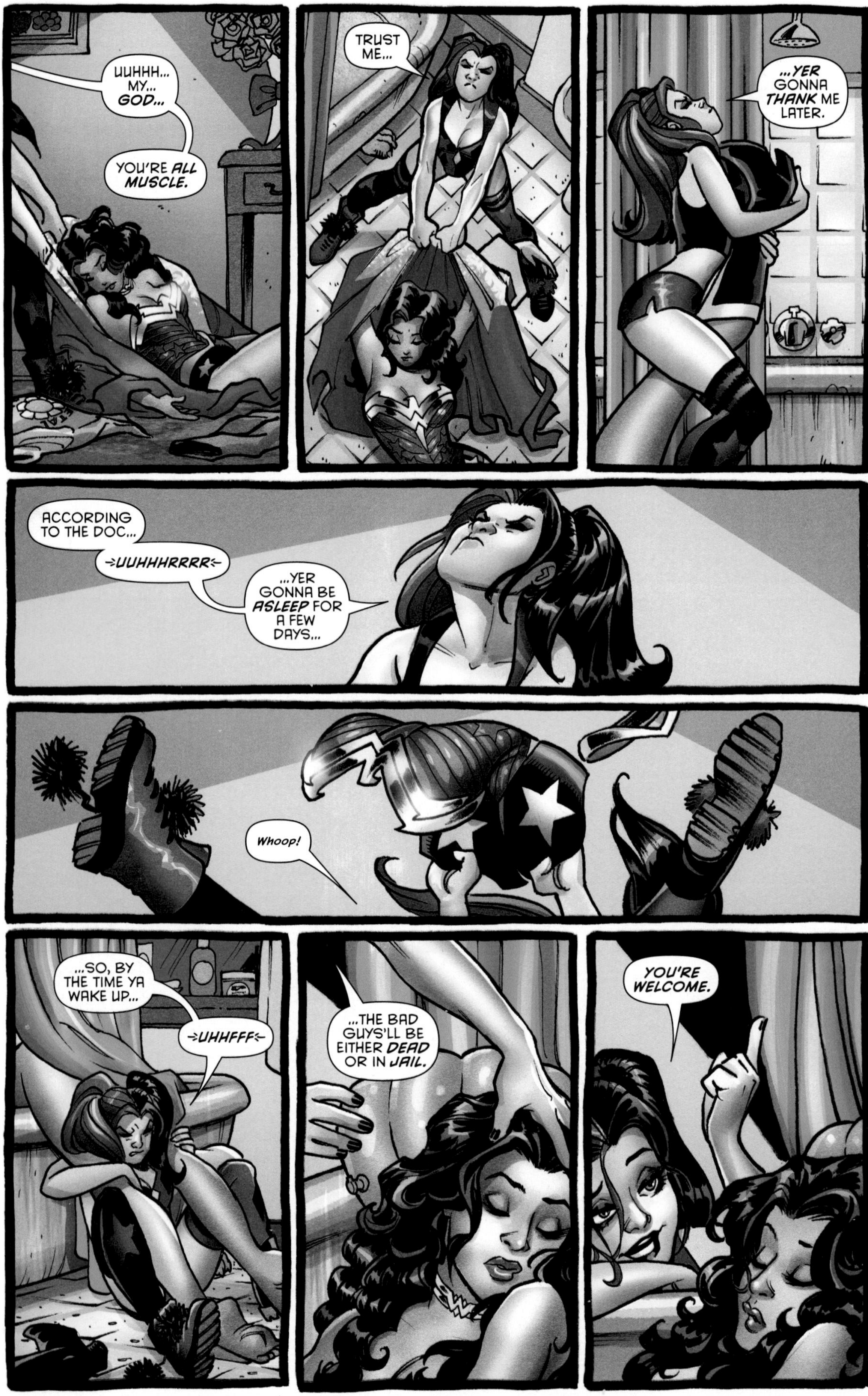
UUHHH... MY... GOD...
YOU'RE ALL MUSCLE.
TRUST ME...
...YER GONNA THANK ME LATER.
ACCORDING TO THE DOC...
UUHHHRRRR
...YER GONNA BE ASLEEP FOR A FEW DAYS...
Whoop!
...SO, BY THE TIME YA WAKE UP...
UHHFFF
...THE BAD GUYS'LL BE EITHER DEAD OR IN JAIL.
YOU'RE WELCOME.

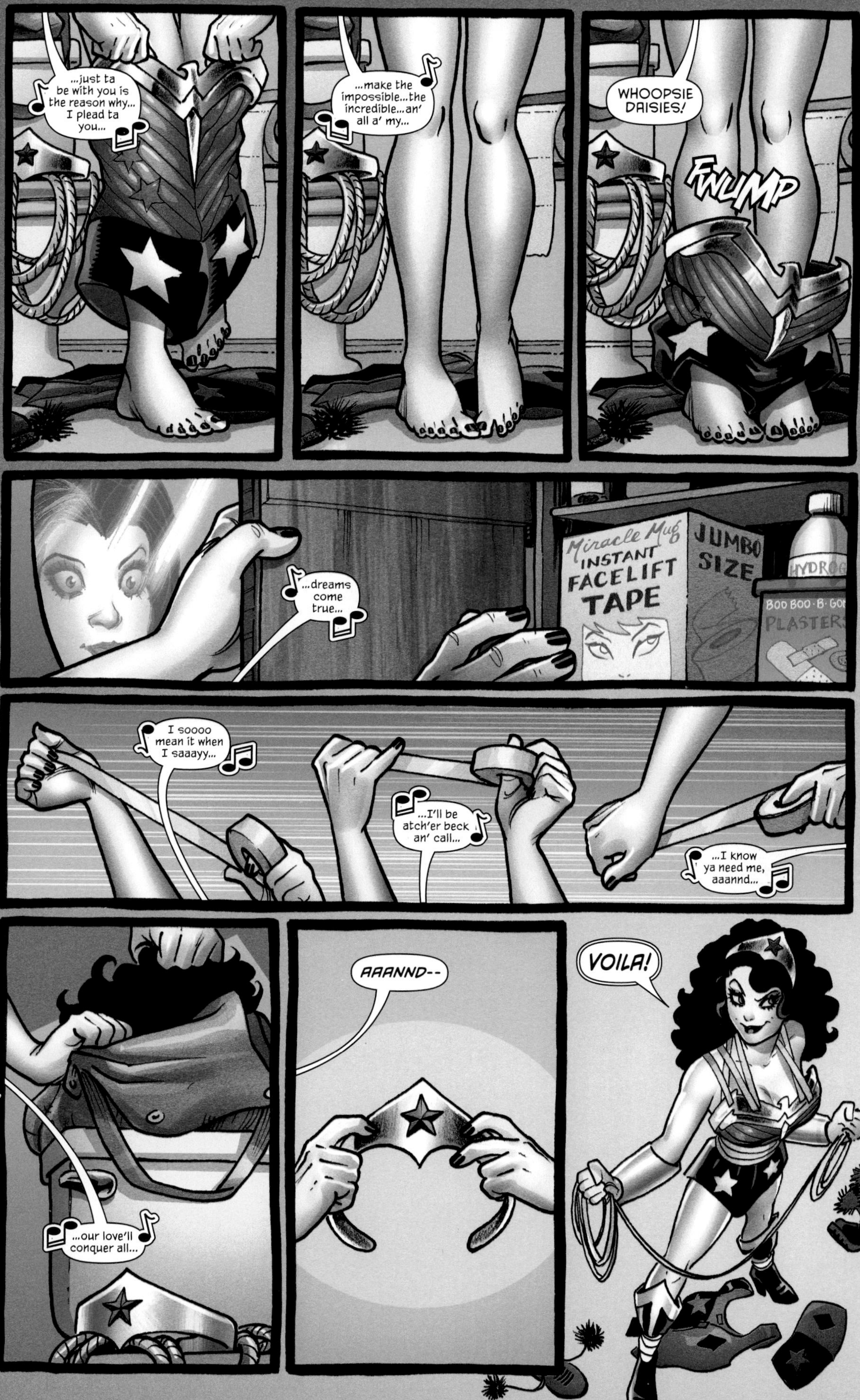
...just ta be with you is the reason why... I plead ta you...
...make the impossible...the incredible...an' all a' my...
WHOOPSIE DAISIES!
FWUMP
...dreams come true...
MIRACLE MUG INSTANT FACELIFT TAPE
JUMBO SIZE
HYDROG
BOO BOO-B-GON PLASTERS
I soooo mean it when I saaayy...
...I'll be atch'er beck an' call...
...I know ya need me, aaannd...
...our love'll conquer all...
AAAANND--
VOILA!

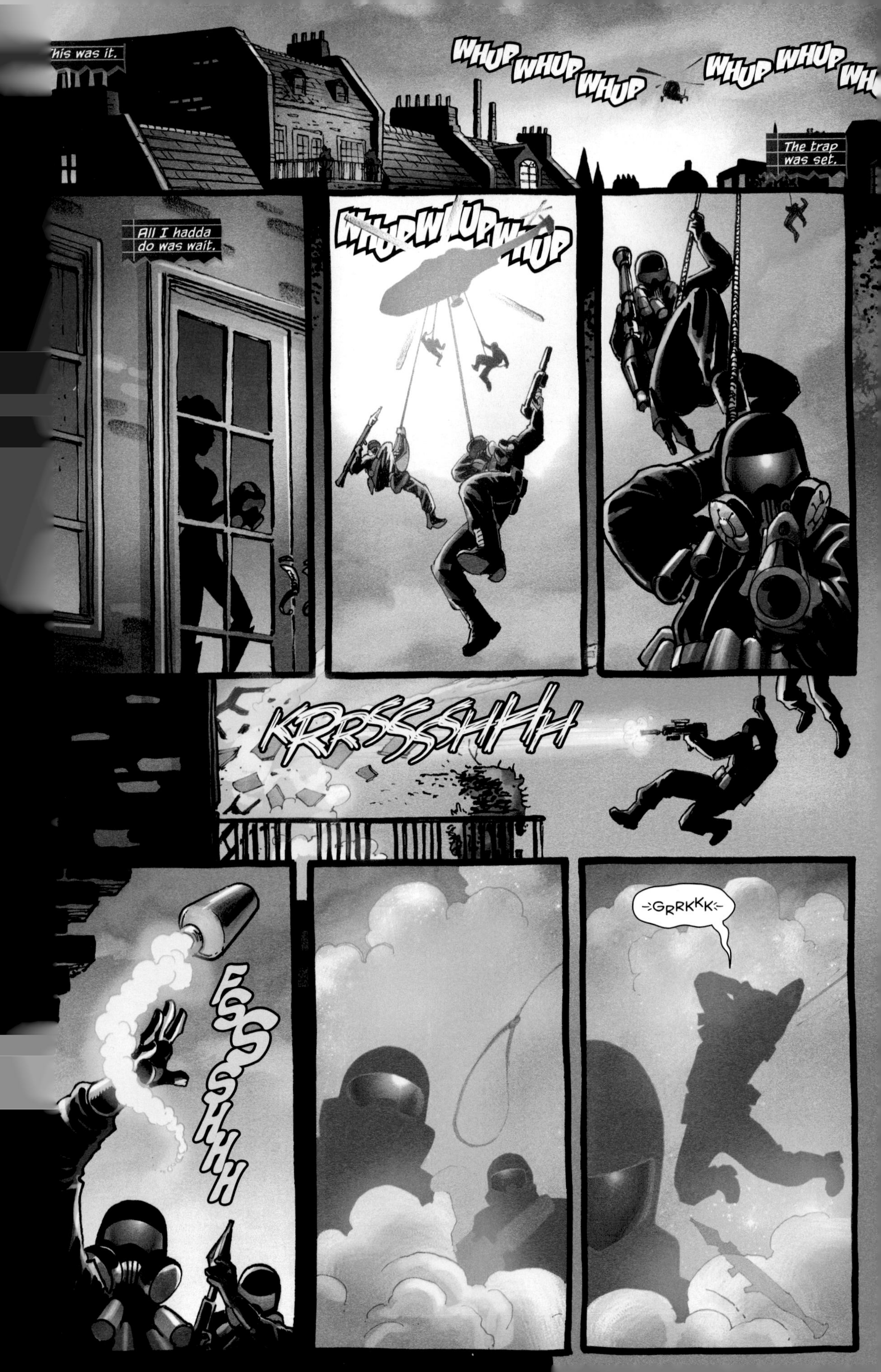
This was it.
WHUP WHUP WHUP
WHUP WHUP WH
The trap was set.
All I hadda do was wait.
WHUP WHUP WHUP
KRRSSSSHHHH
FSSSHHH
GRRKKK

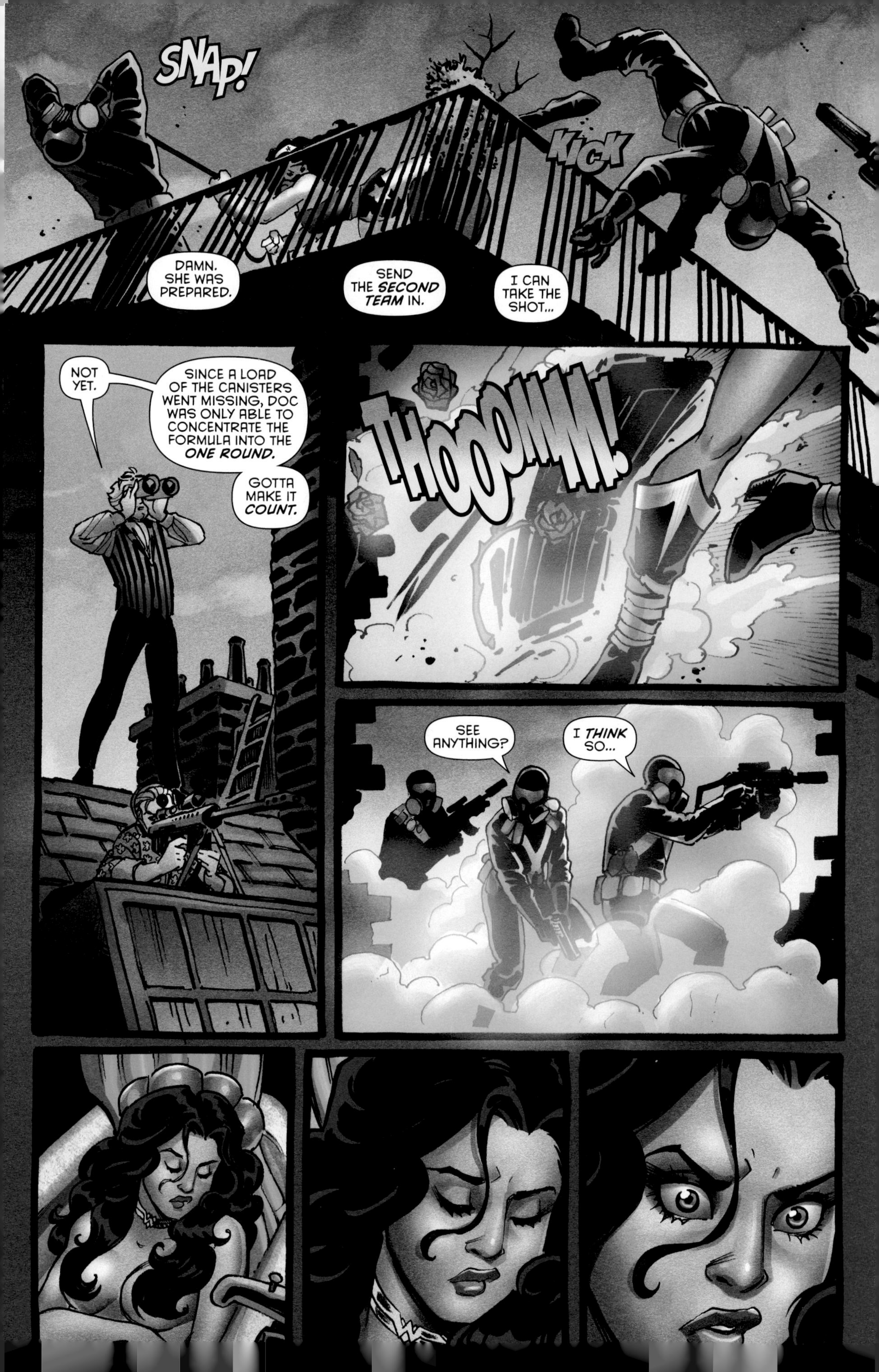
SNAP!
KICK
DAMN. SHE WAS PREPARED.
SEND THE SECOND TEAM IN.
I CAN TAKE THE SHOT...
NOT YET.
SINCE A LOAD OF THE CANISTERS WENT MISSING, DOC WAS ONLY ABLE TO CONCENTRATE THE FORMULA INTO THE ONE ROUND.
GOTTA MAKE IT COUNT.
THOOOMMM!
SEE ANYTHING?
I THINK SO...

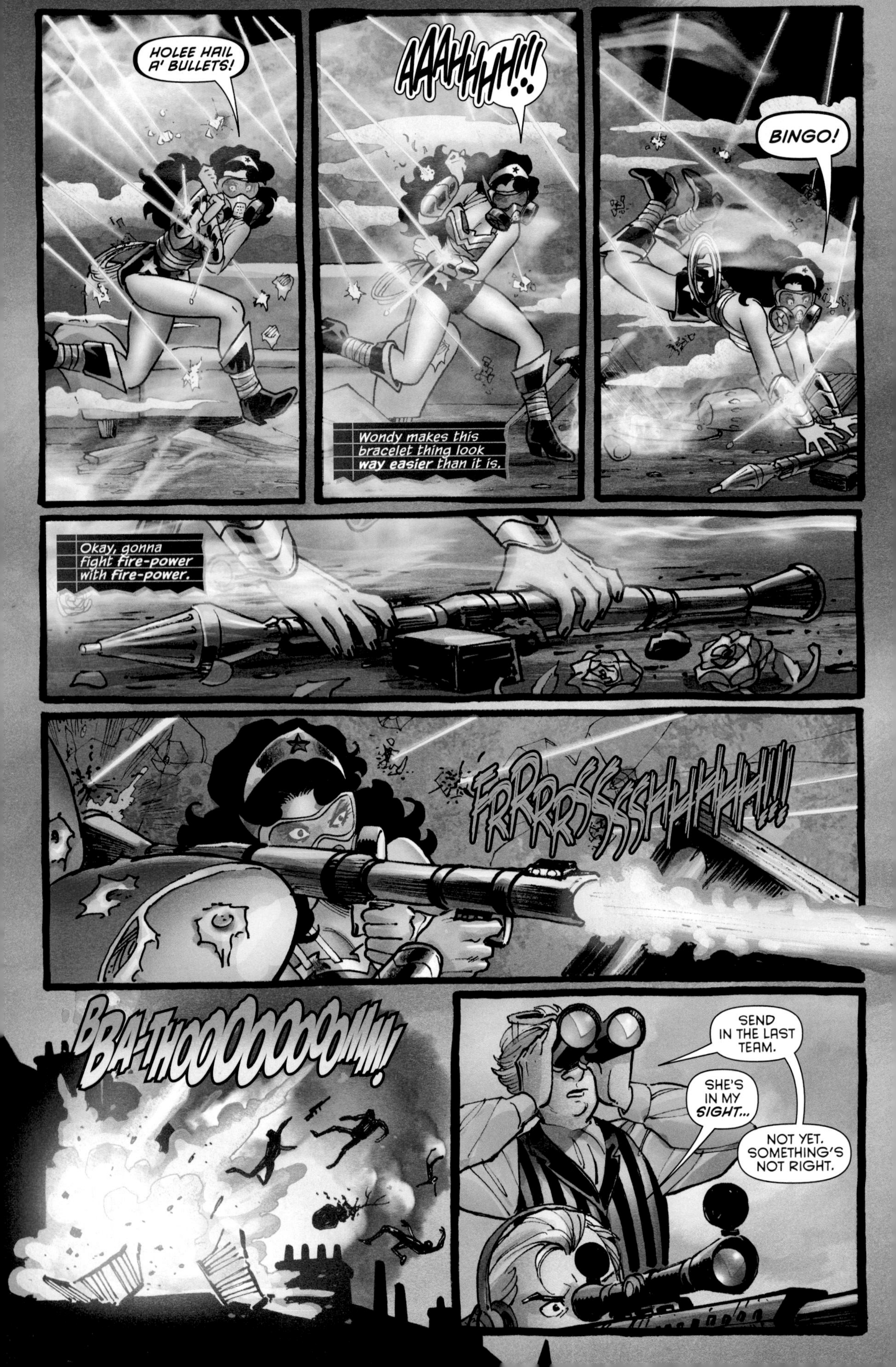
HOLEE HAIL A' BULLETS!
AAAHHHH!!!
Wondy makes this bracelet thing look way easier than it is.
BINGO!
Okay, gonna fight fire-power with fire-power.
FRRRRSSSSSHHHHH!!!
BBA-THOOOOOOOOMM!
SEND IN THE LAST TEAM.
SHE'S IN MY SIGHT...
NOT YET. SOMETHING'S NOT RIGHT.

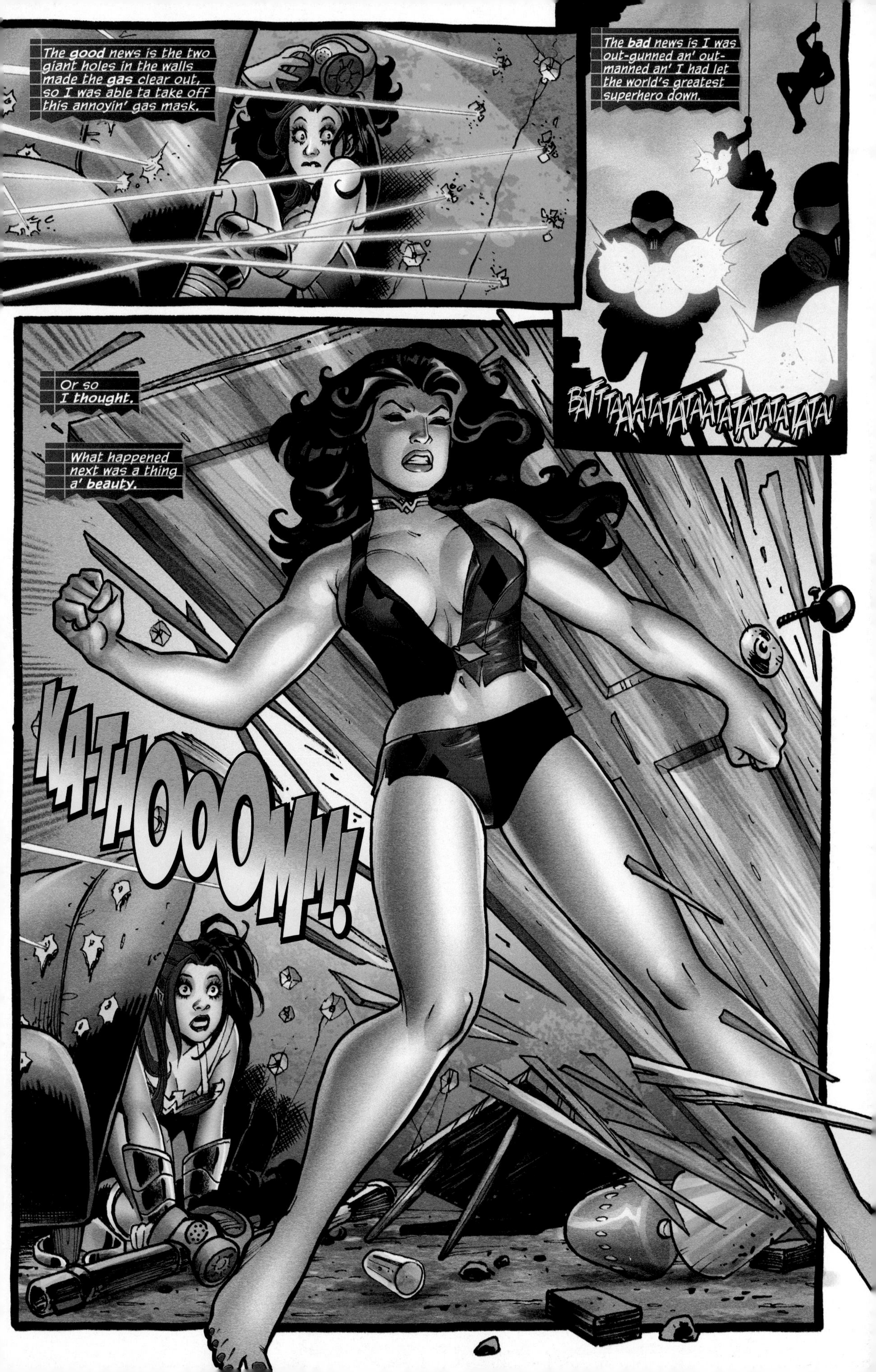
The good news is the two giant holes in the walls made the gas clear out, so I was able ta take off this annoyin' gas mask.
The bad news is I was out-gunned an' out-manned an' I had let the world's greatest superhero down.
BATTTAAATATATAATATATATATATA!
Or so I thought.
What happened next was a thing a' beauty.
KA-THOOOMM!

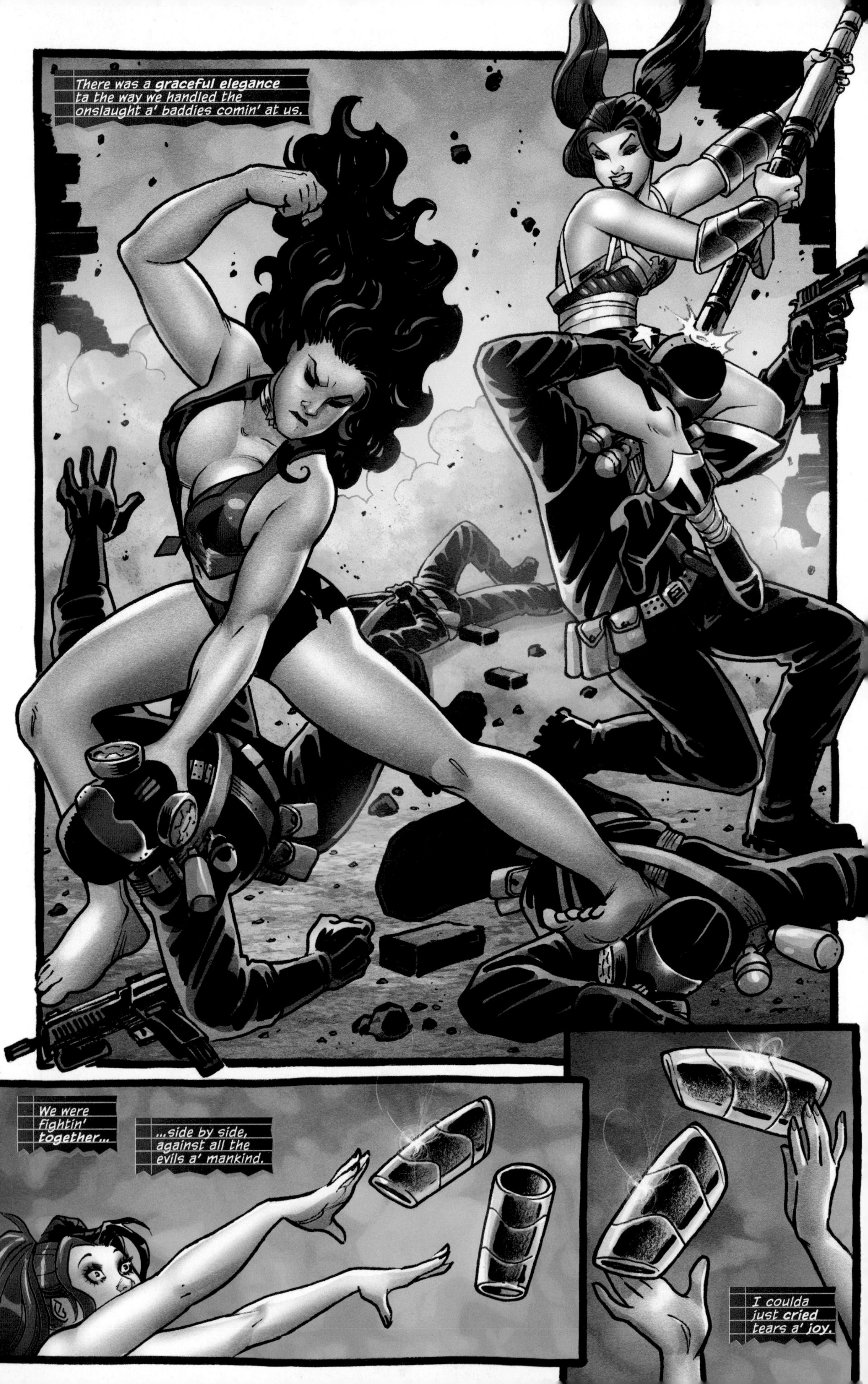
There was a **graceful elegance** ta the way we handled the onslaught a' baddies comin' at us.
We were fightin' **together**...
...side by side, against all the evils a' mankind.
I coulda just **cried** tears a' joy.

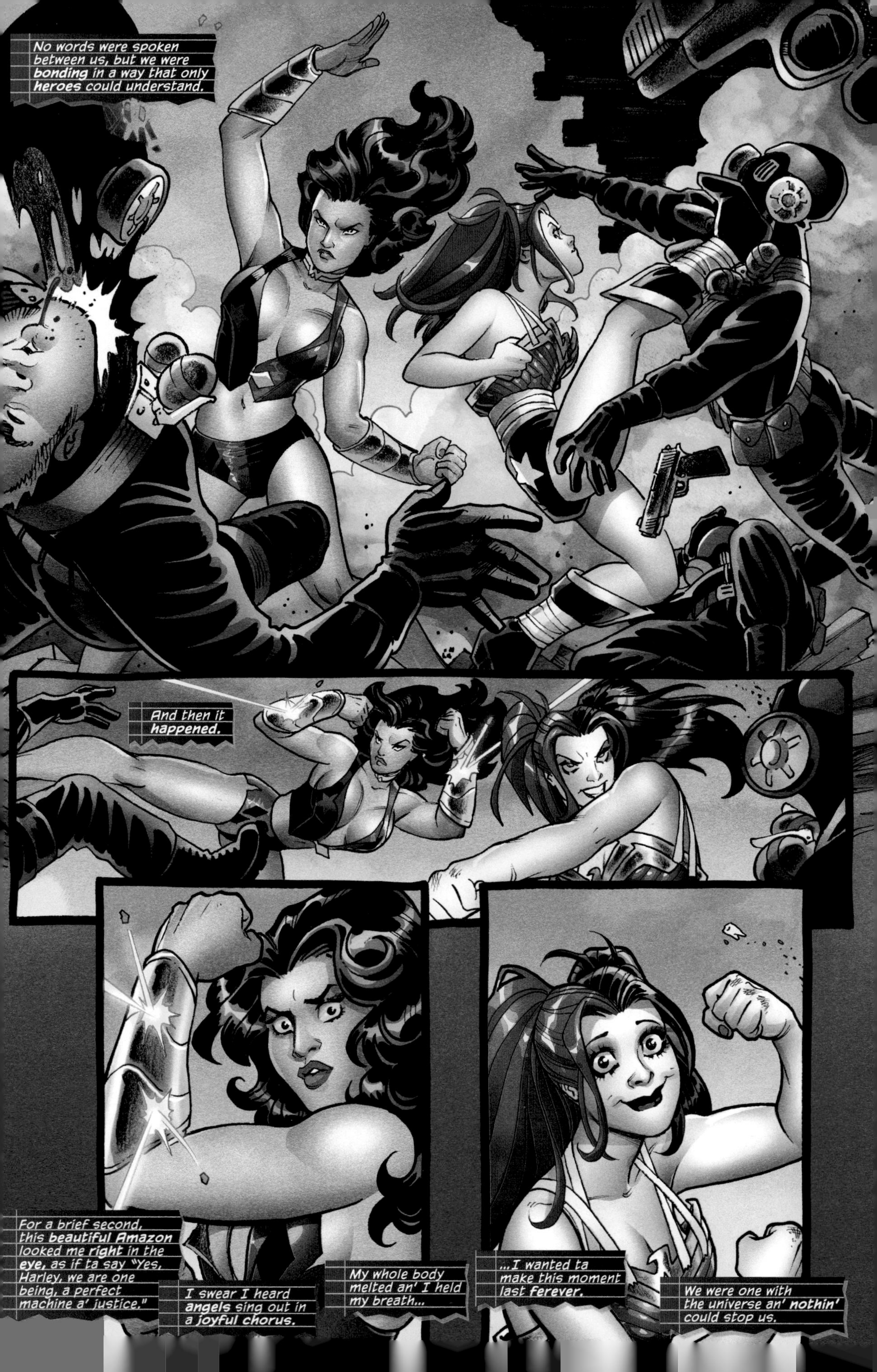
No words were spoken between us, but we were bonding in a way that only heroes could understand.
And then it happened.
For a brief second, this beautiful Amazon looked me right in the eye, as if ta say "Yes, Harley, we are one being, a perfect machine a' justice."
I swear I heard angels sing out in a joyful chorus.
My whole body melted an' I held my breath...
...I wanted ta make this moment last ferever.
We were one with the universe an' nothin' could stop us.

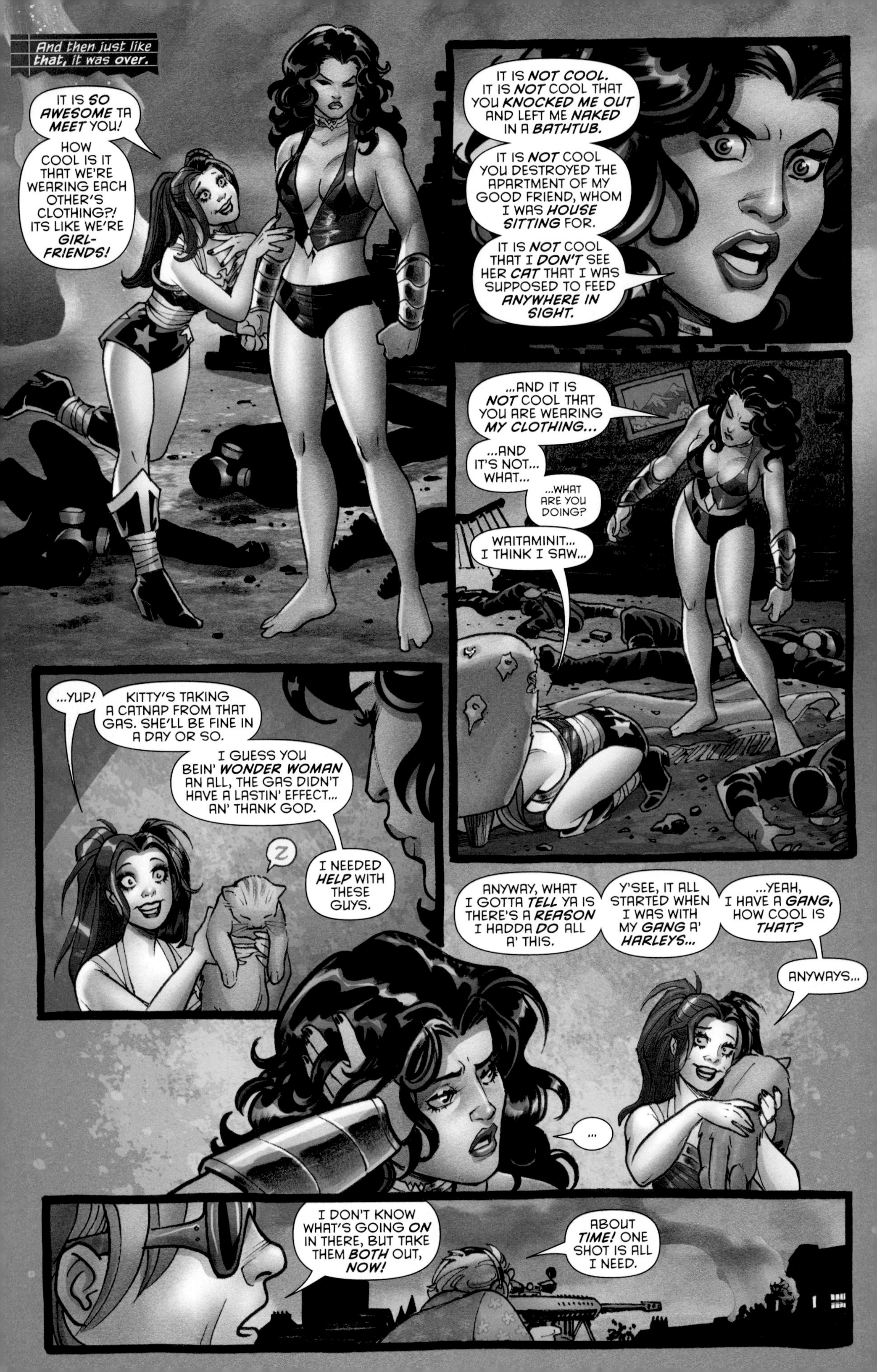

And then just like that, it was over.
IT IS SO AWESOME TA MEET YOU!
HOW COOL IS IT THAT WE'RE WEARING EACH OTHER'S CLOTHING?! ITS LIKE WE'RE GIRL-FRIENDS!
IT IS NOT COOL. IT IS NOT COOL THAT YOU KNOCKED ME OUT AND LEFT ME NAKED IN A BATHTUB.
IT IS NOT COOL YOU DESTROYED THE APARTMENT OF MY GOOD FRIEND, WHOM I WAS HOUSE SITTING FOR.
IT IS NOT COOL THAT I DON'T SEE HER CAT THAT I WAS SUPPOSED TO FEED ANYWHERE IN SIGHT.
...AND IT IS NOT COOL THAT YOU ARE WEARING MY CLOTHING...
...AND IT'S NOT... WHAT...
...WHAT ARE YOU DOING?
WAITAMINIT... I THINK I SAW...
...YUP!
KITTY'S TAKING A CATNAP FROM THAT GAS. SHE'LL BE FINE IN A DAY OR SO.
I GUESS YOU BEIN' WONDER WOMAN AN ALL, THE GAS DIDN'T HAVE A LASTIN' EFFECT... AN' THANK GOD.
Z
I NEEDED HELP WITH THESE GUYS.
ANYWAY, WHAT I GOTTA TELL YA IS THERE'S A REASON I HADDA DO ALL A' THIS.
Y'SEE, IT ALL STARTED WHEN I WAS WITH MY GANG A' HARLEYS...
...YEAH, I HAVE A GANG, HOW COOL IS THAT?
ANYWAYS...
...
I DON'T KNOW WHAT'S GOING ON IN THERE, BUT TAKE THEM BOTH OUT, NOW!
ABOUT TIME! ONE SHOT IS ALL I NEED.

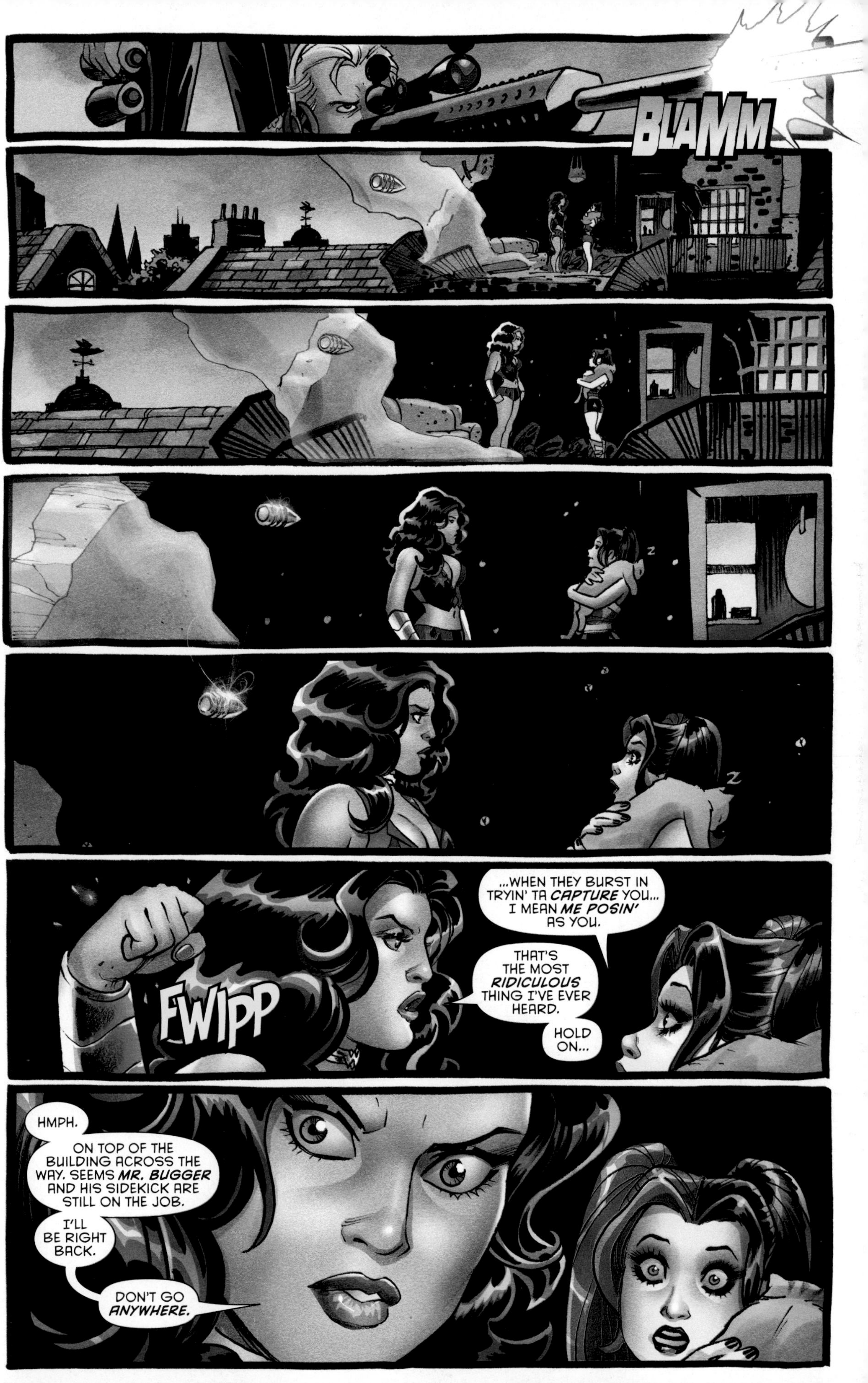
BLAMM
FWIPP
...WHEN THEY BURST IN TRYIN' TA *CAPTURE* YOU... I MEAN *ME POSIN'* AS YOU.
THAT'S THE MOST *RIDICULOUS* THING I'VE EVER HEARD.
HOLD ON...
HMPH.
ON TOP OF THE BUILDING ACROSS THE WAY. SEEMS *MR. BUGGER* AND HIS SIDEKICK ARE STILL ON THE JOB.
I'LL BE RIGHT BACK.
DON'T GO *ANYWHERE.*

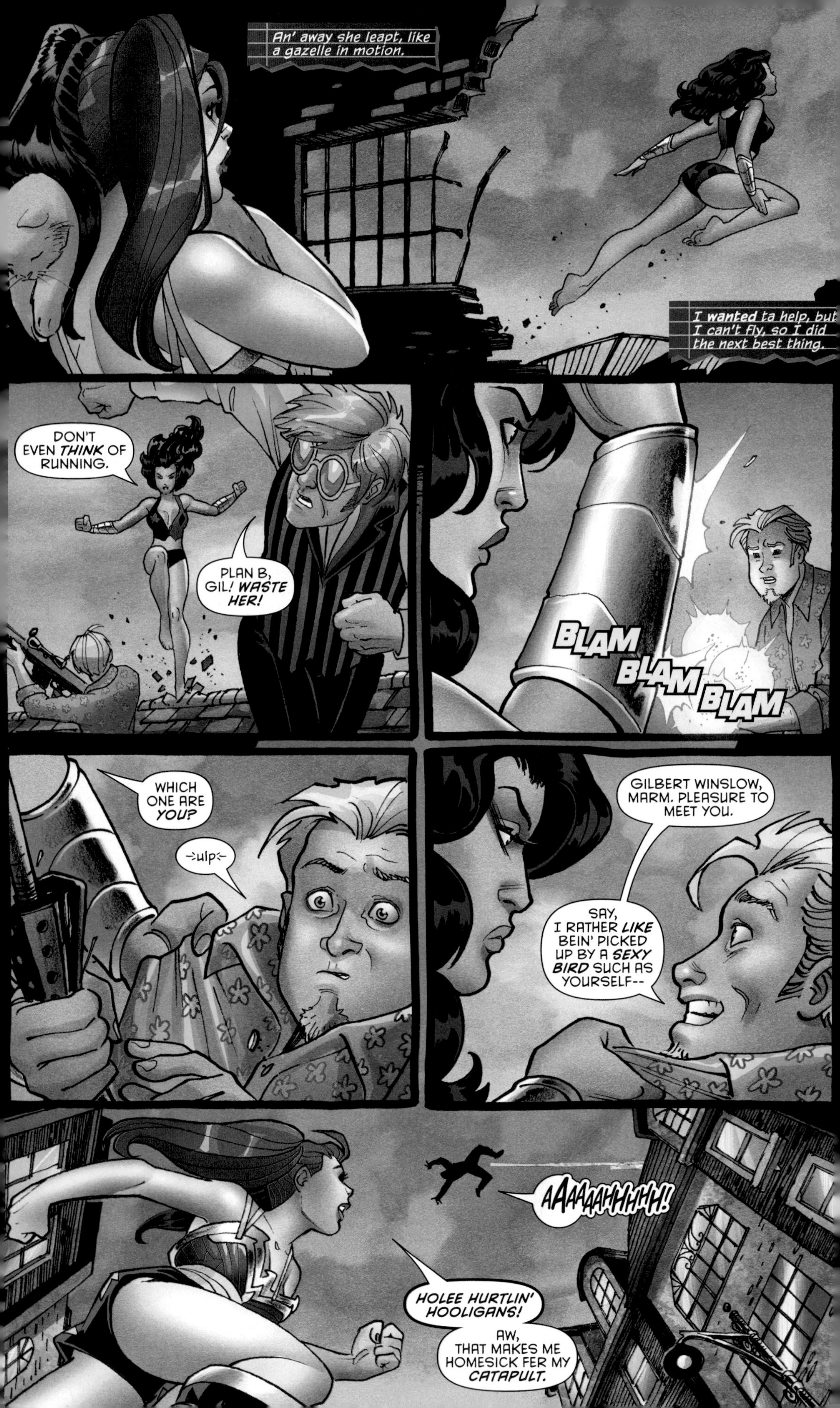

An' away she leapt, like a gazelle in motion.
I wanted ta help, but I can't fly, so I did the next best thing.
DON'T EVEN THINK OF RUNNING.
PLAN B, GIL! WASTE HER!
BLAM BLAM BLAM
WHICH ONE ARE YOU?
-ulp-
GILBERT WINSLOW, MARM. PLEASURE TO MEET YOU.
SAY, I RATHER LIKE BEIN' PICKED UP BY A SEXY BIRD SUCH AS YOURSELF--
AAAAAAHHHHHH!
HOLEE HURTLIN' HOOLIGANS!
AW, THAT MAKES ME HOMESICK FER MY CATAPULT.

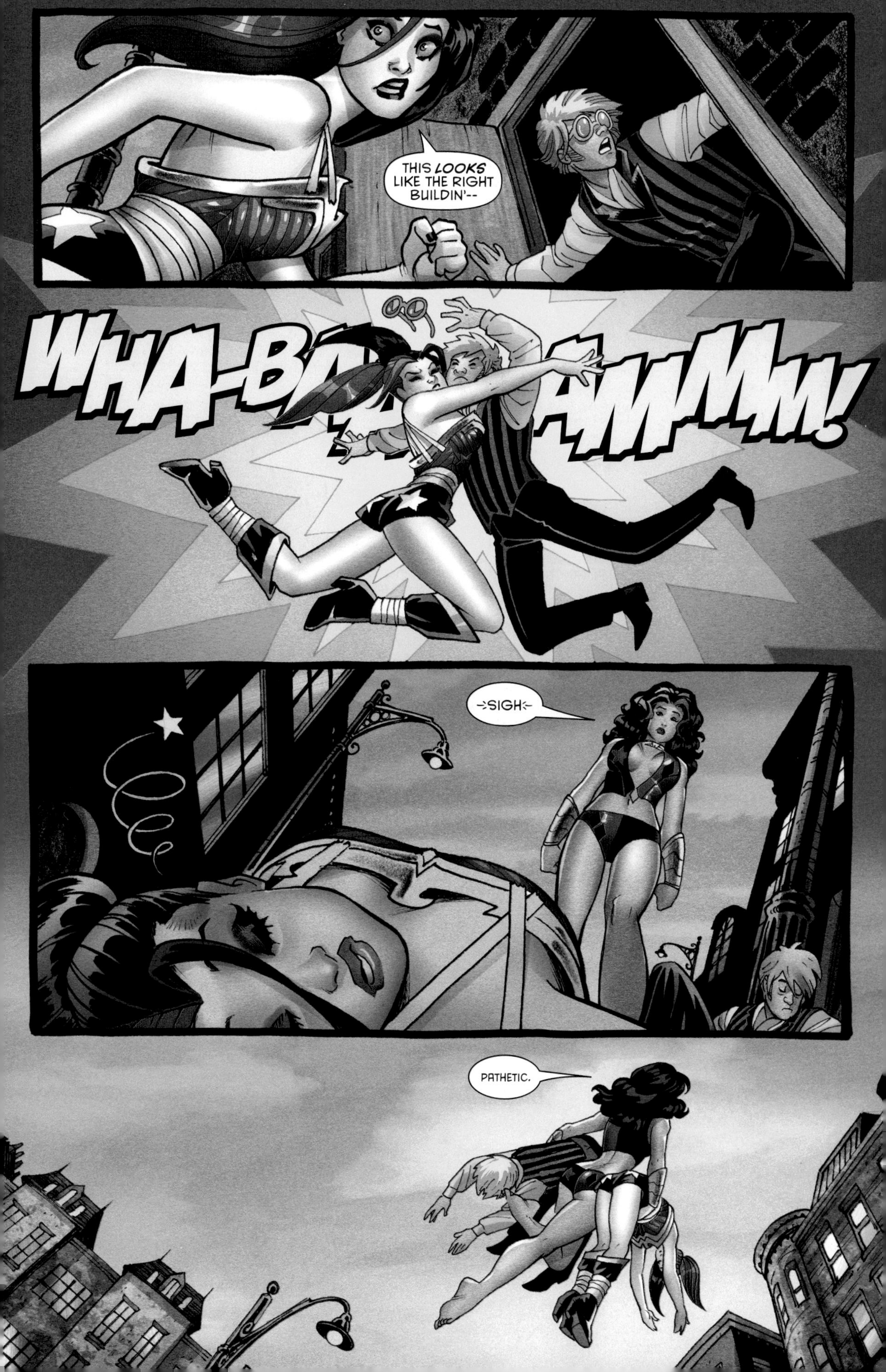
THIS *LOOKS* LIKE THE RIGHT BUILDIN'--
-SIGH-
PATHETIC.

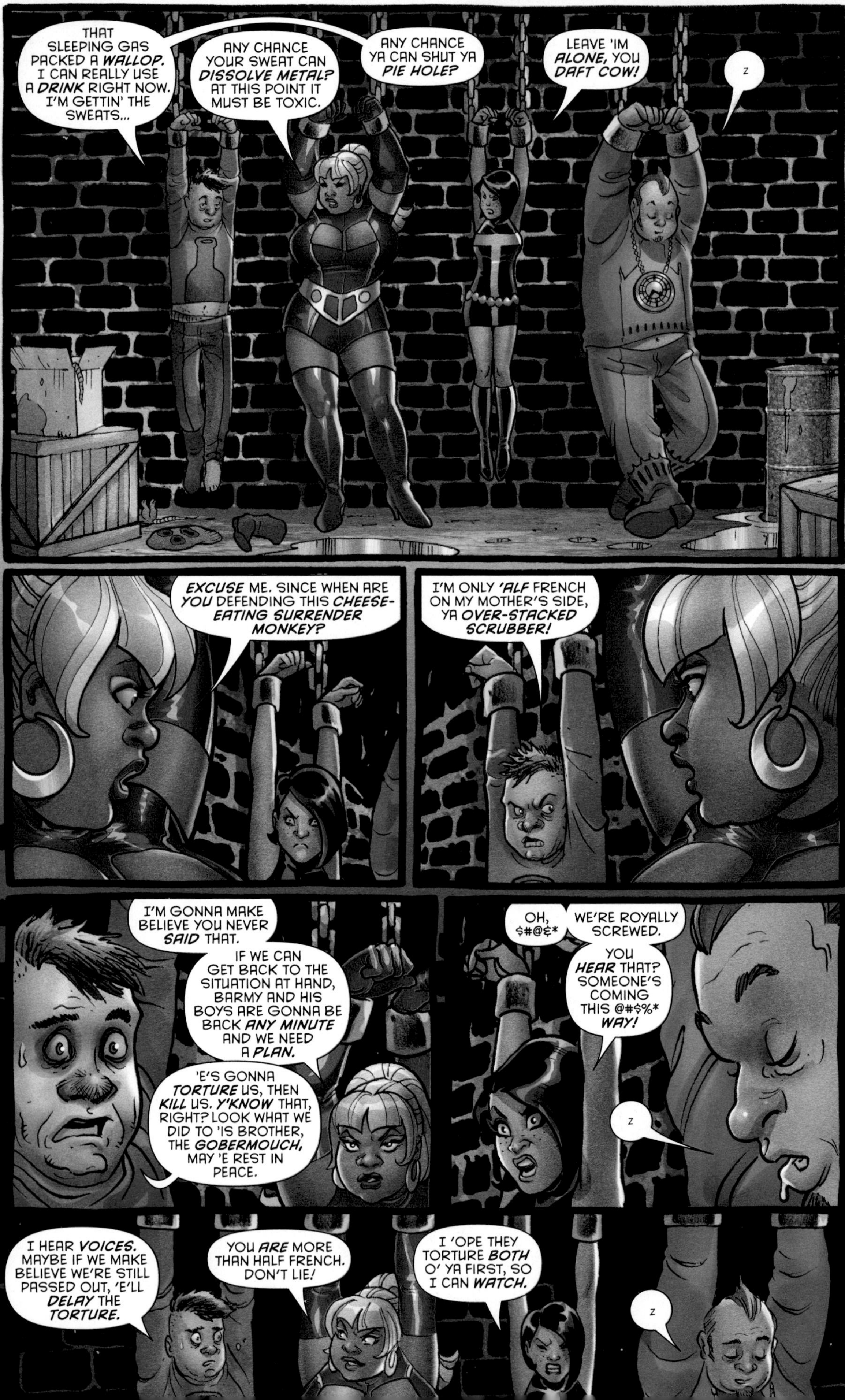
THAT SLEEPING GAS PACKED A WALLOP. I CAN REALLY USE A DRINK RIGHT NOW. I'M GETTIN' THE SWEATS...
ANY CHANCE YOUR SWEAT CAN DISSOLVE METAL? AT THIS POINT IT MUST BE TOXIC.
ANY CHANCE YA CAN SHUT YA PIE HOLE?
LEAVE 'IM ALONE, YOU DAFT COW!
Z
EXCUSE ME. SINCE WHEN ARE YOU DEFENDING THIS CHEESE-EATING SURRENDER MONKEY?
I'M ONLY 'ALF FRENCH ON MY MOTHER'S SIDE, YA OVER-STACKED SCRUBBER!
I'M GONNA MAKE BELIEVE YOU NEVER SAID THAT.
IF WE CAN GET BACK TO THE SITUATION AT HAND, BARMY AND HIS BOYS ARE GONNA BE BACK ANY MINUTE AND WE NEED A PLAN.
'E'S GONNA TORTURE US, THEN KILL US. Y'KNOW THAT, RIGHT? LOOK WHAT WE DID TO 'IS BROTHER, THE GOBERMOUCH, MAY 'E REST IN PEACE.
OH, $#@&*
WE'RE ROYALLY SCREWED.
YOU HEAR THAT? SOMEONE'S COMING THIS @#$%* WAY!
Z
I HEAR VOICES. MAYBE IF WE MAKE BELIEVE WE'RE STILL PASSED OUT, 'E'LL DELAY THE TORTURE.
YOU ARE MORE THAN HALF FRENCH. DON'T LIE!
I 'OPE THEY TORTURE BOTH O' YA FIRST, SO I CAN WATCH.
Z

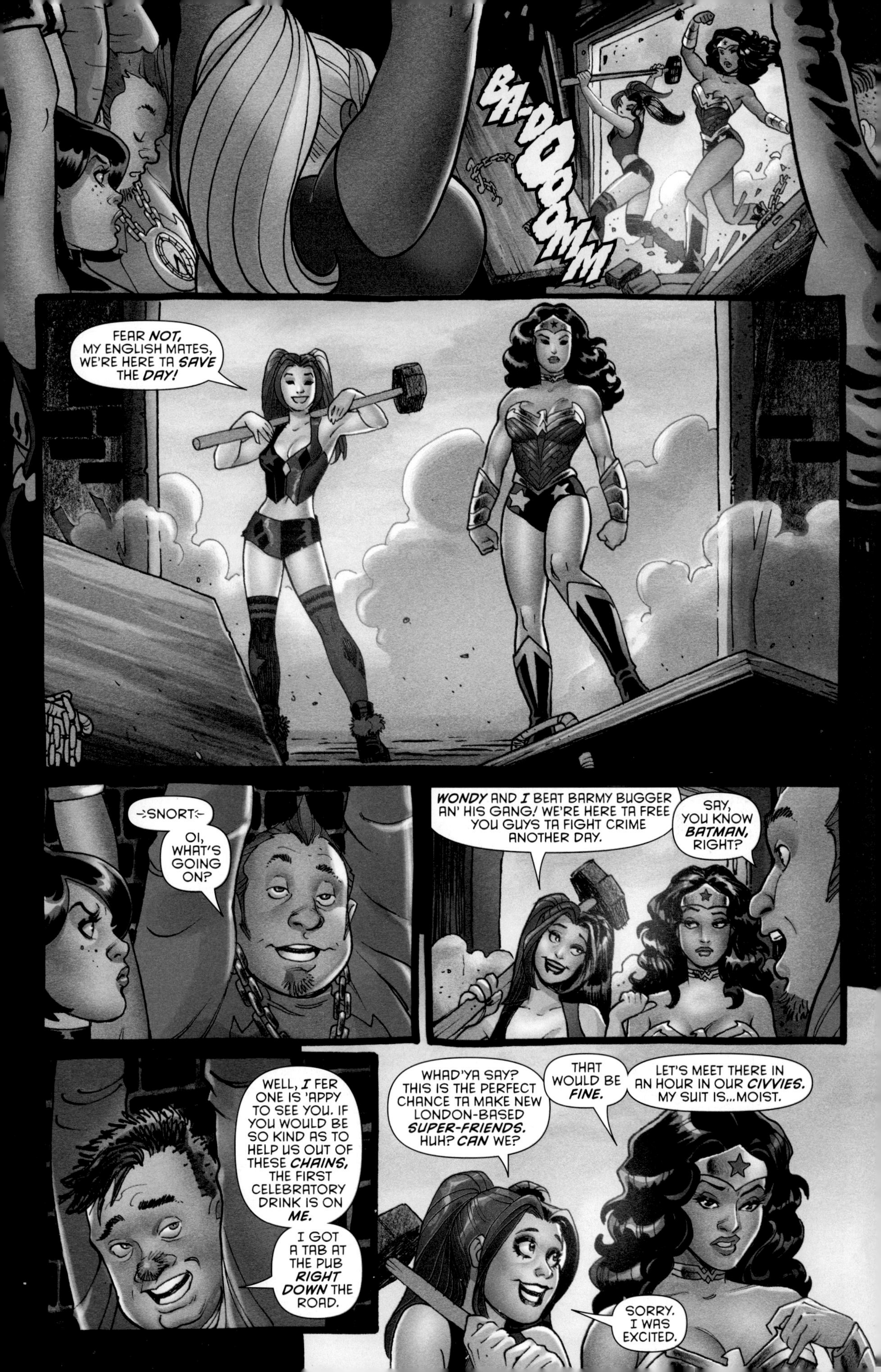
BA-DOOOMM
FEAR NOT, MY ENGLISH MATES, WE'RE HERE TA SAVE THE DAY!
-SNORT-
OI, WHAT'S GOING ON?
WONDY AND I BEAT BARMY BUGGER AN' HIS GANG! WE'RE HERE TA FREE YOU GUYS TA FIGHT CRIME ANOTHER DAY.
SAY, YOU KNOW BATMAN, RIGHT?
WELL, I FER ONE IS 'APPY TO SEE YOU. IF YOU WOULD BE SO KIND AS TO HELP US OUT OF THESE CHAINS, THE FIRST CELEBRATORY DRINK IS ON ME.
I GOT A TAB AT THE PUB RIGHT DOWN THE ROAD.
WHAD'YA SAY? THIS IS THE PERFECT CHANCE TA MAKE NEW LONDON-BASED SUPER-FRIENDS. HUH? CAN WE?
THAT WOULD BE FINE.
LET'S MEET THERE IN AN HOUR IN OUR CIVVIES. MY SUIT IS...MOIST.
SORRY. I WAS EXCITED.

THE BRITISH INQUISITION

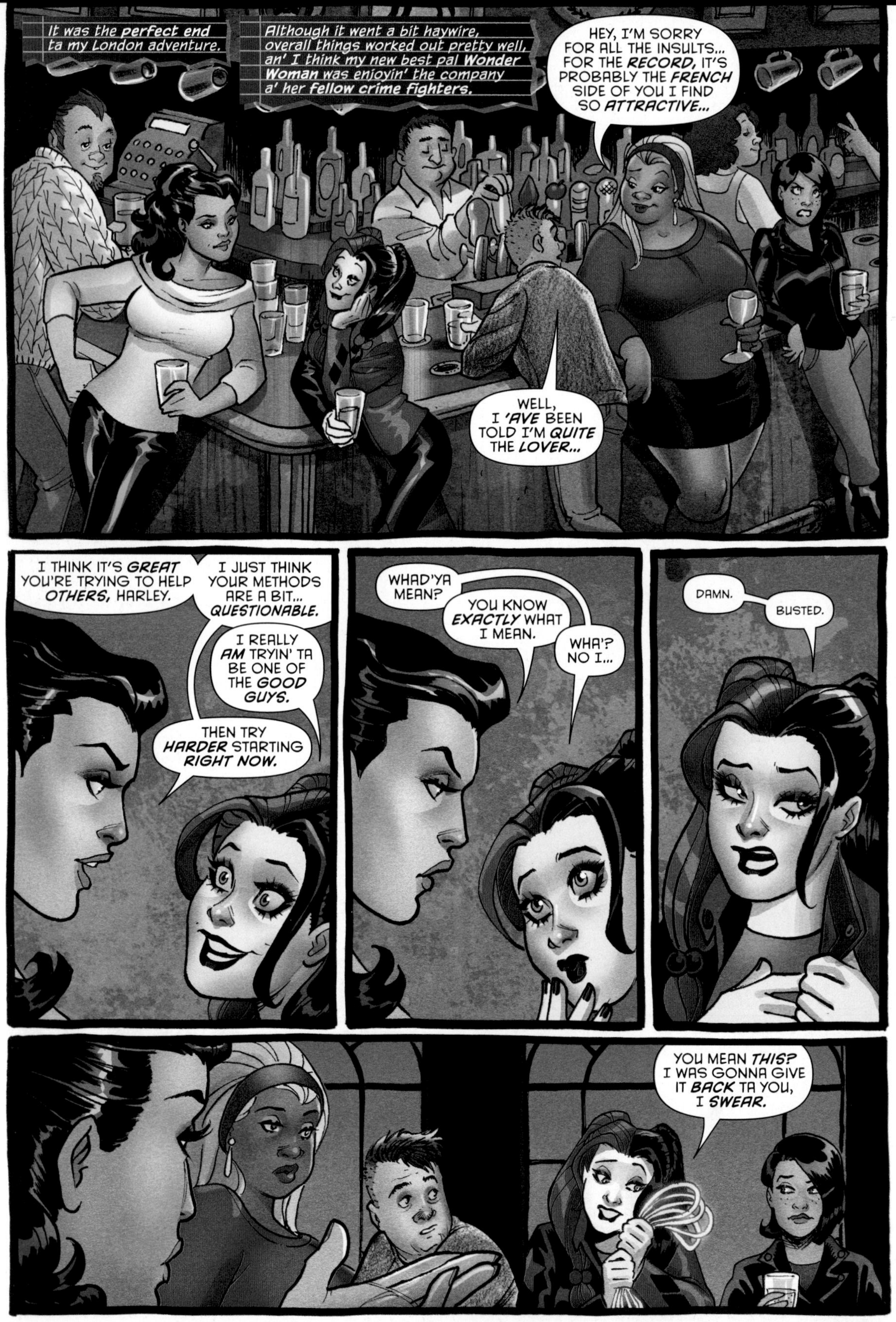

It was the perfect end ta my London adventure.
Although it went a bit haywire, overall things worked out pretty well, an' I think my new best pal Wonder Woman was enjoyin' the company a' her fellow crime fighters.
HEY, I'M SORRY FOR ALL THE INSULTS... FOR THE RECORD, IT'S PROBABLY THE FRENCH SIDE OF YOU I FIND SO ATTRACTIVE...
WELL, I 'AVE BEEN TOLD I'M QUITE THE LOVER...
I THINK IT'S GREAT YOU'RE TRYING TO HELP OTHERS, HARLEY.
I JUST THINK YOUR METHODS ARE A BIT... QUESTIONABLE.
I REALLY AM TRYIN' TA BE ONE OF THE GOOD GUYS.
THEN TRY HARDER STARTING RIGHT NOW.
WHAD'YA MEAN?
YOU KNOW EXACTLY WHAT I MEAN.
WHA'? NO I...
DAMN.
BUSTED.
YOU MEAN THIS? I WAS GONNA GIVE IT BACK TA YOU, I SWEAR.

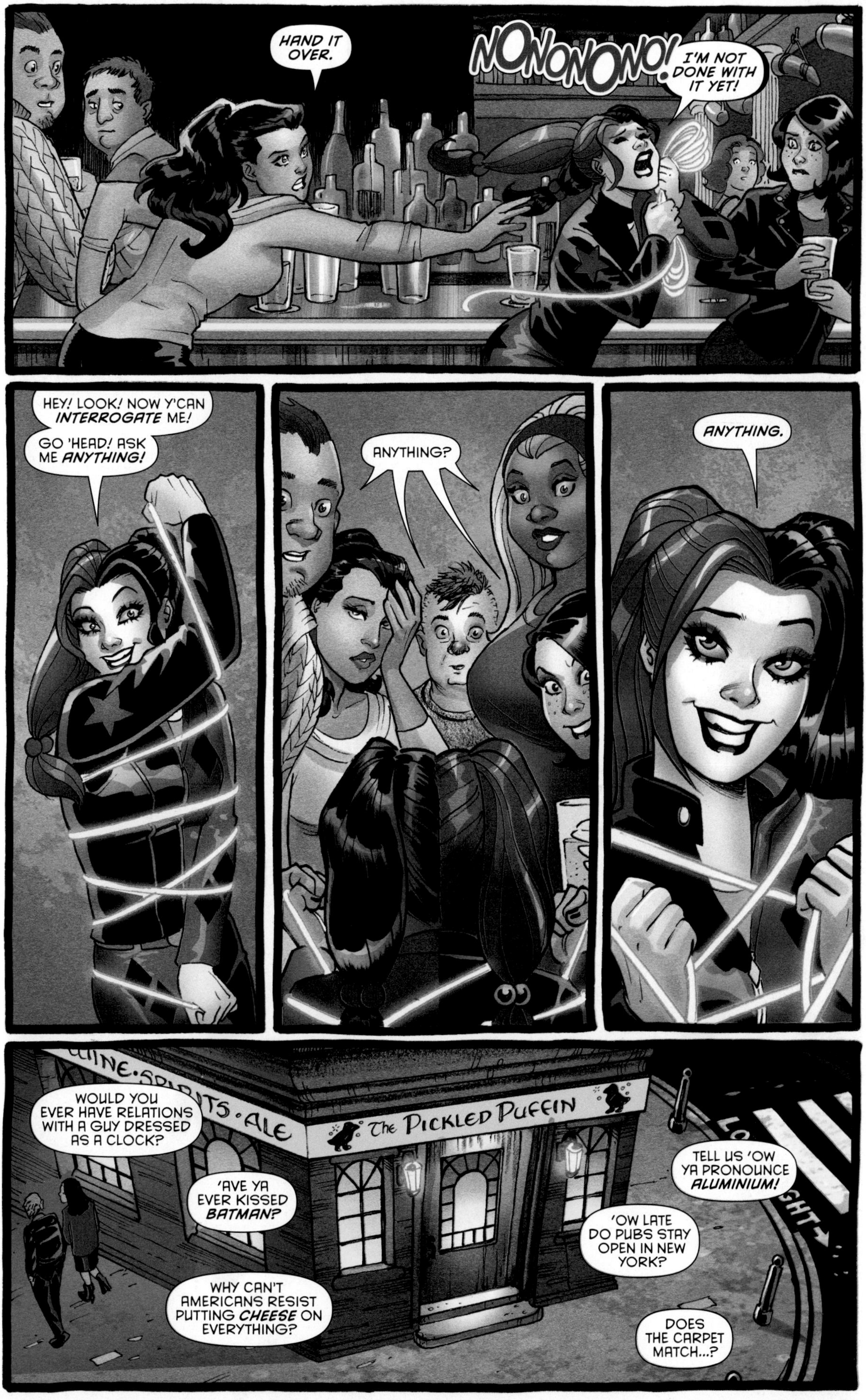
HAND IT OVER.
NONONONONO!
I'M NOT DONE WITH IT YET!
HEY! LOOK! NOW Y'CAN INTERROGATE ME!
GO 'HEAD! ASK ME ANYTHING!
ANYTHING?
ANYTHING.
WINE · SPIRITS · ALE
The Pickled Puffin
WOULD YOU EVER HAVE RELATIONS WITH A GUY DRESSED AS A CLOCK?
'AVE YA EVER KISSED BATMAN?
WHY CAN'T AMERICANS RESIST PUTTING CHEESE ON EVERYTHING?
TELL US 'OW YA PRONOUNCE ALUMINIUM!
'OW LATE DO PUBS STAY OPEN IN NEW YORK?
DOES THE CARPET MATCH...?

AND BOB'S YOUR UNCLE

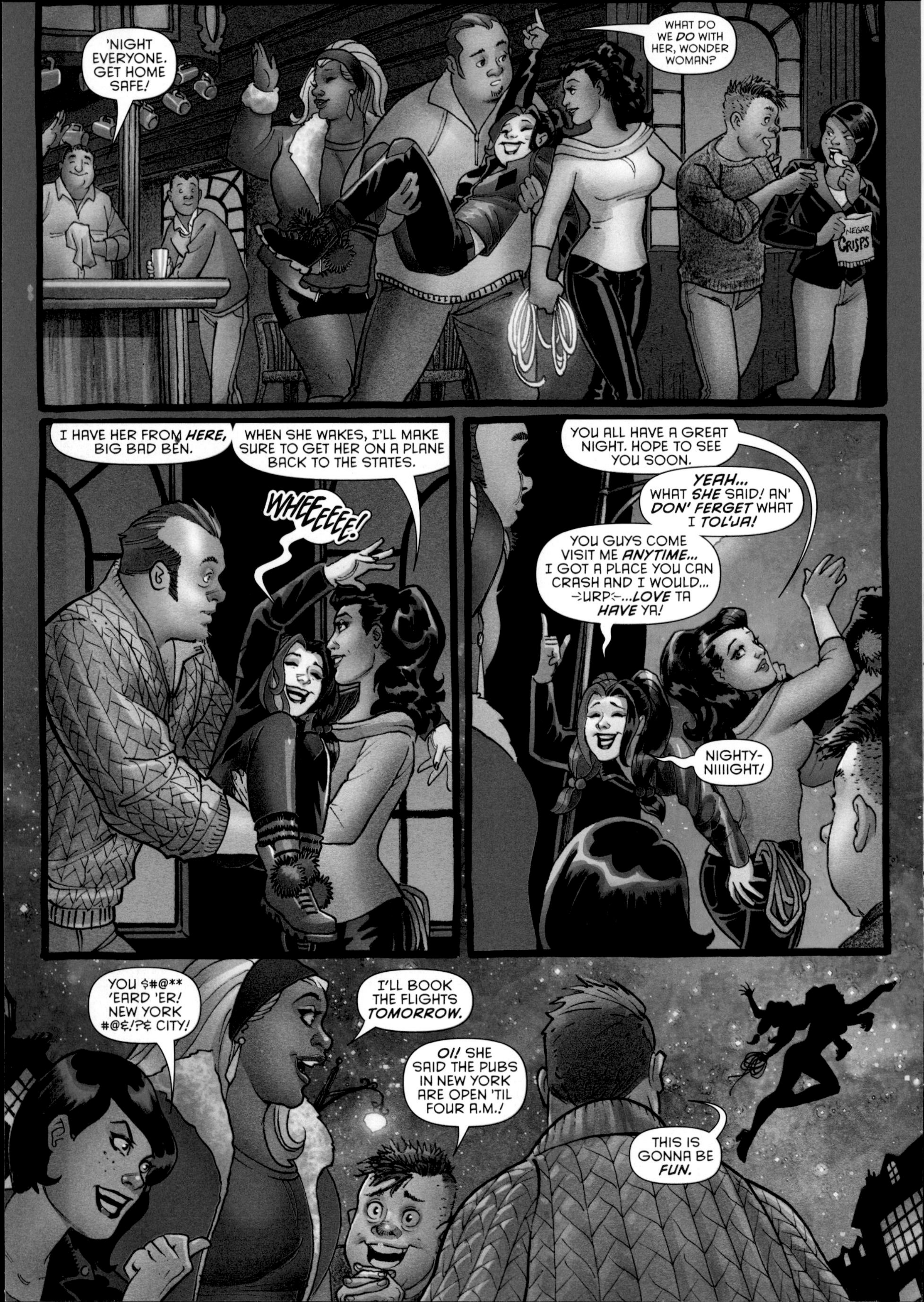
'NIGHT EVERYONE. GET HOME SAFE!
WHAT DO WE *DO* WITH HER, WONDER WOMAN?
NEGAR CRISPS
I HAVE HER FROM *HERE,* BIG BAD BEN.
WHEN SHE WAKES, I'LL MAKE SURE TO GET HER ON A PLANE BACK TO THE STATES.
WHEEEEEE!
YOU ALL HAVE A GREAT NIGHT. HOPE TO SEE YOU SOON.
YEAH... WHAT *SHE* SAID! AN' *DON' FERGET* WHAT I *TOL'JA!*
YOU GUYS COME VISIT ME *ANYTIME...* I GOT A PLACE YOU CAN CRASH AND I WOULD... ->URP<-...*LOVE* TA *HAVE* YA!
NIGHTY-NIIIIGHT!
YOU $#@** 'EARD 'ER! NEW YORK #@&!?& CITY!
I'LL BOOK THE FLIGHTS *TOMORROW.*
OI! SHE SAID THE PUBS IN NEW YORK ARE OPEN 'TIL FOUR A.M.!
THIS IS GONNA BE *FUN.*

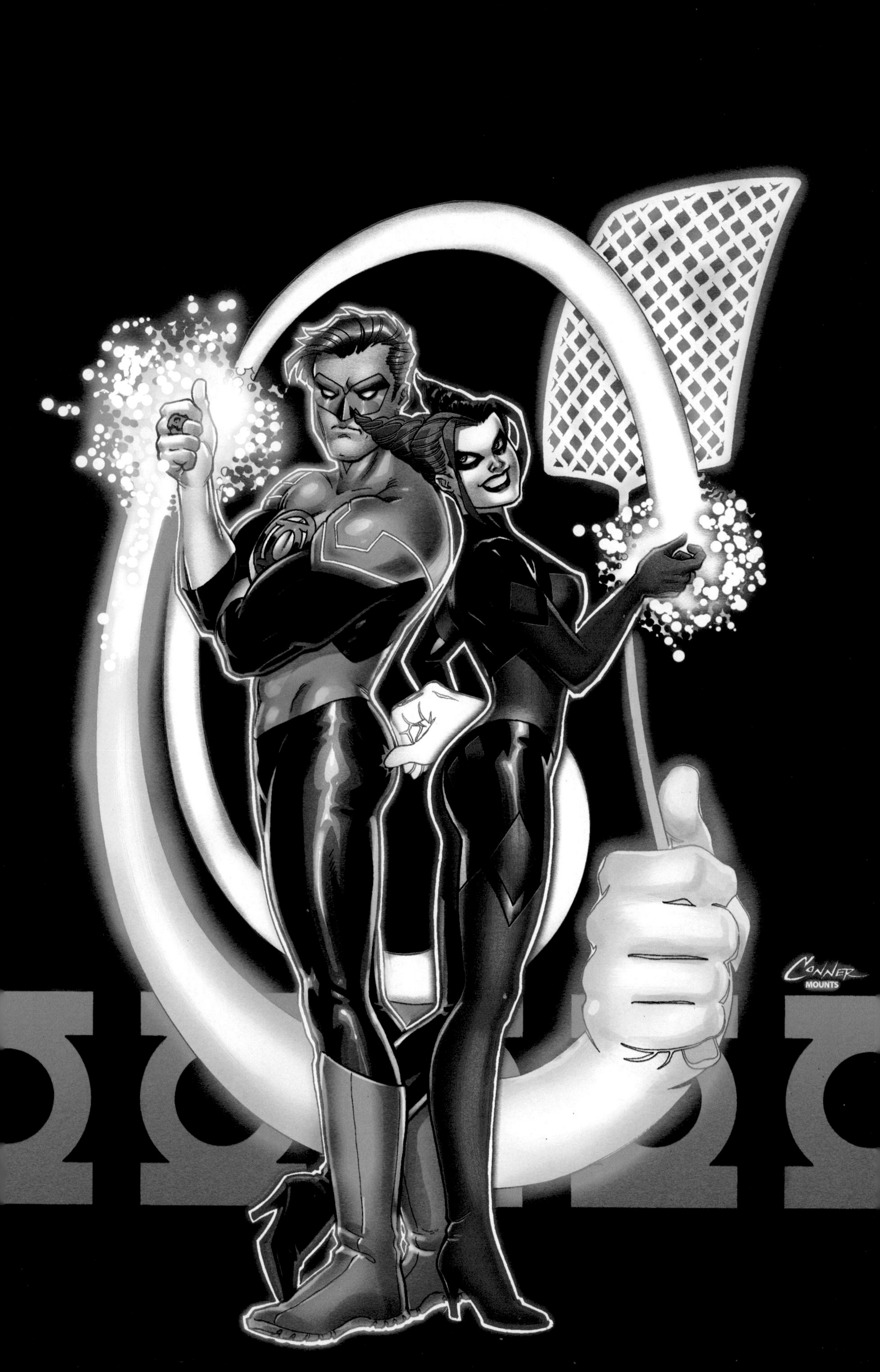
CONNER
MOUNTS

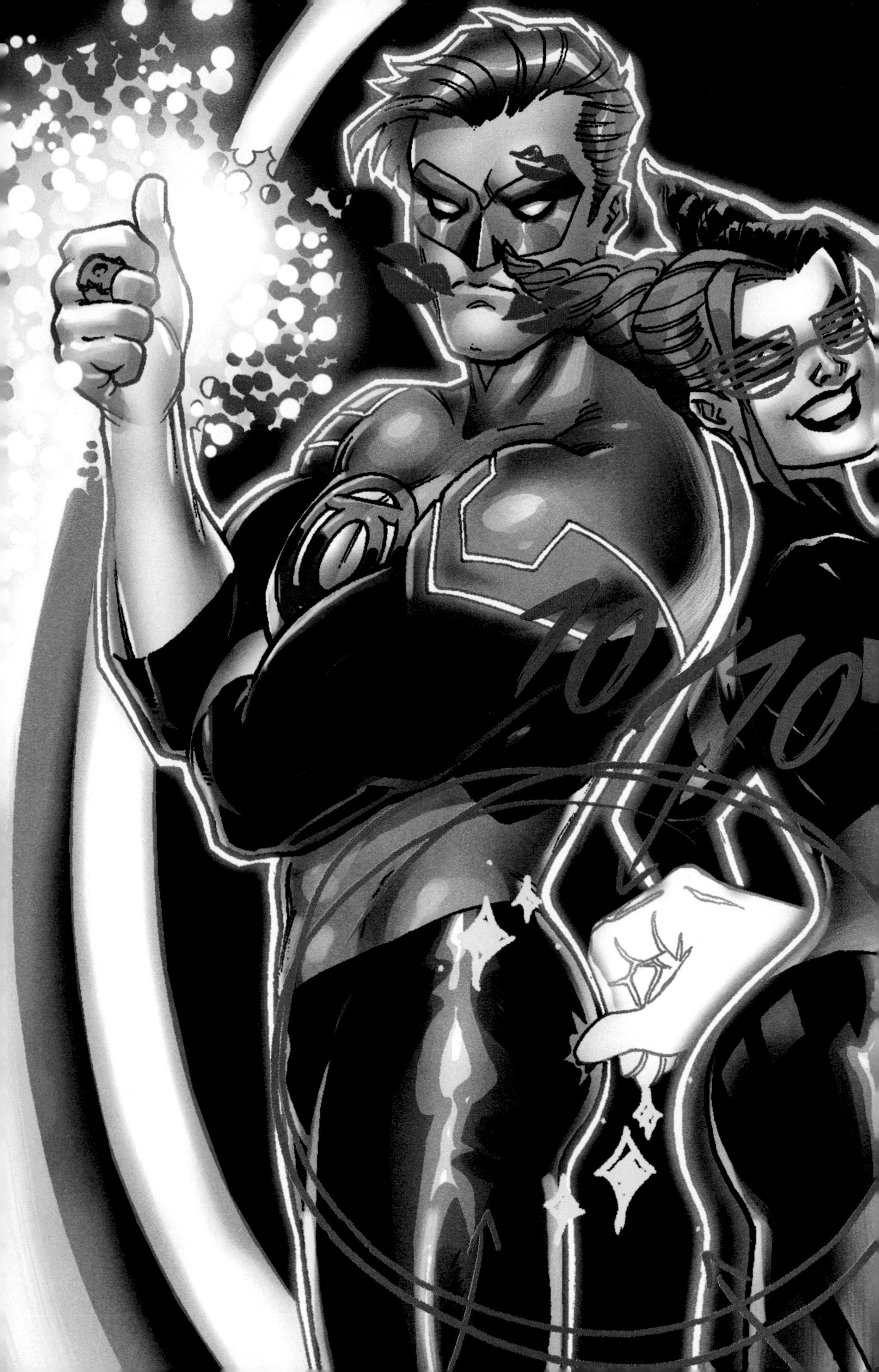
10/10

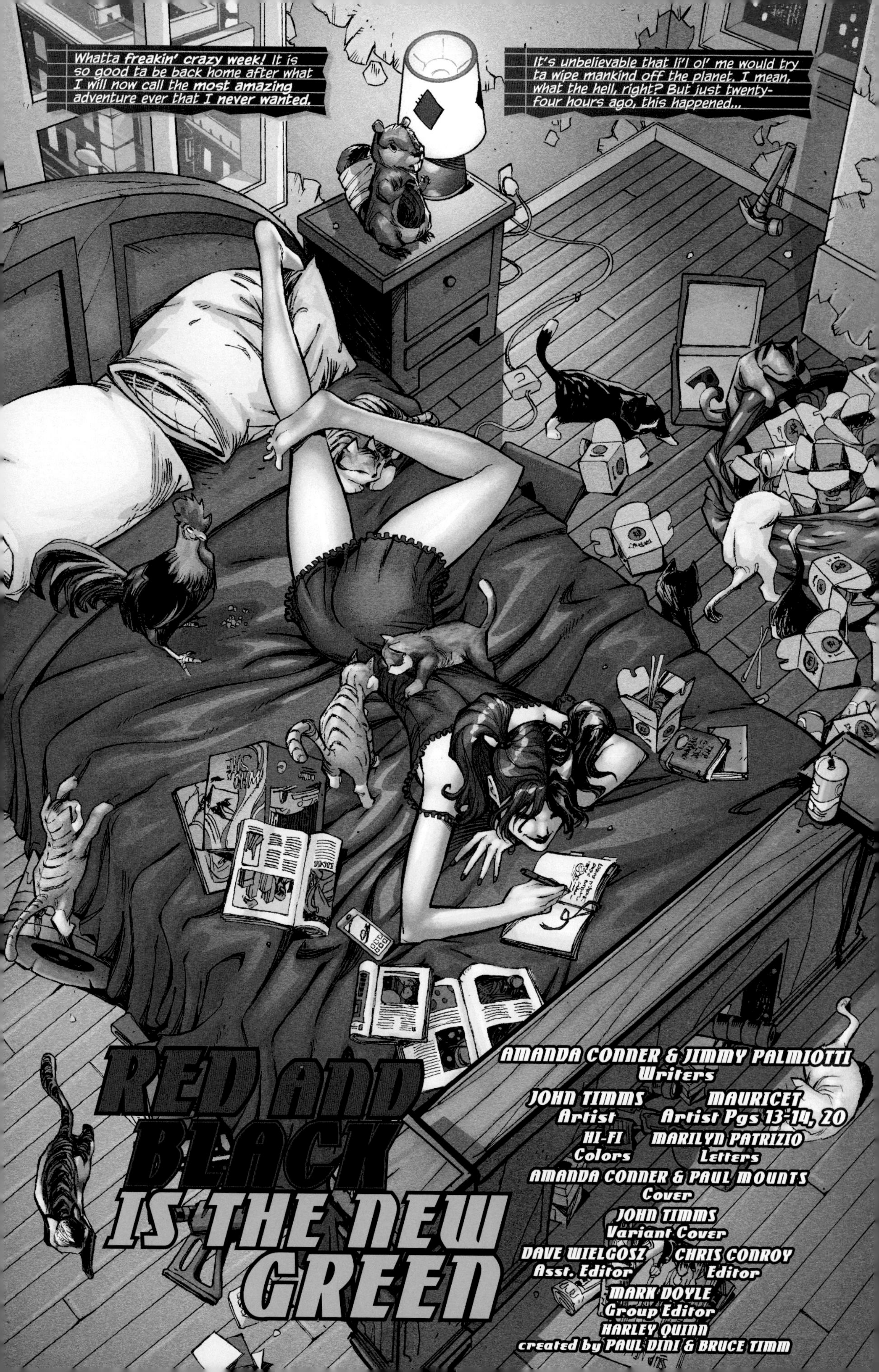
Whatta freakin' crazy week! It is so good ta be back home after what I will now call the most amazing adventure ever that I never wanted.
It's unbelievable that li'l ol' me would try ta wipe mankind off the planet. I mean, what the hell, right? But just twenty-four hours ago, this happened...
RED AND BLACK IS THE NEW GREEN
AMANDA CONNER & JIMMY PALMIOTTI Writers
JOHN TIMMS Artist
MAURICET Artist Pgs 13-14, 20
HI-FI Colors
MARILYN PATRIZIO Letters
AMANDA CONNER & PAUL MOUNTS Cover
JOHN TIMMS Variant Cover
DAVE WIELGOSZ Asst. Editor
CHRIS CONROY Editor
MARK DOYLE Group Editor
HARLEY QUINN created by PAUL DINI & BRUCE TIMM

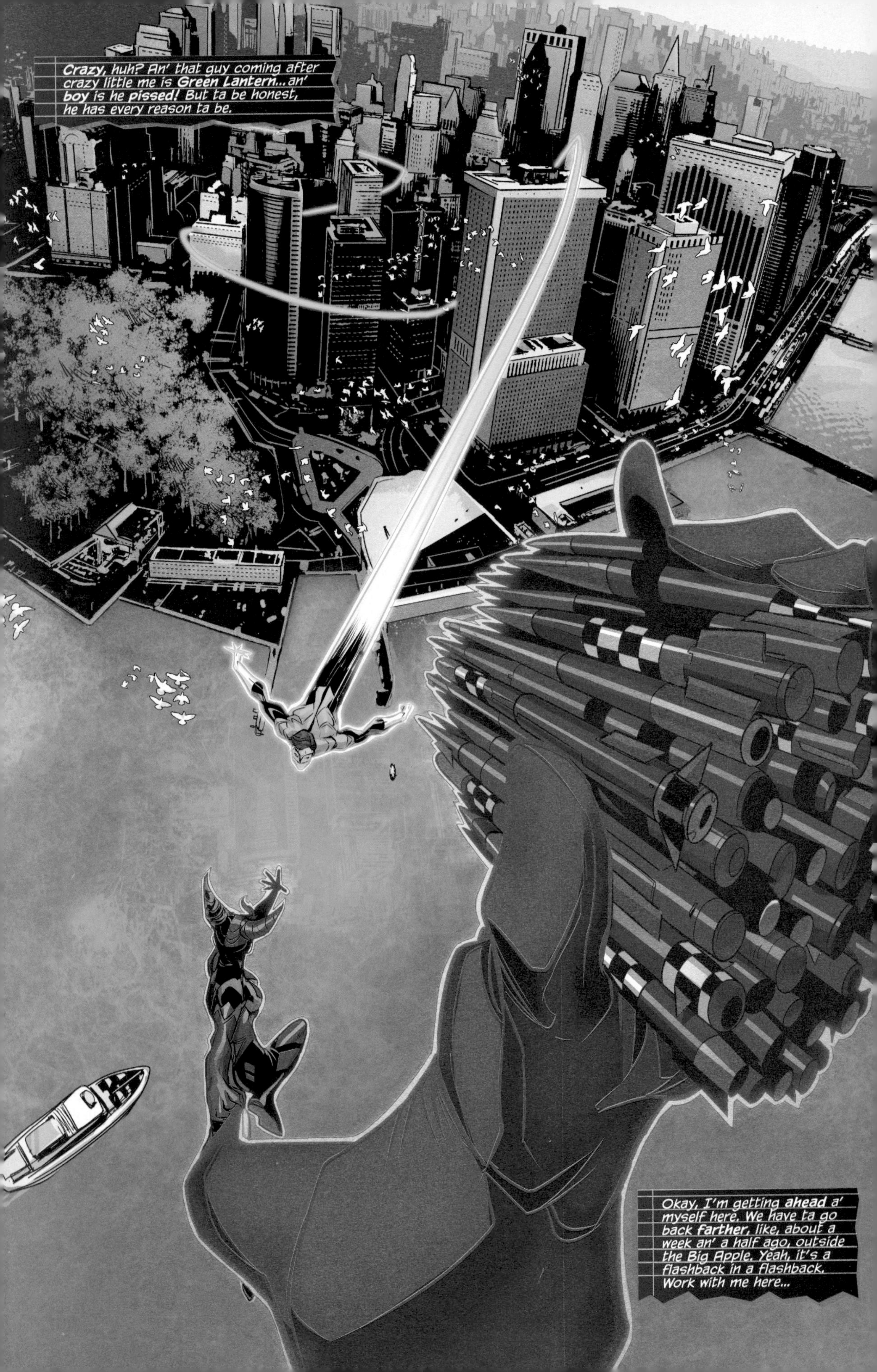
Crazy, huh? An' that guy coming after crazy little me is Green Lantern...an' boy is he pissed! But ta be honest, he has every reason ta be.
Okay, I'm getting ahead a' myself here. We have ta go back farther, like, about a week an' a half ago, outside the Big Apple. Yeah, it's a flashback in a flashback. Work with me here...

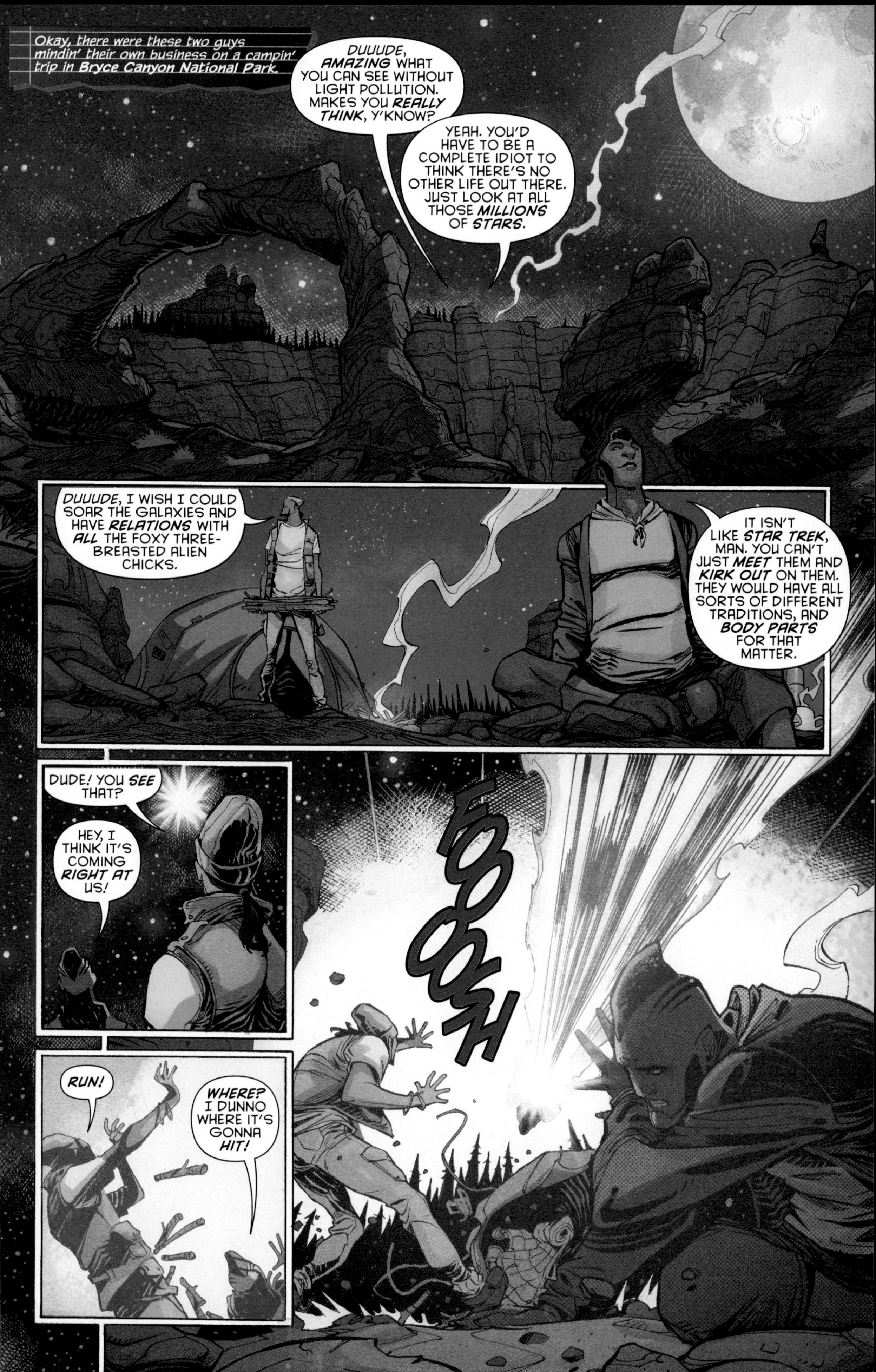
Okay, there were these two guys mindin' their own business on a campin' trip in Bryce Canyon National Park.
DUUUDE, AMAZING WHAT YOU CAN SEE WITHOUT LIGHT POLLUTION. MAKES YOU REALLY THINK, Y'KNOW?
YEAH. YOU'D HAVE TO BE A COMPLETE IDIOT TO THINK THERE'S NO OTHER LIFE OUT THERE. JUST LOOK AT ALL THOSE MILLIONS OF STARS.
DUUUDE, I WISH I COULD SOAR THE GALAXIES AND HAVE RELATIONS WITH ALL THE FOXY THREE-BREASTED ALIEN CHICKS.
IT ISN'T LIKE STAR TREK, MAN. YOU CAN'T JUST MEET THEM AND KIRK OUT ON THEM. THEY WOULD HAVE ALL SORTS OF DIFFERENT TRADITIONS, AND BODY PARTS FOR THAT MATTER.
DUDE! YOU SEE THAT?
HEY, I THINK IT'S COMING RIGHT AT US!
FOOOOOOSH
RUN!
WHERE? I DUNNO WHERE IT'S GONNA HIT!

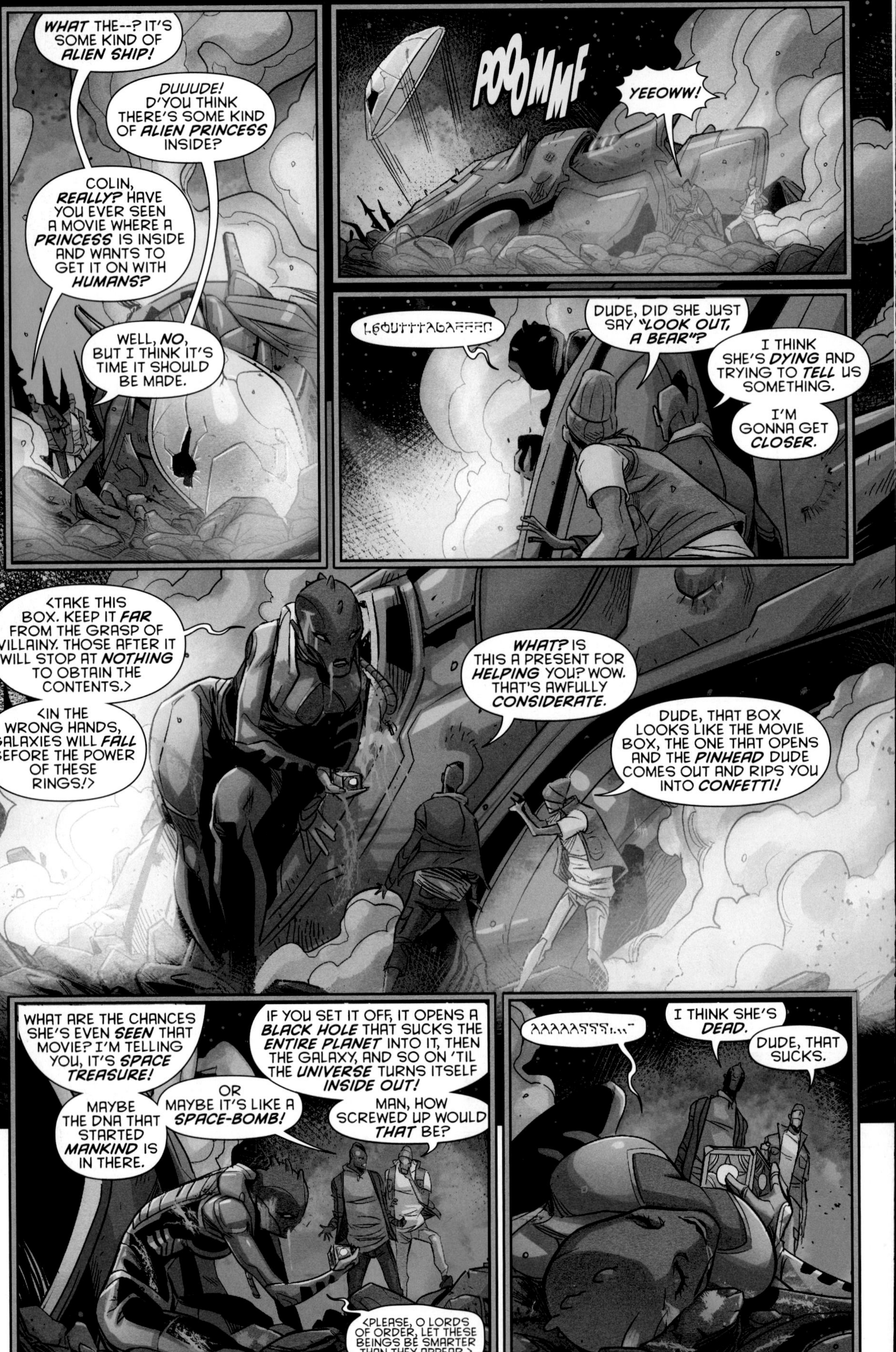
WHAT THE--? IT'S SOME KIND OF ALIEN SHIP!
DUUUDE! D'YOU THINK THERE'S SOME KIND OF ALIEN PRINCESS INSIDE?
COLIN, REALLY? HAVE YOU EVER SEEN A MOVIE WHERE A PRINCESS IS INSIDE AND WANTS TO GET IT ON WITH HUMANS?
WELL, NO, BUT I THINK IT'S TIME IT SHOULD BE MADE.
POOOMMF
YEEOWW!
DUDE, DID SHE JUST SAY "LOOK OUT, A BEAR"?
I THINK SHE'S DYING AND TRYING TO TELL US SOMETHING.
I'M GONNA GET CLOSER.
<TAKE THIS BOX. KEEP IT FAR FROM THE GRASP OF VILLAINY. THOSE AFTER IT WILL STOP AT NOTHING TO OBTAIN THE CONTENTS.>
<IN THE WRONG HANDS, GALAXIES WILL FALL BEFORE THE POWER OF THESE RINGS!>
WHAT? IS THIS A PRESENT FOR HELPING YOU? WOW. THAT'S AWFULLY CONSIDERATE.
DUDE, THAT BOX LOOKS LIKE THE MOVIE BOX, THE ONE THAT OPENS AND THE PINHEAD DUDE COMES OUT AND RIPS YOU INTO CONFETTI!
WHAT ARE THE CHANCES SHE'S EVEN SEEN THAT MOVIE? I'M TELLING YOU, IT'S SPACE TREASURE!
MAYBE THE DNA THAT STARTED MANKIND IS IN THERE.
OR MAYBE IT'S LIKE A SPACE-BOMB!
IF YOU SET IT OFF, IT OPENS A BLACK HOLE THAT SUCKS THE ENTIRE PLANET INTO IT, THEN THE GALAXY, AND SO ON 'TIL THE UNIVERSE TURNS ITSELF INSIDE OUT!
MAN, HOW SCREWED UP WOULD THAT BE?
<PLEASE, O LORDS OF ORDER, LET THESE BEINGS BE SMARTER THAN THEY APPEAR.>
I THINK SHE'S DEAD.
DUDE, THAT SUCKS.

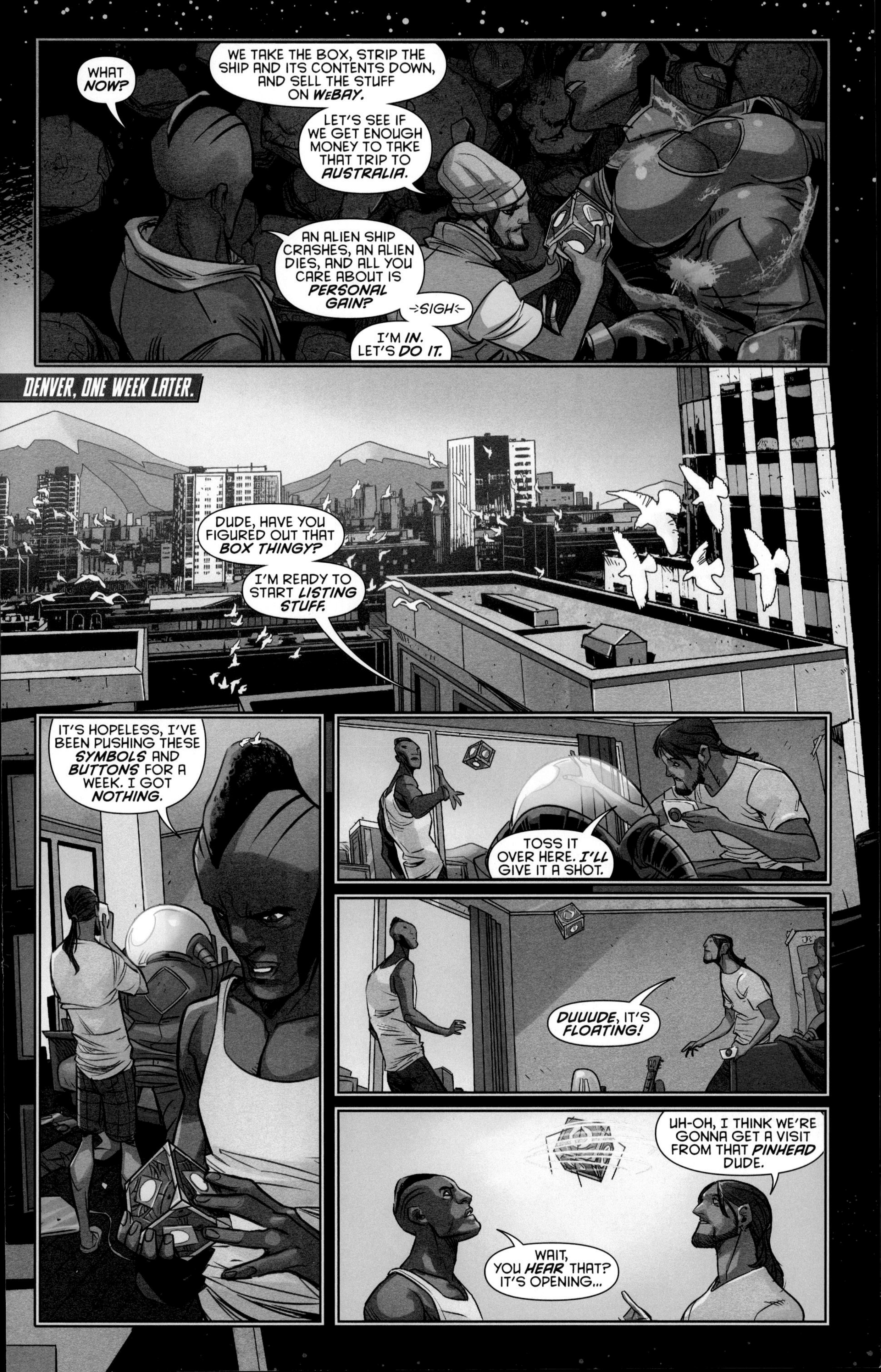
WHAT NOW?
WE TAKE THE BOX, STRIP THE SHIP AND ITS CONTENTS DOWN, AND SELL THE STUFF ON WeBAY.
LET'S SEE IF WE GET ENOUGH MONEY TO TAKE THAT TRIP TO AUSTRALIA.
AN ALIEN SHIP CRASHES, AN ALIEN DIES, AND ALL YOU CARE ABOUT IS PERSONAL GAIN?
SIGH
I'M IN. LET'S DO IT.
DENVER, ONE WEEK LATER.
DUDE, HAVE YOU FIGURED OUT THAT BOX THINGY?
I'M READY TO START LISTING STUFF.
IT'S HOPELESS, I'VE BEEN PUSHING THESE SYMBOLS AND BUTTONS FOR A WEEK. I GOT NOTHING.
TOSS IT OVER HERE. I'LL GIVE IT A SHOT.
DUUUDE, IT'S FLOATING!
UH-OH, I THINK WE'RE GONNA GET A VISIT FROM THAT PINHEAD DUDE.
WAIT, YOU HEAR THAT? IT'S OPENING...

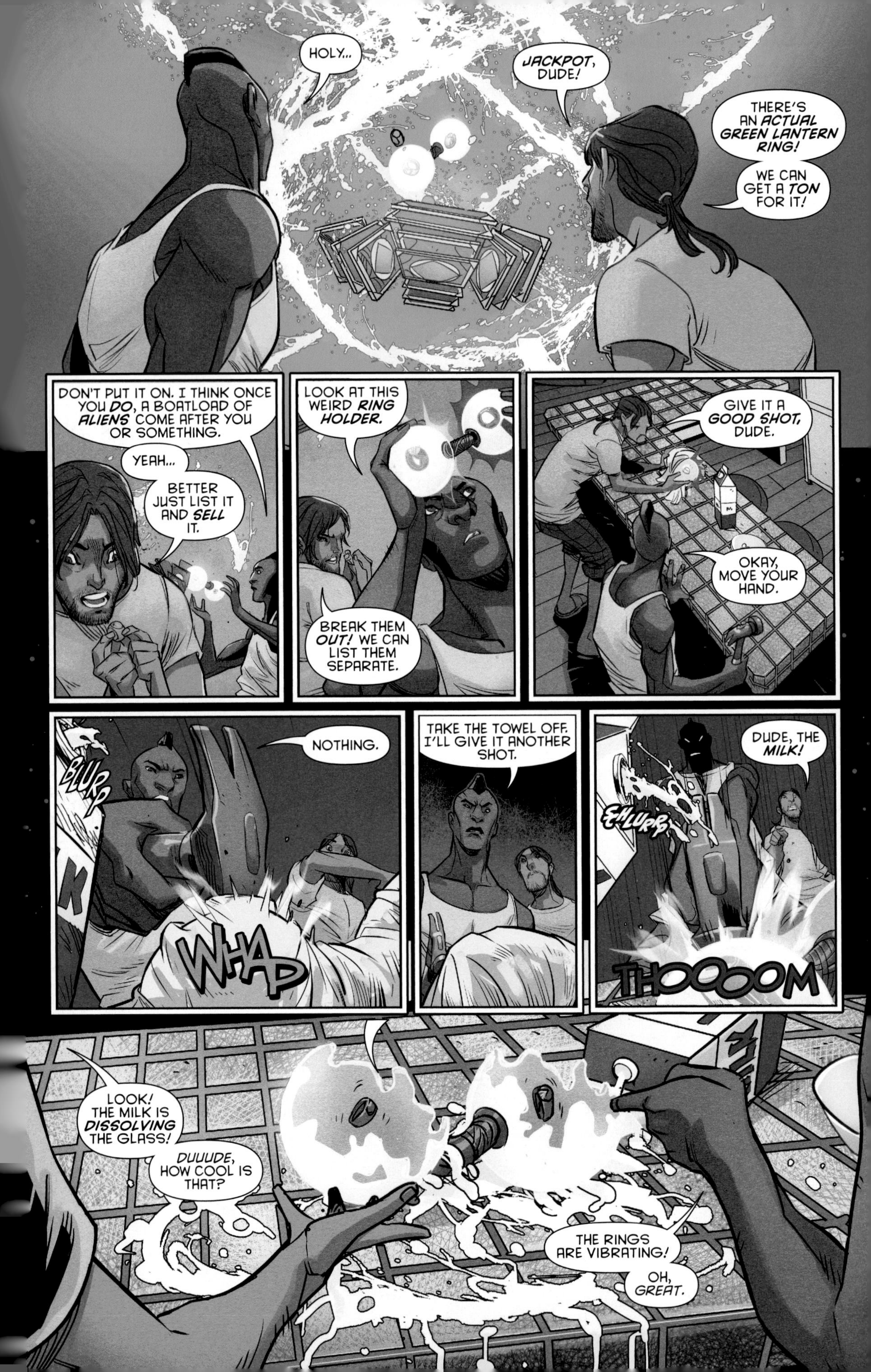

HOLY...
JACKPOT, DUDE!
THERE'S AN ACTUAL GREEN LANTERN RING!
WE CAN GET A TON FOR IT!
DON'T PUT IT ON. I THINK ONCE YOU DO, A BOATLOAD OF ALIENS COME AFTER YOU OR SOMETHING.
YEAH...
BETTER JUST LIST IT AND SELL IT.
LOOK AT THIS WEIRD RING HOLDER.
BREAK THEM OUT! WE CAN LIST THEM SEPARATE.
GIVE IT A GOOD SHOT, DUDE.
OKAY, MOVE YOUR HAND.
BLURP
NOTHING.
WHAP
TAKE THE TOWEL OFF. I'LL GIVE IT ANOTHER SHOT.
DUDE, THE MILK!
EHLURP
THOOOOOM
LOOK! THE MILK IS DISSOLVING THE GLASS!
DUUUDE, HOW COOL IS THAT?
THE RINGS ARE VIBRATING!
OH, GREAT.

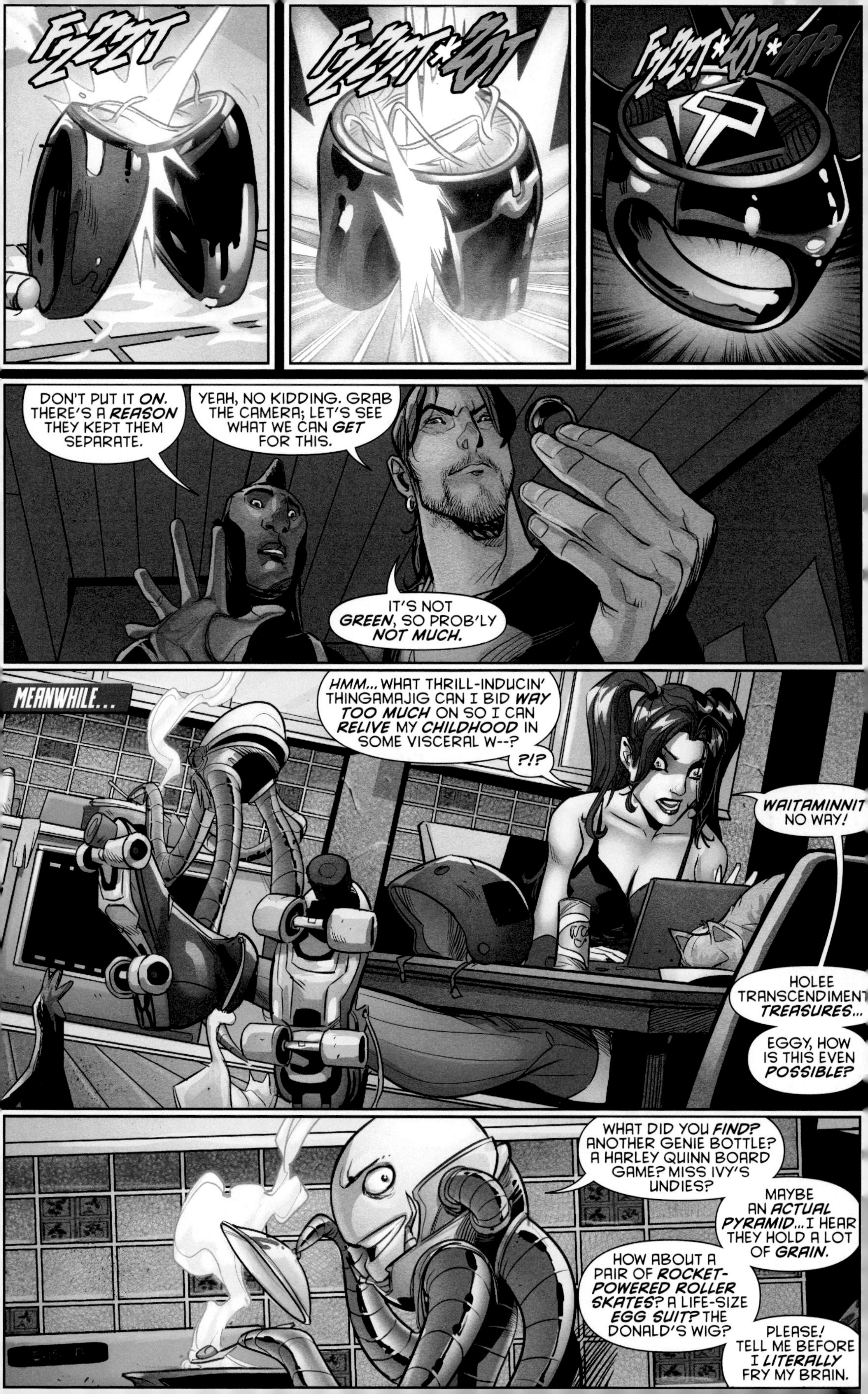
FZZZT
FZZZT*ZOT
FZZZT*ZOT*PAPP
DON'T PUT IT ON. THERE'S A REASON THEY KEPT THEM SEPARATE.
YEAH, NO KIDDING. GRAB THE CAMERA; LET'S SEE WHAT WE CAN GET FOR THIS.
IT'S NOT GREEN, SO PROB'LY NOT MUCH.
MEANWHILE...
HMM... WHAT THRILL-INDUCIN' THINGAMAJIG CAN I BID WAY TOO MUCH ON SO I CAN RELIVE MY CHILDHOOD IN SOME VISCERAL W--?
?!?
WAITAMINNIT NO WAY!
HOLEE TRANSCENDIMENT TREASURES...
EGGY, HOW IS THIS EVEN POSSIBLE?
WHAT DID YOU FIND? ANOTHER GENIE BOTTLE? A HARLEY QUINN BOARD GAME? MISS IVY'S UNDIES?
MAYBE AN ACTUAL PYRAMID... I HEAR THEY HOLD A LOT OF GRAIN.
HOW ABOUT A PAIR OF ROCKET-POWERED ROLLER SKATES? A LIFE-SIZE EGG SUIT? THE DONALD'S WIG?
PLEASE! TELL ME BEFORE I LITERALLY FRY MY BRAIN.

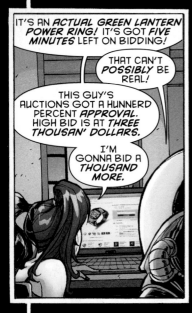

IT'S AN *ACTUAL GREEN LANTERN POWER RING!* IT'S GOT *FIVE MINUTES* LEFT ON BIDDING!

THAT CAN'T *POSSIBLY* BE REAL!

THIS GUY'S AUCTIONS GOT A HUNNERD PERCENT *APPROVAL.* HIGH BID IS AT *THREE THOUSAN' DOLLARS.*

I'M GONNA BID A *THOUSAND* MORE.

FOUR MORE MINUTES AND YOU'RE *MINE,* MY SWEET EMERALD BEAUTY!

DING GEOFF JOHNS

WHAT?! I'M BEING OUTBID BY *"SHOPAHARLIC"?*

NO WAY. NOT HAPPENING.

OUTBID? OUTBID?! OH, *YEAH?* HOW DOES *TEN GRAND* SOUND?

OH *NO.*

TEN GRAND? HOW ABOUT *THIRTY GRAND,* BUDDY?

DC RULES

TAKE THIS *FIFTY GRAND* AN' *SHOVE IT!*

OH MY GOODNESS. THIS IS A MISTAKE.

MISS HARLEY, *PLEASE!*

I *NEVER* LOSE WHEN I WEAR MY *LUCKY LANTERN* SHIRT...

...OKAY...

A *HUNDRED GRAND.* LET'S SEE YOU BEAT *THAT* BID, BOZO!

DC RULES

OOOOO! FINE! A *HUNNERT AN' FIFTY GRAND!* SUCK ON *THAT,* PAL!

UGGHH...

HE ONLY HAS *TWENNY SECONDS* LEFT! HA! I GOT THIS!

TWO HUNDRED GRAND... AND *THREE...*

TWO...

ONE...

IT'S *MINE!*

MINE!

ALL...

DC RULES

...MINE...

OH BOY. WHAT DID I JUST DO?

MY WIFE IS GONNA KILL ME.

NOoOoOo!

I LOST THE BID.

HOW COULD THIS *HAPPEN...?*

DING

HUH?

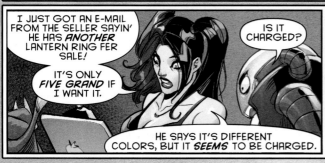

I JUST GOT AN E-MAIL FROM THE SELLER SAYIN' HE HAS *ANOTHER* LANTERN RING FER SALE!

IT'S ONLY *FIVE GRAND* IF I WANT IT.

IS IT *CHARGED?*

HE SAYS IT'S DIFFERENT COLORS, BUT IT *SEEMS* TO BE CHARGED.

I DON'T CARE. I *WANT* IT!

SOLD.

enter

THE NEXT DAY, IN THE MOJAVE DESERT...

SO, *HAL JORDAN,* HOW DO YOU FEEL TO BE ZE FIRST AMERICAN TO TEST ZE SAJ-45?

WELL, *NO ONE* WAS MORE SURPRISED AT MY BEING ASKED THAN *ME.*

BUT I MUST SAY, KATARINA, WHY SO *FORMAL?*

VHAT HAPPENED LAST NIGHT EES BUSINESS BETWEEN *US.* ZE TEST RUN TODAY EES BUSINESS BETWEEN OUR *COUNTRIES.*

IF THINGS GO AS *SMOOTHLY* AS LAST NIGHT, I SEE OUR NATIONS HAVING A *VERY* LONG-LASTING, FAVORABLE RELATIONSHIP.

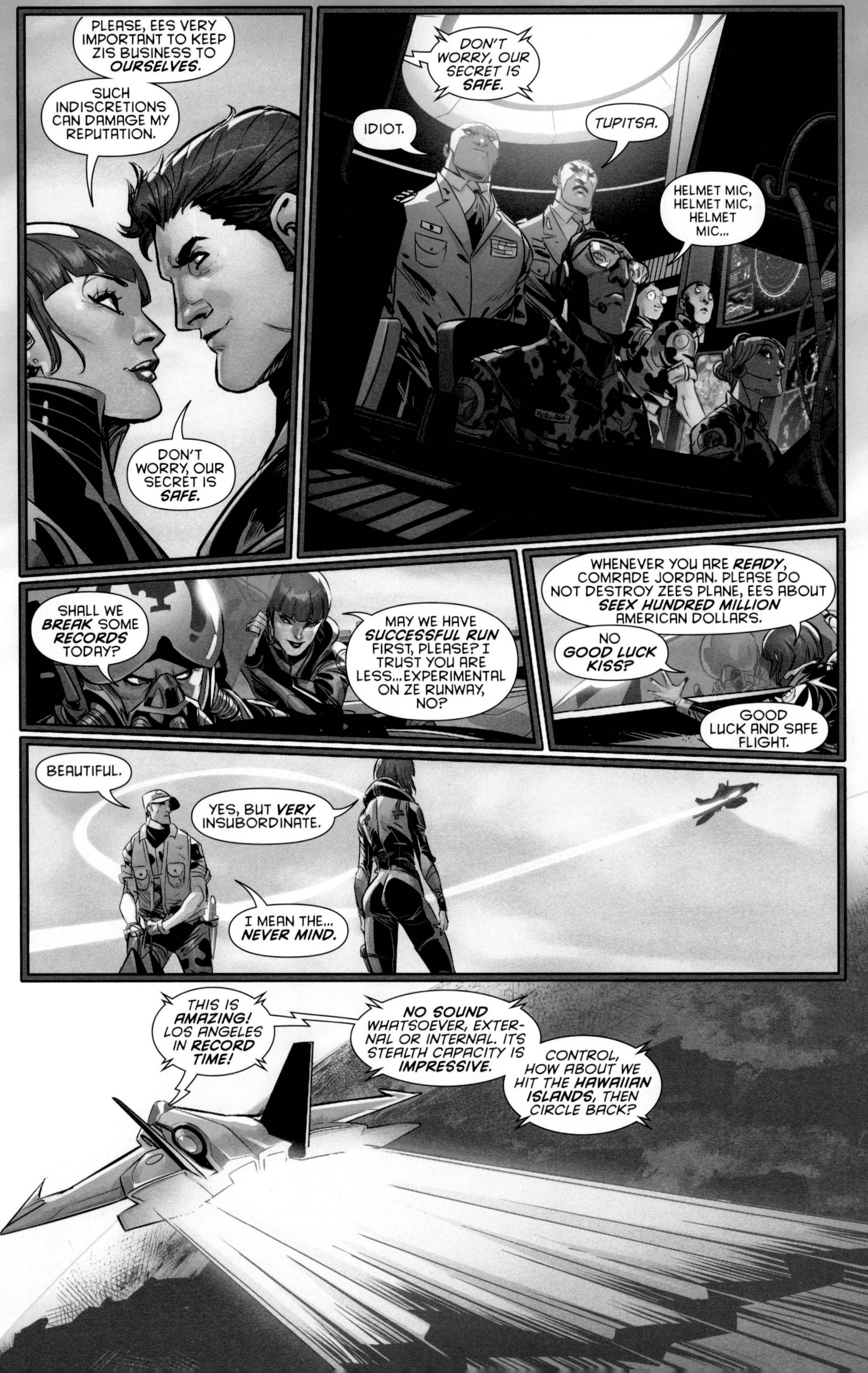
PLEASE, EES VERY IMPORTANT TO KEEP ZIS BUSINESS TO OURSELVES.
SUCH INDISCRETIONS CAN DAMAGE MY REPUTATION.
DON'T WORRY, OUR SECRET IS SAFE.
DON'T WORRY, OUR SECRET IS SAFE.
IDIOT.
TUPITSA.
HELMET MIC, HELMET MIC, HELMET MIC...
SHALL WE BREAK SOME RECORDS TODAY?
MAY WE HAVE SUCCESSFUL RUN FIRST, PLEASE? I TRUST YOU ARE LESS...EXPERIMENTAL ON ZE RUNWAY, NO?
WHENEVER YOU ARE READY, COMRADE JORDAN. PLEASE DO NOT DESTROY ZEES PLANE, EES ABOUT SEEX HUNDRED MILLION AMERICAN DOLLARS.
NO GOOD LUCK KISS?
GOOD LUCK AND SAFE FLIGHT.
BEAUTIFUL.
YES, BUT VERY INSUBORDINATE.
I MEAN THE... NEVER MIND.
THIS IS AMAZING! LOS ANGELES IN RECORD TIME!
NO SOUND WHATSOEVER, EXTERNAL OR INTERNAL. ITS STEALTH CAPACITY IS IMPRESSIVE.
CONTROL, HOW ABOUT WE HIT THE HAWAIIAN ISLANDS, THEN CIRCLE BACK?

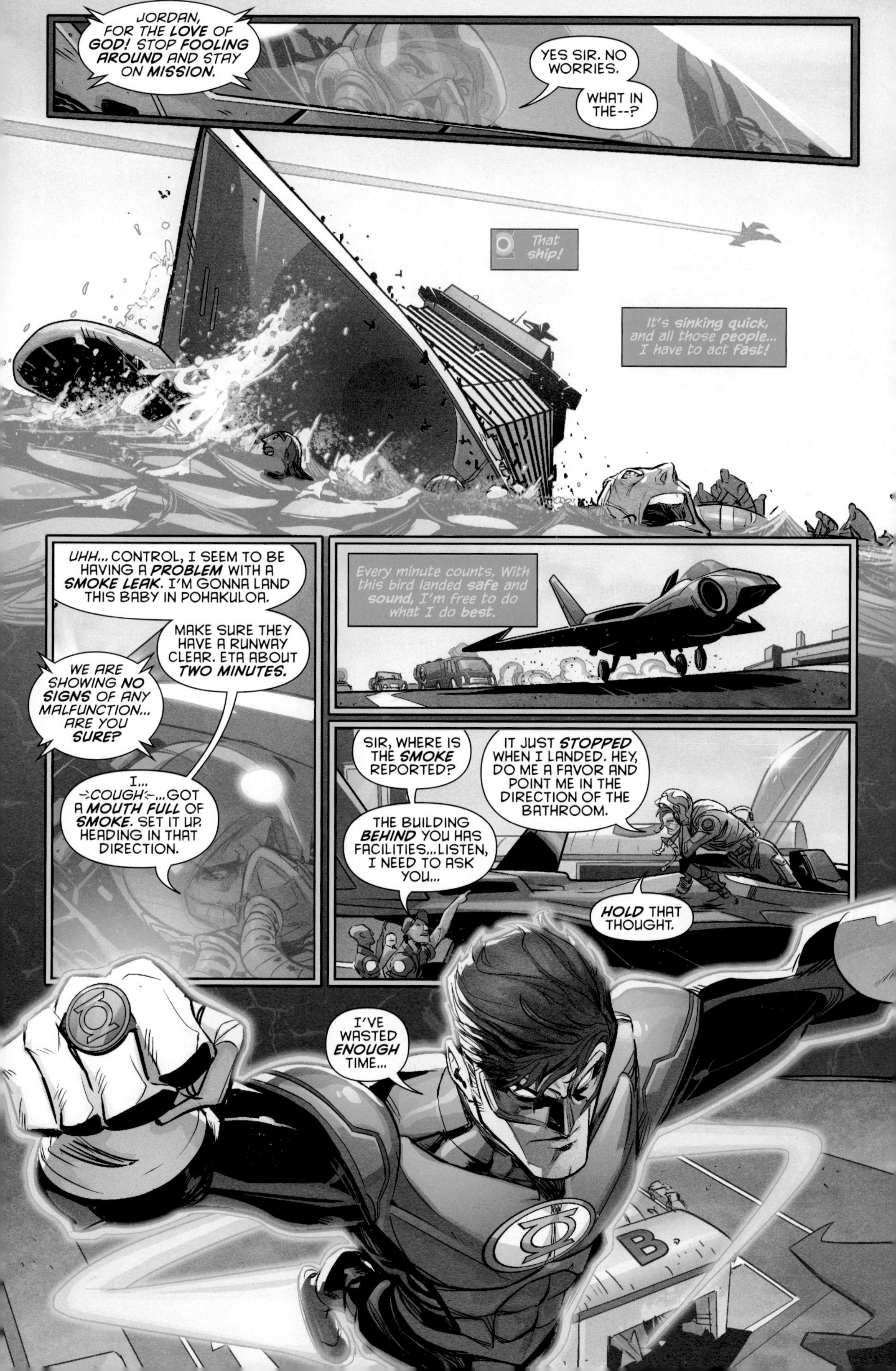

JORDAN, FOR THE LOVE OF GOD! STOP FOOLING AROUND AND STAY ON MISSION.
YES SIR. NO WORRIES.
WHAT IN THE--?
That ship!
It's sinking quick, and all those people... I have to act fast!
UHH... CONTROL, I SEEM TO BE HAVING A PROBLEM WITH A SMOKE LEAK. I'M GONNA LAND THIS BABY IN POHAKULOA.
MAKE SURE THEY HAVE A RUNWAY CLEAR. ETA ABOUT TWO MINUTES.
WE ARE SHOWING NO SIGNS OF ANY MALFUNCTION... ARE YOU SURE?
I... ⇒COUGH⇐...GOT A MOUTH FULL OF SMOKE. SET IT UP. HEADING IN THAT DIRECTION.
Every minute counts. With this bird landed safe and sound, I'm free to do what I do best.
SIR, WHERE IS THE SMOKE REPORTED?
IT JUST STOPPED WHEN I LANDED. HEY, DO ME A FAVOR AND POINT ME IN THE DIRECTION OF THE BATHROOM.
THE BUILDING BEHIND YOU HAS FACILITIES...LISTEN, I NEED TO ASK YOU...
HOLD THAT THOUGHT.
I'VE WASTED ENOUGH TIME...

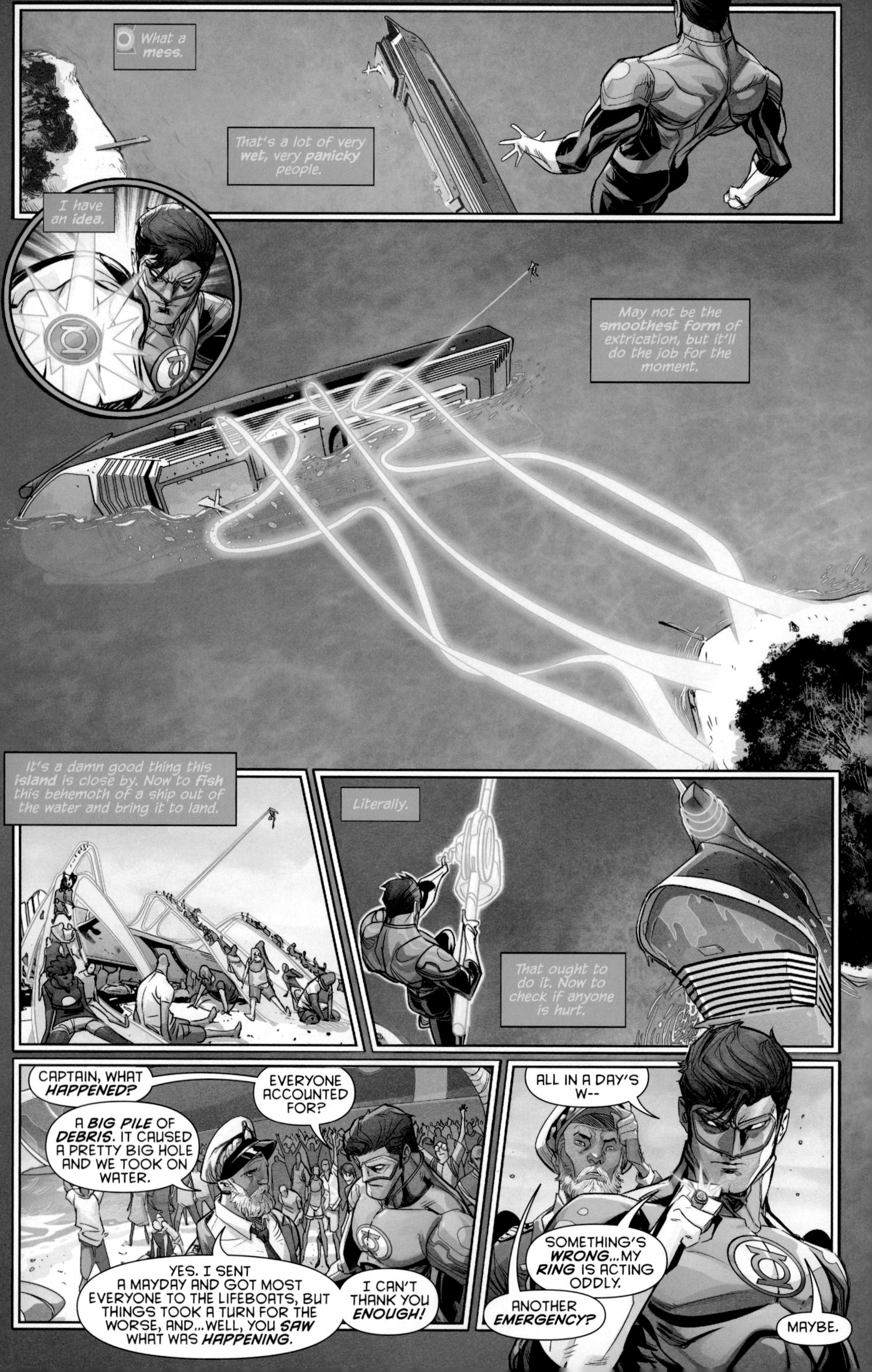
What a mess.
That's a lot of very wet, very panicky people.
I have an idea.
May not be the smoothest form of extrication, but it'll do the job for the moment.
It's a damn good thing this island is close by. Now to fish this behemoth of a ship out of the water and bring it to land.
Literally.
That ought to do it. Now to check if anyone is hurt.
CAPTAIN, WHAT HAPPENED?
A BIG PILE OF DEBRIS. IT CAUSED A PRETTY BIG HOLE AND WE TOOK ON WATER.
EVERYONE ACCOUNTED FOR?
YES. I SENT A MAYDAY AND GOT MOST EVERYONE TO THE LIFEBOATS, BUT THINGS TOOK A TURN FOR THE WORSE, AND...WELL, YOU SAW WHAT WAS HAPPENING.
I CAN'T THANK YOU ENOUGH!
ALL IN A DAY'S W--
SOMETHING'S WRONG...MY RING IS ACTING ODDLY.
ANOTHER EMERGENCY?
MAYBE.

NEW YORK #$%€!' CITY

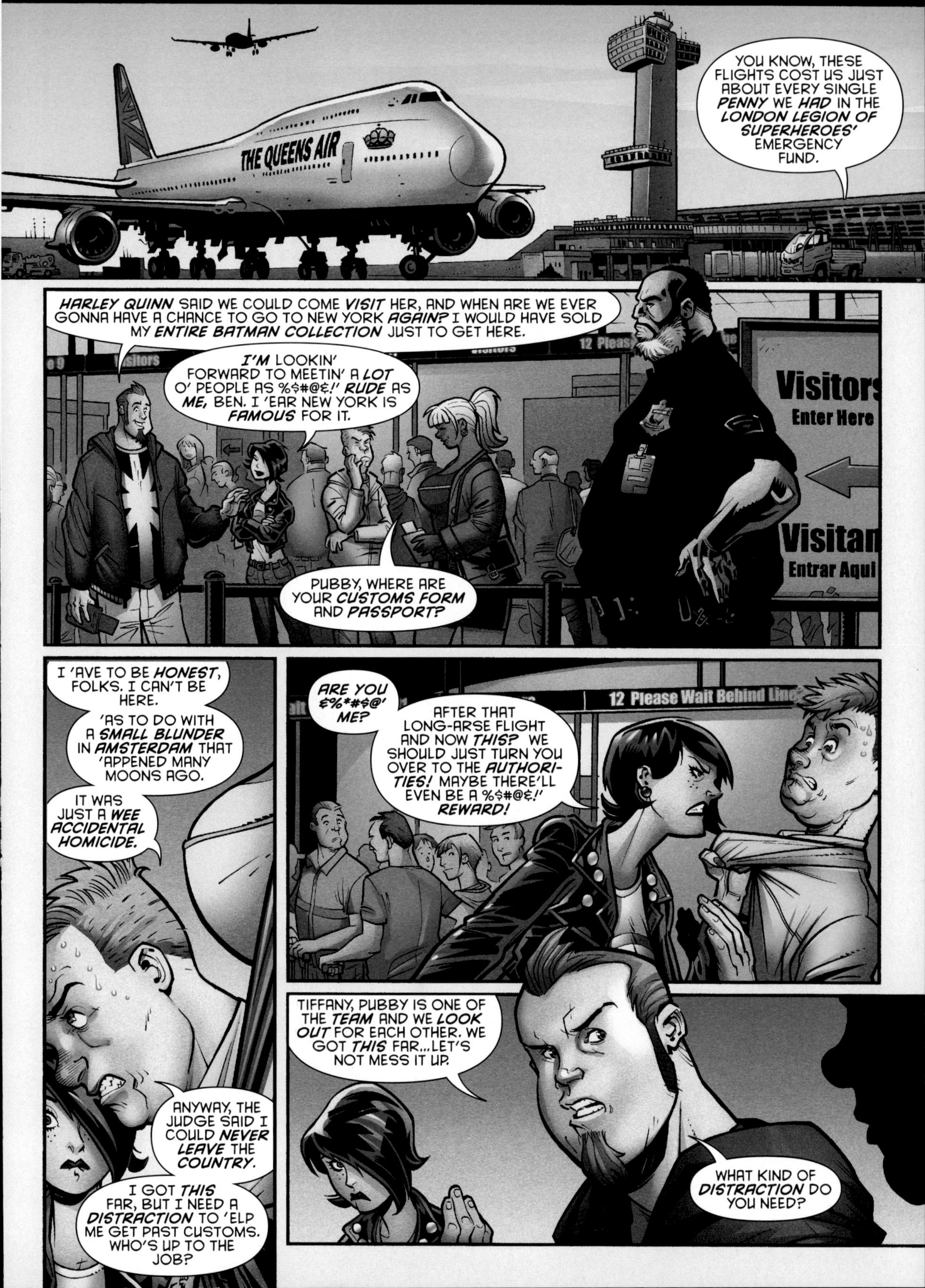
THE QUEENS AIR
YOU KNOW, THESE FLIGHTS COST US JUST ABOUT EVERY SINGLE PENNY WE HAD IN THE LONDON LEGION OF SUPERHEROES' EMERGENCY FUND.
HARLEY QUINN SAID WE COULD COME VISIT HER, AND WHEN ARE WE EVER GONNA HAVE A CHANCE TO GO TO NEW YORK AGAIN? I WOULD HAVE SOLD MY ENTIRE BATMAN COLLECTION JUST TO GET HERE.
I'M LOOKIN' FORWARD TO MEETIN' A LOT O' PEOPLE AS %$#@€!' RUDE AS ME, BEN. I 'EAR NEW YORK IS FAMOUS FOR IT.
Visitors
Visitors Enter Here
Visitantes Entrar Aqui
PUBBY, WHERE ARE YOUR CUSTOMS FORM AND PASSPORT?
I 'AVE TO BE HONEST, FOLKS. I CAN'T BE HERE.
'AS TO DO WITH A SMALL BLUNDER IN AMSTERDAM THAT 'APPENED MANY MOONS AGO.
IT WAS JUST A WEE ACCIDENTAL HOMICIDE.
ANYWAY, THE JUDGE SAID I COULD NEVER LEAVE THE COUNTRY.
I GOT THIS FAR, BUT I NEED A DISTRACTION TO 'ELP ME GET PAST CUSTOMS. WHO'S UP TO THE JOB?
12 Please Wait Behind Line
ARE YOU €%*#$@' ME?
AFTER THAT LONG-ARSE FLIGHT AND NOW THIS? WE SHOULD JUST TURN YOU OVER TO THE AUTHORITIES! MAYBE THERE'LL EVEN BE A %$#@€!' REWARD!
TIFFANY, PUBBY IS ONE OF THE TEAM AND WE LOOK OUT FOR EACH OTHER. WE GOT THIS FAR...LET'S NOT MESS IT UP.
WHAT KIND OF DISTRACTION DO YOU NEED?

WELL, I THINK I JUST *CACKED* IN ME *KECKS*.

ALL THOSE FREE DRINKS THEY WERE POURIN' AND THAT FISH DINNER FINALLY SWAM *DOWNSTREAM*, IF YOU GET MY MEANIN'.

SIR, PLEASE STEP OUT OF THE LINE AND *FOLLOW US.*

WOULD WE BE MAKIN' A BEE-LINE TO THE BOG?

YES, THEN TO A *SHOWER* AND A STERILE ROOM FOR *INTERROGATION.*

KEEP THE CAB ON *HOLD* 'TIL I GET *BACK.*

@#$%**!

WE SHOULD *DO* SOMETHING.

YOU *HEARD* HIM, DOUBLE DECKER. WE'LL WAIT OUTSIDE.

HOW ARE YOU *DOING* IN THERE, SIR?

I PERFORM BETTER *WITHOUT* AN ATTENTIVE AUDIENCE RIGHT OUTSIDE ME LAVVY.

FINE, WE'LL WAIT OUTSIDE. I CAN *USE* A FRESH WHIFF OF OXYGEN.

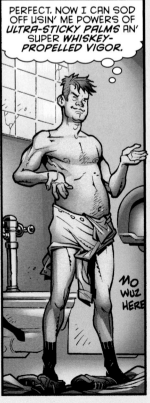

PERFECT. NOW I CAN SOD OFF USIN' ME POWERS OF *ULTRA-STICKY PALMS* AN' SUPER *WHISKEY-PROPELLED VIGOR.*

MO WUZ HERE

OI! EASY PEASY FER THE PLUCKY *PUB CRAWLER.*

I COULD DO WITH A *DRINK* AFTER THIS.

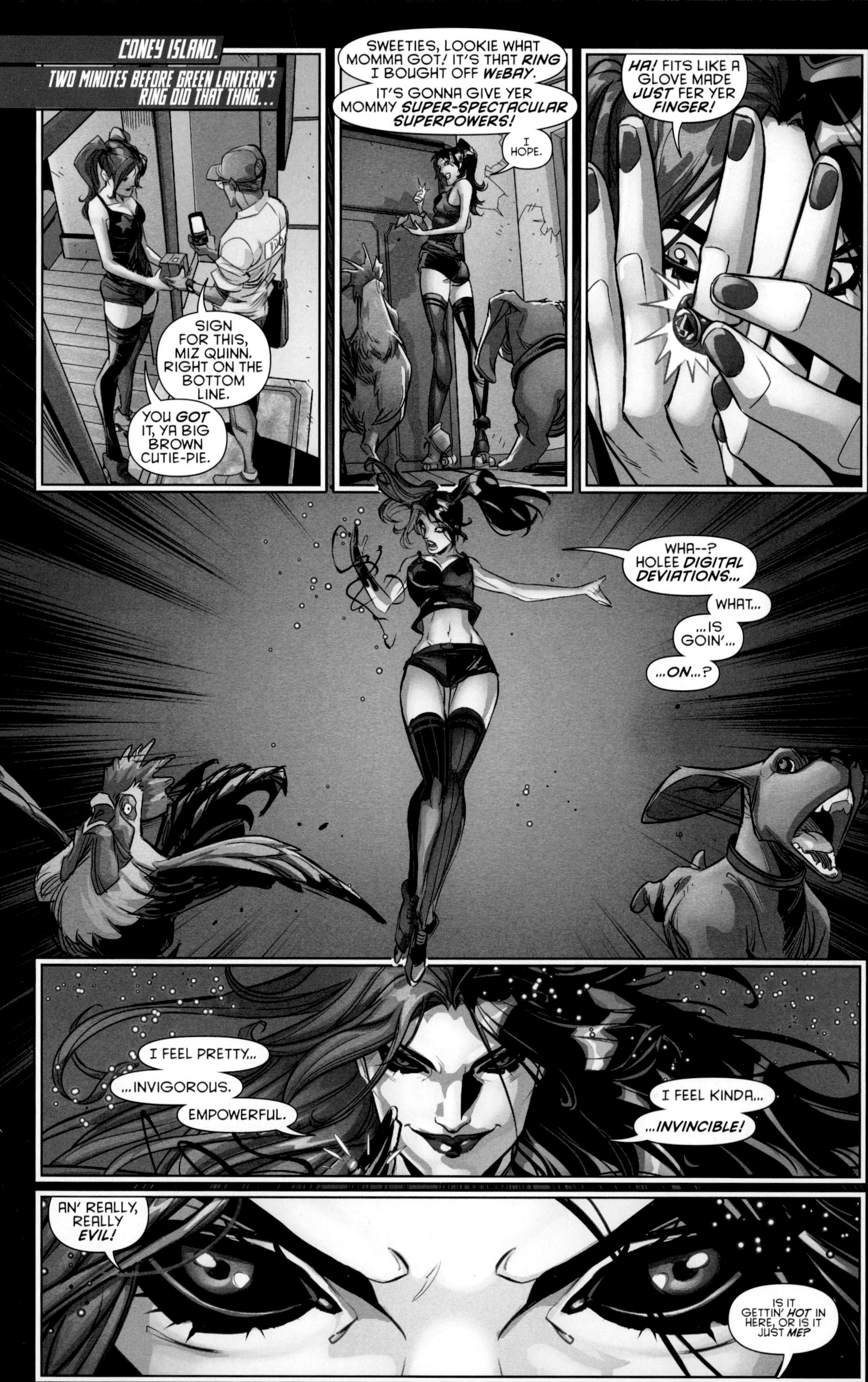

CONEY ISLAND.
TWO MINUTES BEFORE GREEN LANTERN'S RING DID THAT THING...
SIGN FOR THIS, MIZ QUINN. RIGHT ON THE BOTTOM LINE.
YOU GOT IT, YA BIG BROWN CUTIE-PIE.
SWEETIES, LOOKIE WHAT MOMMA GOT! IT'S THAT RING I BOUGHT OFF WEBAY.
IT'S GONNA GIVE YER MOMMY SUPER-SPECTACULAR SUPERPOWERS!
I HOPE.
HA! FITS LIKE A GLOVE MADE JUST FER YER FINGER!
WHA--? HOLEE DIGITAL DEVIATIONS...
WHAT...
...IS GOIN'...
...ON...?
I FEEL PRETTY...
...INVIGOROUS.
EMPOWERFUL.
I FEEL KINDA...
...INVINCIBLE!
AN' REALLY, REALLY EVIL!
IS IT GETTIN' HOT IN HERE, OR IS IT JUST ME?

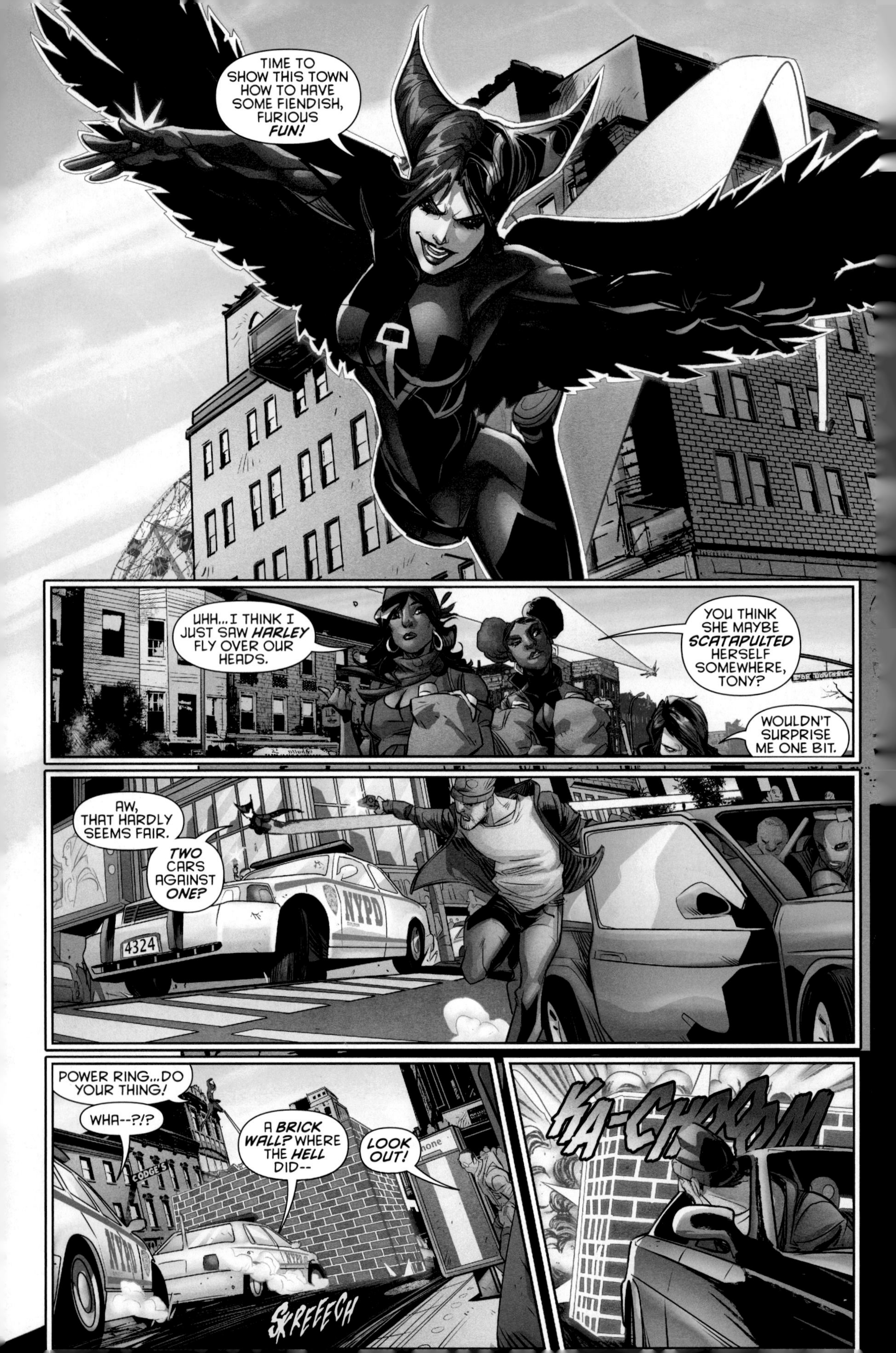

TIME TO SHOW THIS TOWN HOW TO HAVE SOME FIENDISH, FURIOUS *FUN!*
UHH... I THINK I JUST SAW *HARLEY* FLY OVER OUR HEADS.
YOU THINK SHE MAYBE *SCATAPULTED* HERSELF SOMEWHERE, TONY?
WOULDN'T SURPRISE ME ONE BIT.
AW, THAT HARDLY SEEMS FAIR.
TWO CARS AGAINST *ONE?*
NYPD
4324
POWER RING... DO YOUR THING!
WHA--?!?
A *BRICK WALL?* WHERE THE *HELL* DID--
LOOK OUT!
CODGE'S
NYPD
SKREEECH
KA-CHOOOM

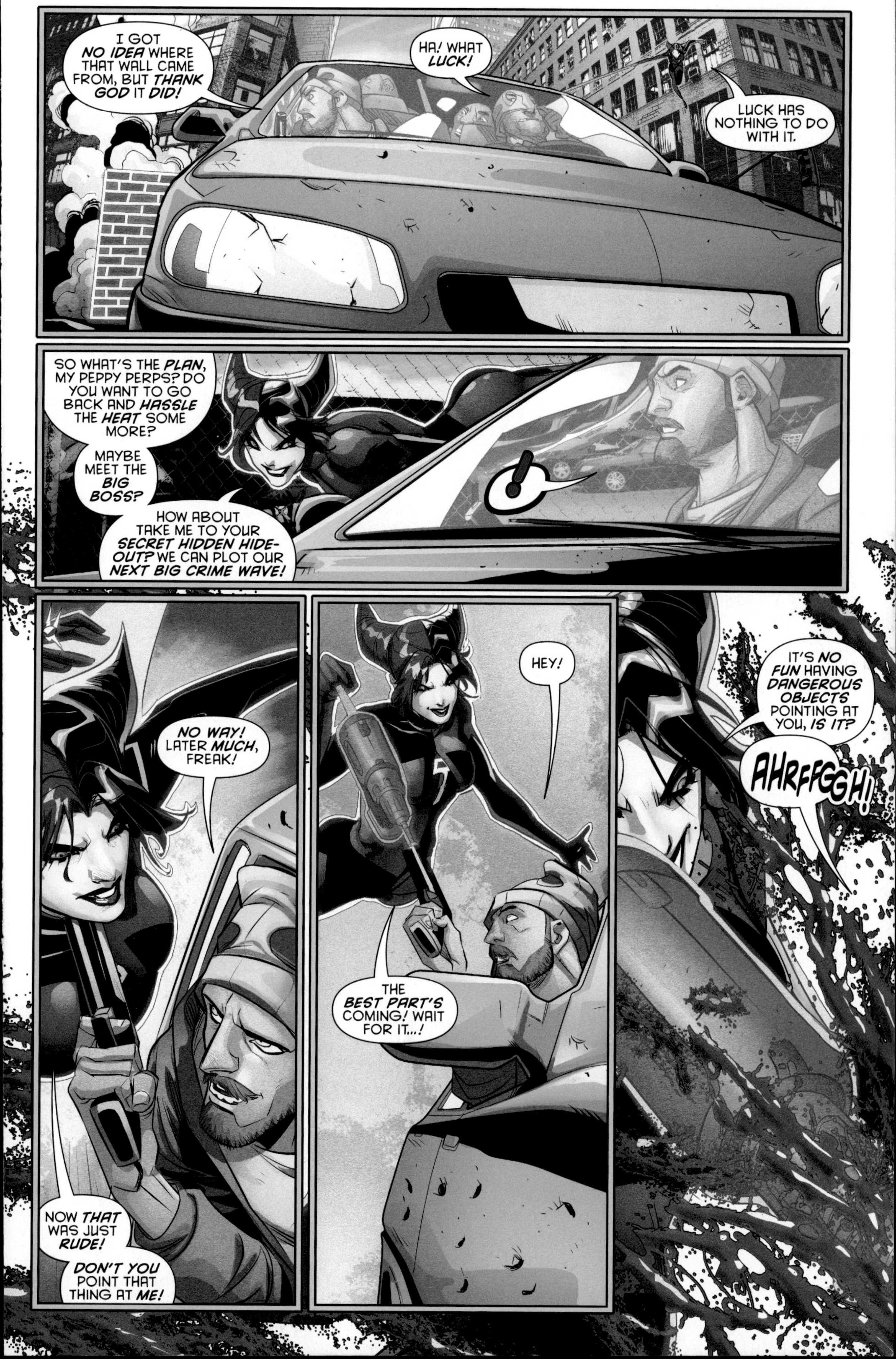
I GOT NO IDEA WHERE THAT WALL CAME FROM, BUT THANK GOD IT DID!
HA! WHAT LUCK!
LUCK HAS NOTHING TO DO WITH IT.
SO WHAT'S THE PLAN, MY PEPPY PERPS? DO YOU WANT TO GO BACK AND HASSLE THE HEAT SOME MORE?
MAYBE MEET THE BIG BOSS?
HOW ABOUT TAKE ME TO YOUR SECRET HIDDEN HIDE-OUT? WE CAN PLOT OUR NEXT BIG CRIME WAVE!
!
NO WAY! LATER MUCH, FREAK!
NOW THAT WAS JUST RUDE!
DON'T YOU POINT THAT THING AT ME!
HEY!
THE BEST PART'S COMING! WAIT FOR IT...!
IT'S NO FUN HAVING DANGEROUS OBJECTS POINTING AT YOU, IS IT?
AHRFFGGH!

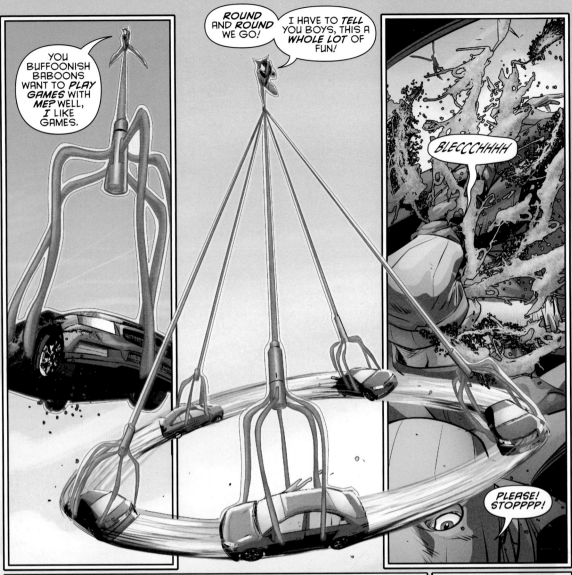

YOU BUFFOONISH BABOONS WANT TO *PLAY GAMES* WITH *ME?* WELL, *I* LIKE GAMES.

ROUND AND *ROUND* WE GO!

I HAVE TO *TELL* YOU BOYS, THIS A *WHOLE LOT* OF FUN!

BLECCCHHHH

PLEASE! STOPPPP!

ARE YOU BOYS *FANS* OF THE *CITY?* HOW ABOUT WE SET IT ON *FIRE?*

BLARCHHHH!!!

PLEASE! LET US GO!

AS YOU *WISH,* MY VOMITY LITTLE VULTURES!

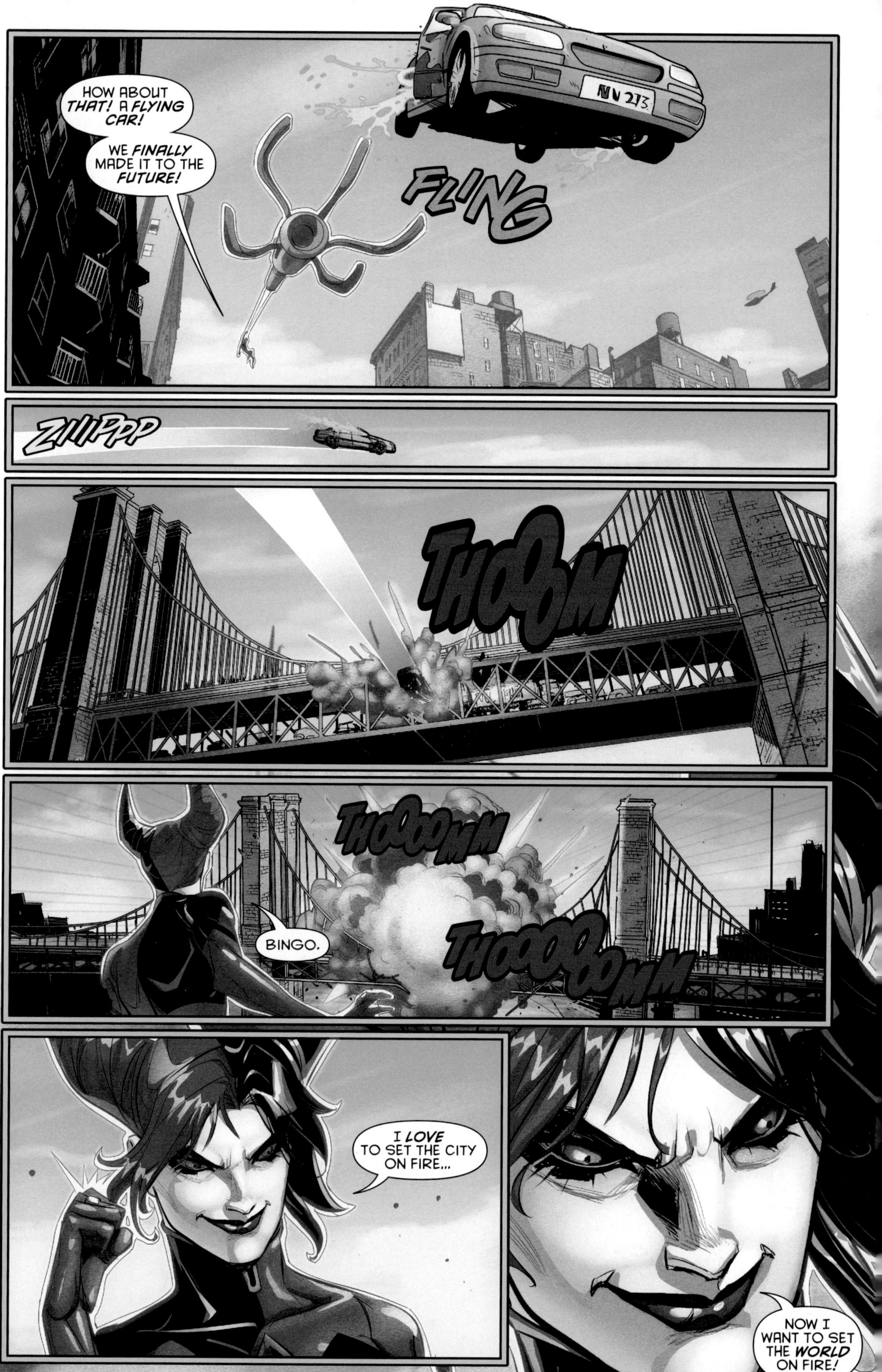
HOW ABOUT THAT! A FLYING CAR!
WE FINALLY MADE IT TO THE FUTURE!
FLING
ZIIIPPP
THOOOM
THOOOOMM
BINGO.
THOOOOOOMM
I LOVE TO SET THE CITY ON FIRE...
NOW I WANT TO SET THE WORLD ON FIRE!

BIG LITTLE TOWN.

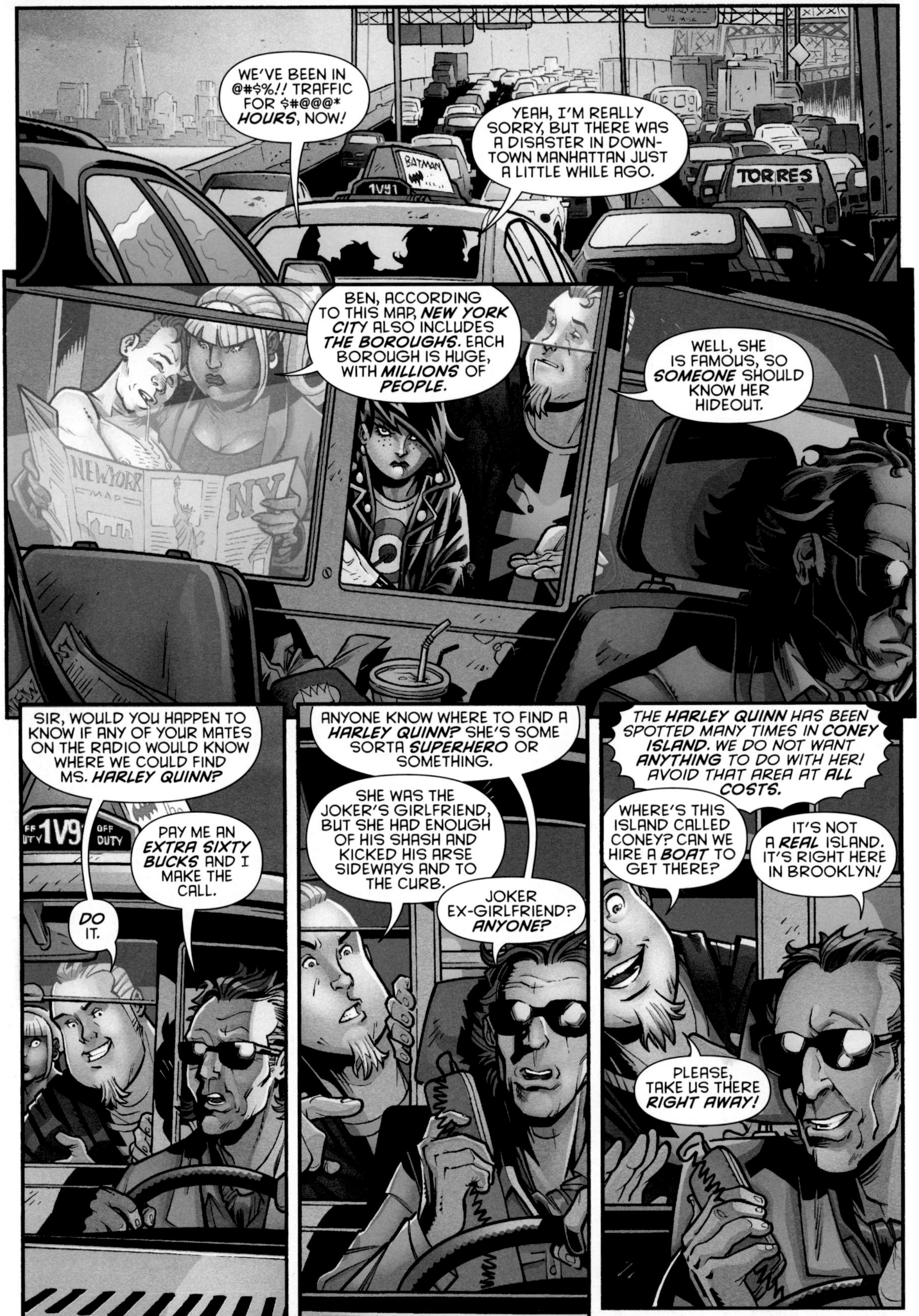

WE'VE BEEN IN @#$%!! TRAFFIC FOR $#@@@* HOURS, NOW!
YEAH, I'M REALLY SORRY, BUT THERE WAS A DISASTER IN DOWN-TOWN MANHATTAN JUST A LITTLE WHILE AGO.
BATMAN
1VY1
TORRES
BEN, ACCORDING TO THIS MAP, NEW YORK CITY ALSO INCLUDES THE BOROUGHS. EACH BOROUGH IS HUGE, WITH MILLIONS OF PEOPLE.
WELL, SHE IS FAMOUS, SO SOMEONE SHOULD KNOW HER HIDEOUT.
NEW YORK MAP
NY
SIR, WOULD YOU HAPPEN TO KNOW IF ANY OF YOUR MATES ON THE RADIO WOULD KNOW WHERE WE COULD FIND MS. HARLEY QUINN?
PAY ME AN EXTRA SIXTY BUCKS AND I MAKE THE CALL.
DO IT.
ANYONE KNOW WHERE TO FIND A HARLEY QUINN? SHE'S SOME SORTA SUPERHERO OR SOMETHING.
SHE WAS THE JOKER'S GIRLFRIEND, BUT SHE HAD ENOUGH OF HIS SHASH AND KICKED HIS ARSE SIDEWAYS AND TO THE CURB.
JOKER EX-GIRLFRIEND? ANYONE?
THE HARLEY QUINN HAS BEEN SPOTTED MANY TIMES IN CONEY ISLAND. WE DO NOT WANT ANYTHING TO DO WITH HER! AVOID THAT AREA AT ALL COSTS.
WHERE'S THIS ISLAND CALLED CONEY? CAN WE HIRE A BOAT TO GET THERE?
IT'S NOT A REAL ISLAND. IT'S RIGHT HERE IN BROOKLYN!
PLEASE, TAKE US THERE RIGHT AWAY!

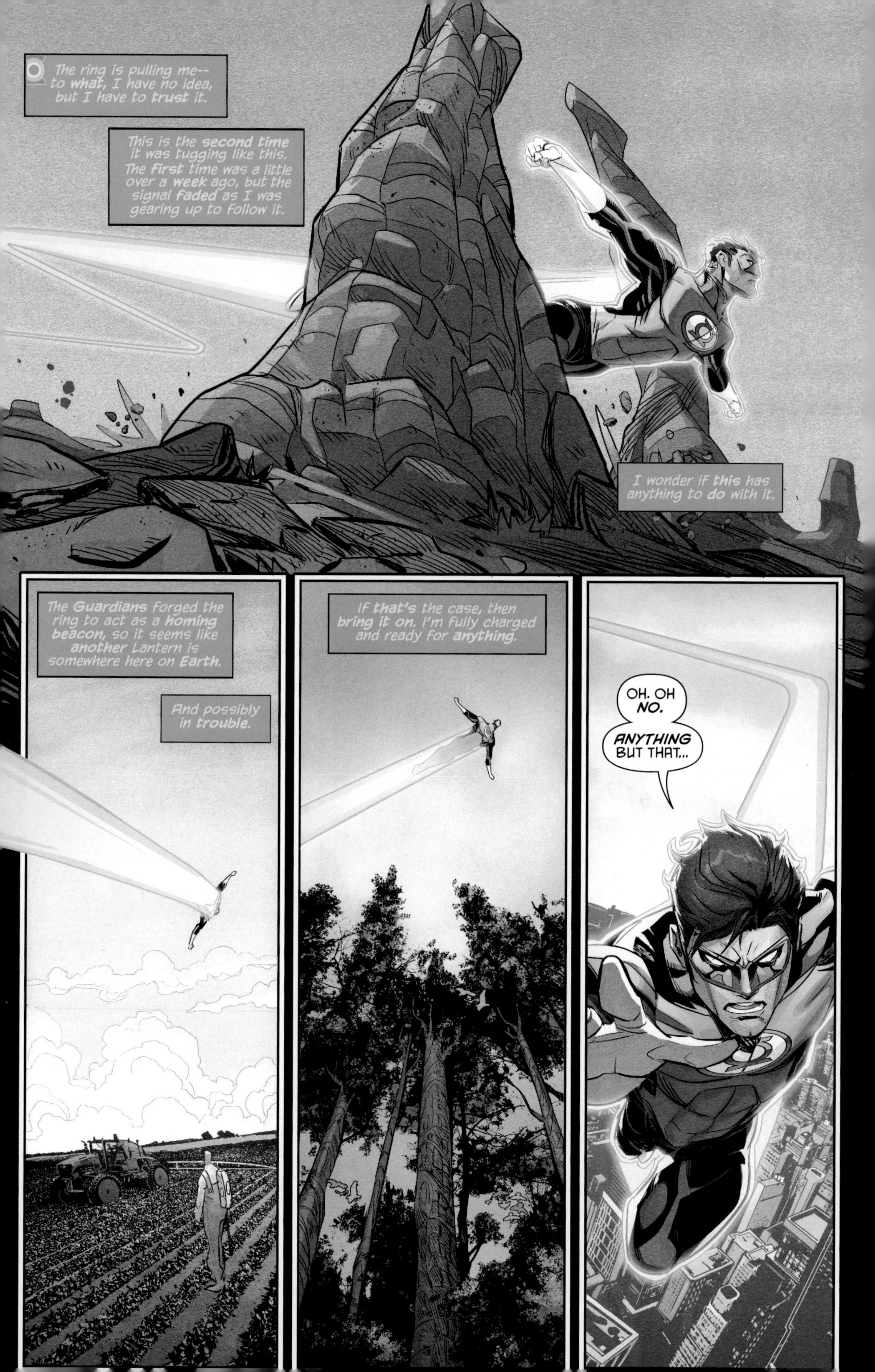
The ring is pulling me-- to what, I have no idea, but I have to trust it.
This is the second time it was tugging like this. The first time was a little over a week ago, but the signal faded as I was gearing up to follow it.
I wonder if this has anything to do with it.
The Guardians forged the ring to act as a homing beacon, so it seems like another Lantern is somewhere here on Earth.
And possibly in trouble.
If that's the case, then bring it on. I'm fully charged and ready for anything.
OH. OH NO.
ANYTHING BUT THAT...

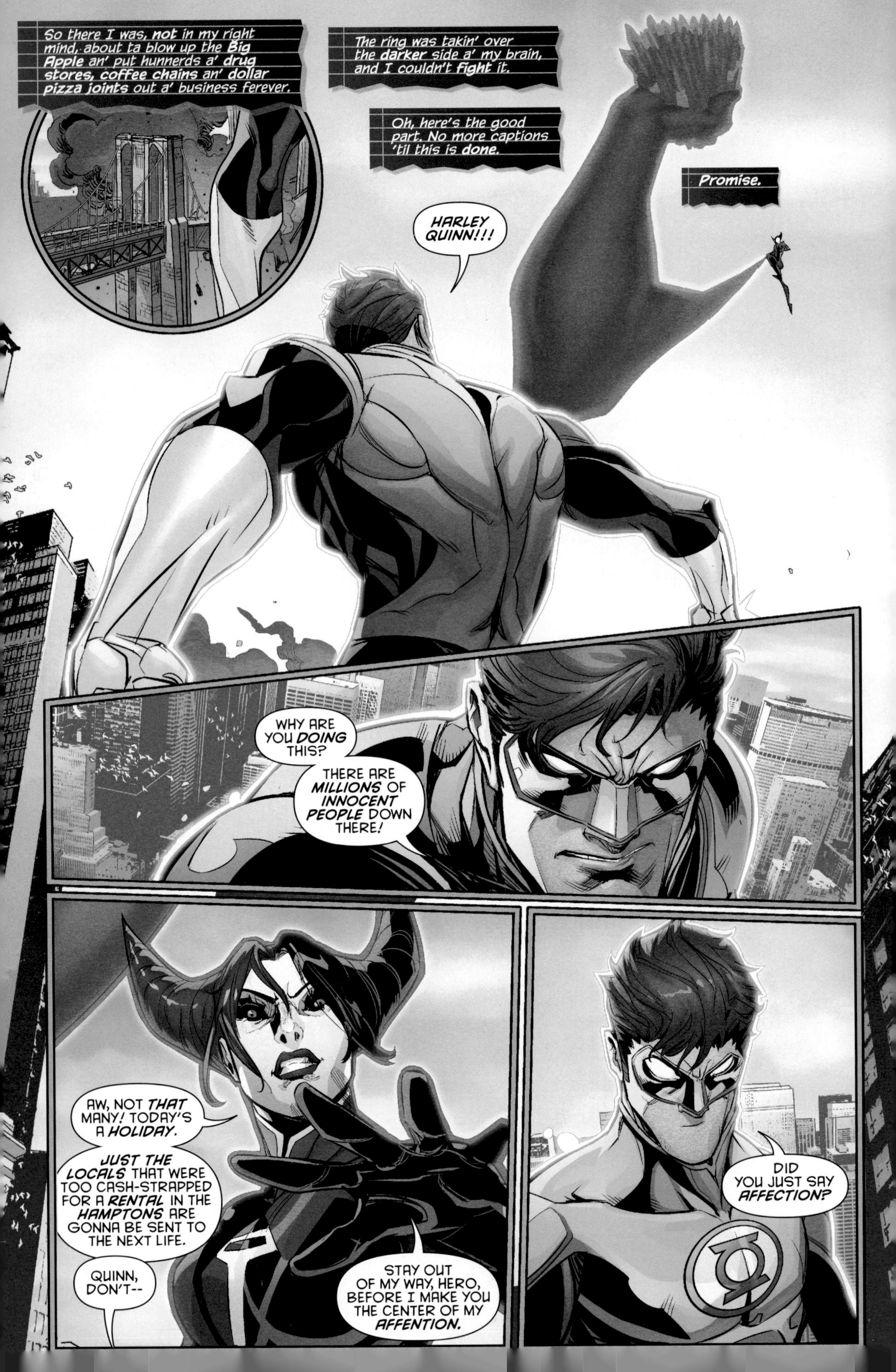
So there I was, not in my right mind, about ta blow up the Big Apple an' put hunnerds a' drug stores, coffee chains an' dollar pizza joints out a' business forever.
The ring was takin' over the darker side a' my brain, and I couldn't fight it.
Oh, here's the good part. No more captions 'til this is done.
Promise.
HARLEY QUINN!!!
WHY ARE YOU DOING THIS?
THERE ARE MILLIONS OF INNOCENT PEOPLE DOWN THERE!
AW, NOT THAT MANY! TODAY'S A HOLIDAY.
JUST THE LOCALS THAT WERE TOO CASH-STRAPPED FOR A RENTAL IN THE HAMPTONS ARE GONNA BE SENT TO THE NEXT LIFE.
QUINN, DON'T--
STAY OUT OF MY WAY, HERO, BEFORE I MAKE YOU THE CENTER OF MY AFFENTION.
DID YOU JUST SAY AFFECTION?

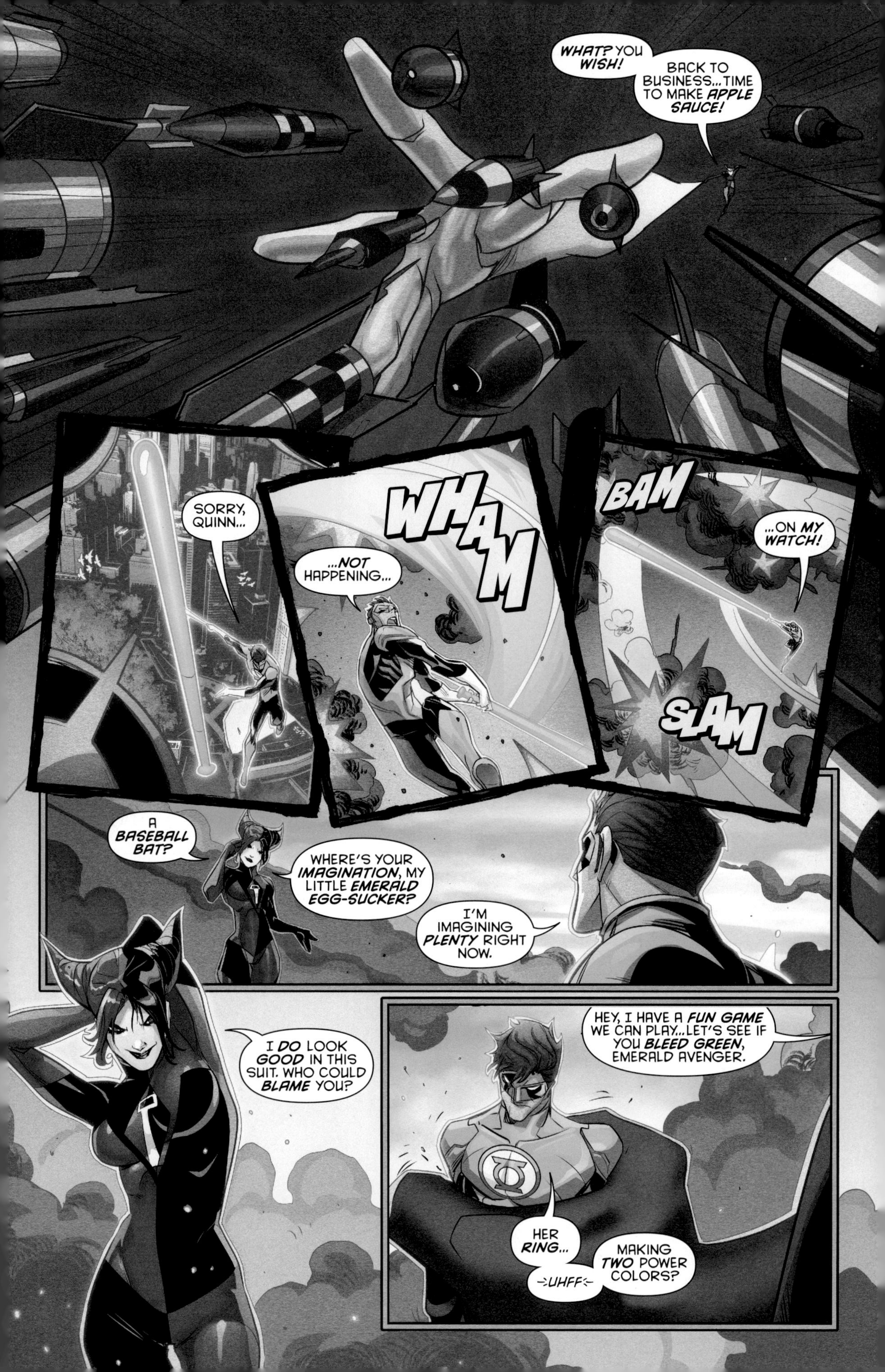

WHAT? YOU WISH!
BACK TO BUSINESS... TIME TO MAKE APPLE SAUCE!
SORRY, QUINN...
WHAM
...NOT HAPPENING...
BAM
...ON MY WATCH!
SLAM
A BASEBALL BAT?
WHERE'S YOUR IMAGINATION, MY LITTLE EMERALD EGG-SUCKER?
I'M IMAGINING PLENTY RIGHT NOW.
I DO LOOK GOOD IN THIS SUIT. WHO COULD BLAME YOU?
HEY, I HAVE A FUN GAME WE CAN PLAY...LET'S SEE IF YOU BLEED GREEN, EMERALD AVENGER.
HER RING...
UHFF
MAKING TWO POWER COLORS?

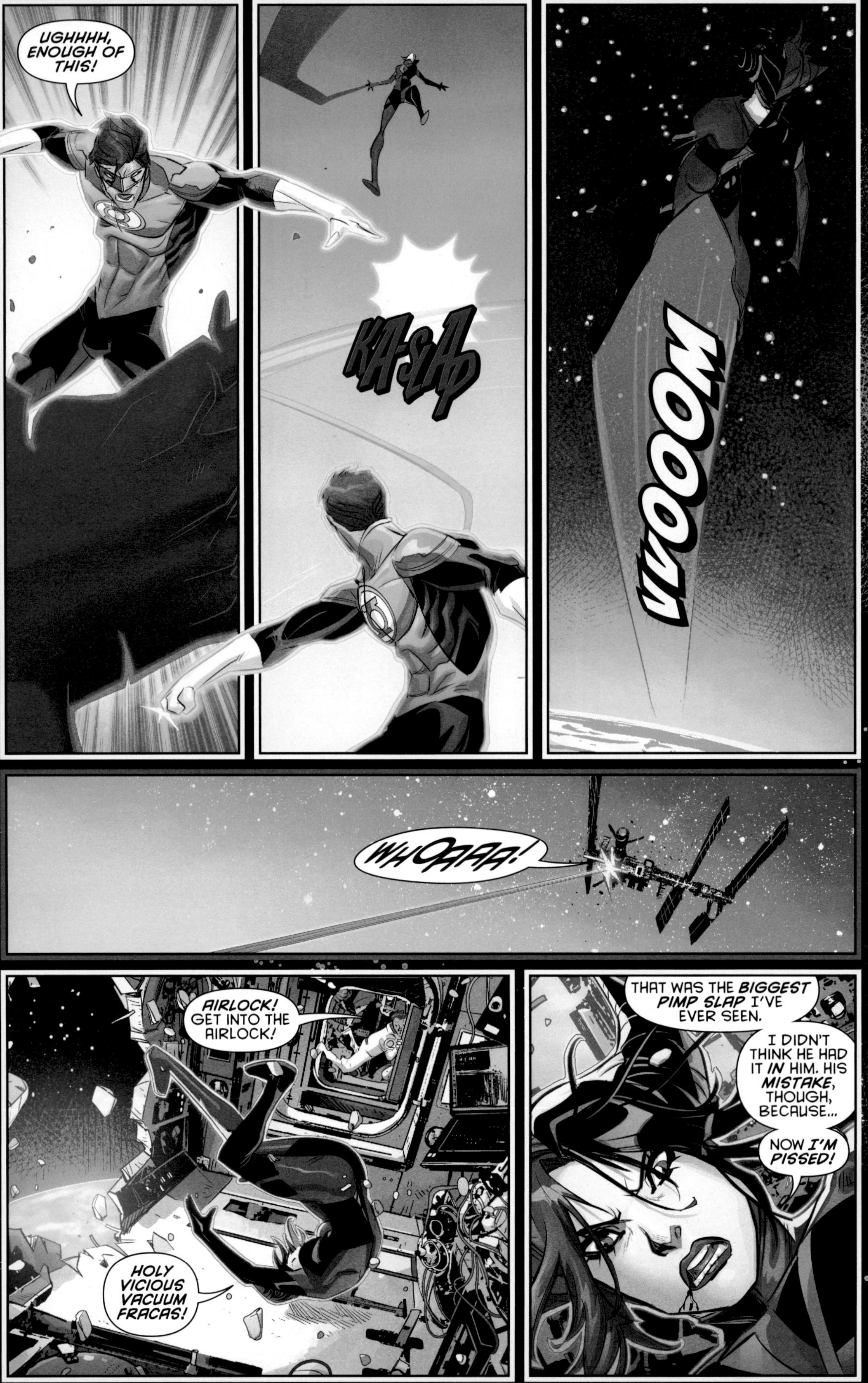

UGHHHH, ENOUGH OF THIS!
KA-SLAP
WOOOOM
WHOAAAA!
AIRLOCK! GET INTO THE AIRLOCK!
HOLY VICIOUS VACUUM FRACAS!
THAT WAS THE *BIGGEST PIMP SLAP* I'VE EVER SEEN.
I DIDN'T THINK HE HAD IT *IN* HIM. HIS *MISTAKE*, THOUGH, BECAUSE...
NOW *I'M PISSED!*

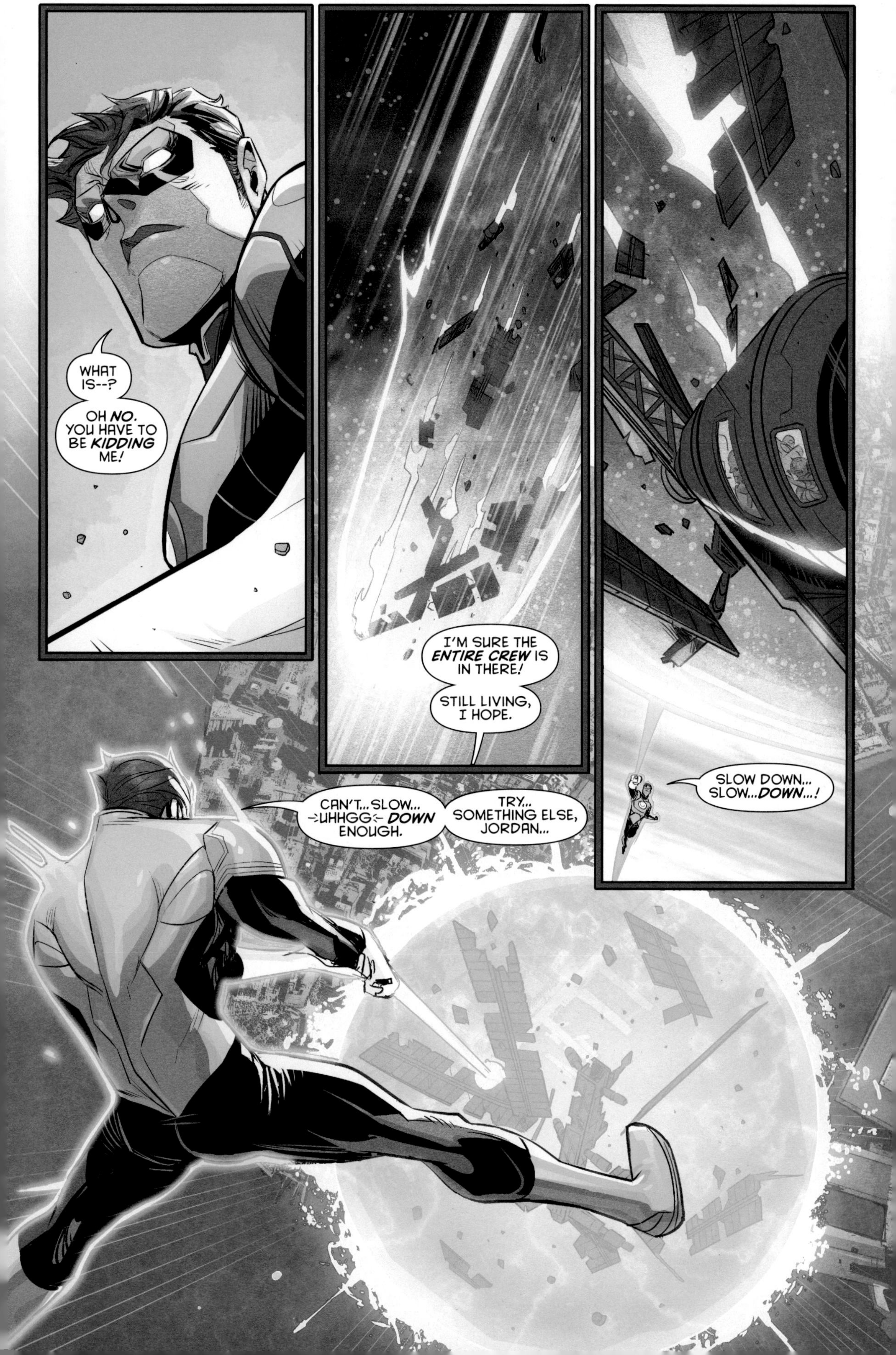
WHAT IS--?
OH NO. YOU HAVE TO BE KIDDING ME!
I'M SURE THE ENTIRE CREW IS IN THERE!
STILL LIVING, I HOPE.
SLOW DOWN... SLOW...DOWN...!
TRY... SOMETHING ELSE, JORDAN...
CAN'T...SLOW... ⇒UHHGG⇐ DOWN ENOUGH.

FOOOMMP

THAT SHOULD DO IT.

ASTRONAUTS ACCOUNTED FOR...

...COAST GUARD'S IN...

...GOOD.

WHOA!

WHAT *NOW*?

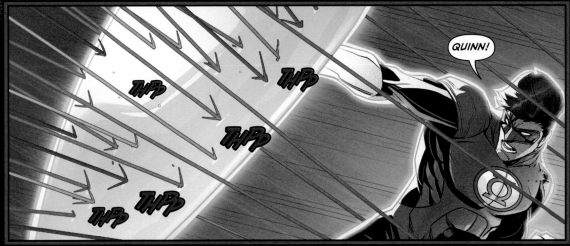

THPP

THPP

THPP

THPP

THPP

QUINN!

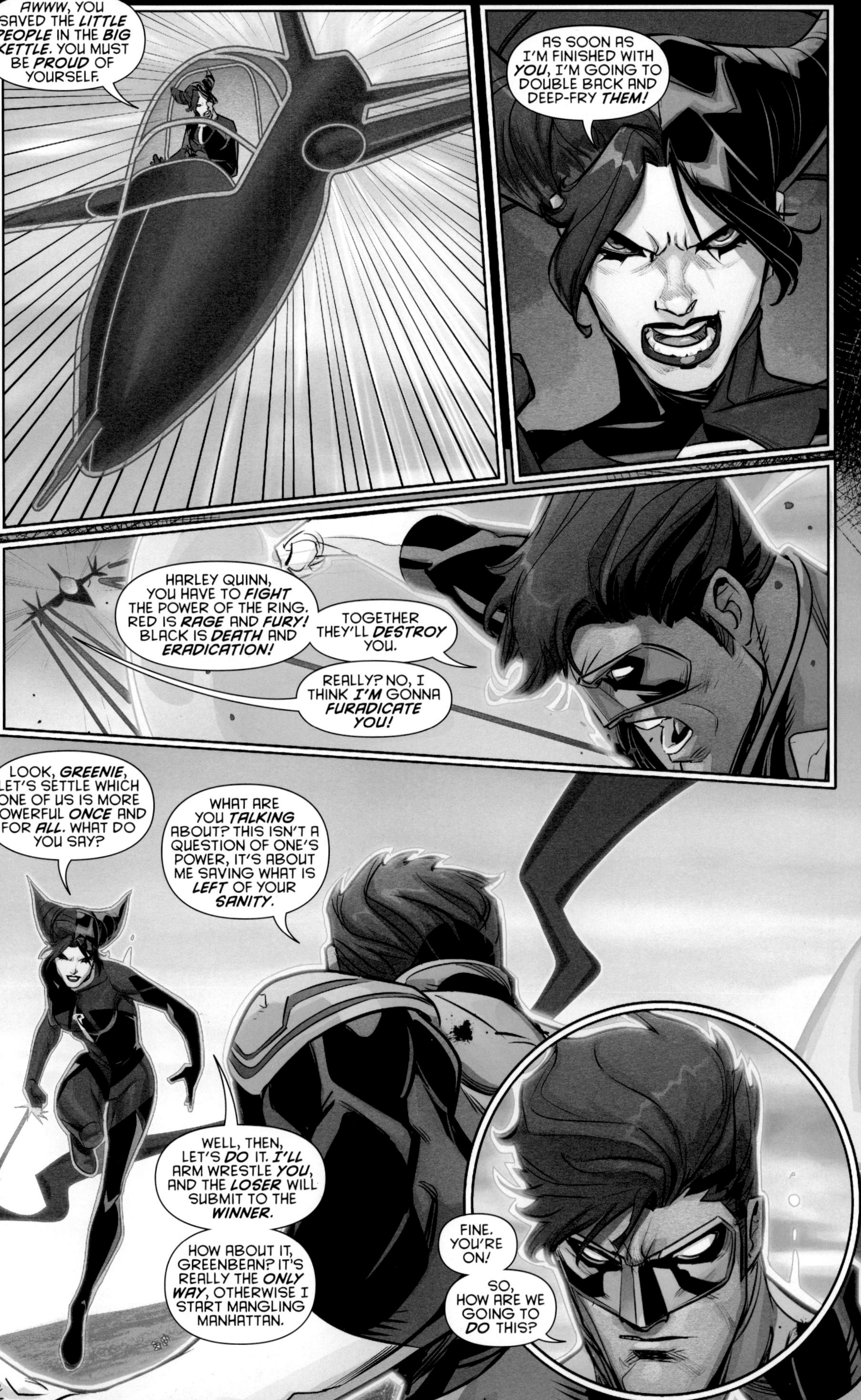
AWWW, YOU SAVED THE *LITTLE PEOPLE* IN THE *BIG KETTLE*. YOU MUST BE *PROUD* OF YOURSELF.
AS SOON AS I'M FINISHED WITH *YOU*, I'M GOING TO DOUBLE BACK AND DEEP-FRY *THEM!*
HARLEY QUINN, YOU HAVE TO *FIGHT* THE POWER OF THE RING. RED IS *RAGE* AND *FURY!* BLACK IS *DEATH* AND *ERADICATION!*
TOGETHER THEY'LL *DESTROY* YOU.
REALLY? NO, I THINK *I'M* GONNA *FURADICATE YOU!*
LOOK, *GREENIE*, LET'S SETTLE WHICH ONE OF US IS MORE POWERFUL *ONCE* AND FOR *ALL*. WHAT DO YOU SAY?
WHAT ARE YOU *TALKING* ABOUT? THIS ISN'T A QUESTION OF ONE'S POWER, IT'S ABOUT ME SAVING WHAT IS *LEFT* OF YOUR *SANITY*.
WELL, THEN, LET'S *DO* IT. *I'LL* ARM WRESTLE *YOU*, AND THE *LOSER* WILL SUBMIT TO THE *WINNER*.
HOW ABOUT IT, GREENBEAN? IT'S REALLY THE *ONLY WAY*, OTHERWISE I START MANGLING MANHATTAN.
FINE. YOU'RE ON!
SO, HOW ARE WE GOING TO *DO* THIS?

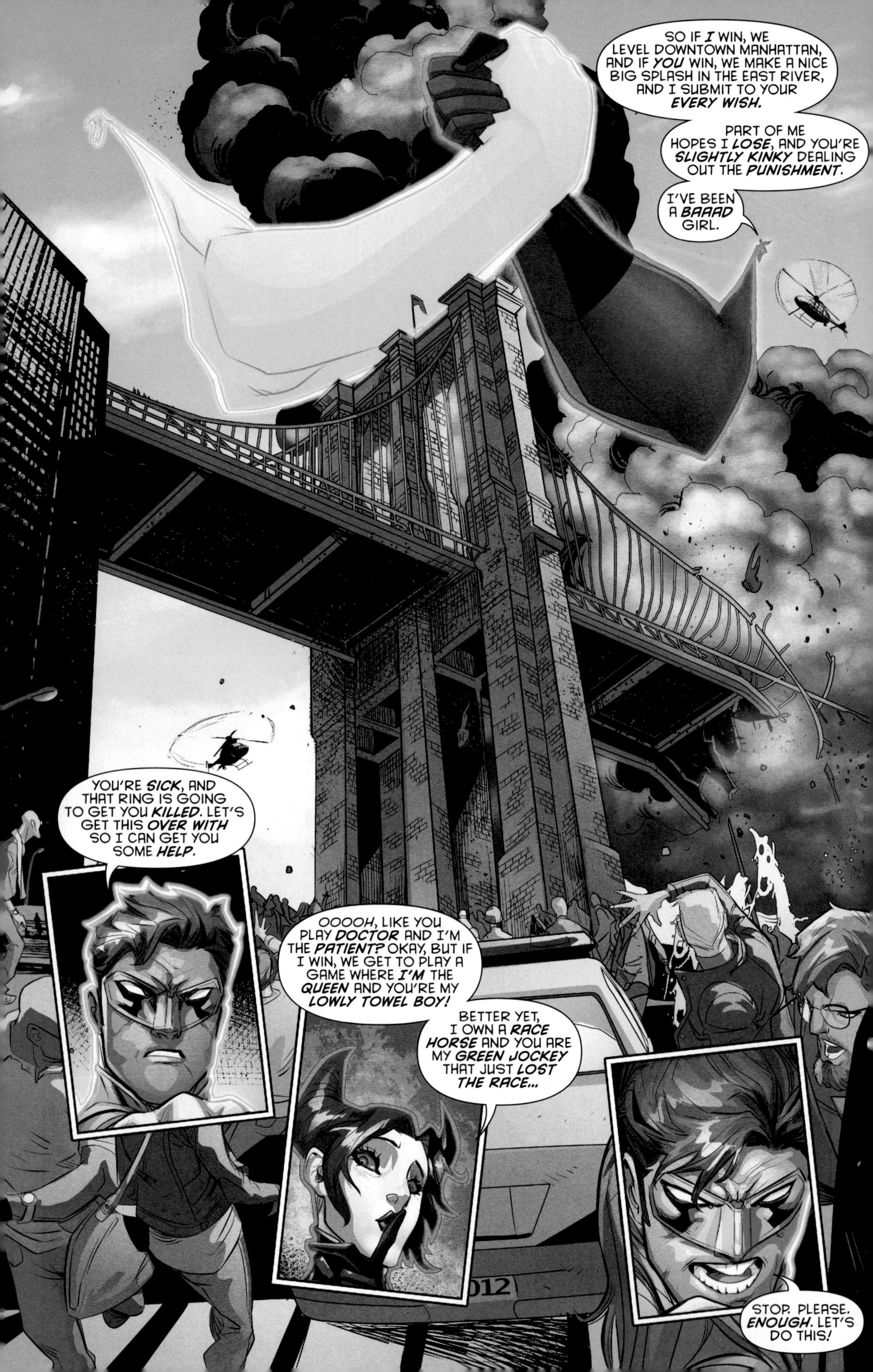
SO IF I WIN, WE LEVEL DOWNTOWN MANHATTAN, AND IF YOU WIN, WE MAKE A NICE BIG SPLASH IN THE EAST RIVER, AND I SUBMIT TO YOUR EVERY WISH.
PART OF ME HOPES I LOSE, AND YOU'RE SLIGHTLY KINKY DEALING OUT THE PUNISHMENT.
I'VE BEEN A BAAAD GIRL.
YOU'RE SICK, AND THAT RING IS GOING TO GET YOU KILLED. LET'S GET THIS OVER WITH SO I CAN GET YOU SOME HELP.
OOOOH, LIKE YOU PLAY DOCTOR AND I'M THE PATIENT? OKAY, BUT IF I WIN, WE GET TO PLAY A GAME WHERE I'M THE QUEEN AND YOU'RE MY LOWLY TOWEL BOY!
BETTER YET, I OWN A RACE HORSE AND YOU ARE MY GREEN JOCKEY THAT JUST LOST THE RACE...
STOP. PLEASE. ENOUGH. LET'S DO THIS!

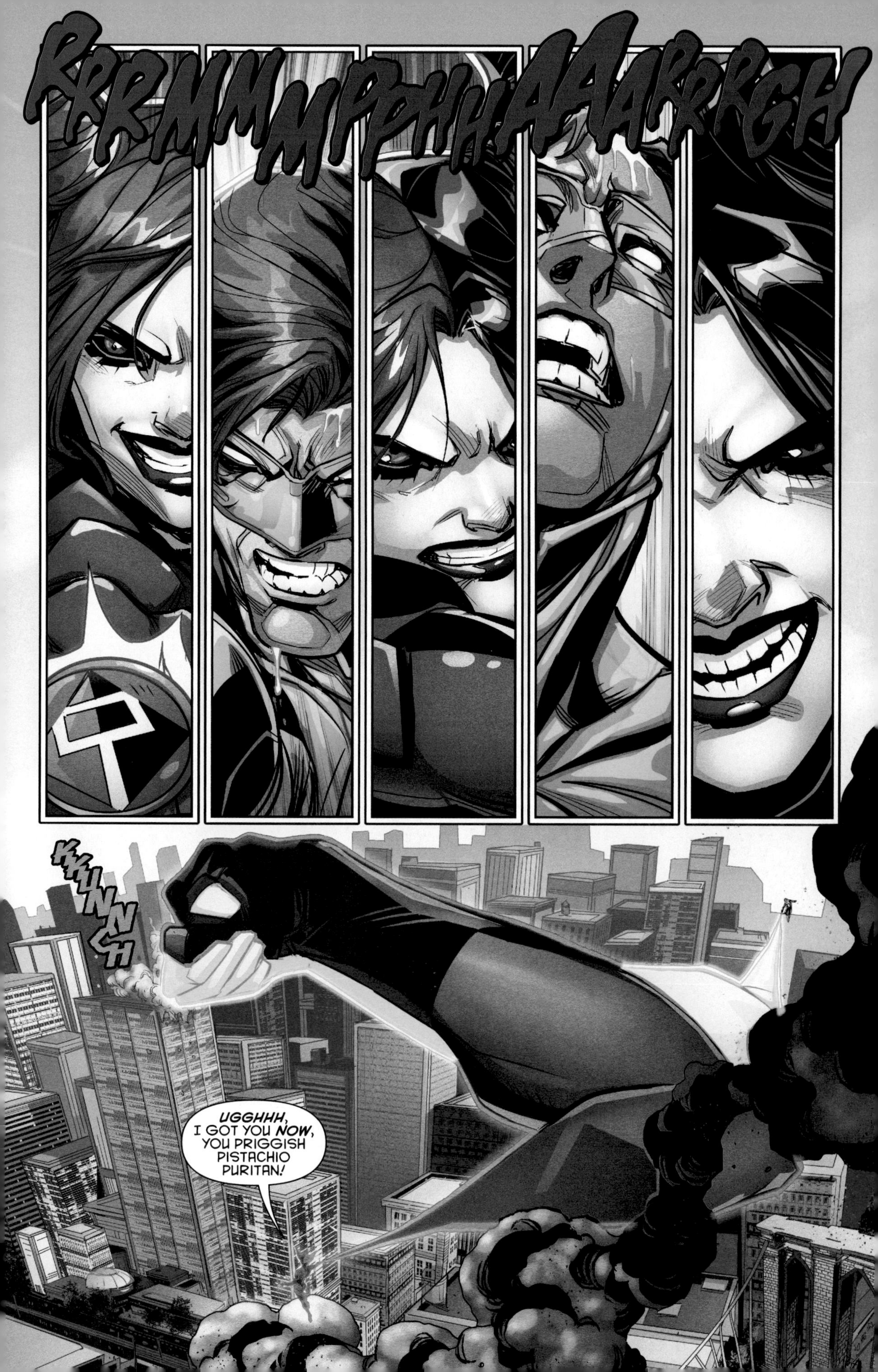
RRRMMMMPPHHAAAARRRGH
KKLUNNCH
UGGHHH, I GOT YOU NOW, YOU PRIGGISH PISTACHIO PURITAN!

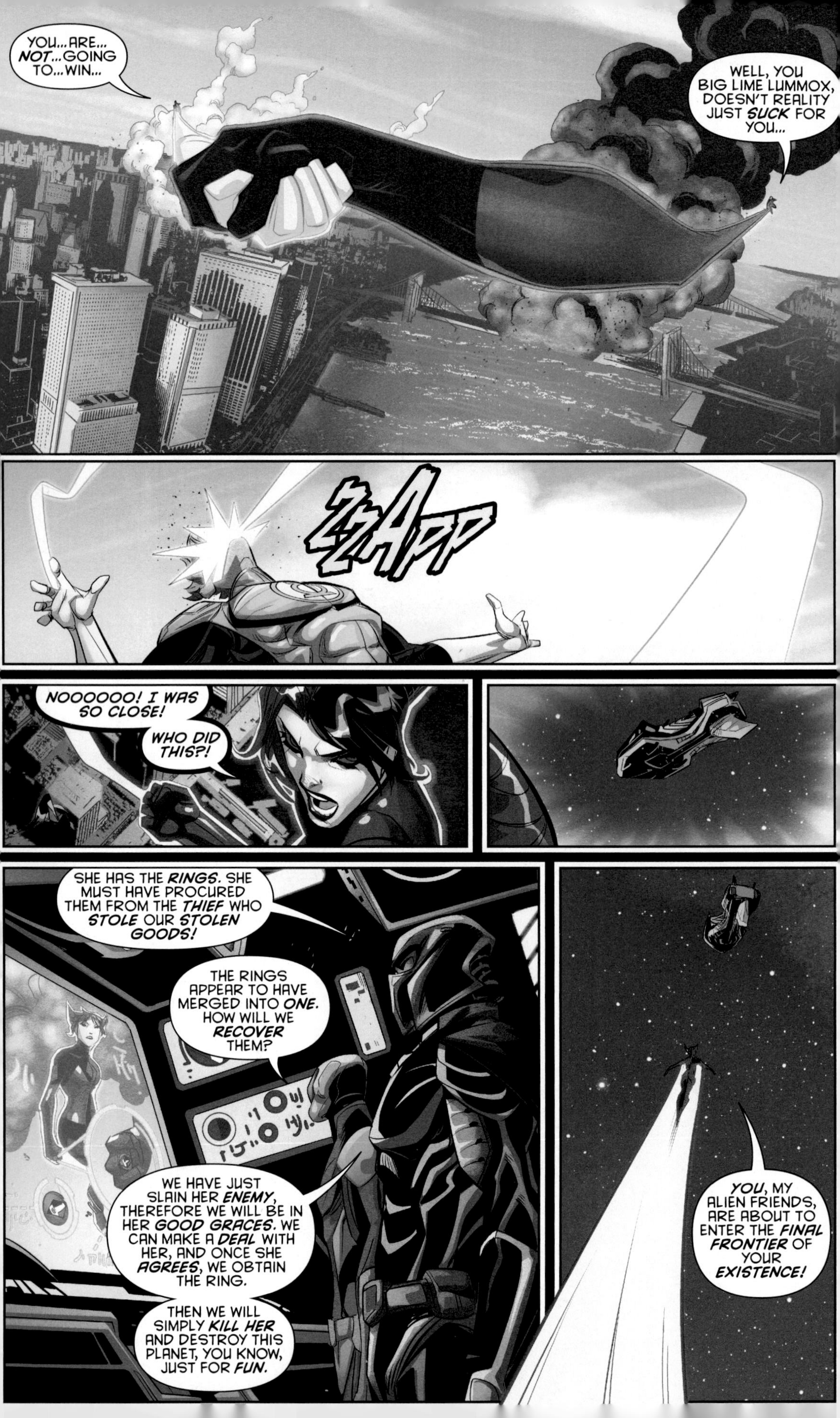

YOU...ARE... NOT...GOING TO...WIN...
WELL, YOU BIG LIME LUMMOX, DOESN'T REALITY JUST SUCK FOR YOU...
ZzAPP
NOOOOOO! I WAS SO CLOSE!
WHO DID THIS?!
SHE HAS THE RINGS. SHE MUST HAVE PROCURED THEM FROM THE THIEF WHO STOLE OUR STOLEN GOODS!
THE RINGS APPEAR TO HAVE MERGED INTO ONE. HOW WILL WE RECOVER THEM?
WE HAVE JUST SLAIN HER ENEMY, THEREFORE WE WILL BE IN HER GOOD GRACES. WE CAN MAKE A DEAL WITH HER, AND ONCE SHE AGREES, WE OBTAIN THE RING.
THEN WE WILL SIMPLY KILL HER AND DESTROY THIS PLANET, YOU KNOW, JUST FOR FUN.
YOU, MY ALIEN FRIENDS, ARE ABOUT TO ENTER THE FINAL FRONTIER OF YOUR EXISTENCE!

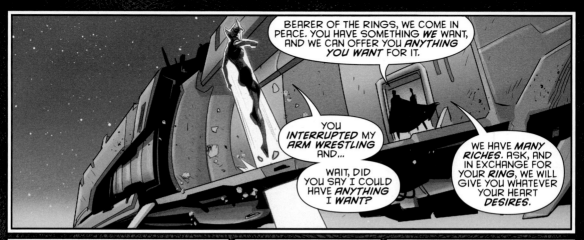

BEARER OF THE RINGS, WE COME IN PEACE. YOU HAVE SOMETHING *WE* WANT, AND WE CAN OFFER YOU *ANYTHING YOU WANT* FOR IT.

YOU *INTERRUPTED* MY *ARM WRESTLING* AND...

WAIT, DID YOU SAY I COULD HAVE *ANYTHING* I WANT?

WE HAVE *MANY* RICHES. ASK, AND IN EXCHANGE FOR YOUR *RING*, WE WILL GIVE YOU WHATEVER YOUR HEART *DESIRES.*

SO, I GIVE YOU THIS RING AND YOU CAN GIVE ME, LET'S SAY, AN *ARMY* OF FIRE-BREATHING *DRAGONS*, OR PERHAPS A MILLION *PEPPERONI PIZZA PIES*?

I AM SURE IF YOU TELL US WHAT A *PEPPERONI PIZZA PIE* IS, WE CAN ACCOMMODATE YOU.

HOW ABOUT A PLANET'S WORTH OF KITTENS AND PUPPIES THAT DON'T *POO*?

AGAIN, IF YOU LET US KNOW WHAT *KITTENS, PUPPIES, AND POO* ARE, WE SHALL MAKE IT HAPPEN.

I...I... -*UGGHH*- WHY AM I SO *TIRED* ALL OF A SUDDEN?

THE RING TAKES A TOLL ON THOSE WHO WIELD ITS POWER. SIMPLY *REMOVE* IT AND GIVE IT TO *ME.* NOT ONLY SHALL YOU FEEL *IMPROVED*, BUT ALL YOUR WISHES WILL BE INDULGED.

WAIT, THE *RING*...IT'S *TALKING* TO ME...

THAT'S...AN *AZAKARIAN WAR SHIP...* SHE HAS NO IDEA...

WE *GOT* YOU BUDDY.

SEEMS THIS RING CAN ALSO READ *MINDS*, AND IT'S TELLING ME YOU ARE *FULL OF IT.* IT MEANING "*POO*".

I DON'T LIKE *LIARS*, ANAKIN.

YOU HAVE *ANY IDEA* WHAT HAPPENS TO *LIARS*?

ENOUGH OF THIS.

ARRGGGHH!

WEAK HUMAN.

THE RING IS *MINE*. NOW NOTHING STANDS IN MY WAY!

*

HUH? WHA'S *HAPPENIN'*? WHERE *AM* I?

WHAT'S BROOKLYN DOIN' WAY DOWN *THERE*, AN' WHY AM I WAY UP *HERE*?

I CAN HELP ANSWER THAT.

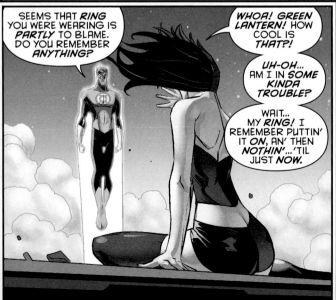

SEEMS THAT *RING* YOU WERE WEARING IS *PARTLY* TO BLAME. DO YOU REMEMBER *ANYTHING*?

WHOA! GREEN LANTERN! HOW COOL IS *THAT*?!

UH-OH... AM I IN *SOME KINDA TROUBLE*?

WAIT... MY *RING*! I REMEMBER PUTTIN' IT *ON*, AN' THEN *NOTHIN'*...'TIL JUST *NOW*.

EEYAAHHH!

SOMEONE STOLE MY *RING*!

THIS SHIP IS AZAKARIAN, AN ALIEN RACE OF *THIEVES* AND *KILLERS*. I AM AFRAID WITH THAT *RING* IN THEIR POSSESSION, *NOTHING GOOD* WILL HAPPEN.

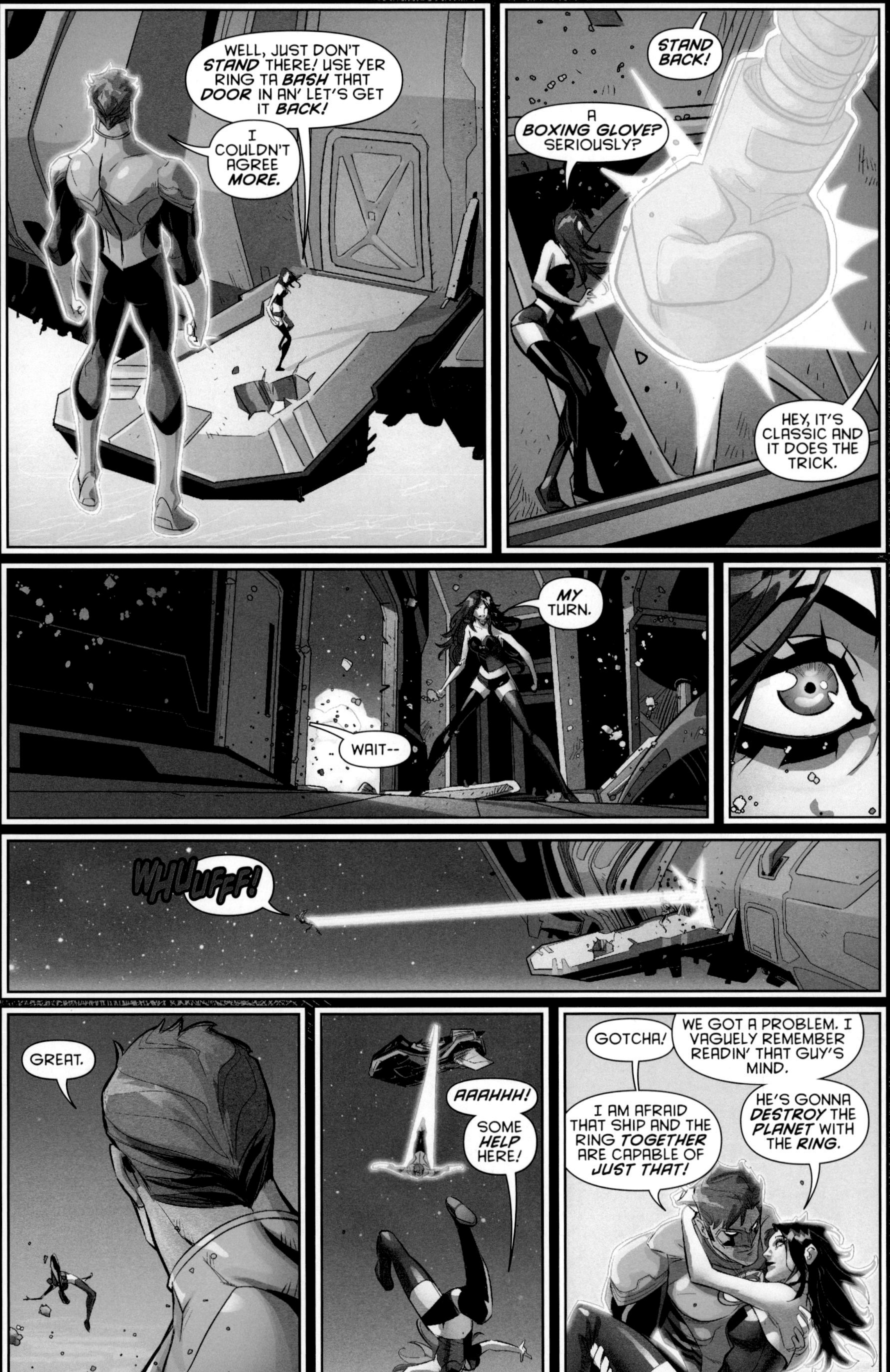
WELL, JUST DON'T STAND THERE! USE YER RING TA BASH THAT DOOR IN AN' LET'S GET IT BACK!
I COULDN'T AGREE MORE.
STAND BACK!
A BOXING GLOVE? SERIOUSLY?
HEY, IT'S CLASSIC AND IT DOES THE TRICK.
MY TURN.
WAIT--
WHUUFFF!
GREAT.
AAAHHH!
SOME HELP HERE!
GOTCHA!
WE GOT A PROBLEM. I VAGUELY REMEMBER READIN' THAT GUY'S MIND.
HE'S GONNA DESTROY THE PLANET WITH THE RING.
I AM AFRAID THAT SHIP AND THE RING TOGETHER ARE CAPABLE OF JUST THAT!

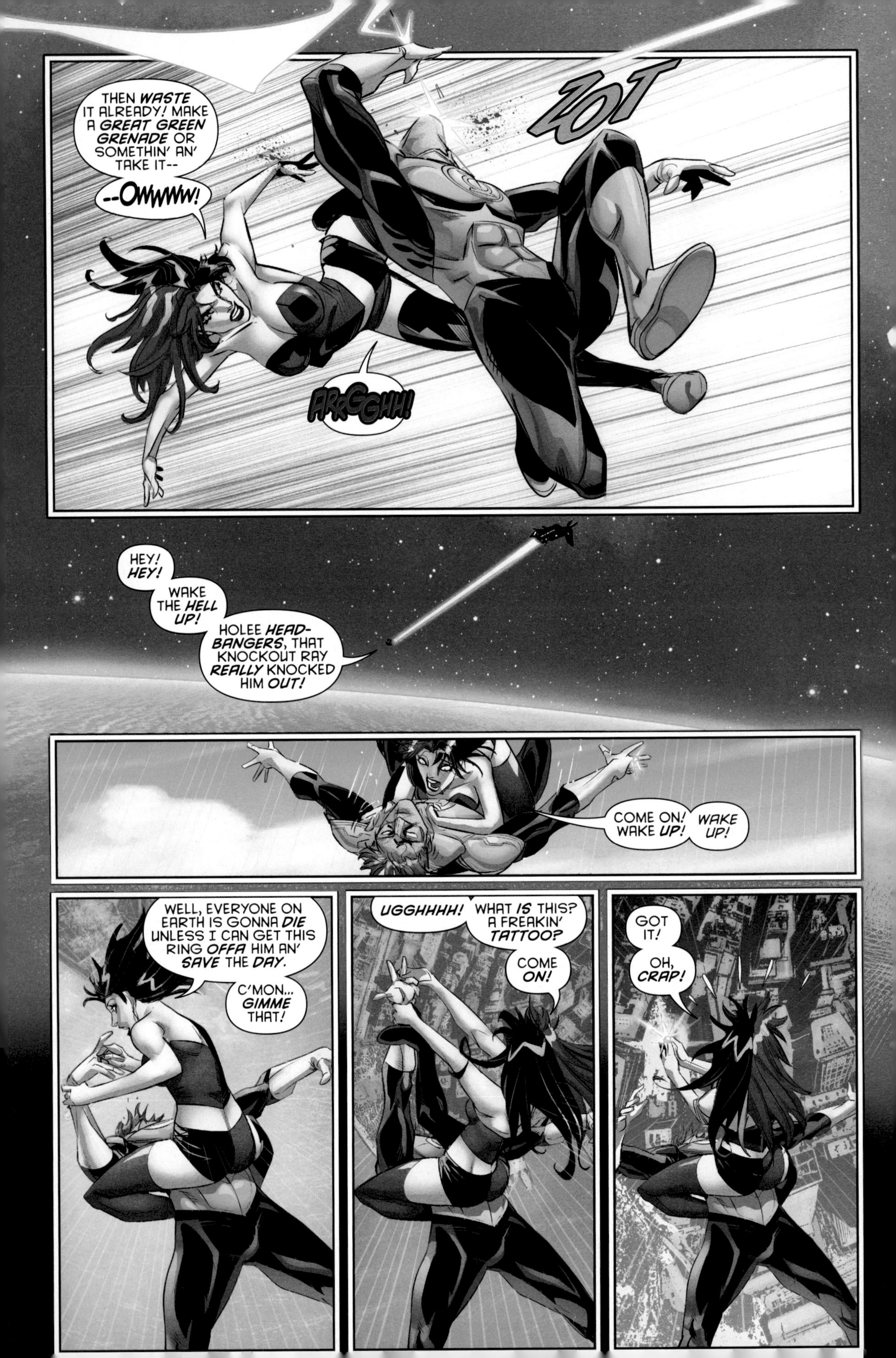

THEN WASTE IT ALREADY! MAKE A GREAT GREEN GRENADE OR SOMETHIN' AN' TAKE IT--
--OWWWW!
ZOT
ARRGGHH!
HEY! HEY!
WAKE THE HELL UP!
HOLEE HEAD-BANGERS, THAT KNOCKOUT RAY REALLY KNOCKED HIM OUT!
COME ON! WAKE UP!
WAKE UP!
WELL, EVERYONE ON EARTH IS GONNA DIE UNLESS I CAN GET THIS RING OFFA HIM AN' SAVE THE DAY.
C'MON... GIMME THAT!
UGGHHHH!
WHAT IS THIS? A FREAKIN' TATTOO?
COME ON!
GOT IT!
OH, CRAP!

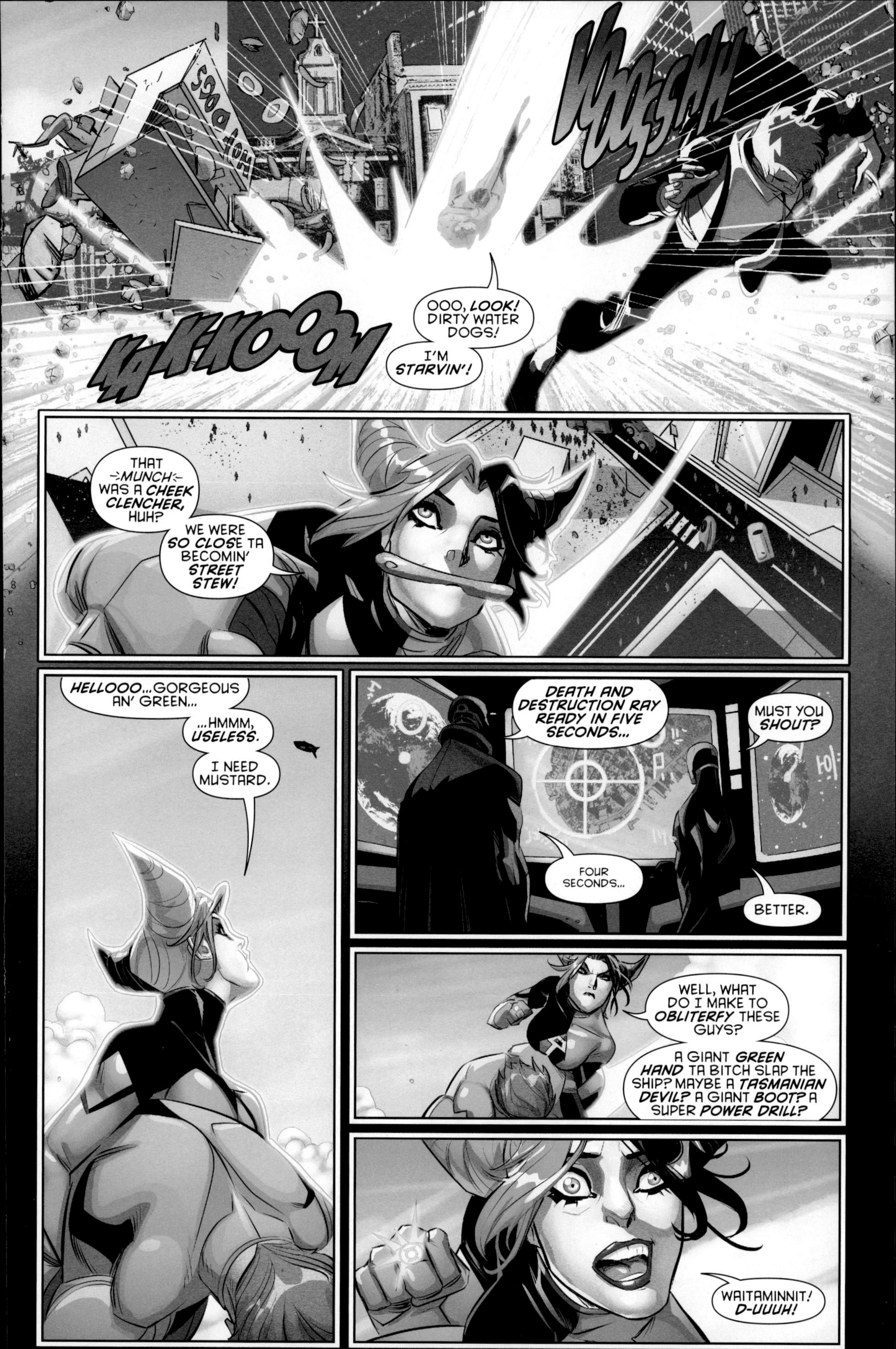
VOOSSHH
KA-K-KOOOOM
OOO, LOOK! DIRTY WATER DOGS!
I'M STARVIN'!
THAT MUNCH WAS A CHEEK CLENCHER, HUH?
WE WERE SO CLOSE TA BECOMIN' STREET STEW!
HELLOOO...GORGEOUS AN' GREEN...
...HMMM, USELESS.
I NEED MUSTARD.
DEATH AND DESTRUCTION RAY READY IN FIVE SECONDS...
MUST YOU SHOUT?
FOUR SECONDS...
BETTER.
WELL, WHAT DO I MAKE TO OBLITERFY THESE GUYS?
A GIANT GREEN HAND TA BITCH SLAP THE SHIP? MAYBE A TASMANIAN DEVIL? A GIANT BOOT? A SUPER POWER DRILL?
WAITAMINNIT! D-UUUH!

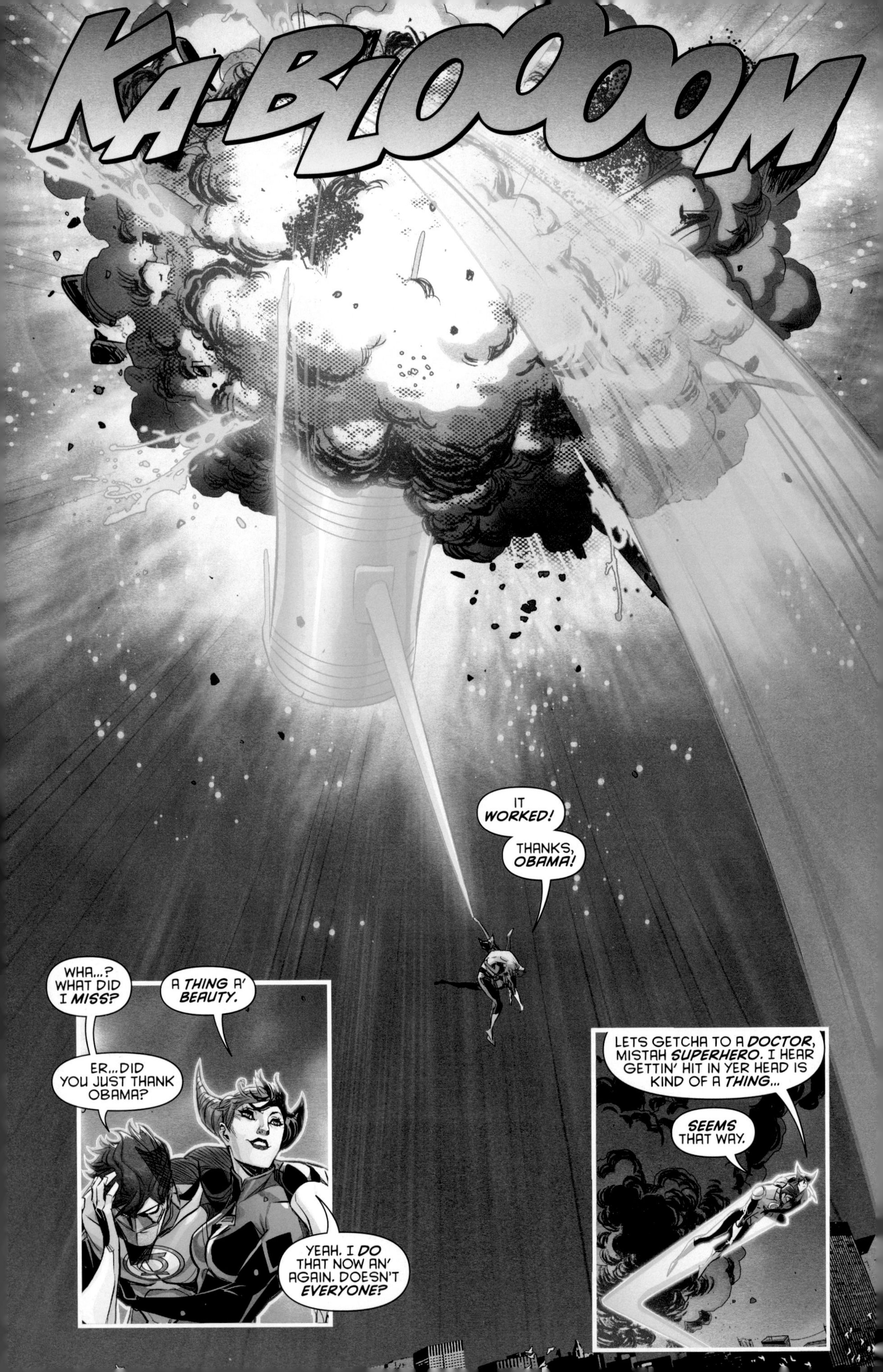
KA-BLOOOOM
IT WORKED!
THANKS, OBAMA!
WHA...? WHAT DID I MISS?
A THING A' BEAUTY.
ER...DID YOU JUST THANK OBAMA?
YEAH. I DO THAT NOW AN' AGAIN. DOESN'T EVERYONE?
LETS GETCHA TO A DOCTOR, MISTAH SUPERHERO. I HEAR GETTIN' HIT IN YER HEAD IS KIND OF A THING...
SEEMS THAT WAY.

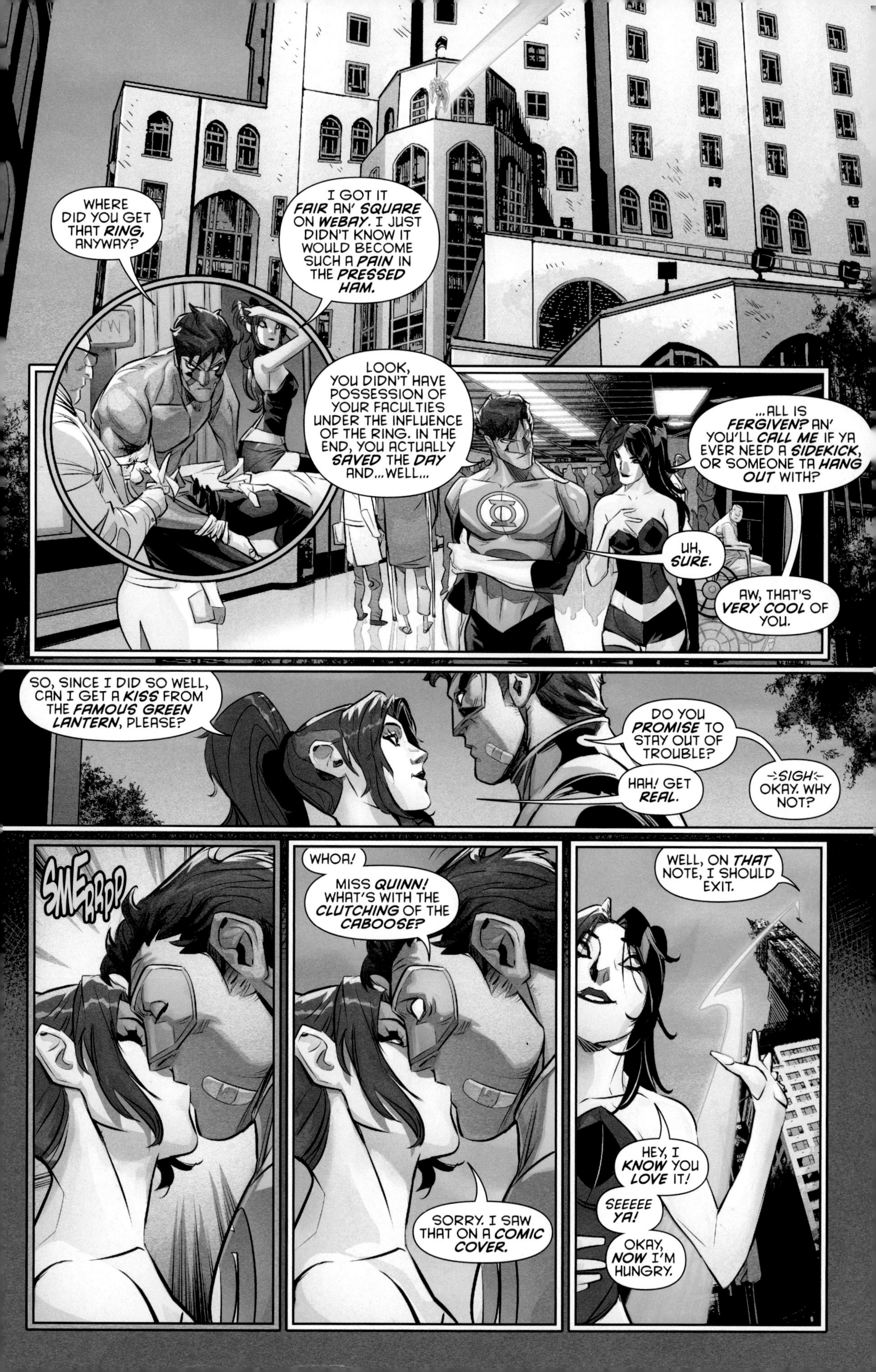
WHERE DID YOU GET THAT RING, ANYWAY?
I GOT IT FAIR AN' SQUARE ON WEBAY. I JUST DIDN'T KNOW IT WOULD BECOME SUCH A PAIN IN THE PRESSED HAM.
LOOK, YOU DIDN'T HAVE POSSESSION OF YOUR FACULTIES UNDER THE INFLUENCE OF THE RING. IN THE END, YOU ACTUALLY SAVED THE DAY AND...WELL...
...ALL IS FERGIVEN? AN' YOU'LL CALL ME IF YA EVER NEED A SIDEKICK, OR SOMEONE TA HANG OUT WITH?
UH, SURE.
AW, THAT'S VERY COOL OF YOU.
SO, SINCE I DID SO WELL, CAN I GET A KISS FROM THE FAMOUS GREEN LANTERN, PLEASE?
DO YOU PROMISE TO STAY OUT OF TROUBLE?
HAH! GET REAL.
-SIGH- OKAY. WHY NOT?
SMERRDP
WHOA!
MISS QUINN! WHAT'S WITH THE CLUTCHING OF THE CABOOSE?
SORRY. I SAW THAT ON A COMIC COVER.
WELL, ON THAT NOTE, I SHOULD EXIT.
HEY, I KNOW YOU LOVE IT!
SEEEEE YA!
OKAY, NOW I'M HUNGRY.

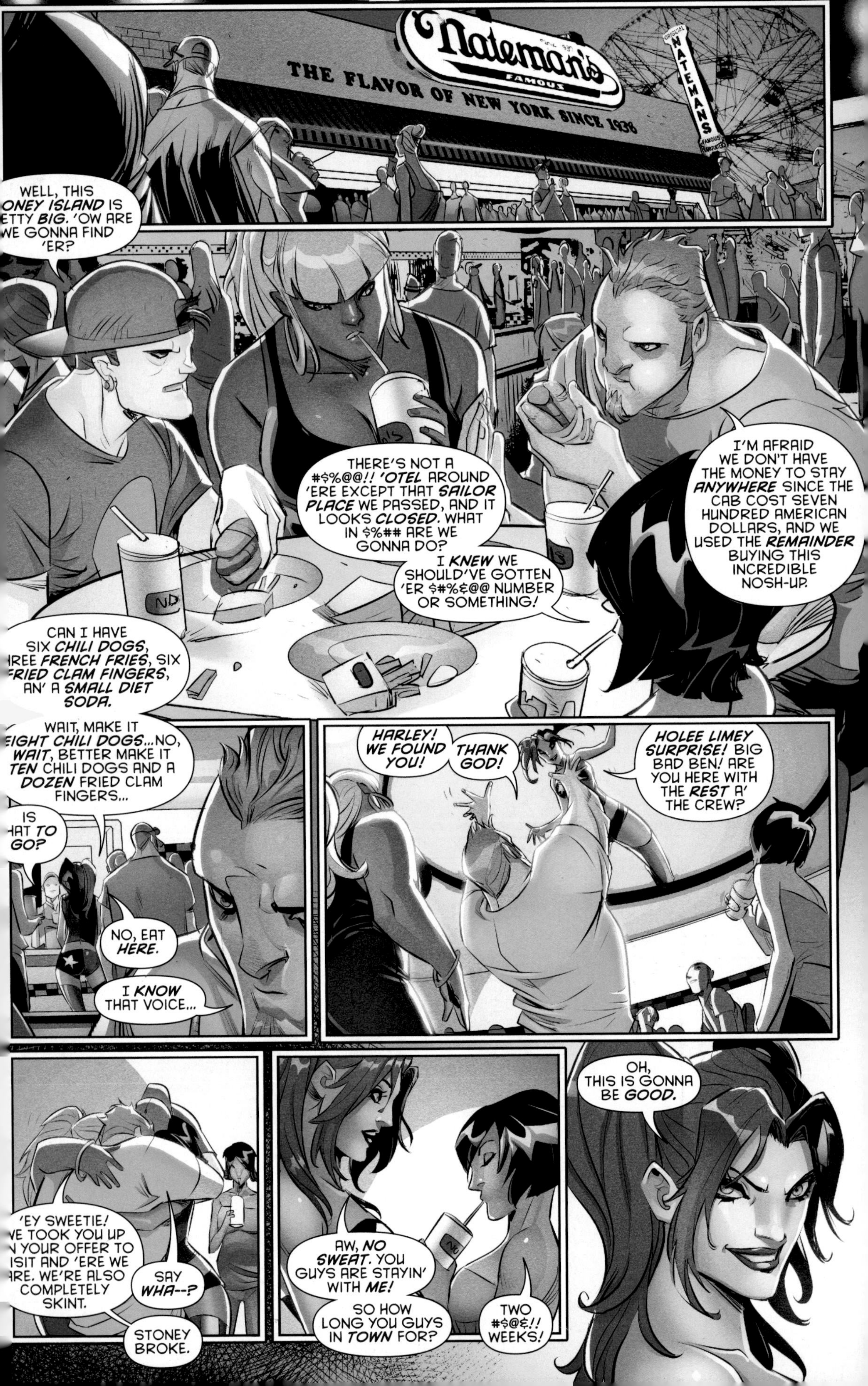
Nateman's
FAMOUS
THE FLAVOR OF NEW YORK SINCE 1936
ORIGINAL NATEMANS FAMOUS
WELL, THIS ONEY ISLAND IS ETTY BIG. 'OW ARE WE GONNA FIND 'ER?
THERE'S NOT A #$%@@!! 'OTEL AROUND 'ERE EXCEPT THAT SAILOR PLACE WE PASSED, AND IT LOOKS CLOSED. WHAT IN $%## ARE WE GONNA DO?
I KNEW WE SHOULD'VE GOTTEN 'ER $#%&@@ NUMBER OR SOMETHING!
I'M AFRAID WE DON'T HAVE THE MONEY TO STAY ANYWHERE SINCE THE CAB COST SEVEN HUNDRED AMERICAN DOLLARS, AND WE USED THE REMAINDER BUYING THIS INCREDIBLE NOSH-UP.
CAN I HAVE SIX CHILI DOGS, HREE FRENCH FRIES, SIX FRIED CLAM FINGERS, AN' A SMALL DIET SODA.
WAIT, MAKE IT EIGHT CHILI DOGS...NO, WAIT, BETTER MAKE IT TEN CHILI DOGS AND A DOZEN FRIED CLAM FINGERS...
IS HAT TO GO?
NO, EAT HERE.
I KNOW THAT VOICE...
HARLEY! WE FOUND YOU!
THANK GOD!
HOLEE LIMEY SURPRISE! BIG BAD BEN! ARE YOU HERE WITH THE REST A' THE CREW?
'EY SWEETIE! WE TOOK YOU UP N YOUR OFFER TO ISIT AND 'ERE WE ARE. WE'RE ALSO COMPLETELY SKINT.
SAY WHA--?
STONEY BROKE.
AW, NO SWEAT. YOU GUYS ARE STAYIN' WITH ME!
SO HOW LONG YOU GUYS IN TOWN FOR?
TWO #$@&!! WEEKS!
OH, THIS IS GONNA BE GOOD.

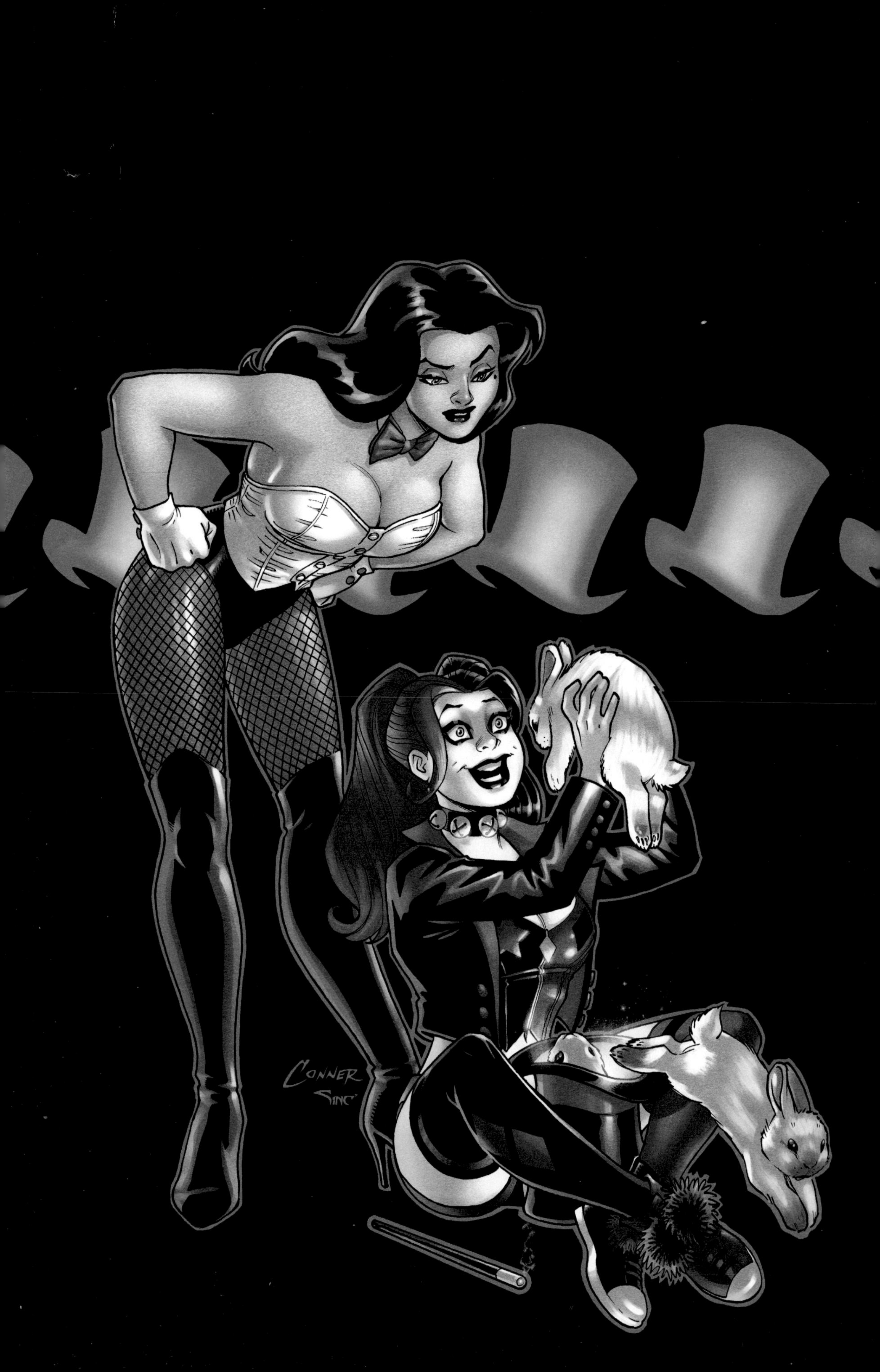
CONNER
SINC'

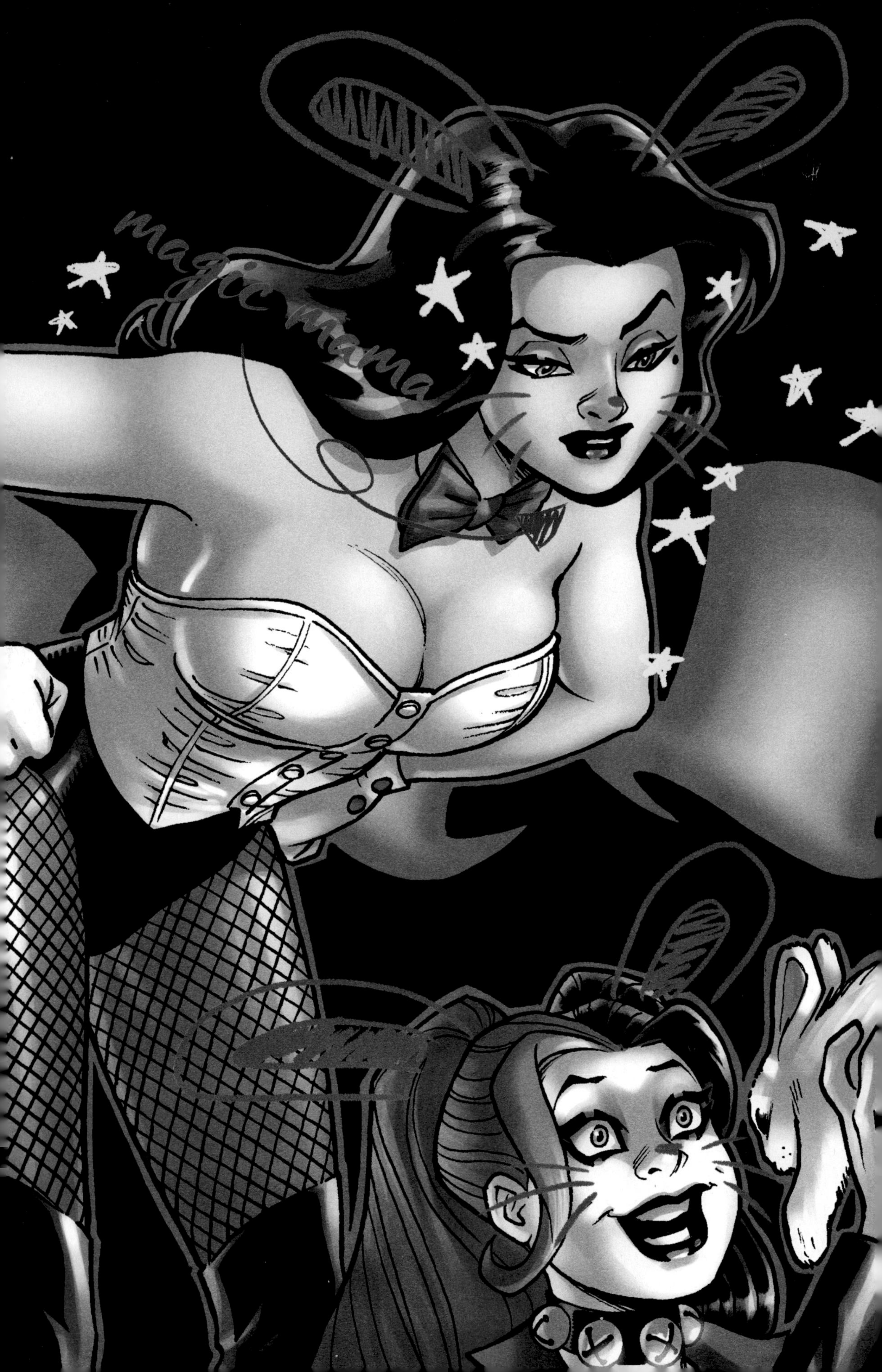
magic mama

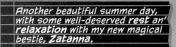

HARLEY QUINN IN DISPIRITED SPIRITS

Another beautiful summer day, with some well-deserved **rest an' relaxation** with my new magical bestie, Zatanna.

After the crazy few days we just had, we damn well **deserve** it.

How crazy, you ask? Lemme explain.

A long time ago, when I was in medical school, I was **workin' late** one night. I had just finished a double shift, when I swear, I kid you **not**, I saw a **ghost** walk out a' the morgue a' the hospital.

I put it off ta exhaustion, but this once non-believer is no more.

It was just a few days ago...

AMANDA CONNER & JIMMY PALMIOTTI **WRITERS**
JOSEPH MICHAEL LINSNER **ARTIST** HI-FI **COLORS** DAVE SHARPE **LETTERS**
AMANDA CONNER & ALEX SINCLAIR **COVER** JOSEPH MICHAEL LINSNER **VARIANT COVER**
DAVE WIELGOSZ **ASST. EDITOR** CHRIS CONROY **EDITOR** MARK DOYLE **GROUP EDITOR**
HARLEY QUINN CREATED BY PAUL DINI & BRUCE TIMM

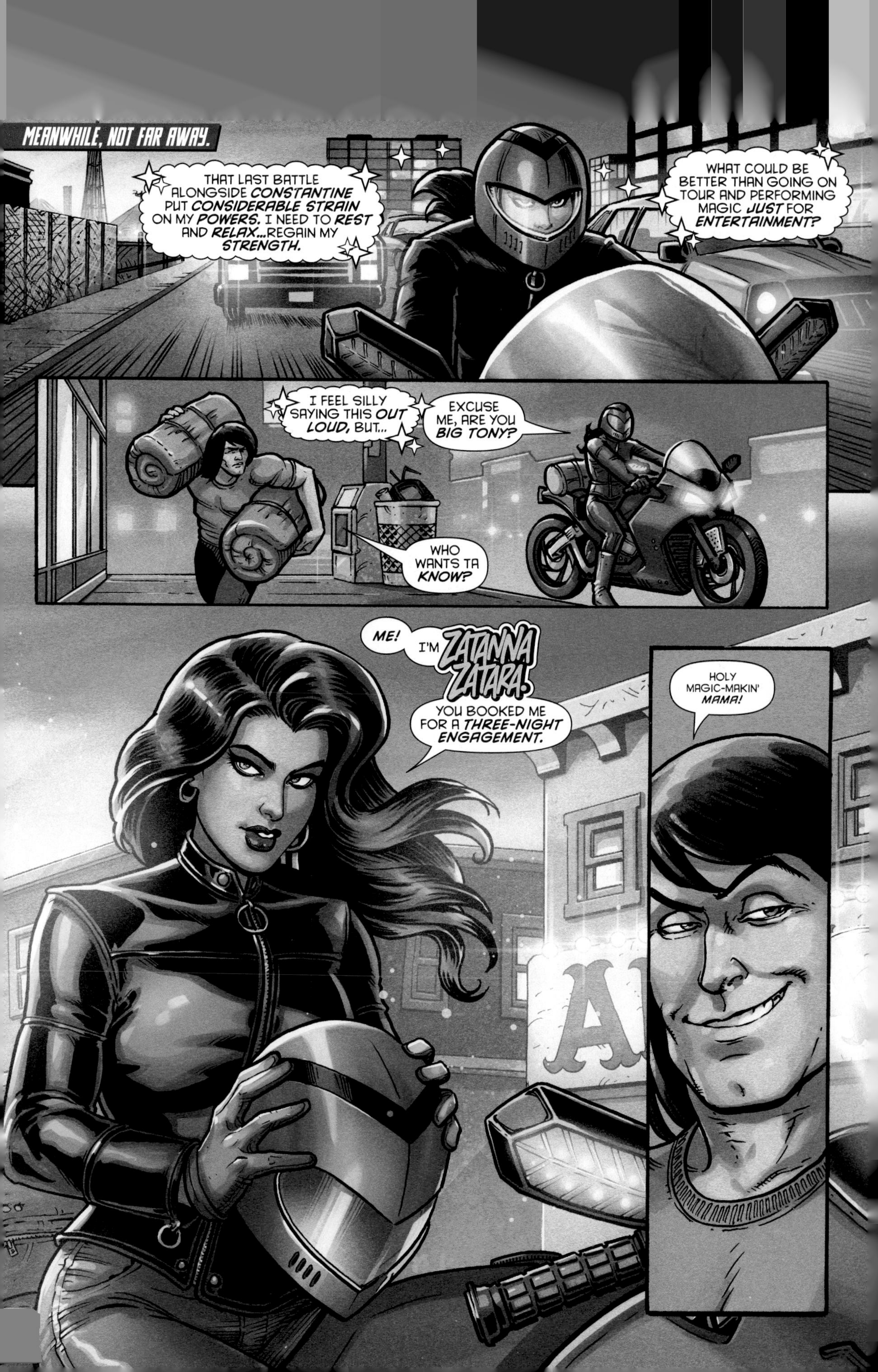
MEANWHILE, NOT FAR AWAY.
THAT LAST BATTLE ALONGSIDE CONSTANTINE PUT CONSIDERABLE STRAIN ON MY POWERS. I NEED TO REST AND RELAX...REGAIN MY STRENGTH.
WHAT COULD BE BETTER THAN GOING ON TOUR AND PERFORMING MAGIC JUST FOR ENTERTAINMENT?
I FEEL SILLY SAYING THIS OUT LOUD, BUT...
EXCUSE ME, ARE YOU BIG TONY?
WHO WANTS TA KNOW?
ME!
I'M ZATANNA ZATARA.
YOU BOOKED ME FOR A THREE-NIGHT ENGAGEMENT.
HOLY MAGIC-MAKIN' MAMA!

BE AFRAID OF THE DARK

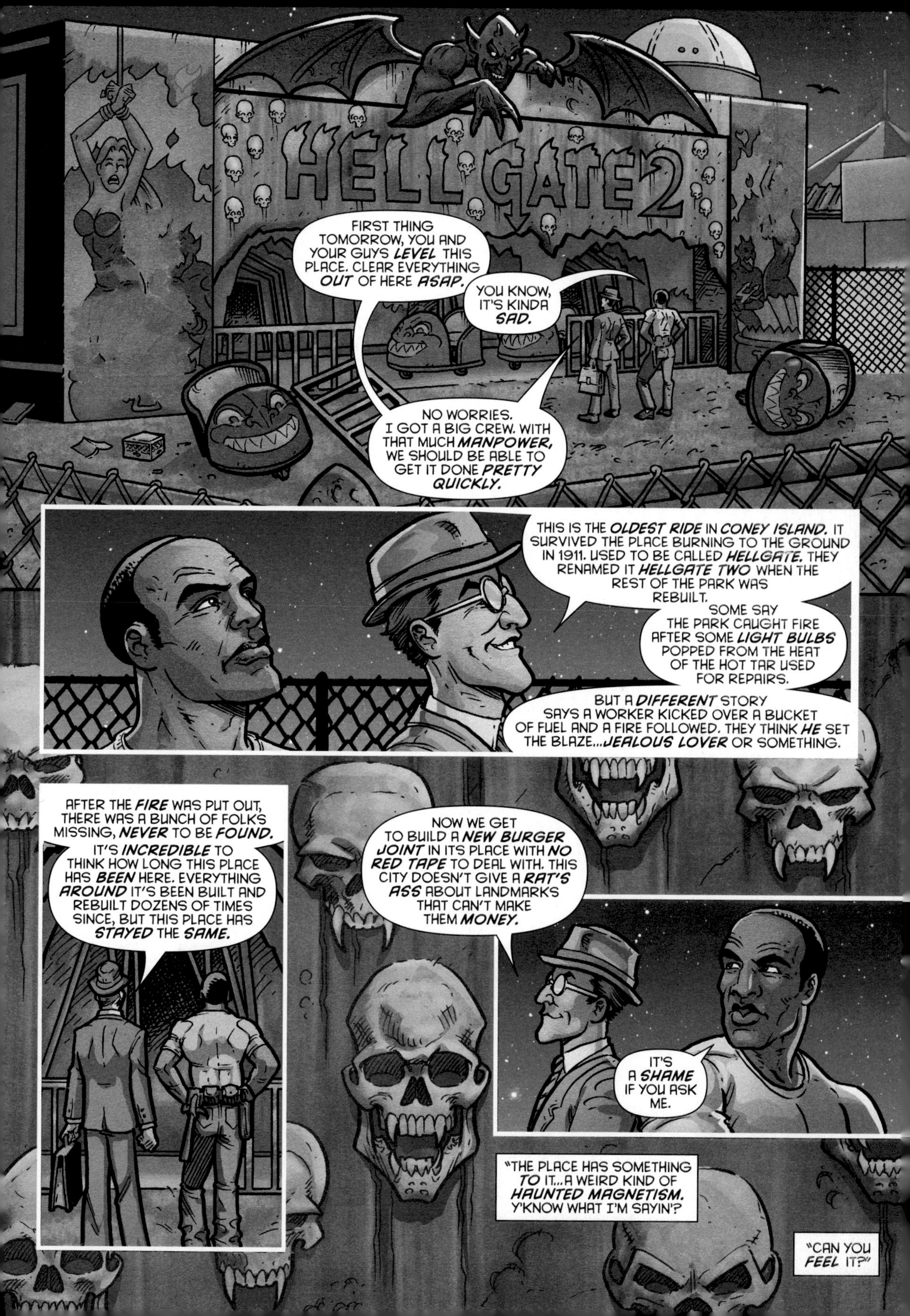

HELL GATE 2
FIRST THING TOMORROW, YOU AND YOUR GUYS *LEVEL* THIS PLACE. CLEAR EVERYTHING *OUT* OF HERE *ASAP.*
YOU KNOW, IT'S KINDA *SAD.*
NO WORRIES. I GOT A BIG CREW. WITH THAT MUCH *MANPOWER,* WE SHOULD BE ABLE TO GET IT DONE *PRETTY QUICKLY.*
THIS IS THE *OLDEST RIDE* IN *CONEY ISLAND.* IT SURVIVED THE PLACE BURNING TO THE GROUND IN 1911. USED TO BE CALLED *HELLGATE.* THEY RENAMED IT *HELLGATE TWO* WHEN THE REST OF THE PARK WAS REBUILT.
SOME SAY THE PARK CAUGHT FIRE AFTER SOME *LIGHT BULBS* POPPED FROM THE HEAT OF THE HOT TAR USED FOR REPAIRS.
BUT A *DIFFERENT* STORY SAYS A WORKER KICKED OVER A BUCKET OF FUEL AND A FIRE FOLLOWED. THEY THINK *HE* SET THE BLAZE...*JEALOUS LOVER* OR SOMETHING.
AFTER THE *FIRE* WAS PUT OUT, THERE WAS A BUNCH OF FOLKS MISSING, *NEVER* TO BE *FOUND.*
IT'S *INCREDIBLE* TO THINK HOW LONG THIS PLACE HAS *BEEN* HERE. EVERYTHING *AROUND* IT'S BEEN BUILT AND REBUILT DOZENS OF TIMES SINCE, BUT THIS PLACE HAS *STAYED* THE *SAME.*
NOW WE GET TO BUILD A *NEW BURGER JOINT* IN ITS PLACE WITH *NO RED TAPE* TO DEAL WITH. THIS CITY DOESN'T GIVE A *RAT'S ASS* ABOUT LANDMARKS THAT CAN'T MAKE THEM *MONEY.*
IT'S A *SHAME* IF YOU ASK ME.
"THE PLACE HAS SOMETHING *TO* IT...A WEIRD KIND OF *HAUNTED MAGNETISM.* Y'KNOW WHAT I'M SAYIN'?
"CAN YOU *FEEL* IT?"

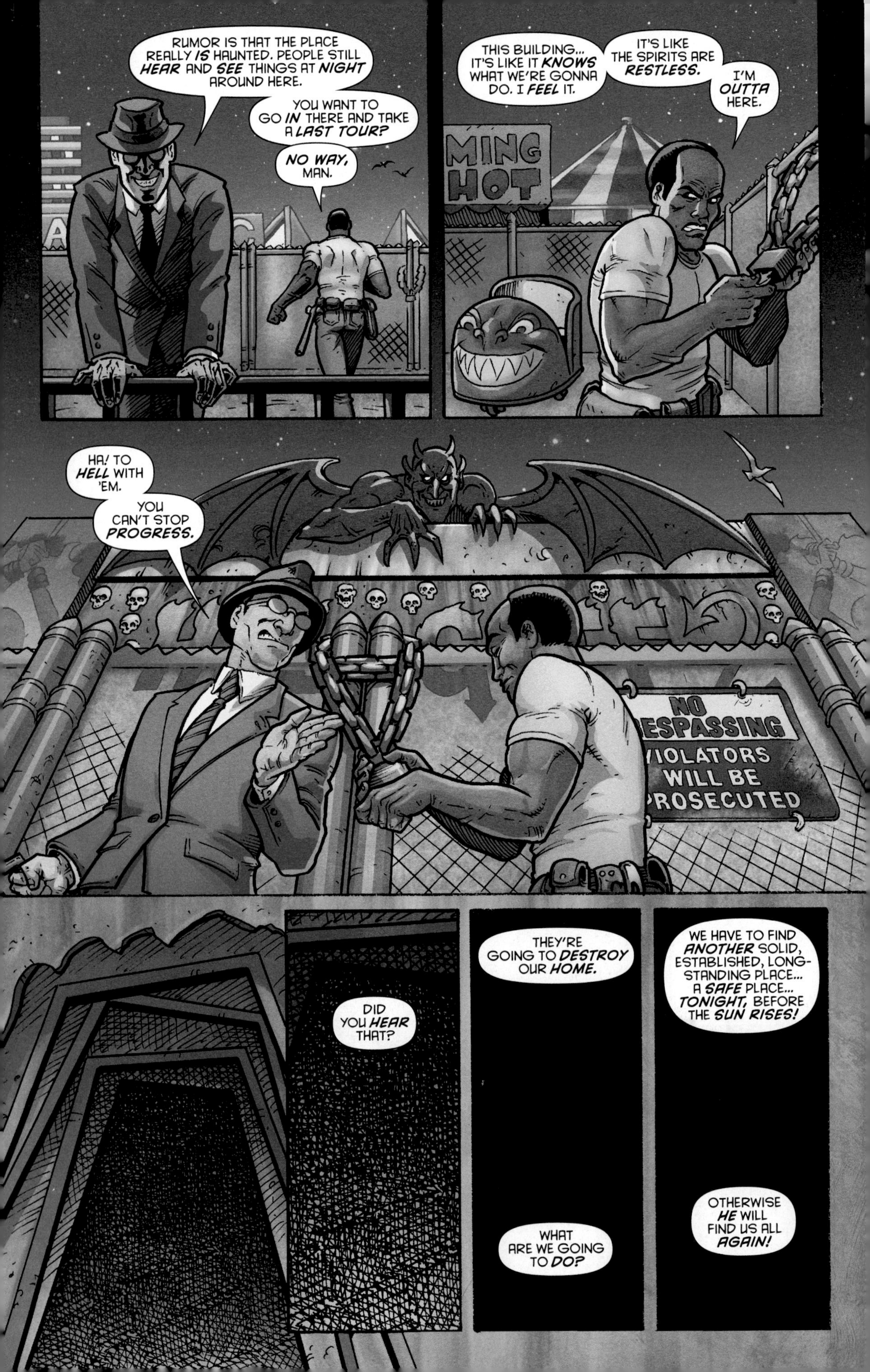
RUMOR IS THAT THE PLACE REALLY *IS* HAUNTED. PEOPLE STILL *HEAR* AND *SEE* THINGS AT *NIGHT* AROUND HERE.
YOU WANT TO GO *IN* THERE AND TAKE A *LAST TOUR?*
NO WAY, MAN.
THIS BUILDING... IT'S LIKE IT *KNOWS* WHAT WE'RE GONNA DO. I *FEEL* IT.
IT'S LIKE THE SPIRITS ARE *RESTLESS.*
I'M *OUTTA* HERE.
MING
HOT
HA! TO *HELL* WITH 'EM.
YOU CAN'T STOP *PROGRESS.*
NO
ESPASSING
VIOLATORS
WILL BE
PROSECUTED
DID YOU *HEAR* THAT?
THEY'RE GOING TO *DESTROY* OUR *HOME.*
WHAT ARE WE GOING TO *DO?*
WE HAVE TO FIND *ANOTHER* SOLID, ESTABLISHED, LONG-STANDING PLACE... A *SAFE* PLACE... *TONIGHT,* BEFORE THE *SUN RISES!*
OTHERWISE *HE* WILL FIND US ALL *AGAIN!*

BEAUTY SLEEP

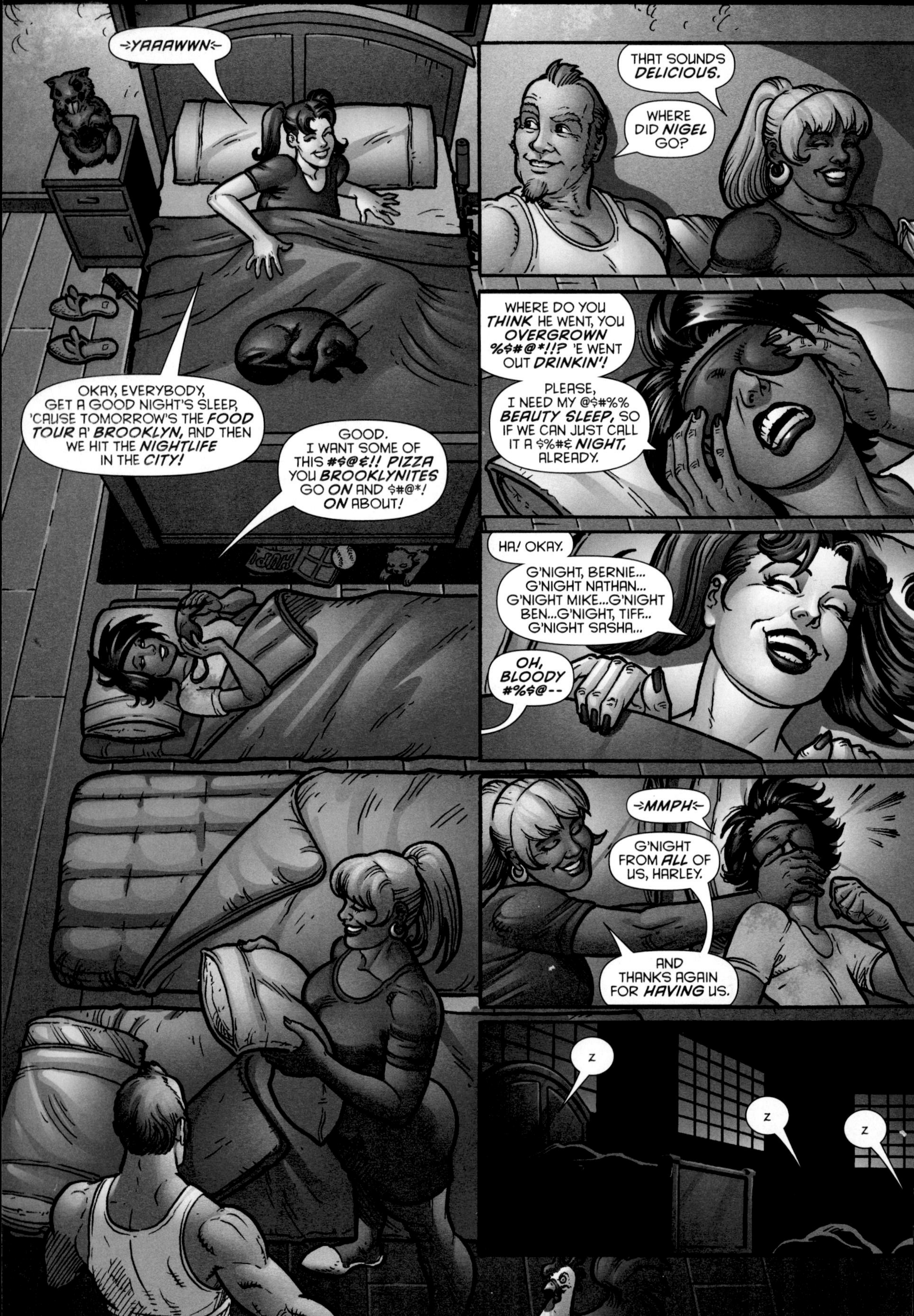

~YAAAWWN~
OKAY, EVERYBODY, GET A GOOD NIGHT'S SLEEP, 'CAUSE TOMORROW'S THE FOOD TOUR A' BROOKLYN, AND THEN WE HIT THE NIGHTLIFE IN THE CITY!
GOOD. I WANT SOME OF THIS #$@€!! PIZZA YOU BROOKLYNITES GO ON AND $#@*! ON ABOUT!
THAT SOUNDS DELICIOUS.
WHERE DID NIGEL GO?
WHERE DO YOU THINK HE WENT, YOU OVERGROWN %$#@*!!? 'E WENT OUT DRINKIN'!
PLEASE, I NEED MY @$#%% BEAUTY SLEEP, SO IF WE CAN JUST CALL IT A $%#€ NIGHT, ALREADY.
HA! OKAY.
G'NIGHT, BERNIE... G'NIGHT NATHAN... G'NIGHT MIKE...G'NIGHT BEN...G'NIGHT, TIFF... G'NIGHT SASHA...
OH, BLOODY #%$@--
~MMPH~
G'NIGHT FROM ALL OF US, HARLEY.
AND THANKS AGAIN FOR HAVING US.
Z
Z
Z

DRINK AND DROP

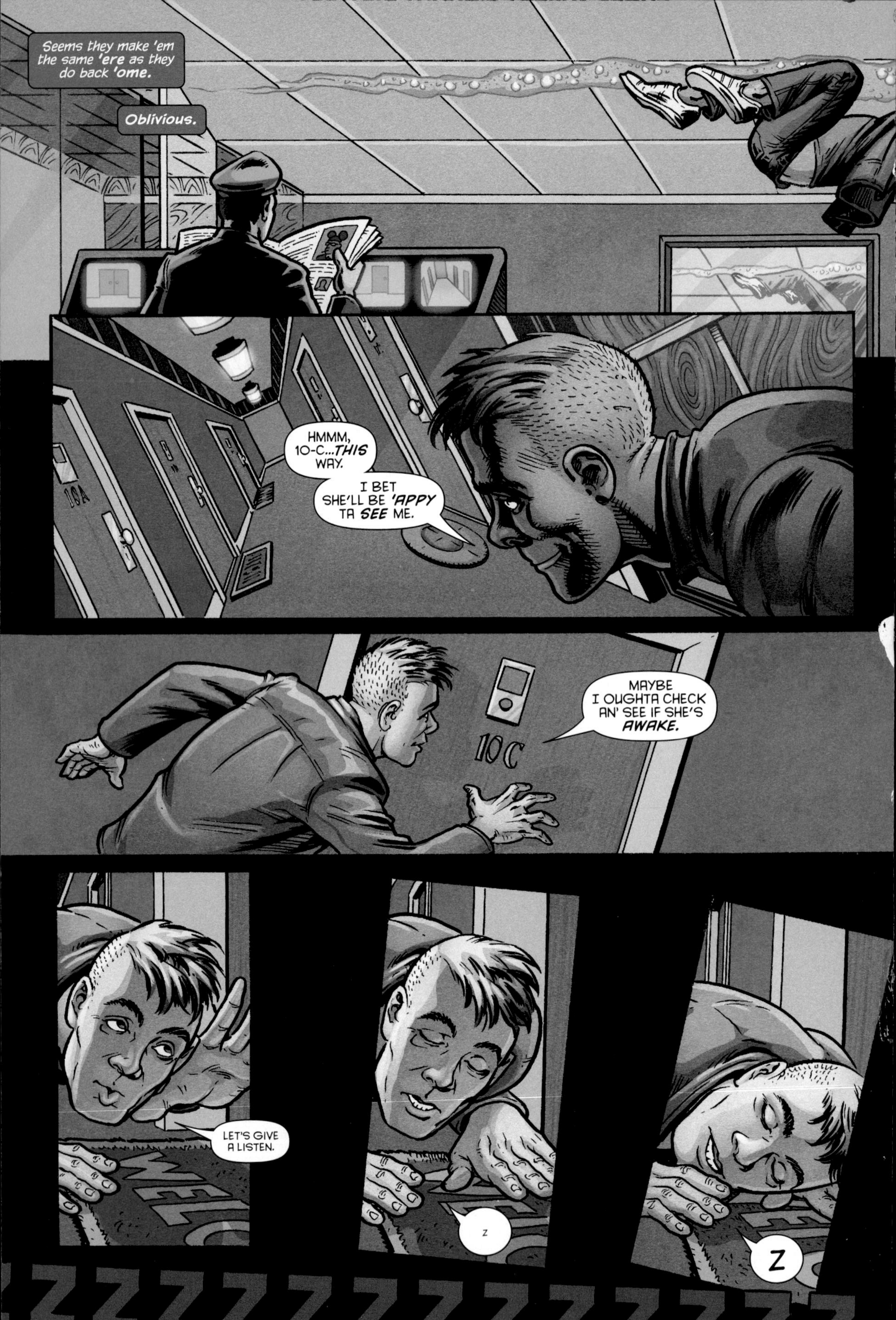
Seems they make 'em the same 'ere as they do back 'ome.
Oblivious.
HMMM, 10-C...THIS WAY.
I BET SHE'LL BE 'APPY TA SEE ME.
10A
MAYBE I OUGHTA CHECK AN' SEE IF SHE'S AWAKE.
10C
LET'S GIVE A LISTEN.
Z
Z

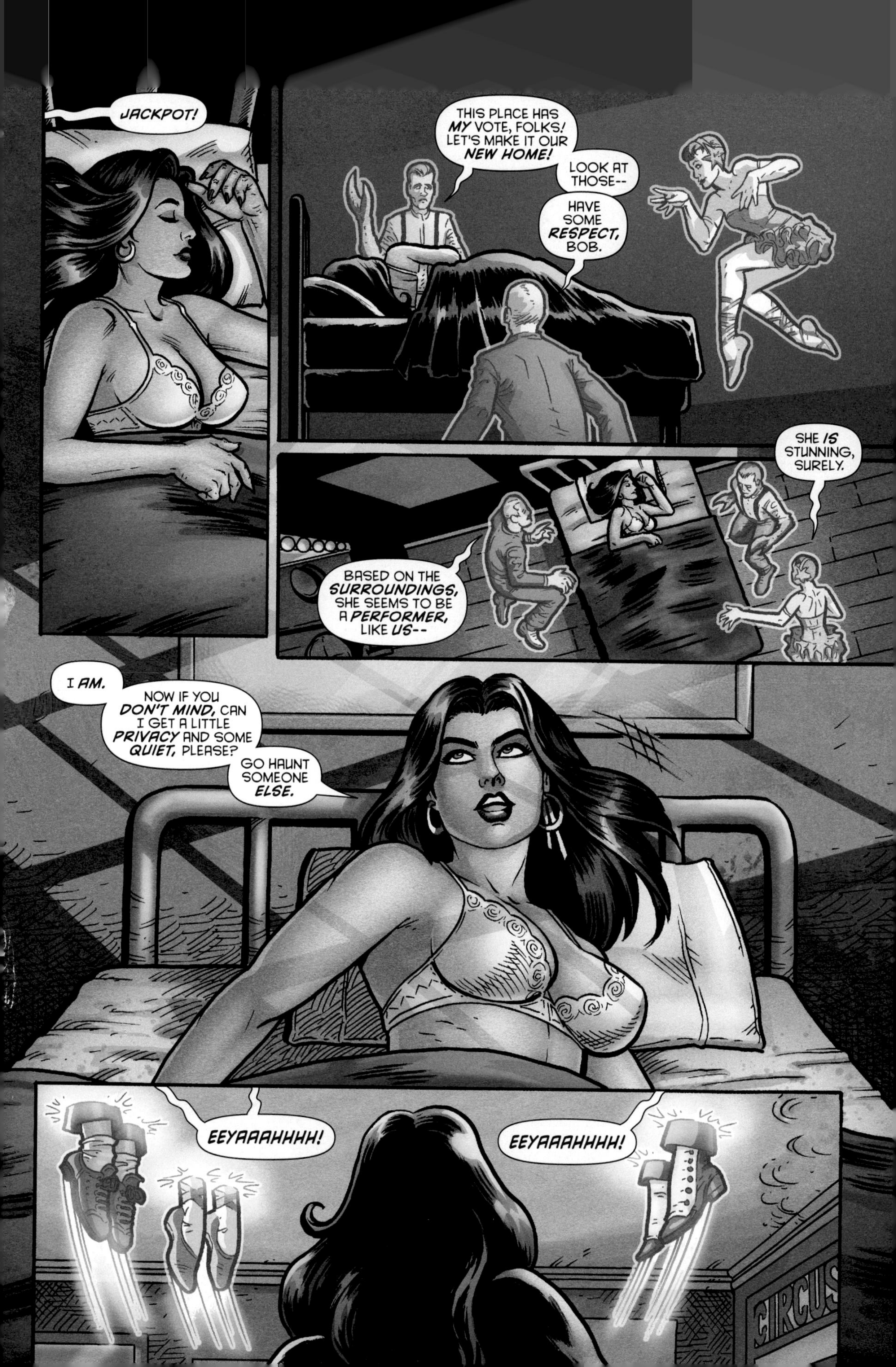
JACKPOT!
THIS PLACE HAS MY VOTE, FOLKS! LET'S MAKE IT OUR NEW HOME!
LOOK AT THOSE--
HAVE SOME RESPECT, BOB.
BASED ON THE SURROUNDINGS, SHE SEEMS TO BE A PERFORMER, LIKE US--
SHE IS STUNNING, SURELY.
I AM.
NOW IF YOU DON'T MIND, CAN I GET A LITTLE PRIVACY AND SOME QUIET, PLEASE?
GO HAUNT SOMEONE ELSE.
EEYAAAHHHH!
EEYAAAHHHH!
CIRCUS

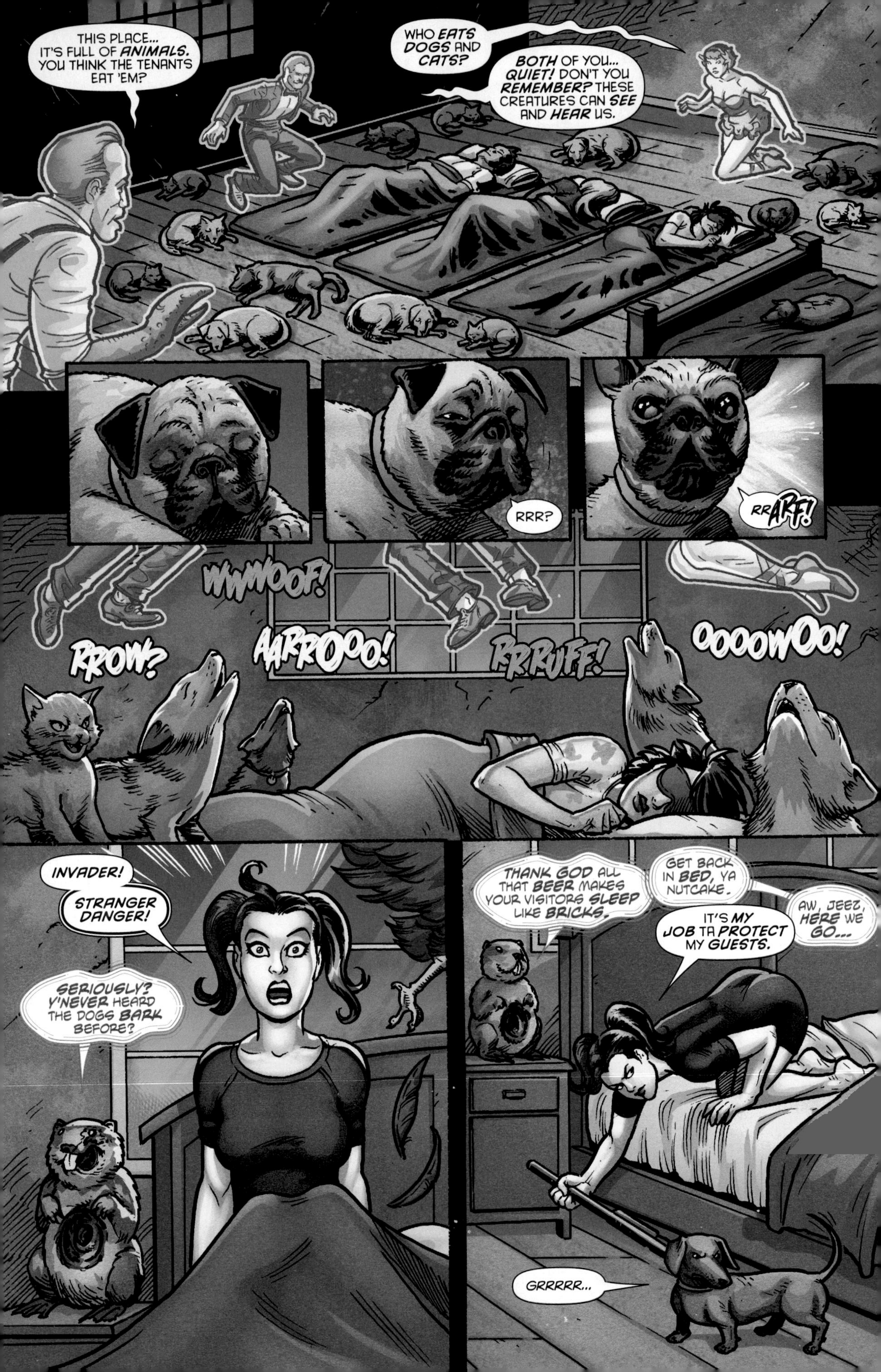

THIS PLACE... IT'S FULL OF ANIMALS. YOU THINK THE TENANTS EAT 'EM?
WHO EATS DOGS AND CATS?
BOTH OF YOU... QUIET! DON'T YOU REMEMBER? THESE CREATURES CAN SEE AND HEAR US.
RRR?
RRARF!
WWWOOF!
RROW?
AARROOO!
RRRUFF!
OOOOWOO!
INVADER!
STRANGER DANGER!
SERIOUSLY? Y'NEVER HEARD THE DOGS BARK BEFORE?
THANK GOD ALL THAT BEER MAKES YOUR VISITORS SLEEP LIKE BRICKS.
GET BACK IN BED, YA NUTCAKE.
IT'S MY JOB TA PROTECT MY GUESTS.
AW, JEEZ, HERE WE GO...
GRRRRR...

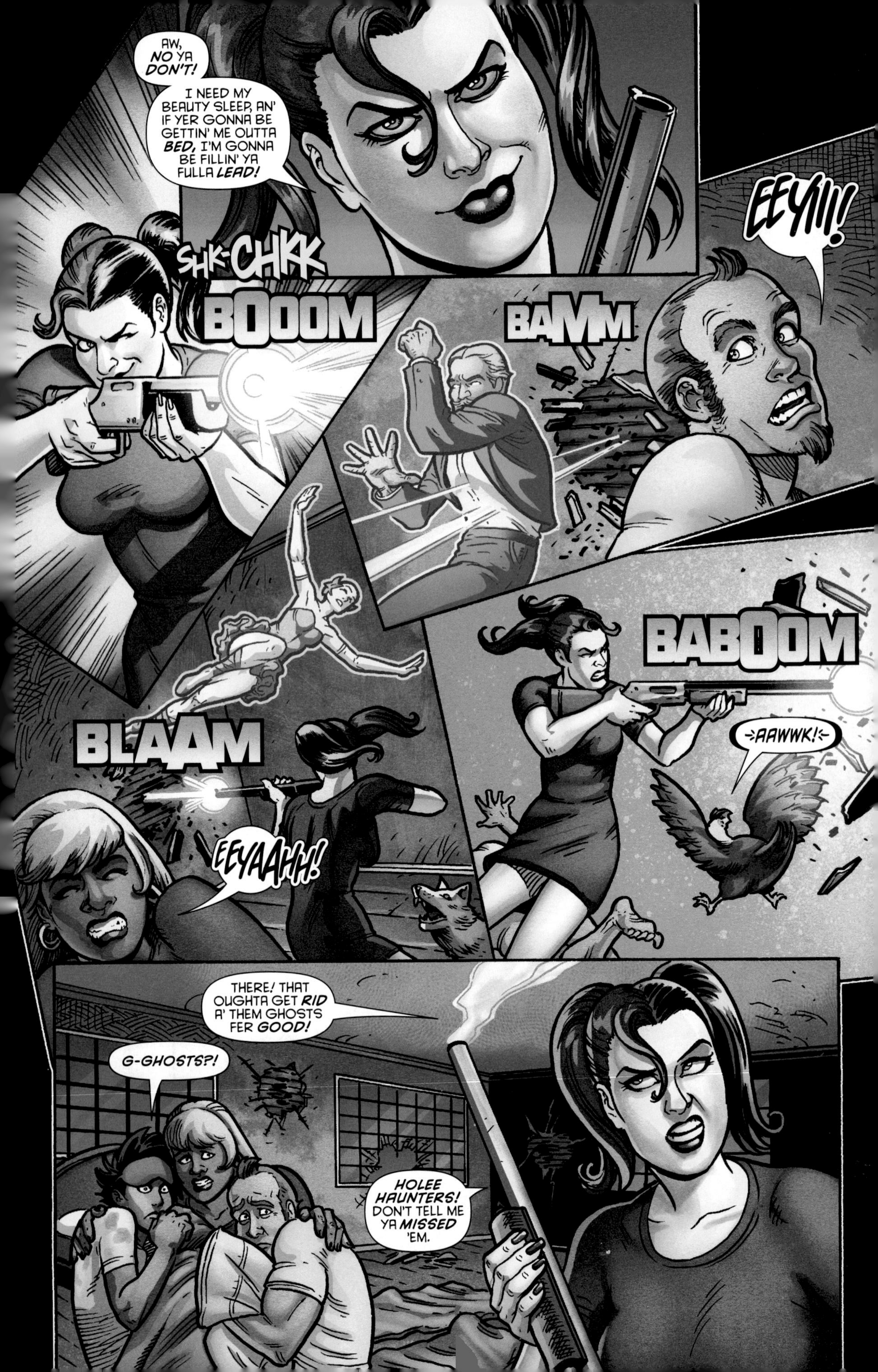
AW, NO YA DON'T!
I NEED MY BEAUTY SLEEP, AN' IF YER GONNA BE GETTIN' ME OUTTA BED, I'M GONNA BE FILLIN' YA FULLA LEAD!
SHK-CHKK
BOOOM
BAMM
EEYIII!
BLAAM
EEYAAHH!
BABOOM
AAWWK!
THERE! THAT OUGHTA GET RID A' THEM GHOSTS FER GOOD!
G-GHOSTS?!
HOLEE HAUNTERS! DON'T TELL ME YA MISSED 'EM.

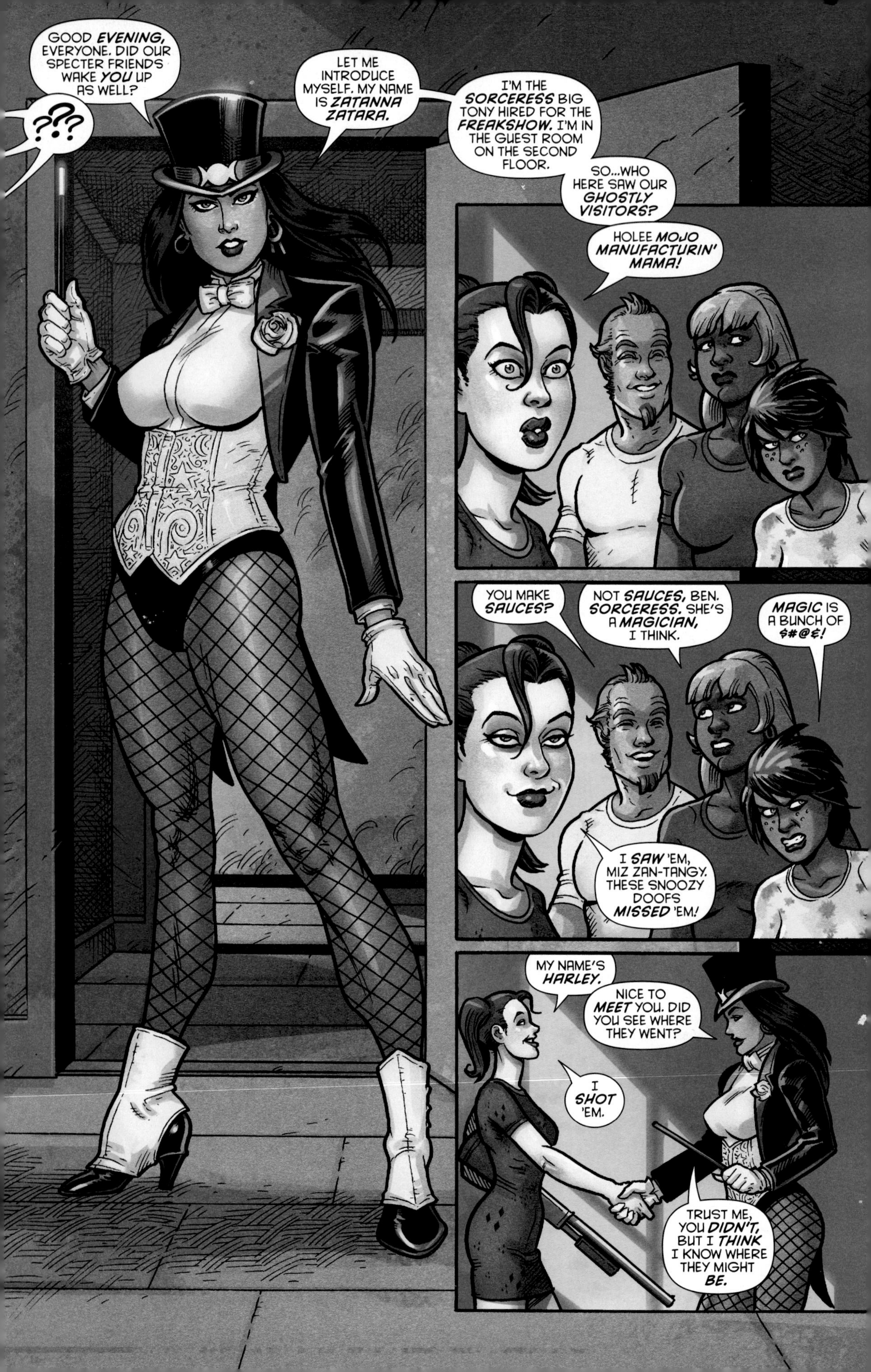

GOOD EVENING, EVERYONE. DID OUR SPECTER FRIENDS WAKE YOU UP AS WELL?
???
LET ME INTRODUCE MYSELF. MY NAME IS ZATANNA ZATARA.
I'M THE SORCERESS BIG TONY HIRED FOR THE FREAKSHOW. I'M IN THE GUEST ROOM ON THE SECOND FLOOR.
SO...WHO HERE SAW OUR GHOSTLY VISITORS?
HOLEE MOJO MANUFACTURIN' MAMA!
YOU MAKE SAUCES?
NOT SAUCES, BEN. SORCERESS. SHE'S A MAGICIAN, I THINK.
MAGIC IS A BUNCH OF $#@€!
I SAW 'EM, MIZ ZAN-TANGY. THESE SNOOZY DOOFS MISSED 'EM!
MY NAME'S HARLEY.
NICE TO MEET YOU. DID YOU SEE WHERE THEY WENT?
I SHOT 'EM.
TRUST ME, YOU DIDN'T, BUT I THINK I KNOW WHERE THEY MIGHT BE.

IF NONE OF YOU *SAW* THEM, THEN YOU REALLY *SHOULD* STAY IN MY ROOM DOWNSTAIRS. WE HAVE *WORK* TO DO HERE.

MAYBE WE CAN *HELP?*

HONESTLY, THE *BEST HELP* WOULD BE TO LET ME DO MY *THING.*

DON'T *ARGUE* WITH 'ER, YOU $%##@, LET'S TAKE THE ROOM, GET SOME SHUT-EYE, AN' LEAVE THESE *NUTBAGS* TO THEIR $@#* *MADNESS.*

MISS *ZATANNA,* CAN YOU PULL A *BUNNY RABBIT* OUT OF YOUR HAT?

EVIG EM A TIBBAR!

BRILLIANT! CAN I *KEEP* HIM?

I DON'T SEE WHY NOT. HARLEY, DO WE HAVE *ROOF ACCESS* HERE?

YEAH, DIRECT. *GIMME* A SECOND.

UM...WHAT ARE YOU *DOING?*

PUTTIN' ON *WORK CLOTHES.* YOU GOT *YOUR* UNIFORM, I NEED *MINE.*

IT'S OKAY, YOU CAN *WATCH.*

WAIT. YOU... YOU'RE *HARLEY QUINN.*

THE *ONE AN' ONLY.*

OH. YOU SHOULD *FIRE* YOUR *PUBLIC RELATIONS* CREW.

AW, DON'T BELIEVE EVERYTHING Y'HEAR...

WELL, *MOST* OF IT, ANYWAYS.

SO WHY D'YA WANNA GO TA THE *ROOF...*AN' WHERE'DJA GET THAT *AWESOME* COSTUME?

I THINK WHAT WE'RE *LOOKING* FOR IS *WAITING* FOR US UP THERE. AS FAR AS THE *SUIT,* I LIKE TO CLASS UP A PLACE.

WELL IT'S *WORKIN'.* I'M FEELING *CLASSY* ALL *OVER.*

THE BAD DEAL

"DOWN THE DEVIL'S MOUTH LEAD A STAIRCASE TO A *DANK, DARK CHAMBER BELOW.* A STRANGE CONFIGURATION OF *CANDLES* AND *SYMBOLS* MARKED THE FLOOR, AND TWO FEARSOME ROBED FIGURES STOOD BY, THEIR GLARES BORING A HOLE THROUGH MY VERY SOUL."

"HE *ASSAILED* ME, HELD ME *DOWN*. THE *ROBED ONES* TORE THE CLOTHES FROM ME AND *BOUND* ME TO THE *FLOOR*."

"I *SCREAMED* AT THE *TOP* OF MY *LUNGS*, 'TIL I THOUGHT I WOULD *BURST*."

"EERIE CHANTS AROSE FROM THE *ROBED ABETTORS*, AND JOLLY MENACED ME WITH A *FEARSOME-LOOKING BLADE*."

"I *FAINTED* FROM FRIGHT."

WHAT *IS* THIS PLACE? JOLLY! I WISH TO *LEAVE* THIS *INSTANT!*

"THEY ONLY SEEMED TO *ENJOY* IT."

AAIEEEEEEEEEEE!!!

I'VE GOT THE REST A' THE STORY FOR YA...

...IF YOU'D *KINDLY REMOVE* YOUR *HEAD* FROM MY *KEISTER!*

HA! SORRY. I'VE NEVER SEEN *GHOST INSIDES* BEFORE.

"RICK AND I WERE WORKING *LATE* THAT NIGHT, BREAKING IN A NEW PERFORMER, WHEN WE HEARD *FAMILIAR SCREAMS* COMING FROM THE *HELLGATE*."

"*FAMILIAR SCREAMS?* HMMM..."

WHY *WERE* THOSE SCREAMS *SO FAMILIAR*, BETTY?

DO TELL!

YOU *BETCHA!*

SAY, IF *I* WAS A LITHE AN' LIMBER TRAPEZE CHICK, AN' A BENDY BALLERINA, *I'D* HAVE A BUNCH A' FUN WITH IT *MYSELF!*

DO GO ON...

MUST I? FINE. I MADE THE *ROUNDS*, OKAY? I WAS A DOORKNOB WHERE EVERYONE GOT A TURN. I WAS A SHAMELESS FLOOZY.

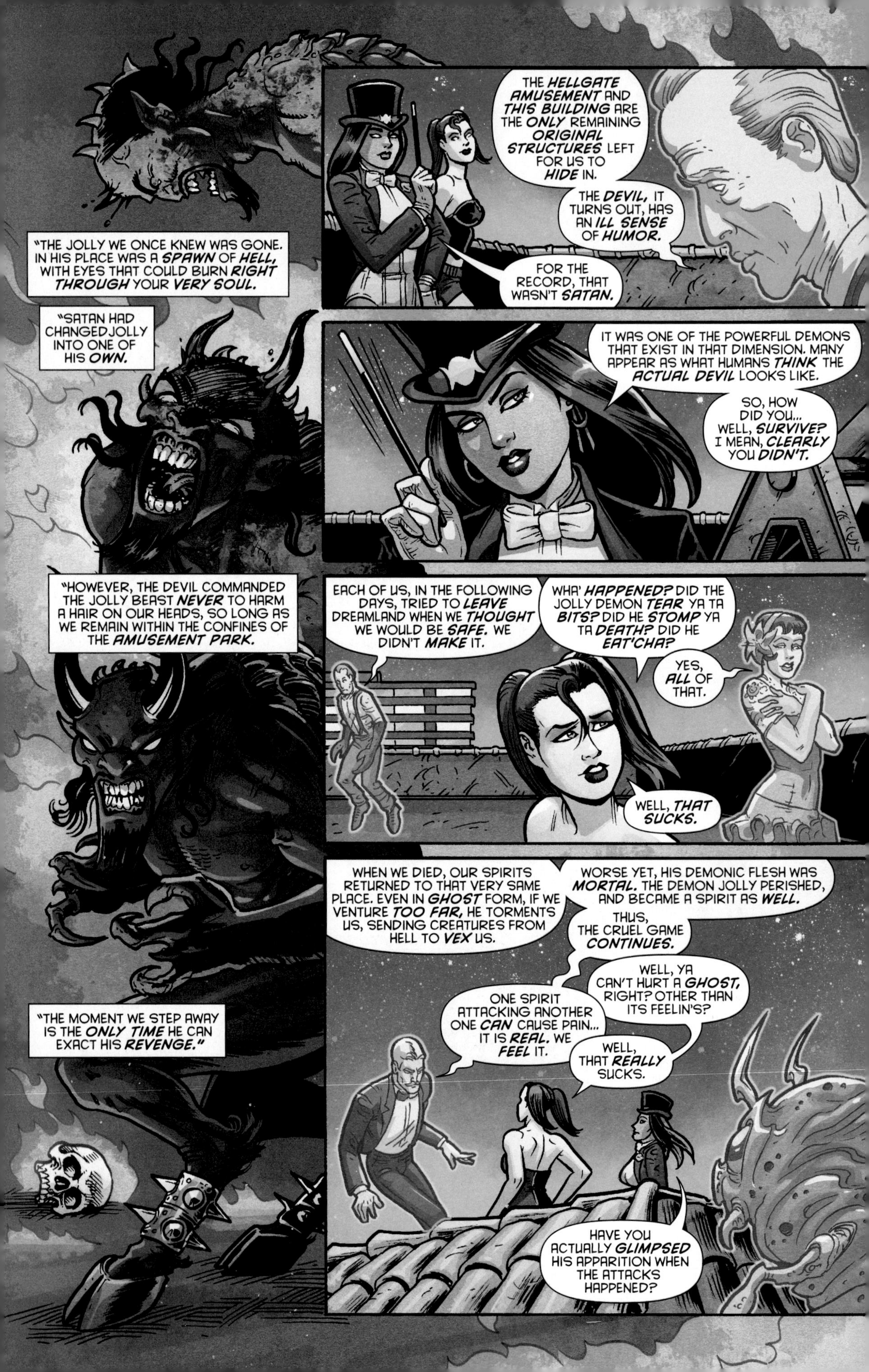

"THE JOLLY WE ONCE KNEW WAS GONE. IN HIS PLACE WAS A SPAWN OF HELL, WITH EYES THAT COULD BURN RIGHT THROUGH YOUR VERY SOUL.
THE HELLGATE AMUSEMENT AND THIS BUILDING ARE THE ONLY REMAINING ORIGINAL STRUCTURES LEFT FOR US TO HIDE IN.
THE DEVIL, IT TURNS OUT, HAS AN ILL SENSE OF HUMOR.
FOR THE RECORD, THAT WASN'T SATAN.
"SATAN HAD CHANGED JOLLY INTO ONE OF HIS OWN.
IT WAS ONE OF THE POWERFUL DEMONS THAT EXIST IN THAT DIMENSION. MANY APPEAR AS WHAT HUMANS THINK THE ACTUAL DEVIL LOOKS LIKE.
SO, HOW DID YOU... WELL, SURVIVE? I MEAN, CLEARLY YOU DIDN'T.
"HOWEVER, THE DEVIL COMMANDED THE JOLLY BEAST NEVER TO HARM A HAIR ON OUR HEADS, SO LONG AS WE REMAIN WITHIN THE CONFINES OF THE AMUSEMENT PARK.
EACH OF US, IN THE FOLLOWING DAYS, TRIED TO LEAVE DREAMLAND WHEN WE THOUGHT WE WOULD BE SAFE. WE DIDN'T MAKE IT.
WHA' HAPPENED? DID THE JOLLY DEMON TEAR YA TA BITS? DID HE STOMP YA TA DEATH? DID HE EAT'CHA?
YES, ALL OF THAT.
WELL, THAT SUCKS.
"THE MOMENT WE STEP AWAY IS THE ONLY TIME HE CAN EXACT HIS REVENGE."
WHEN WE DIED, OUR SPIRITS RETURNED TO THAT VERY SAME PLACE. EVEN IN GHOST FORM, IF WE VENTURE TOO FAR, HE TORMENTS US, SENDING CREATURES FROM HELL TO VEX US.
WORSE YET, HIS DEMONIC FLESH WAS MORTAL. THE DEMON JOLLY PERISHED, AND BECAME A SPIRIT AS WELL.
THUS, THE CRUEL GAME CONTINUES.
WELL, YA CAN'T HURT A GHOST, RIGHT? OTHER THAN ITS FEELIN'S?
ONE SPIRIT ATTACKING ANOTHER ONE CAN CAUSE PAIN... IT IS REAL. WE FEEL IT.
WELL, THAT REALLY SUCKS.
HAVE YOU ACTUALLY GLIMPSED HIS APPARITION WHEN THE ATTACKS HAPPENED?

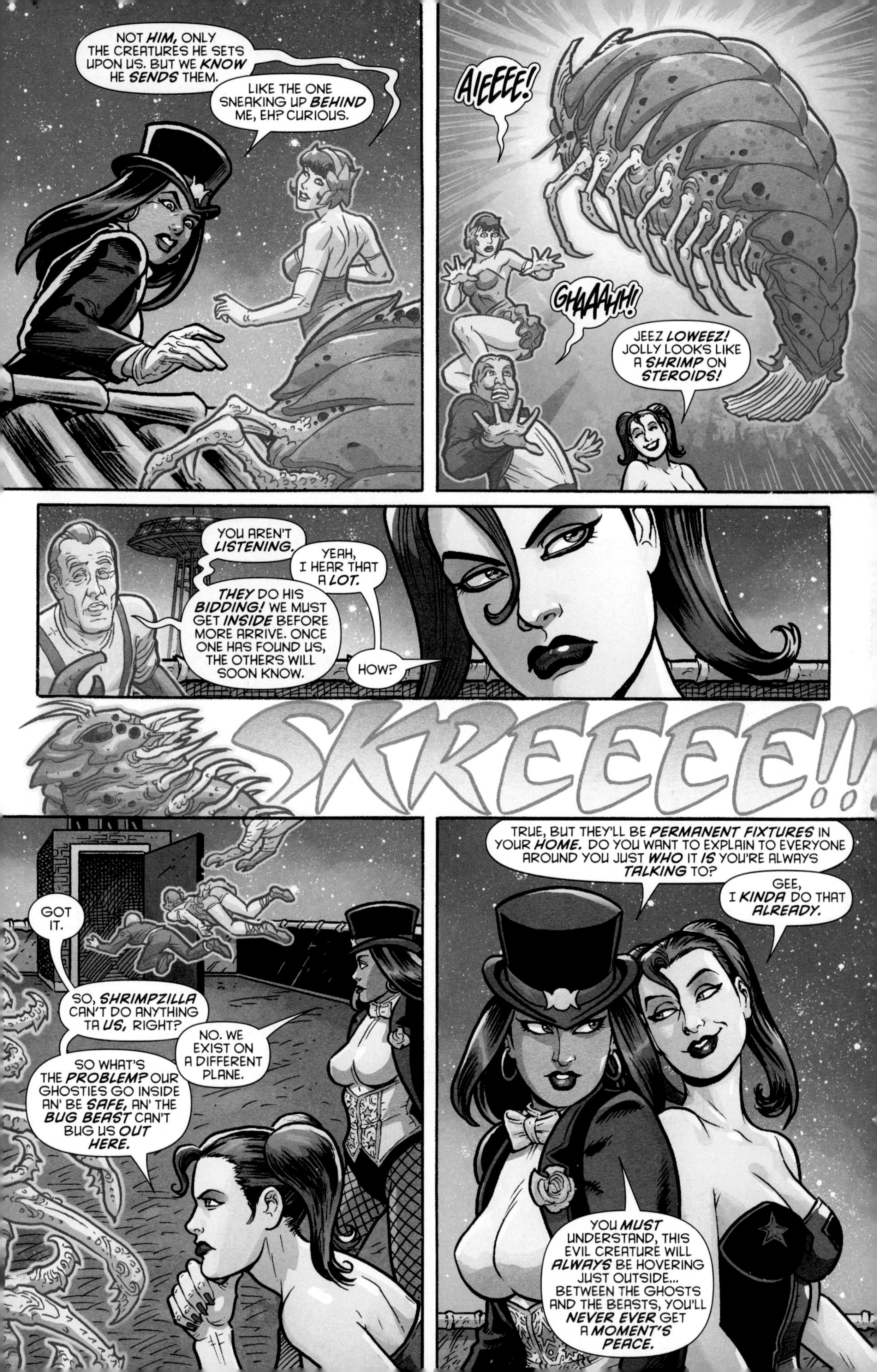
NOT HIM, ONLY THE CREATURES HE SETS UPON US. BUT WE KNOW HE SENDS THEM.
LIKE THE ONE SNEAKING UP BEHIND ME, EH? CURIOUS.
AIEEEE!
GHAAAHH!
JEEZ LOWEEZ! JOLLY LOOKS LIKE A SHRIMP ON STEROIDS!
YOU AREN'T LISTENING.
YEAH, I HEAR THAT A LOT.
THEY DO HIS BIDDING! WE MUST GET INSIDE BEFORE MORE ARRIVE. ONCE ONE HAS FOUND US, THE OTHERS WILL SOON KNOW.
HOW?
SKREEEE!!
GOT IT.
SO, SHRIMPZILLA CAN'T DO ANYTHING TA US, RIGHT?
NO. WE EXIST ON A DIFFERENT PLANE.
SO WHAT'S THE PROBLEM? OUR GHOSTIES GO INSIDE AN' BE SAFE, AN' THE BUG BEAST CAN'T BUG US OUT HERE.
TRUE, BUT THEY'LL BE PERMANENT FIXTURES IN YOUR HOME. DO YOU WANT TO EXPLAIN TO EVERYONE AROUND YOU JUST WHO IT IS YOU'RE ALWAYS TALKING TO?
GEE, I KINDA DO THAT ALREADY.
YOU MUST UNDERSTAND, THIS EVIL CREATURE WILL ALWAYS BE HOVERING JUST OUTSIDE... BETWEEN THE GHOSTS AND THE BEASTS, YOU'LL NEVER EVER GET A MOMENT'S PEACE.

GHOST BUSTED

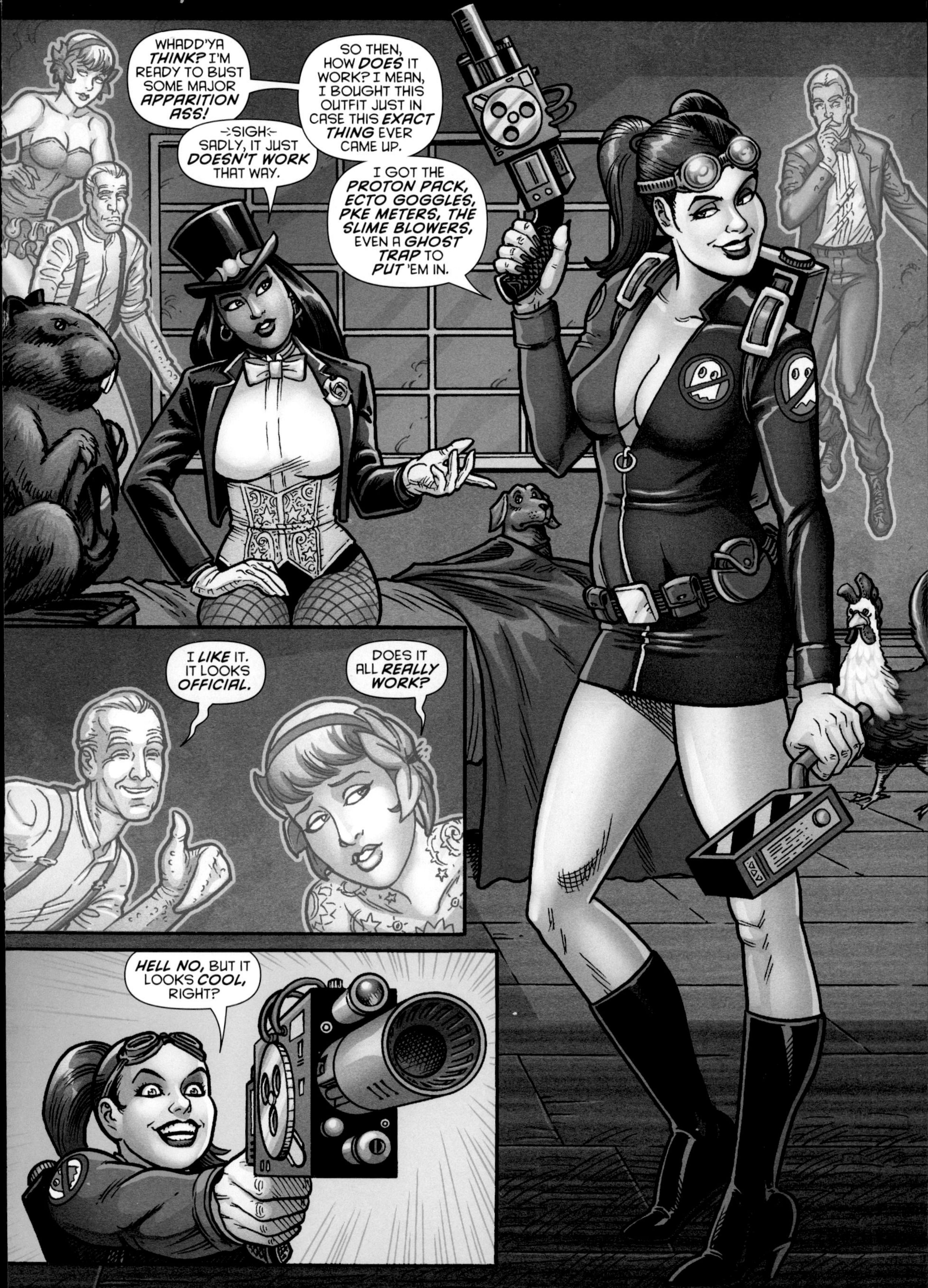

WHADD'YA THINK? I'M READY TO BUST SOME MAJOR APPARITION ASS!
SO THEN, HOW DOES IT WORK? I MEAN, I BOUGHT THIS OUTFIT JUST IN CASE THIS EXACT THING EVER CAME UP.
-SIGH- SADLY, IT JUST DOESN'T WORK THAT WAY.
I GOT THE PROTON PACK, ECTO GOGGLES, PKE METERS, THE SLIME BLOWERS, EVEN A GHOST TRAP TO PUT 'EM IN.
I LIKE IT. IT LOOKS OFFICIAL.
DOES IT ALL REALLY WORK?
HELL NO, BUT IT LOOKS COOL, RIGHT?

BIRDS OF A FEATHER

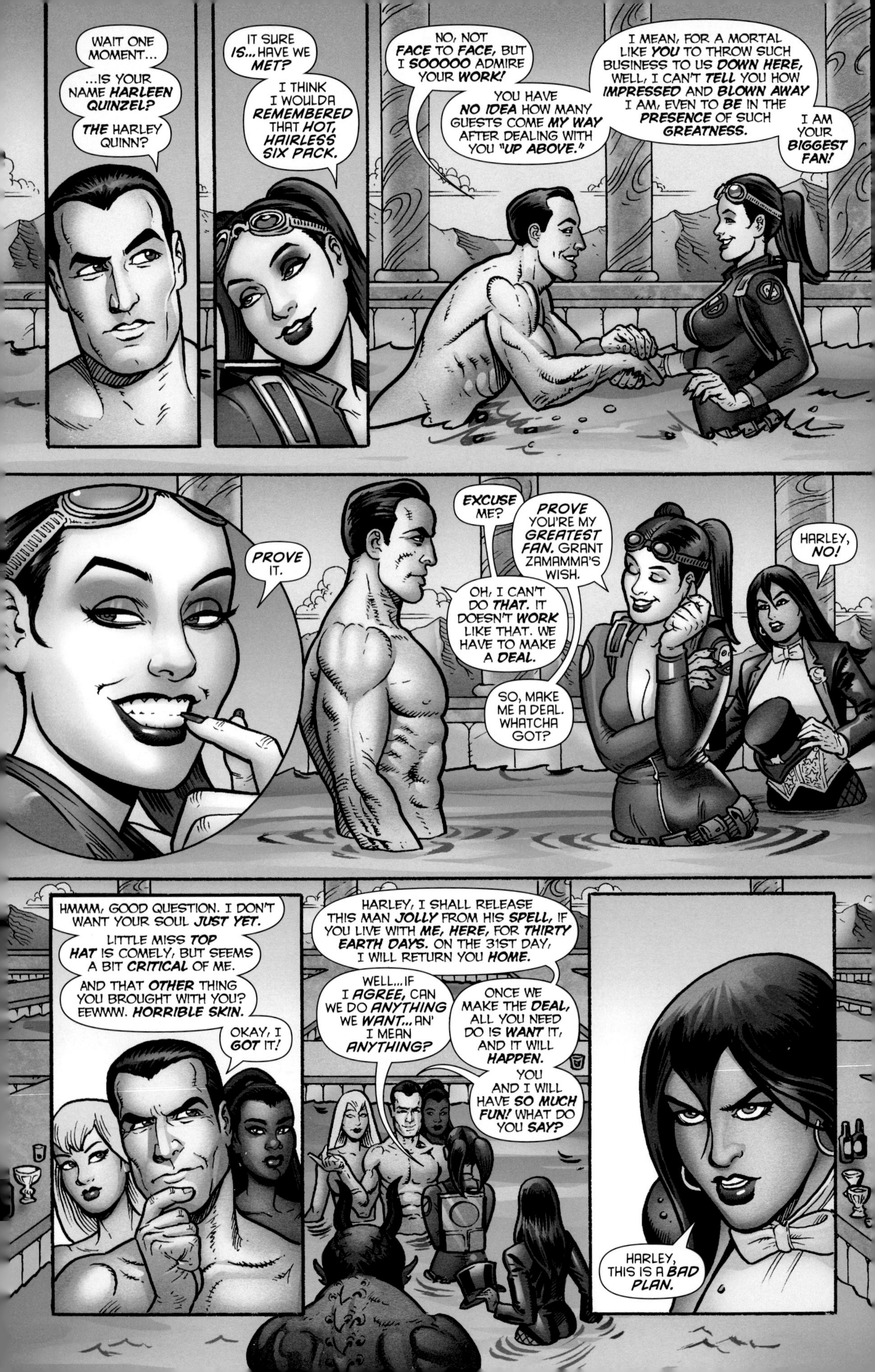

WAIT ONE MOMENT...
...IS YOUR NAME HARLEEN QUINZEL?
THE HARLEY QUINN?
IT SURE IS... HAVE WE MET?
I THINK I WOULDA REMEMBERED THAT HOT, HAIRLESS SIX PACK.
NO, NOT FACE TO FACE, BUT I SOOOOO ADMIRE YOUR WORK!
YOU HAVE NO IDEA HOW MANY GUESTS COME MY WAY AFTER DEALING WITH YOU "UP ABOVE."
I MEAN, FOR A MORTAL LIKE YOU TO THROW SUCH BUSINESS TO US DOWN HERE, WELL, I CAN'T TELL YOU HOW IMPRESSED AND BLOWN AWAY I AM, EVEN TO BE IN THE PRESENCE OF SUCH GREATNESS.
I AM YOUR BIGGEST FAN!
PROVE IT.
EXCUSE ME?
PROVE YOU'RE MY GREATEST FAN. GRANT ZAMAMMA'S WISH.
HARLEY, NO!
OH, I CAN'T DO THAT. IT DOESN'T WORK LIKE THAT. WE HAVE TO MAKE A DEAL.
SO, MAKE ME A DEAL. WHATCHA GOT?
HMMM, GOOD QUESTION. I DON'T WANT YOUR SOUL JUST YET.
LITTLE MISS TOP HAT IS COMELY, BUT SEEMS A BIT CRITICAL OF ME.
AND THAT OTHER THING YOU BROUGHT WITH YOU? EEWWW. HORRIBLE SKIN.
OKAY, I GOT IT!
HARLEY, I SHALL RELEASE THIS MAN JOLLY FROM HIS SPELL, IF YOU LIVE WITH ME, HERE, FOR THIRTY EARTH DAYS. ON THE 31ST DAY, I WILL RETURN YOU HOME.
WELL... IF I AGREE, CAN WE DO ANYTHING WE WANT... AN' I MEAN ANYTHING?
ONCE WE MAKE THE DEAL, ALL YOU NEED DO IS WANT IT, AND IT WILL HAPPEN.
YOU AND I WILL HAVE SO MUCH FUN! WHAT DO YOU SAY?
HARLEY, THIS IS A BAD PLAN.

QUICK TURNAROUND

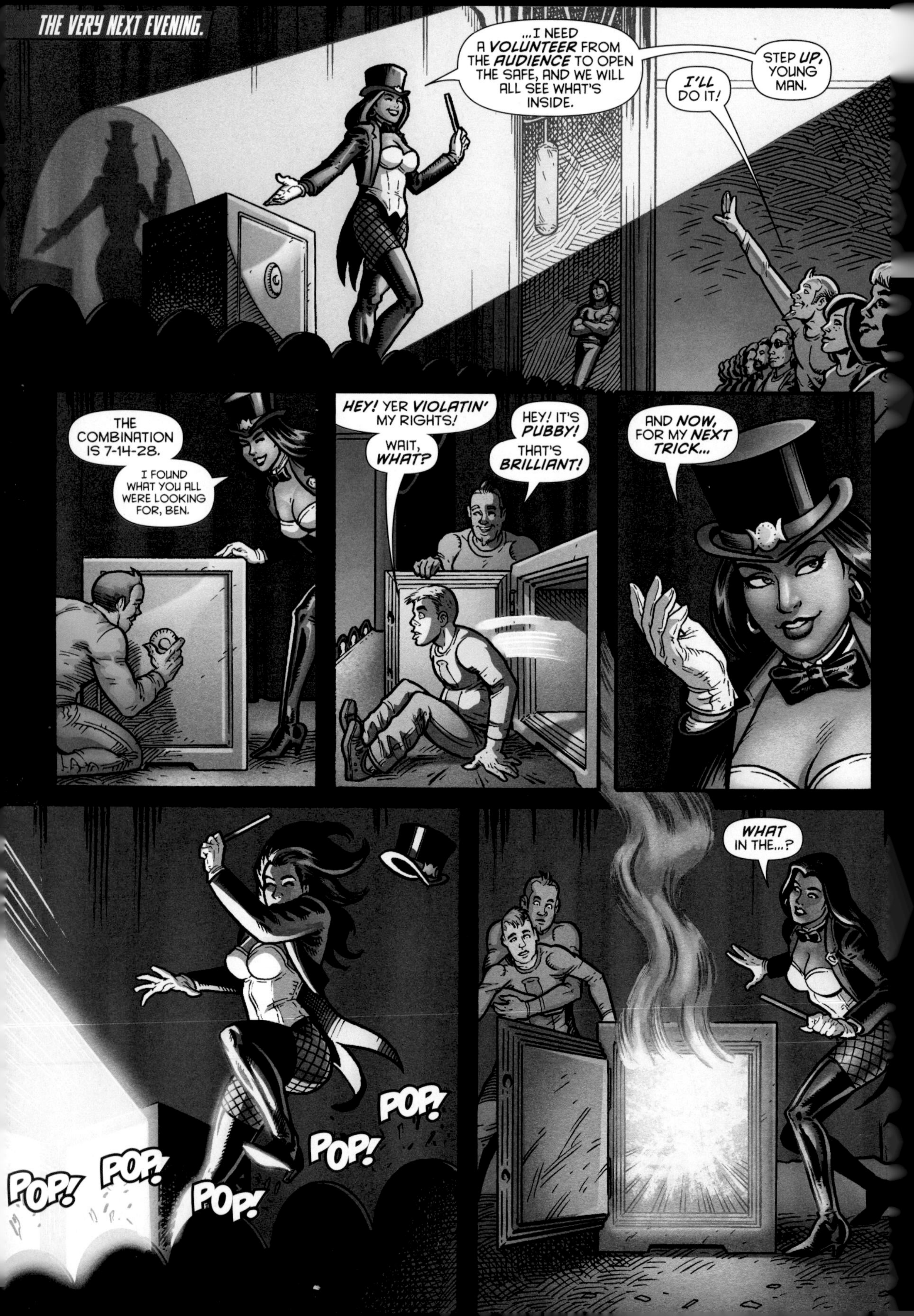

THE VERY NEXT EVENING.
...I NEED A VOLUNTEER FROM THE AUDIENCE TO OPEN THE SAFE, AND WE WILL ALL SEE WHAT'S INSIDE.
I'LL DO IT!
STEP UP, YOUNG MAN.
THE COMBINATION IS 7-14-28.
I FOUND WHAT YOU ALL WERE LOOKING FOR, BEN.
HEY! YER VIOLATIN' MY RIGHTS!
WAIT, WHAT?
HEY! IT'S PUBBY! THAT'S BRILLIANT!
AND NOW, FOR MY NEXT TRICK...
POP!
POP!
POP!
POP!
POP!
WHAT IN THE...?

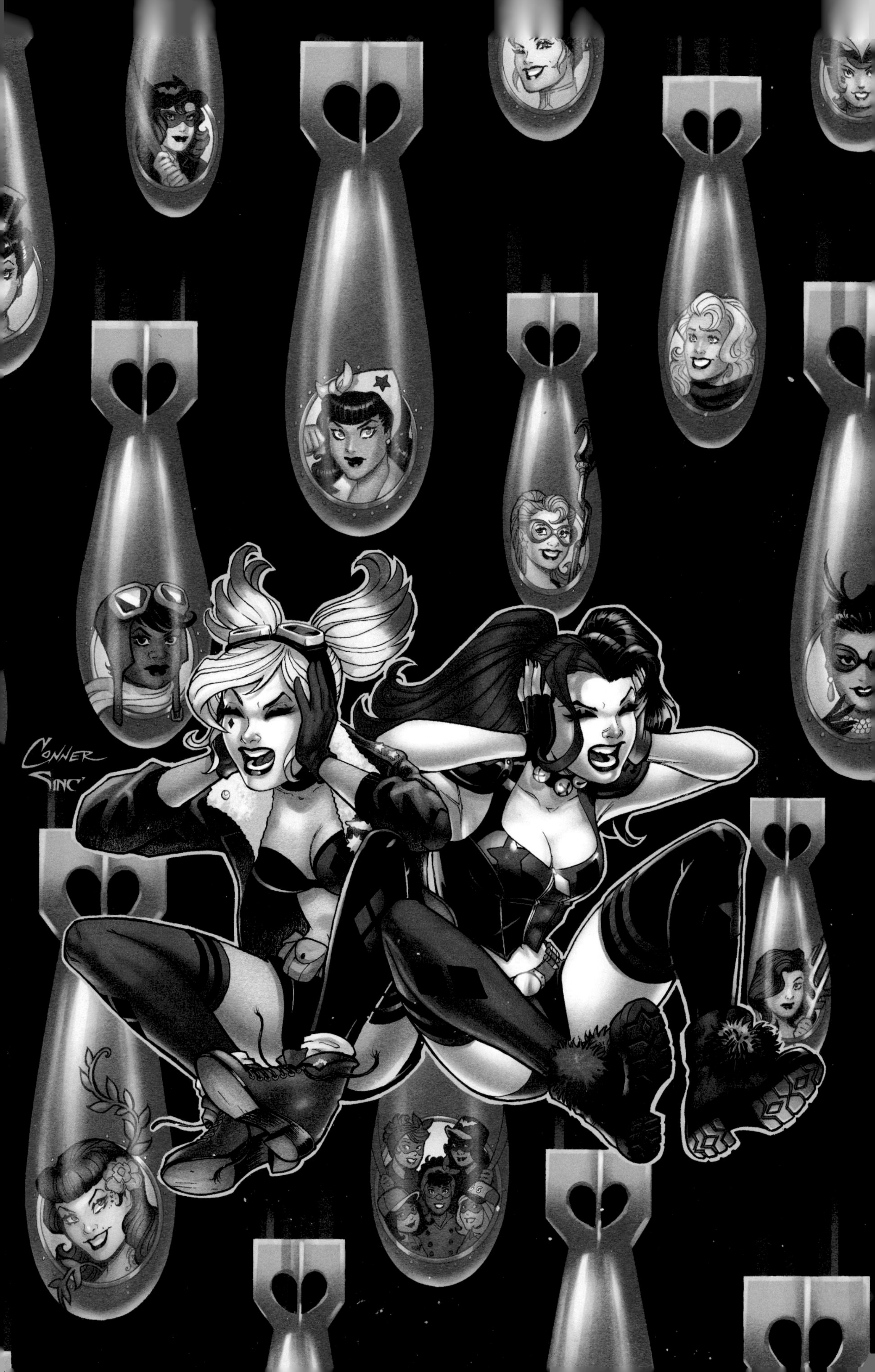
CONNER
SINC'

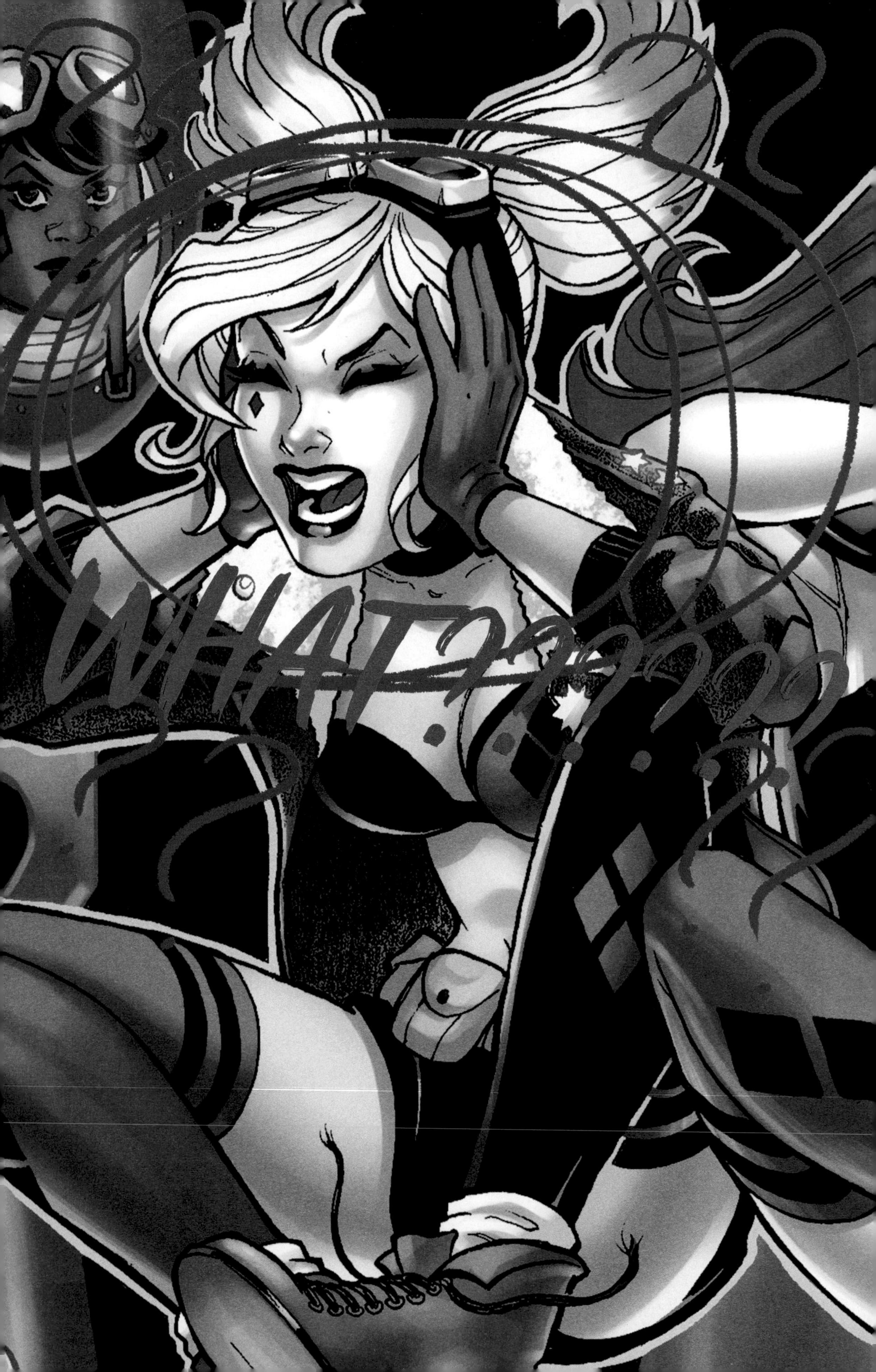
WHAT???

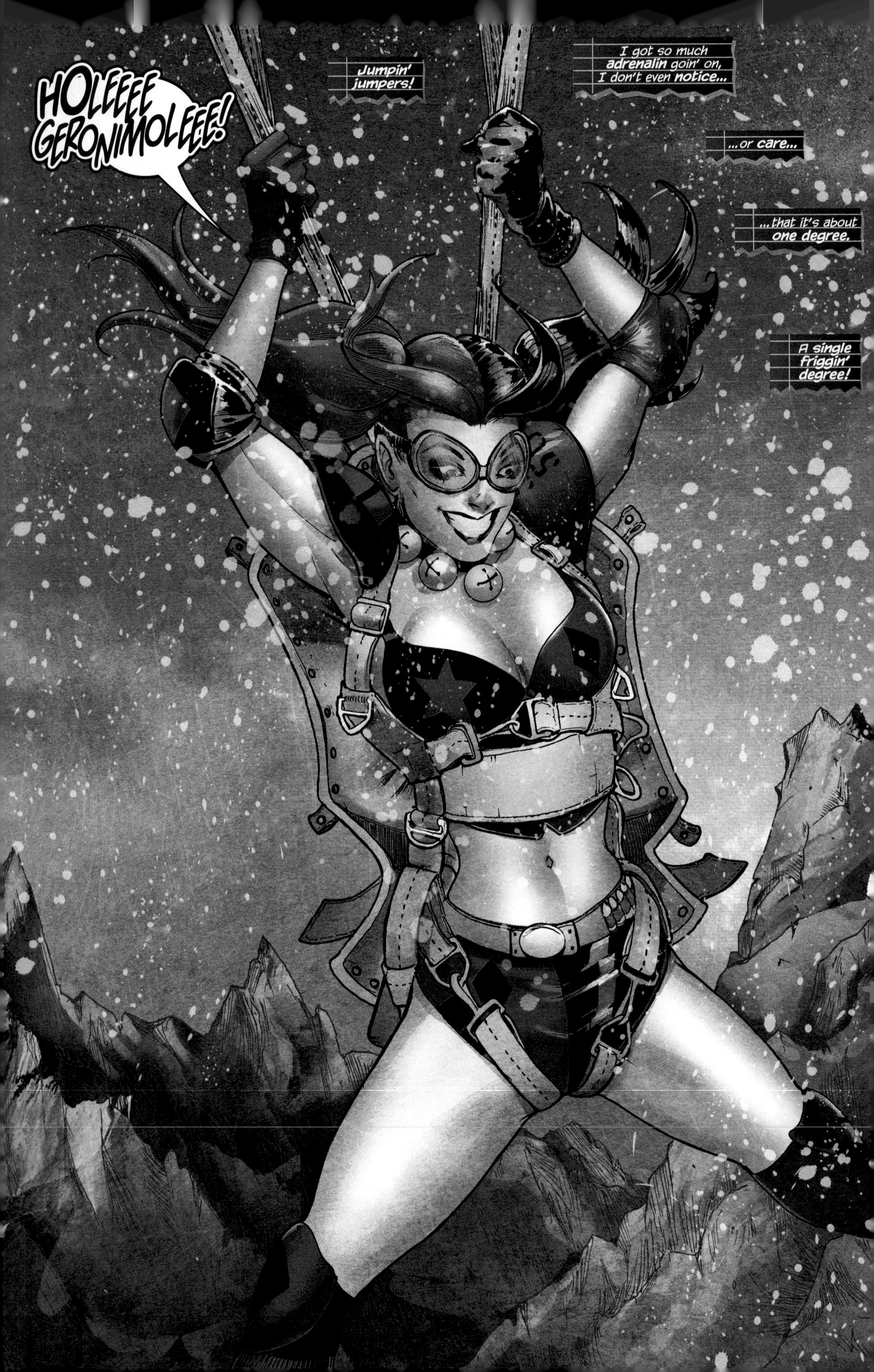
HOLEEEE GERONIMOLEEE!
Jumpin' jumpers!
I got so much adrenalin goin' on, I don't even notice...
...or care...
...that it's about one degree.
A single friggin' degree!

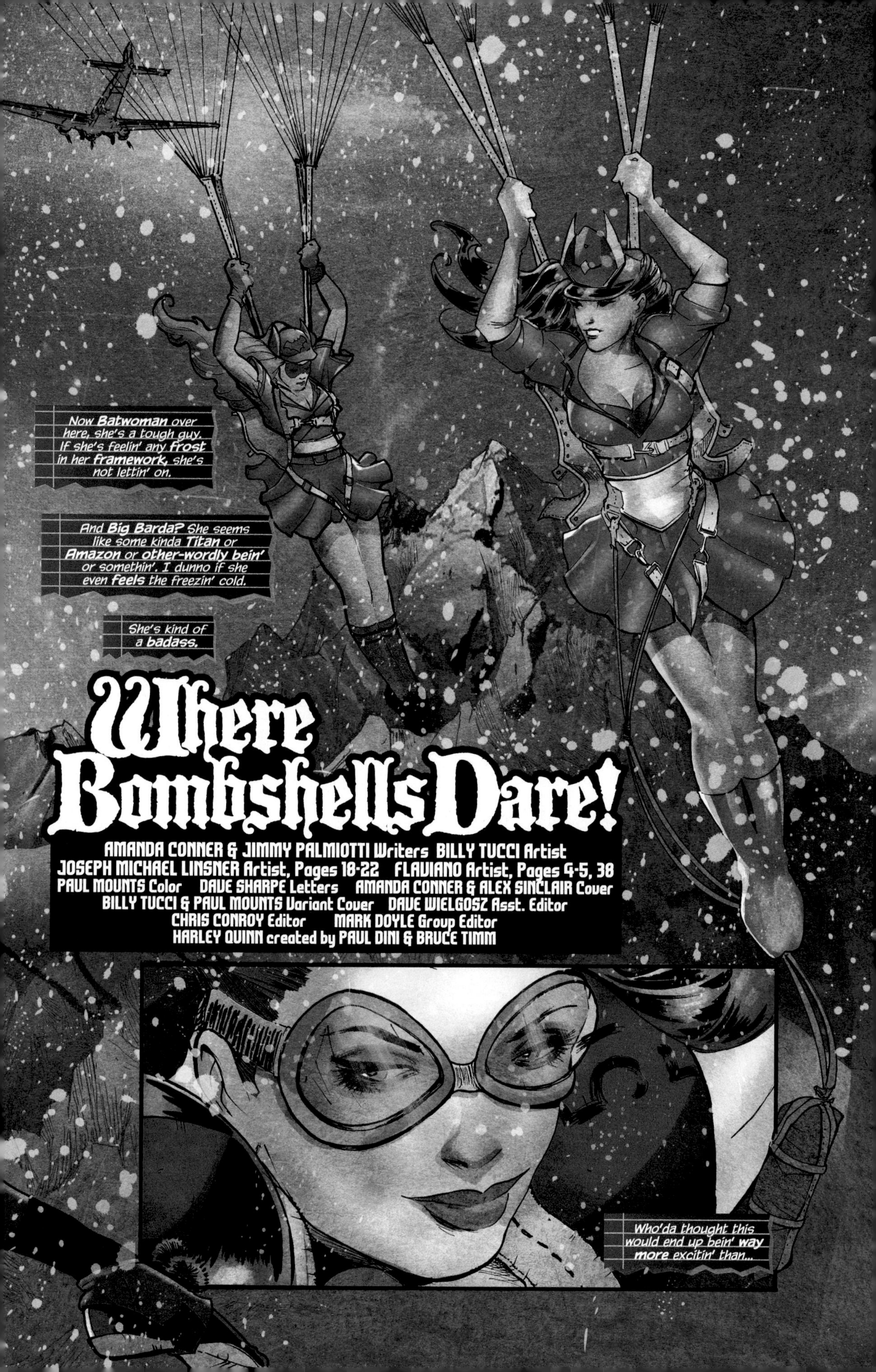

Now Batwoman over here, she's a tough guy. If she's feelin' any frost in her framework, she's not lettin' on.
And Big Barda? She seems like some kinda Titan or Amazon or other-wordly bein' or somethin'. I dunno if she even feels the freezin' cold.
She's kind of a badass.
Where Bombshells Dare!
AMANDA CONNER & JIMMY PALMIOTTI Writers BILLY TUCCI Artist
JOSEPH MICHAEL LINSNER Artist, Pages 18-22 FLAVIANO Artist, Pages 4-5, 38
PAUL MOUNTS Color DAVE SHARPE Letters AMANDA CONNER & ALEX SINCLAIR Cover
BILLY TUCCI & PAUL MOUNTS Variant Cover DAVE WIELGOSZ Asst. Editor
CHRIS CONROY Editor MARK DOYLE Group Editor
HARLEY QUINN created by PAUL DINI & BRUCE TIMM
Who'da thought this would end up bein' way more excitin' than...

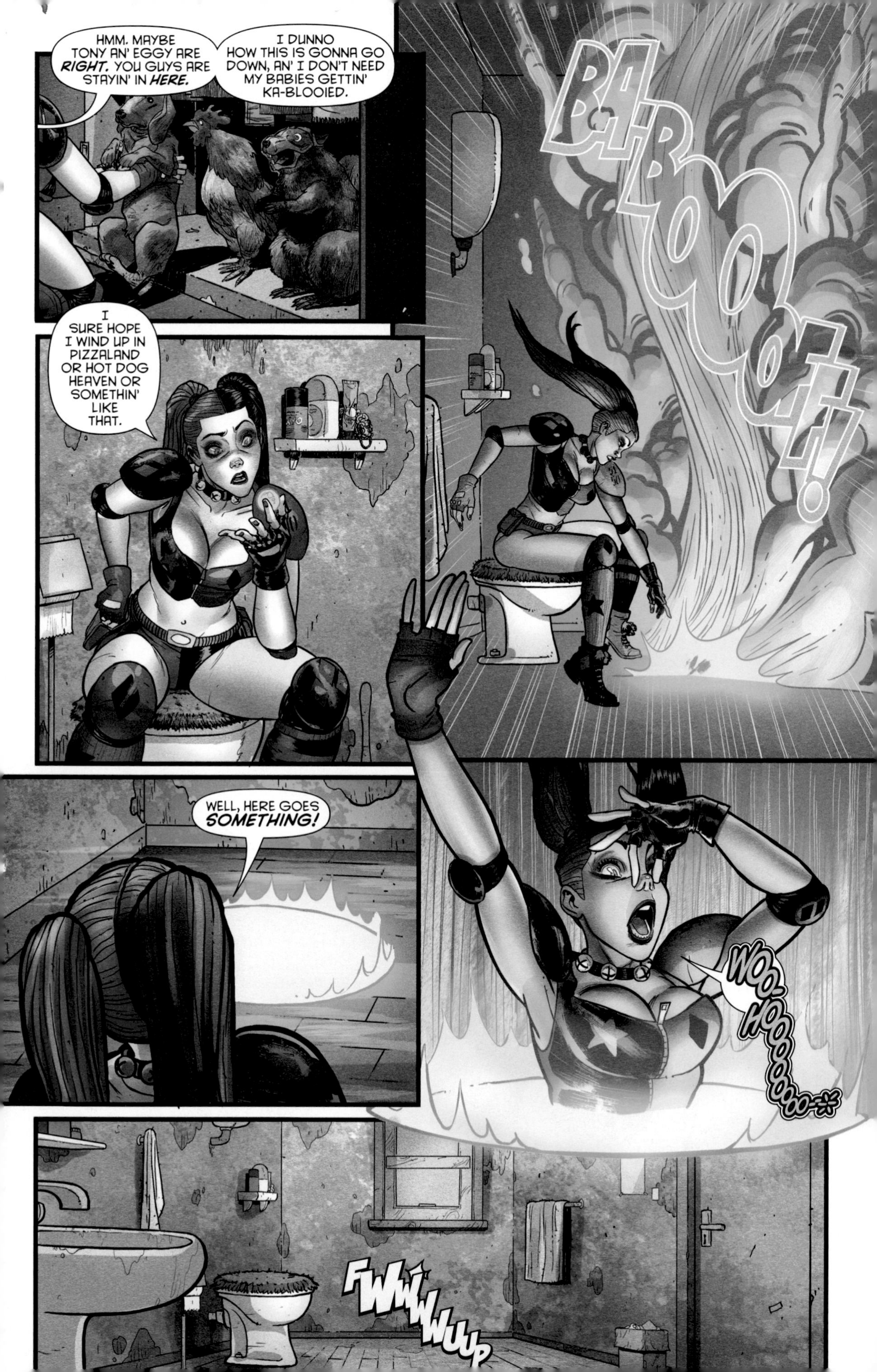

HMM. MAYBE TONY AN' EGGY ARE RIGHT. YOU GUYS ARE STAYIN' IN HERE.
I DUNNO HOW THIS IS GONNA GO DOWN, AN' I DON'T NEED MY BABIES GETTIN' KA-BLOOIED.
BABOOOOOOM!
I SURE HOPE I WIND UP IN PIZZALAND OR HOT DOG HEAVEN OR SOMETHIN' LIKE THAT.
WELL, HERE GOES SOMETHING!
WOO-HOOOOOOOO-
FWWWWUUP

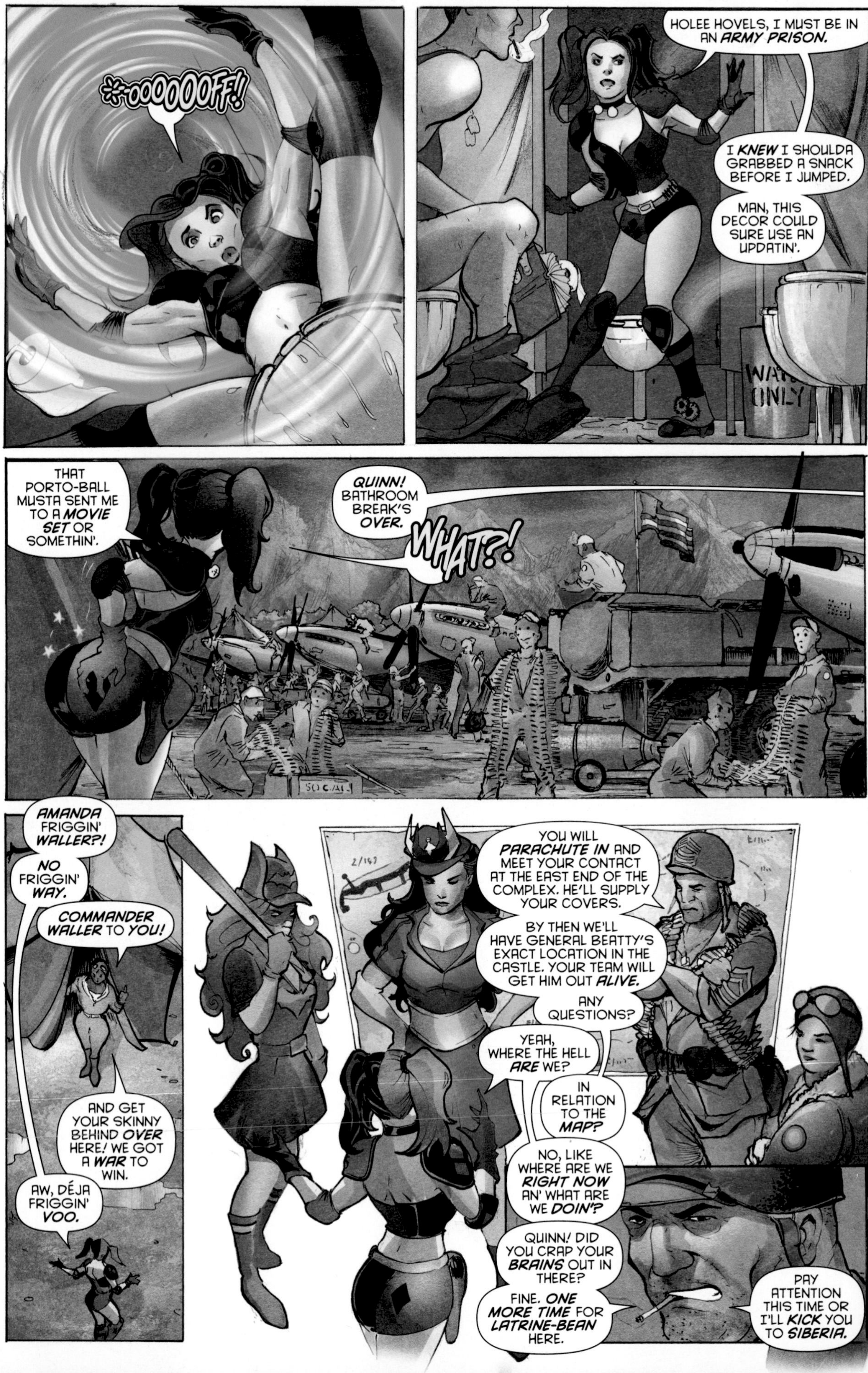

-OOOOOOFF!!
HOLEE HOVELS, I MUST BE IN AN ARMY PRISON.
I KNEW I SHOULDA GRABBED A SNACK BEFORE I JUMPED.
MAN, THIS DECOR COULD SURE USE AN UPDATIN'.
WATER ONLY
THAT PORTO-BALL MUSTA SENT ME TO A MOVIE SET OR SOMETHIN'.
QUINN! BATHROOM BREAK'S OVER.
WHAT?!
50 CAL
AMANDA FRIGGIN' WALLER?!
NO FRIGGIN' WAY.
COMMANDER WALLER TO YOU!
AND GET YOUR SKINNY BEHIND OVER HERE! WE GOT A WAR TO WIN.
AW, DÉJA FRIGGIN' VOO.
YOU WILL PARACHUTE IN AND MEET YOUR CONTACT AT THE EAST END OF THE COMPLEX. HE'LL SUPPLY YOUR COVERS.
BY THEN WE'LL HAVE GENERAL BEATTY'S EXACT LOCATION IN THE CASTLE. YOUR TEAM WILL GET HIM OUT ALIVE.
ANY QUESTIONS?
YEAH, WHERE THE HELL ARE WE?
IN RELATION TO THE MAP?
NO, LIKE WHERE ARE WE RIGHT NOW AN' WHAT ARE WE DOIN'?
QUINN! DID YOU CRAP YOUR BRAINS OUT IN THERE?
FINE. ONE MORE TIME FOR LATRINE-BEAN HERE.
PAY ATTENTION THIS TIME OR I'LL KICK YOU TO SIBERIA.

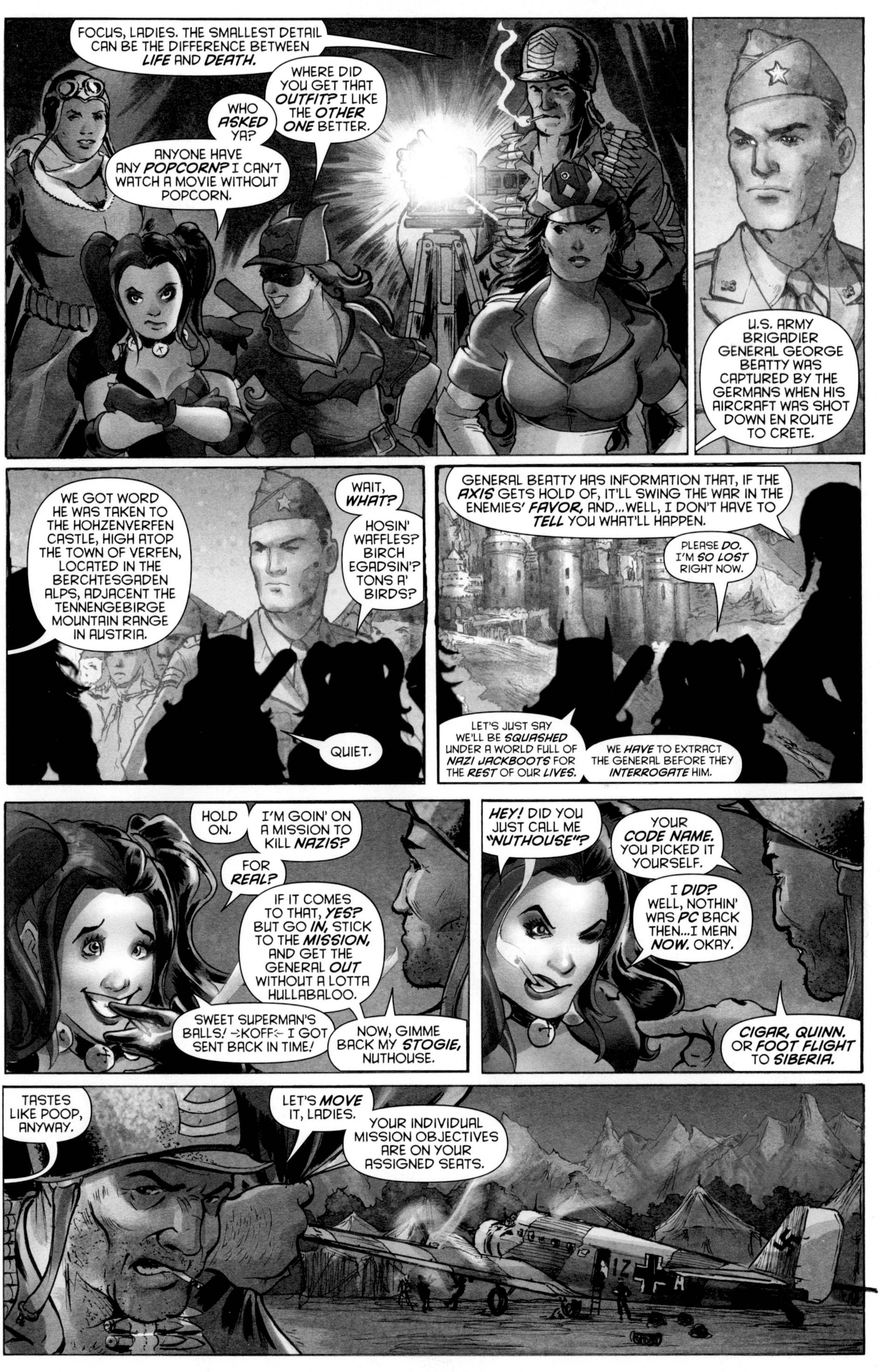

FOCUS, LADIES. THE SMALLEST DETAIL CAN BE THE DIFFERENCE BETWEEN *LIFE* AND *DEATH.*
WHERE DID YOU GET THAT *OUTFIT?* I LIKE THE *OTHER ONE* BETTER.
WHO *ASKED* YA?
ANYONE HAVE ANY *POPCORN?* I CAN'T WATCH A MOVIE WITHOUT POPCORN.
U.S. ARMY BRIGADIER GENERAL GEORGE BEATTY WAS CAPTURED BY THE GERMANS WHEN HIS AIRCRAFT WAS SHOT DOWN EN ROUTE TO CRETE.
WE GOT WORD HE WAS TAKEN TO THE HOHZENVERFEN CASTLE, HIGH ATOP THE TOWN OF VERFEN, LOCATED IN THE BERCHTESGADEN ALPS, ADJACENT THE TENNENGEBIRGE MOUNTAIN RANGE IN AUSTRIA.
WAIT, *WHAT?*
HOSIN' WAFFLES? BIRCH EGADSIN'? TONS A' BIRDS?
QUIET.
GENERAL BEATTY HAS INFORMATION THAT, IF THE *AXIS* GETS HOLD OF, IT'LL SWING THE WAR IN THE ENEMIES' *FAVOR,* AND...WELL, I DON'T HAVE TO *TELL* YOU WHAT'LL HAPPEN.
PLEASE *DO.* I'M *SO LOST* RIGHT NOW.
LET'S JUST SAY WE'LL BE *SQUASHED* UNDER A WORLD FULL OF *NAZI JACKBOOTS* FOR THE *REST* OF OUR *LIVES.*
WE *HAVE* TO EXTRACT THE GENERAL BEFORE THEY *INTERROGATE* HIM.
HOLD ON.
I'M GOIN' ON A MISSION TO KILL *NAZIS?*
FOR *REAL?*
IF IT COMES TO THAT, *YES?* BUT GO *IN,* STICK TO THE *MISSION,* AND GET THE GENERAL *OUT* WITHOUT A LOTTA HULLABALOO.
SWEET SUPERMAN'S BALLS! →KOFF← I GOT SENT BACK IN TIME!
NOW, GIMME BACK MY *STOGIE,* NUTHOUSE.
HEY! DID YOU JUST CALL ME *"NUTHOUSE"?*
YOUR *CODE NAME.* YOU PICKED IT YOURSELF.
I *DID?* WELL, NOTHIN' WAS *PC* BACK THEN...I MEAN *NOW.* OKAY.
CIGAR, QUINN. OR *FOOT FLIGHT* TO *SIBERIA.*
TASTES LIKE POOP, ANYWAY.
LET'S *MOVE* IT, LADIES.
YOUR INDIVIDUAL MISSION OBJECTIVES ARE ON YOUR ASSIGNED SEATS.

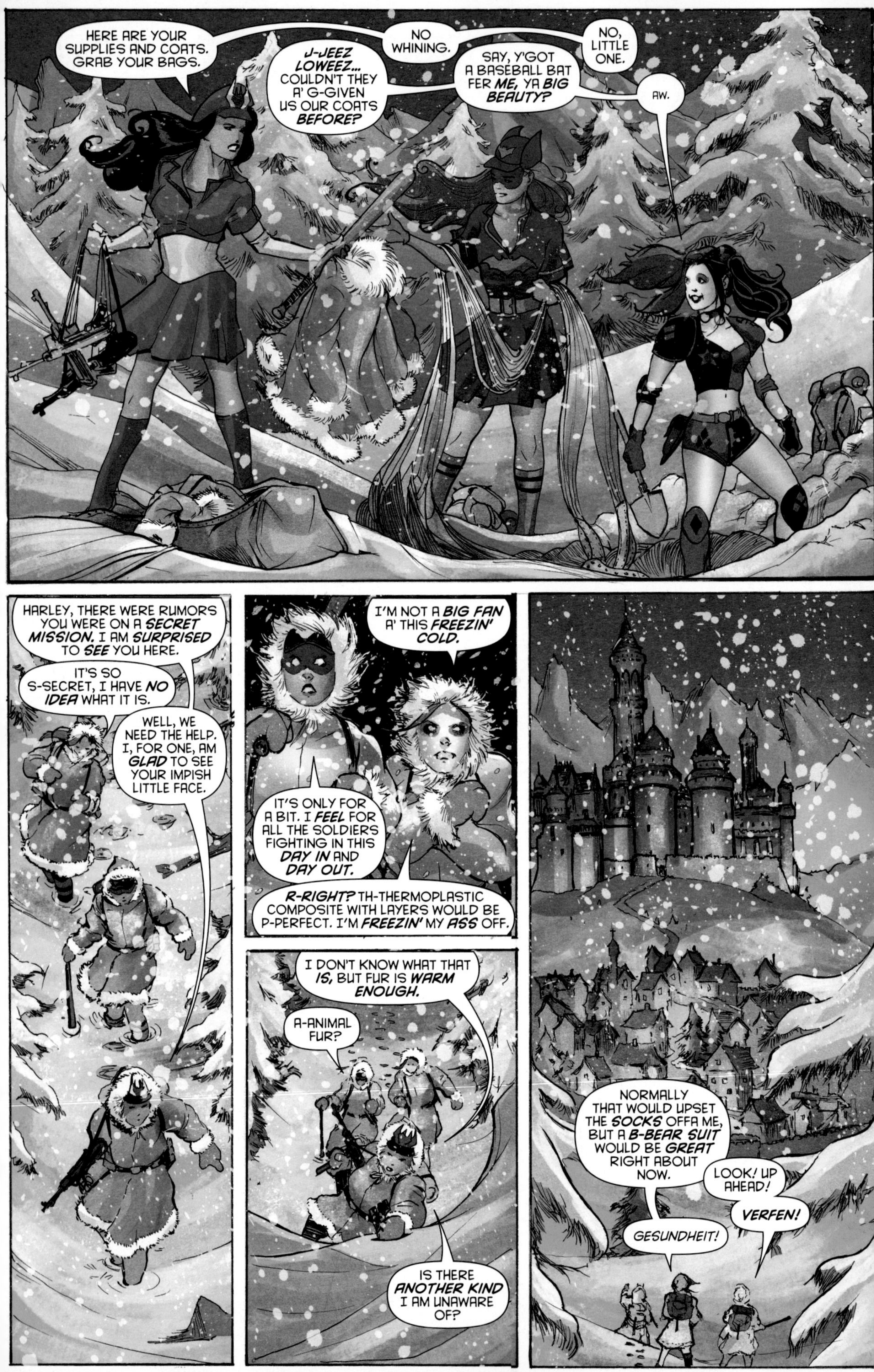
HERE ARE YOUR SUPPLIES AND COATS. GRAB YOUR BAGS.
J-JEEZ LOWEEZ... COULDN'T THEY A' G-GIVEN US OUR COATS BEFORE?
NO WHINING.
SAY, Y'GOT A BASEBALL BAT FER ME, YA BIG BEAUTY?
NO, LITTLE ONE.
AW.
HARLEY, THERE WERE RUMORS YOU WERE ON A SECRET MISSION. I AM SURPRISED TO SEE YOU HERE.
IT'S SO S-SECRET, I HAVE NO IDEA WHAT IT IS.
WELL, WE NEED THE HELP. I, FOR ONE, AM GLAD TO SEE YOUR IMPISH LITTLE FACE.
I'M NOT A BIG FAN A' THIS FREEZIN' COLD.
IT'S ONLY FOR A BIT. I FEEL FOR ALL THE SOLDIERS FIGHTING IN THIS DAY IN AND DAY OUT.
R-RIGHT? TH-THERMOPLASTIC COMPOSITE WITH LAYERS WOULD BE P-PERFECT. I'M FREEZIN' MY ASS OFF.
I DON'T KNOW WHAT THAT IS, BUT FUR IS WARM ENOUGH.
A-ANIMAL FUR?
IS THERE ANOTHER KIND I AM UNAWARE OF?
NORMALLY THAT WOULD UPSET THE SOCKS OFFA ME, BUT A B-BEAR SUIT WOULD BE GREAT RIGHT ABOUT NOW.
LOOK! UP AHEAD!
VERFEN!
GESUNDHEIT!

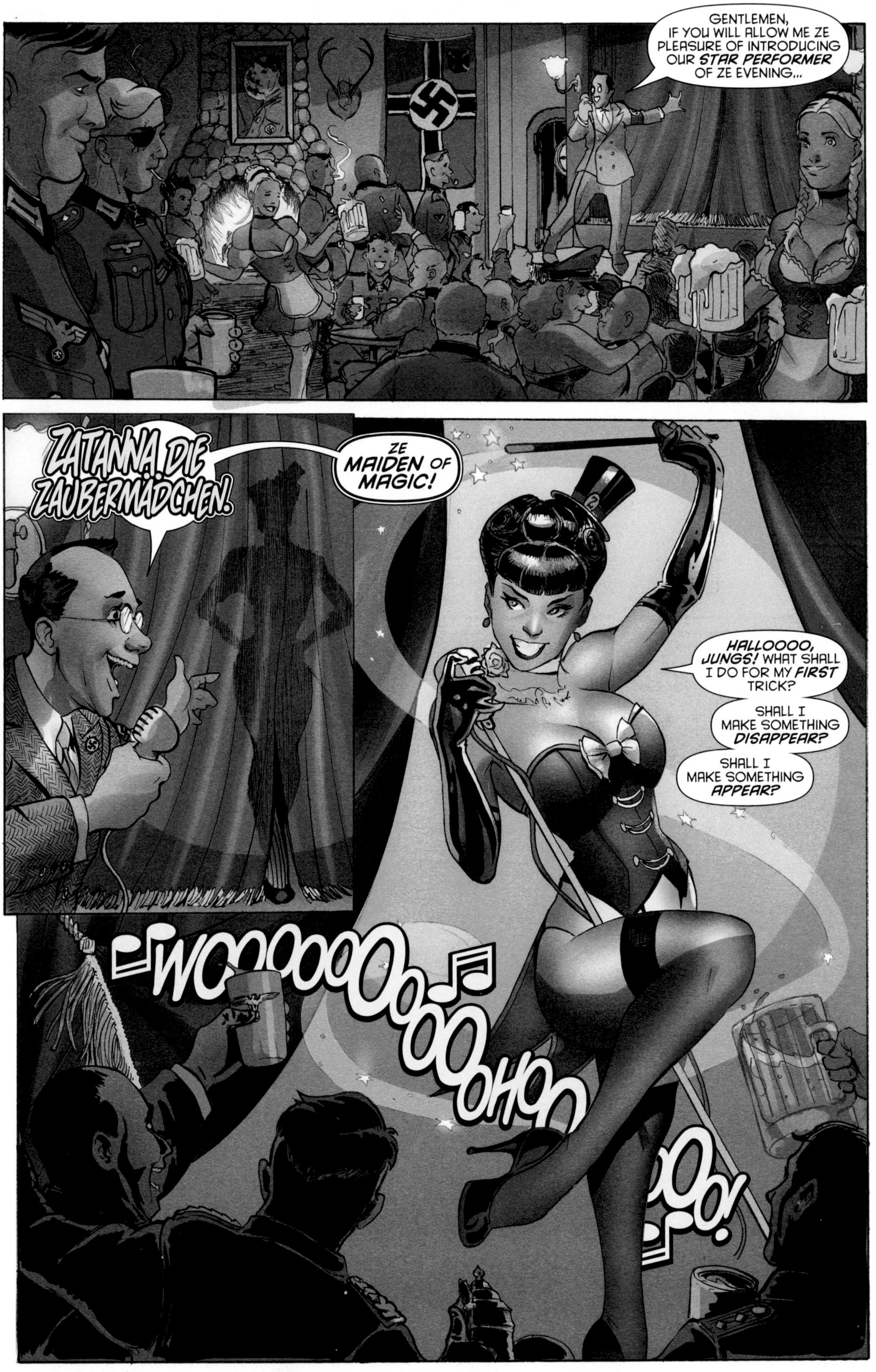
GENTLEMEN, IF YOU WILL ALLOW ME ZE PLEASURE OF INTRODUCING OUR STAR PERFORMER OF ZE EVENING...
ZATANNA DIE ZAUBERMÄDCHEN!
ZE MAIDEN OF MAGIC!
HALLOOOO, JUNGS! WHAT SHALL I DO FOR MY FIRST TRICK?
SHALL I MAKE SOMETHING DISAPPEAR?
SHALL I MAKE SOMETHING APPEAR?
WOOOOOOOOOOOOHOOOOOO!

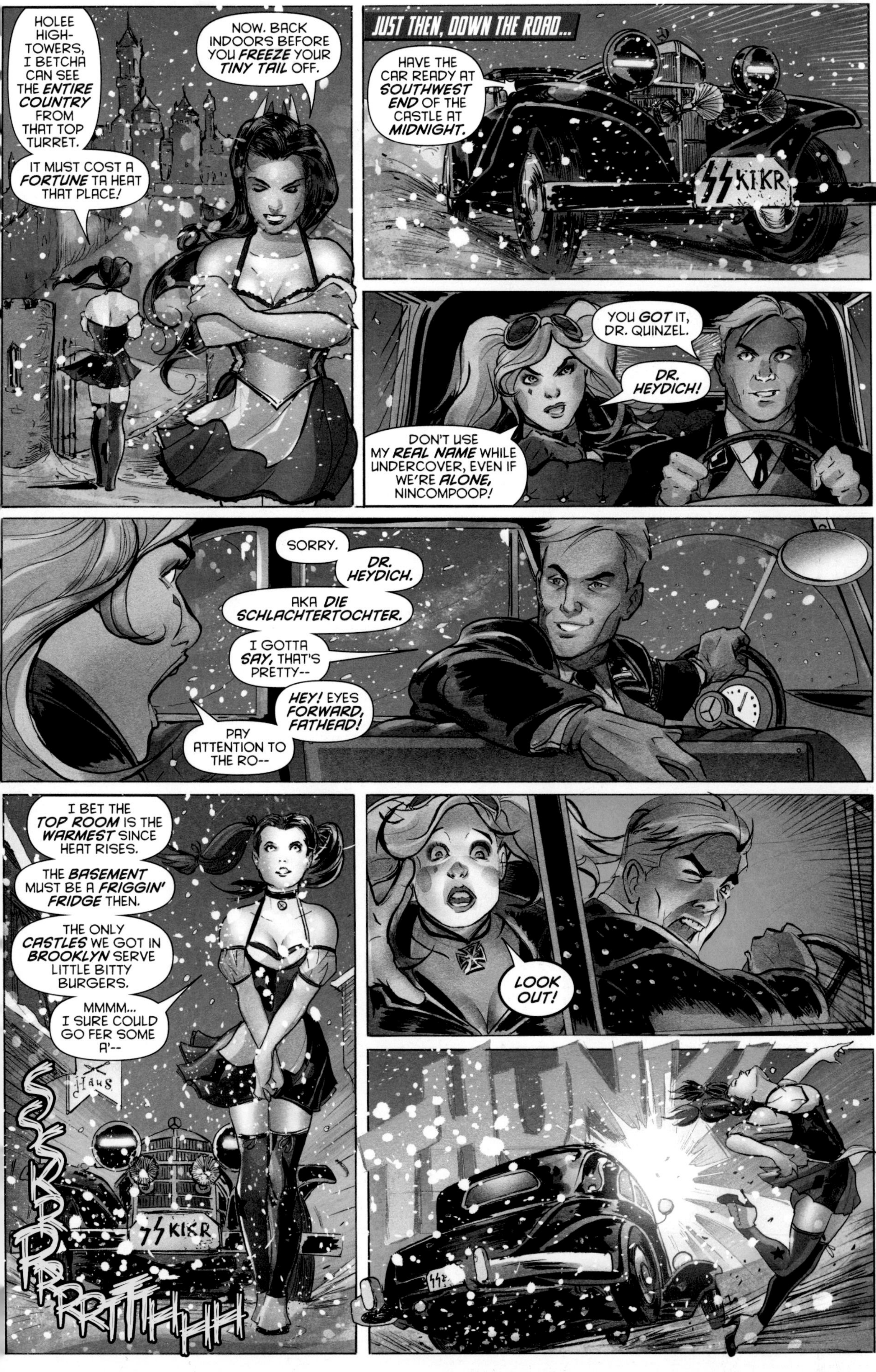
HOLEE HIGH-TOWERS, I BETCHA CAN SEE THE ENTIRE COUNTRY FROM THAT TOP TURRET.
IT MUST COST A FORTUNE TA HEAT THAT PLACE!
NOW. BACK INDOORS BEFORE YOU FREEZE YOUR TINY TAIL OFF.
JUST THEN, DOWN THE ROAD...
HAVE THE CAR READY AT SOUTHWEST END OF THE CASTLE AT MIDNIGHT.
SS KIKR
YOU GOT IT, DR. QUINZEL.
DR. HEYDICH!
DON'T USE MY REAL NAME WHILE UNDERCOVER, EVEN IF WE'RE ALONE, NINCOMPOOP!
SORRY.
DR. HEYDICH.
AKA DIE SCHLACHTERTOCHTER.
I GOTTA SAY, THAT'S PRETTY--
HEY! EYES FORWARD, FATHEAD!
PAY ATTENTION TO THE RO--
I BET THE TOP ROOM IS THE WARMEST SINCE HEAT RISES.
THE BASEMENT MUST BE A FRIGGIN' FRIDGE THEN.
THE ONLY CASTLES WE GOT IN BROOKLYN SERVE LITTLE BITTY BURGERS.
MMMM... I SURE COULD GO FER SOME A'--
Haus
SS KIKR
SSKRRRRRTTTHHHH
LOOK OUT!
THUNK!

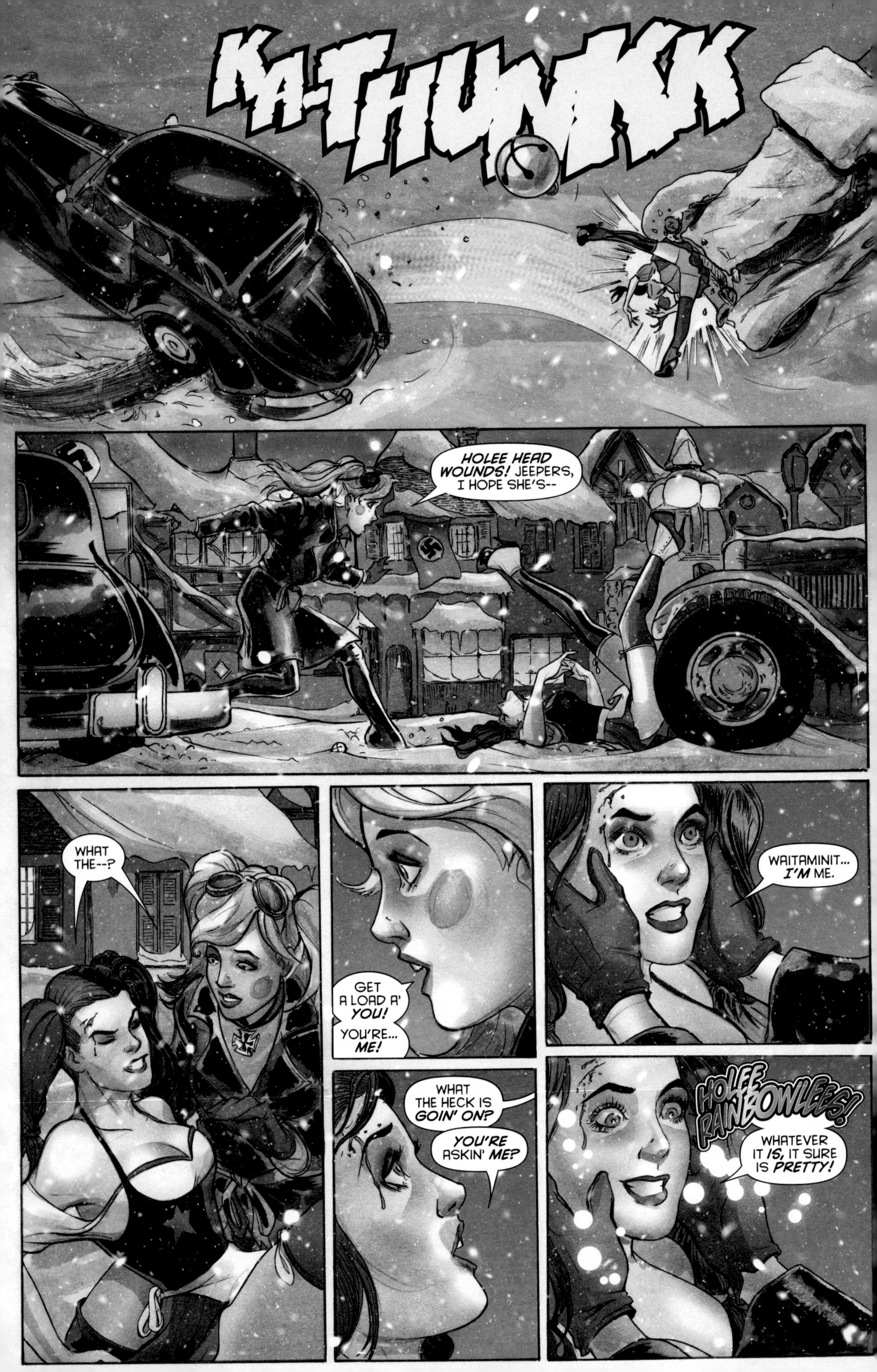
KA-THUNKKK
HOLEE HEAD WOUNDS! JEEPERS, I HOPE SHE'S--
WHAT THE--?
GET A LOAD A' YOU!
YOU'RE... ME!
WAITAMINIT... I'M ME.
WHAT THE HECK IS GOIN' ON?
YOU'RE ASKIN' ME?
HOLEE RAINBOWLEES!
WHATEVER IT IS, IT SURE IS PRETTY!

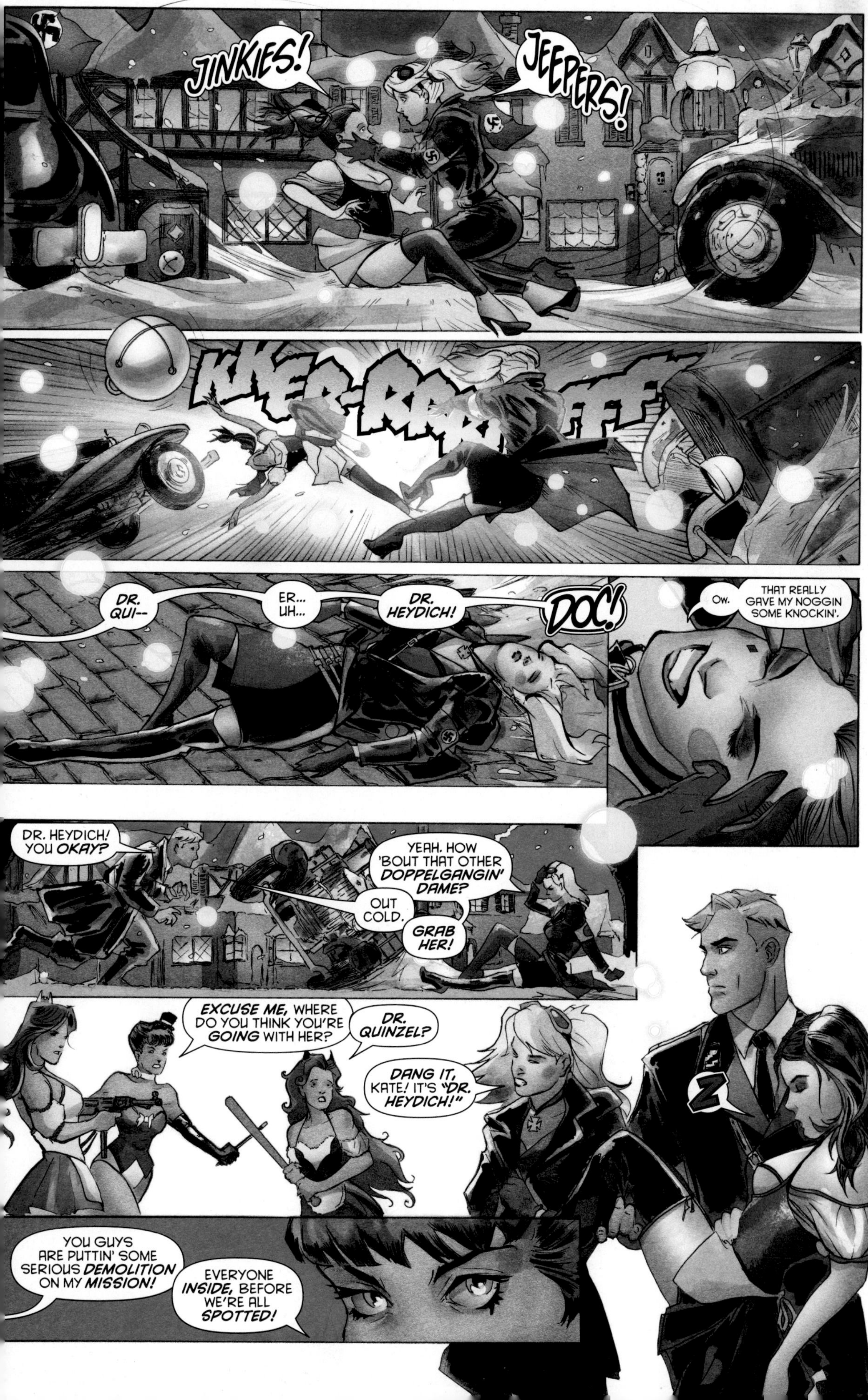
JINKIES!
JEEPERS!
DR. QUI--
ER... UH...
DR. HEYDICH!
DOC!
Ow.
THAT REALLY GAVE MY NOGGIN SOME KNOCKIN'.
DR. HEYDICH! YOU OKAY?
YEAH. HOW 'BOUT THAT OTHER DOPPELGANGIN' DAME?
OUT COLD.
GRAB HER!
EXCUSE ME, WHERE DO YOU THINK YOU'RE GOING WITH HER?
DR. QUINZEL?
DANG IT, KATE! IT'S "DR. HEYDICH!"
YOU GUYS ARE PUTTIN' SOME SERIOUS DEMOLITION ON MY MISSION!
EVERYONE INSIDE, BEFORE WE'RE ALL SPOTTED!

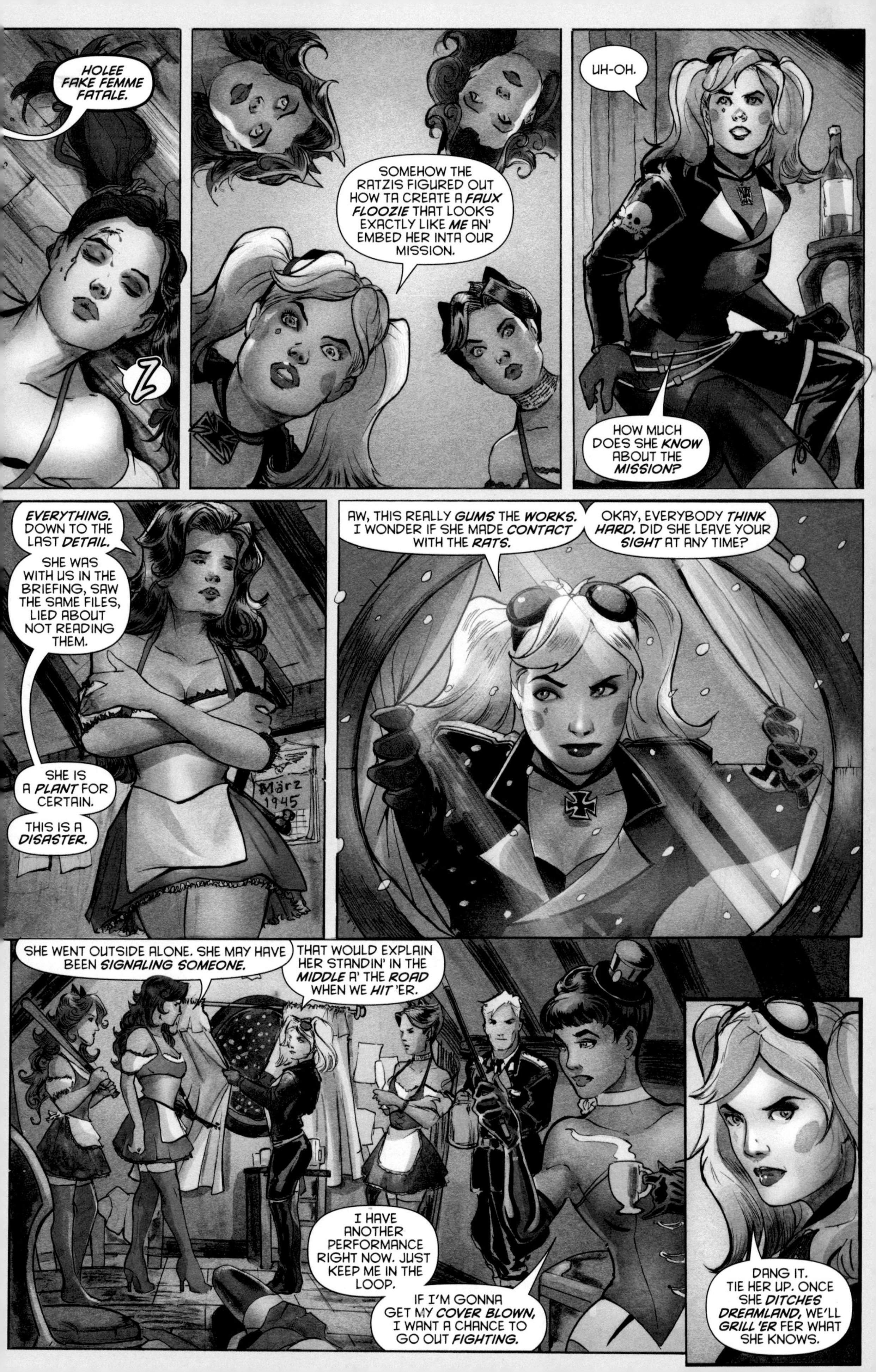
HOLEE FAKE FEMME FATALE.
Z
SOMEHOW THE RATZIS FIGURED OUT HOW TA CREATE A FAUX FLOOZIE THAT LOOKS EXACTLY LIKE ME AN' EMBED HER INTA OUR MISSION.
UH-OH.
HOW MUCH DOES SHE KNOW ABOUT THE MISSION?
EVERYTHING. DOWN TO THE LAST DETAIL.
SHE WAS WITH US IN THE BRIEFING, SAW THE SAME FILES, LIED ABOUT NOT READING THEM.
SHE IS A PLANT FOR CERTAIN.
THIS IS A DISASTER.
März 1945
AW, THIS REALLY GUMS THE WORKS. I WONDER IF SHE MADE CONTACT WITH THE RATS.
OKAY, EVERYBODY THINK HARD. DID SHE LEAVE YOUR SIGHT AT ANY TIME?
SHE WENT OUTSIDE ALONE. SHE MAY HAVE BEEN SIGNALING SOMEONE.
THAT WOULD EXPLAIN HER STANDIN' IN THE MIDDLE A' THE ROAD WHEN WE HIT 'ER.
I HAVE ANOTHER PERFORMANCE RIGHT NOW. JUST KEEP ME IN THE LOOP.
IF I'M GONNA GET MY COVER BLOWN, I WANT A CHANCE TO GO OUT FIGHTING.
DANG IT. TIE HER UP. ONCE SHE DITCHES DREAMLAND, WE'LL GRILL 'ER FER WHAT SHE KNOWS.

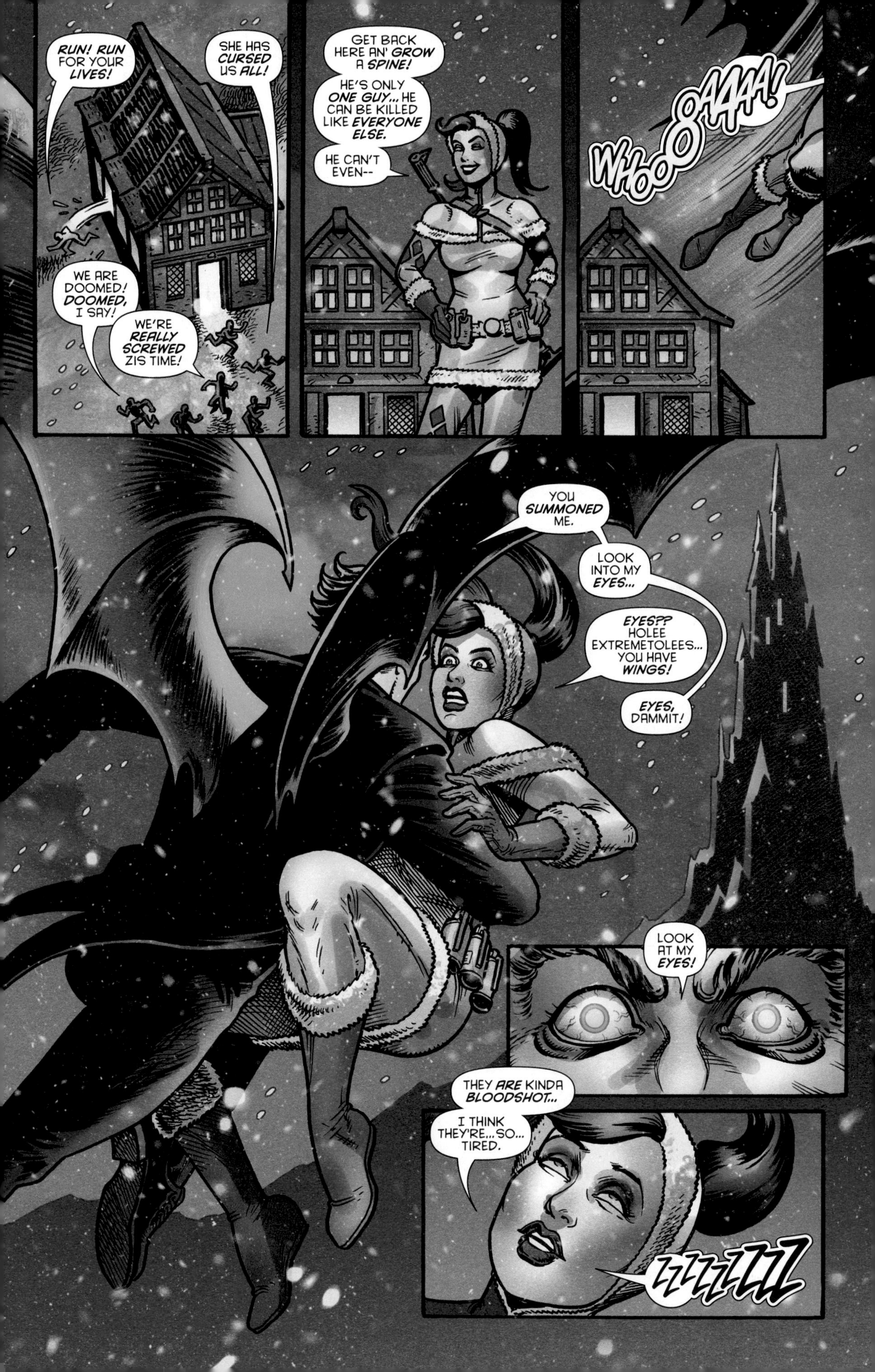
RUN! RUN FOR YOUR LIVES!
SHE HAS CURSED US ALL!
WE ARE DOOMED! DOOMED, I SAY!
WE'RE REALLY SCREWED ZIS TIME!
GET BACK HERE AN' GROW A SPINE!
HE'S ONLY ONE GUY... HE CAN BE KILLED LIKE EVERYONE ELSE.
HE CAN'T EVEN--
WHOOOOAAAA!
YOU SUMMONED ME.
LOOK INTO MY EYES...
EYES?? HOLEE EXTREMETOLEES... YOU HAVE WINGS!
EYES, DAMMIT!
LOOK AT MY EYES!
THEY ARE KINDA BLOODSHOT...
I THINK THEY'RE... SO... TIRED.
ZZZZZZZZ

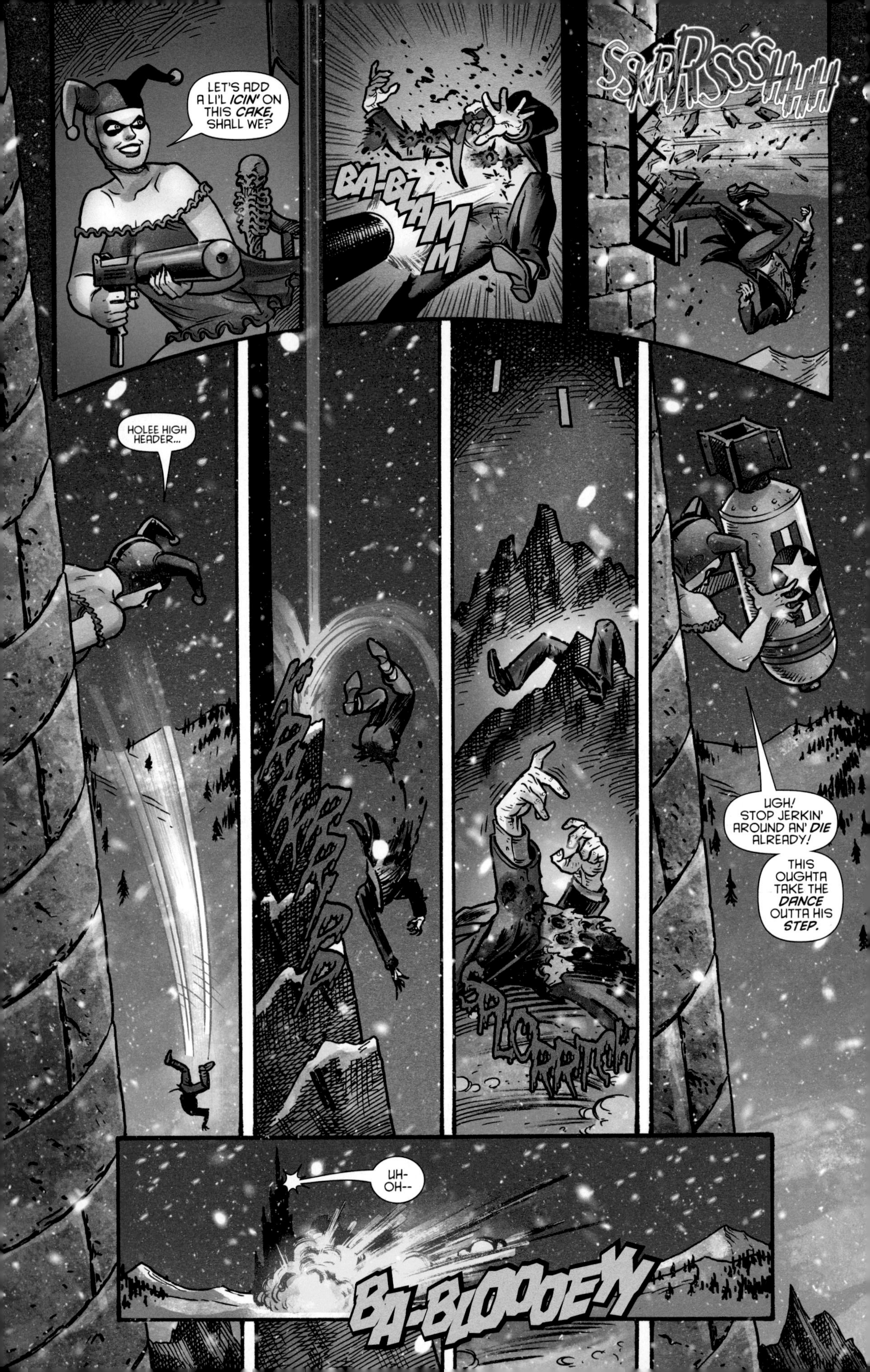
LET'S ADD A LI'L *ICIN'* ON THIS *CAKE,* SHALL WE?
BA-BLAMMM
SSKRRRSSSHHH
HOLEE HIGH HEADER...
SPLORRRCH
UGH! STOP JERKIN' AROUND AN' *DIE* ALREADY!
THIS OUGHTA TAKE THE *DANCE* OUTTA HIS *STEP.*
UH-OH--
BA-BLOOOOEY

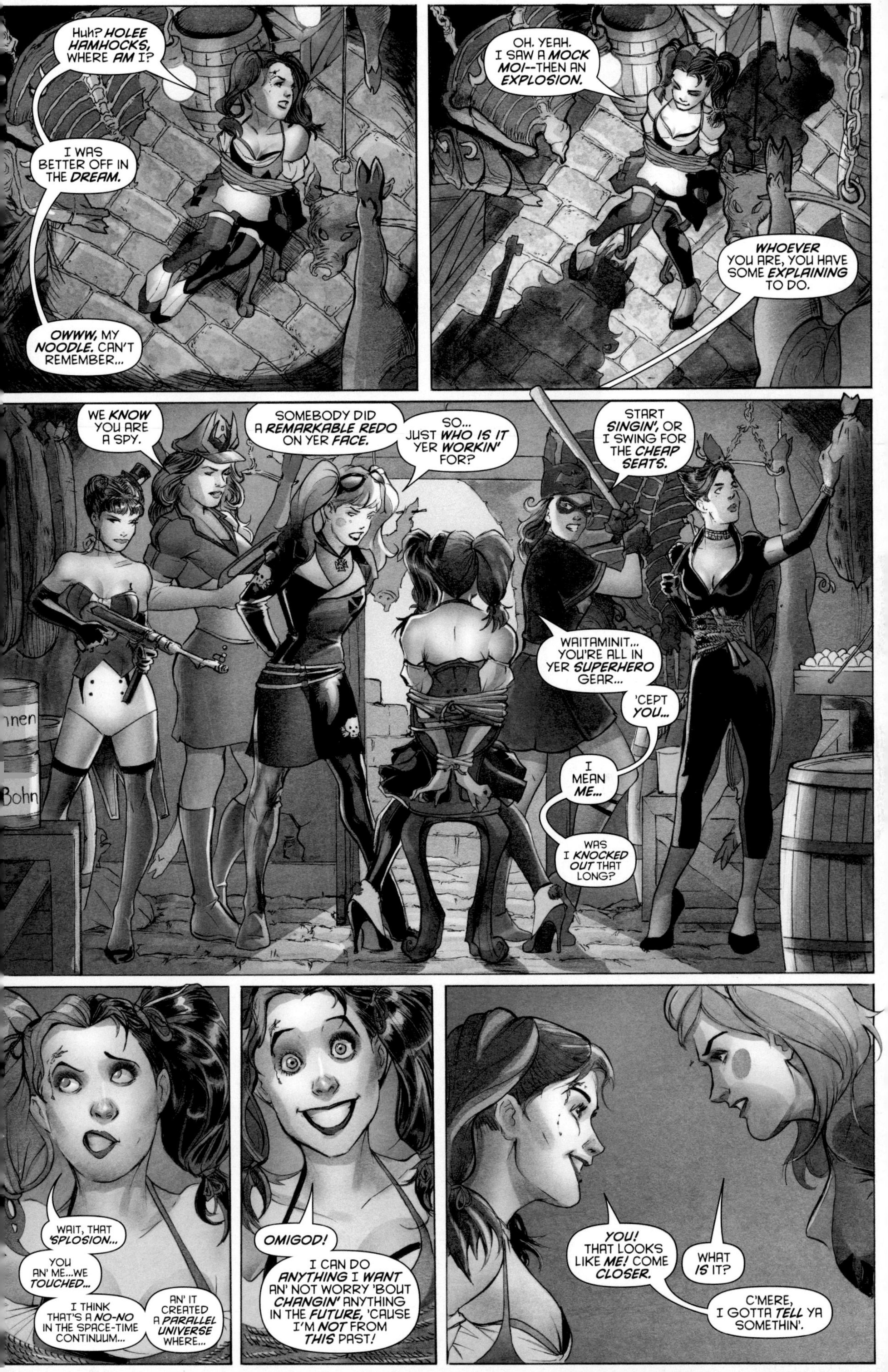

Huh? HOLEE HAMHOCKS, WHERE AM I?
I WAS BETTER OFF IN THE DREAM.
OWWW, MY NOODLE. CAN'T REMEMBER...
OH. YEAH. I SAW A MOCK MOI--THEN AN EXPLOSION.
WHOEVER YOU ARE, YOU HAVE SOME EXPLAINING TO DO.
WE KNOW YOU ARE A SPY.
SOMEBODY DID A REMARKABLE REDO ON YER FACE.
SO... JUST WHO IS IT YER WORKIN' FOR?
START SINGIN', OR I SWING FOR THE CHEAP SEATS.
WAITAMINIT... YOU'RE ALL IN YER SUPERHERO GEAR...
'CEPT YOU...
I MEAN ME...
WAS I KNOCKED OUT THAT LONG?
WAIT, THAT 'SPLOSION...
YOU AN' ME...WE TOUCHED...
I THINK THAT'S A NO-NO IN THE SPACE-TIME CONTINUUM...
AN' IT CREATED A PARALLEL UNIVERSE WHERE...
OMIGOD!
I CAN DO ANYTHING I WANT AN' NOT WORRY 'BOUT CHANGIN' ANYTHING IN THE FUTURE, 'CAUSE I'M NOT FROM THIS PAST!
YOU! THAT LOOKS LIKE ME! COME CLOSER.
WHAT IS IT?
C'MERE, I GOTTA TELL YA SOMETHIN'.

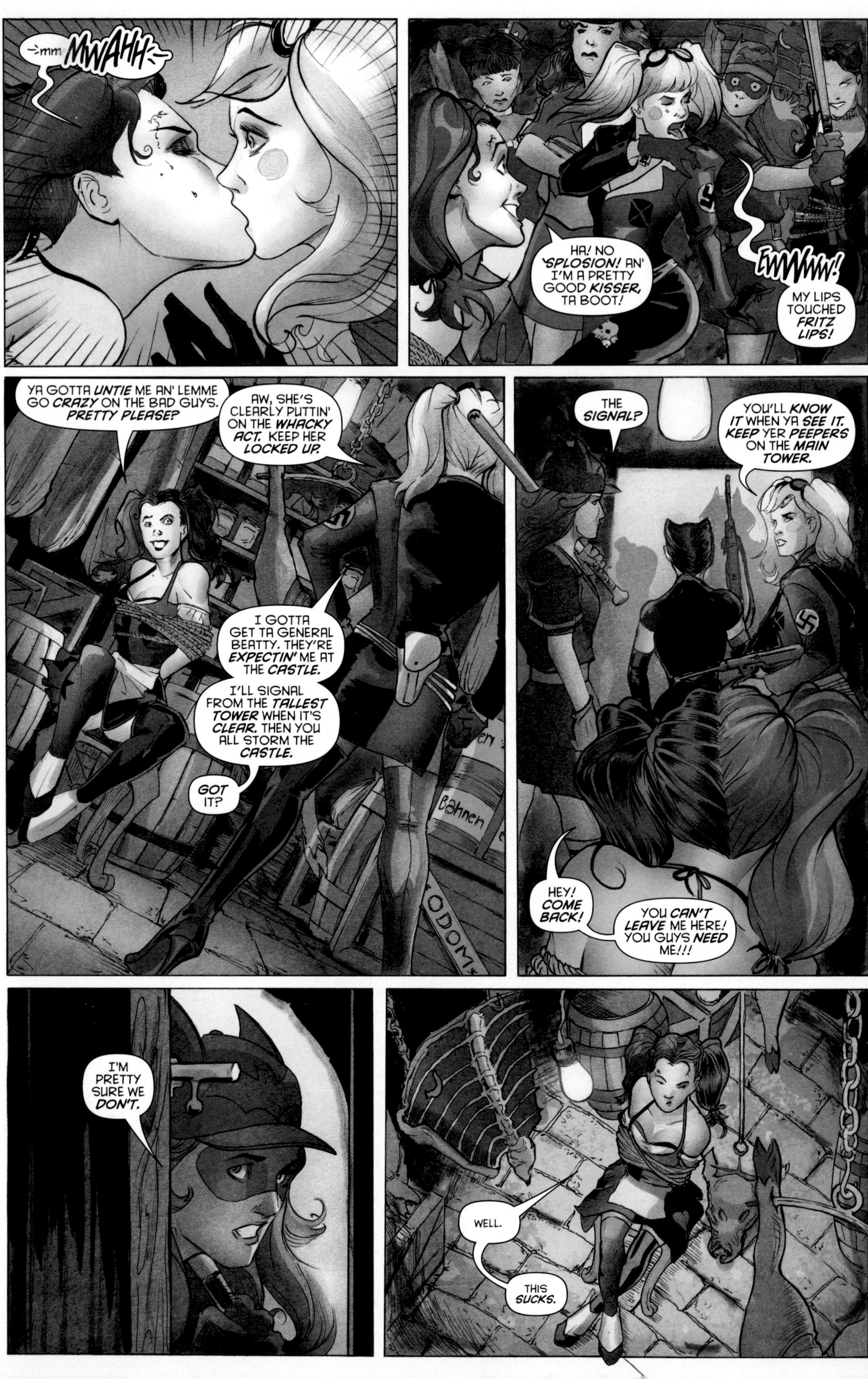

mm MWAHH
HA! NO 'SPLOSION! AN' I'M A PRETTY GOOD KISSER, TA BOOT!
EWWWW!
MY LIPS TOUCHED FRITZ LIPS!
YA GOTTA UNTIE ME AN' LEMME GO CRAZY ON THE BAD GUYS. PRETTY PLEASE?
AW, SHE'S CLEARLY PUTTIN' ON THE WHACKY ACT. KEEP HER LOCKED UP.
I GOTTA GET TA GENERAL BEATTY. THEY'RE EXPECTIN' ME AT THE CASTLE.
I'LL SIGNAL FROM THE TALLEST TOWER WHEN IT'S CLEAR. THEN YOU ALL STORM THE CASTLE.
GOT IT?
Bohnen
THE SIGNAL?
YOU'LL KNOW IT WHEN YA SEE IT. KEEP YER PEEPERS ON THE MAIN TOWER.
HEY! COME BACK!
YOU CAN'T LEAVE ME HERE! YOU GUYS NEED ME!!!
I'M PRETTY SURE WE DON'T.
WELL.
THIS SUCKS.

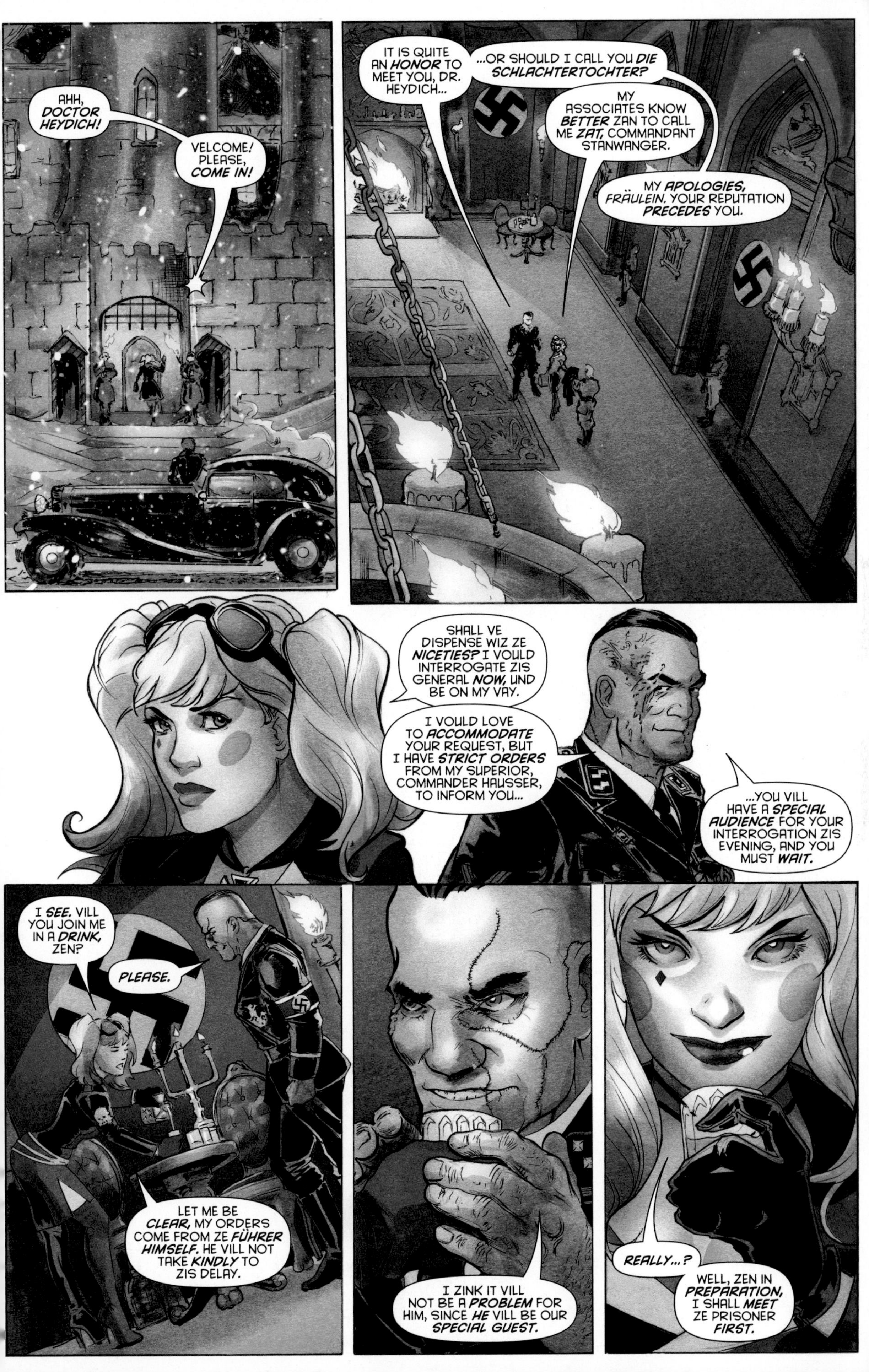
AHH, DOCTOR HEYDICH!
VELCOME! PLEASE, COME IN!
IT IS QUITE AN HONOR TO MEET YOU, DR. HEYDICH...
...OR SHOULD I CALL YOU DIE SCHLACHTERTOCHTER?
MY ASSOCIATES KNOW BETTER ZAN TO CALL ME ZAT, COMMANDANT STANWANGER.
MY APOLOGIES, FRÄULEIN. YOUR REPUTATION PRECEDES YOU.
SHALL VE DISPENSE WIZ ZE NICETIES? I VOULD INTERROGATE ZIS GENERAL NOW, UND BE ON MY VAY.
I VOULD LOVE TO ACCOMMODATE YOUR REQUEST, BUT I HAVE STRICT ORDERS FROM MY SUPERIOR, COMMANDER HAUSSER, TO INFORM YOU...
...YOU VILL HAVE A SPECIAL AUDIENCE FOR YOUR INTERROGATION ZIS EVENING, AND YOU MUST WAIT.
I SEE. VILL YOU JOIN ME IN A DRINK, ZEN?
PLEASE.
LET ME BE CLEAR, MY ORDERS COME FROM ZE FÜHRER HIMSELF. HE VILL NOT TAKE KINDLY TO ZIS DELAY.
I ZINK IT VILL NOT BE A PROBLEM FOR HIM, SINCE HE VILL BE OUR SPECIAL GUEST.
REALLY...?
WELL, ZEN IN PREPARATION, I SHALL MEET ZE PRISONER FIRST.

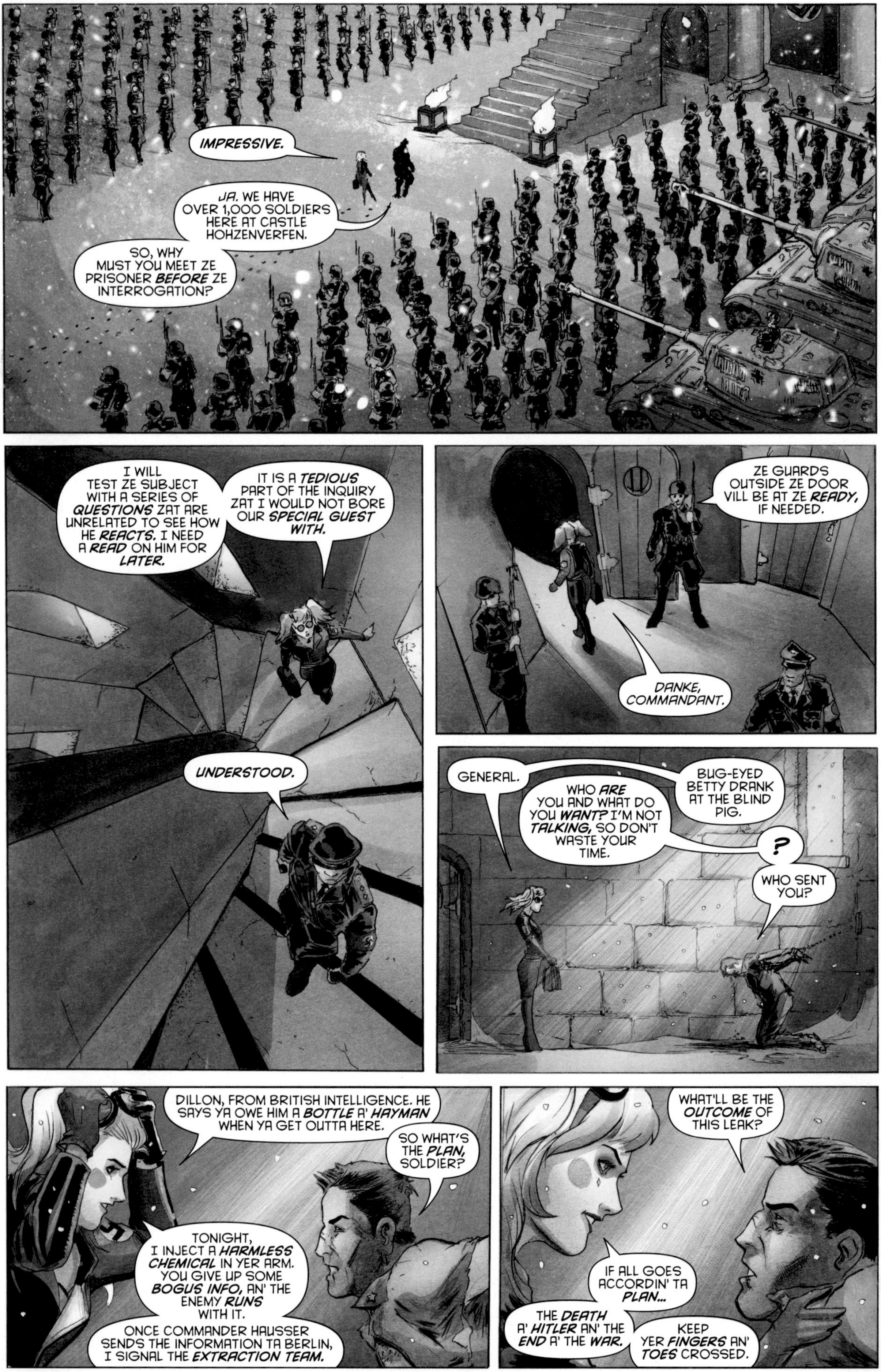
IMPRESSIVE.
JA. WE HAVE OVER 1,000 SOLDIERS HERE AT CASTLE HOHZENVERFEN.
SO, WHY MUST YOU MEET ZE PRISONER BEFORE ZE INTERROGATION?
I WILL TEST ZE SUBJECT WITH A SERIES OF QUESTIONS ZAT ARE UNRELATED TO SEE HOW HE REACTS. I NEED A READ ON HIM FOR LATER.
IT IS A TEDIOUS PART OF THE INQUIRY ZAT I WOULD NOT BORE OUR SPECIAL GUEST WITH.
UNDERSTOOD.
ZE GUARDS OUTSIDE ZE DOOR VILL BE AT ZE READY, IF NEEDED.
DANKE, COMMANDANT.
GENERAL.
BUG-EYED BETTY DRANK AT THE BLIND PIG.
WHO ARE YOU AND WHAT DO YOU WANT? I'M NOT TALKING, SO DON'T WASTE YOUR TIME.
?
WHO SENT YOU?
DILLON, FROM BRITISH INTELLIGENCE. HE SAYS YA OWE HIM A BOTTLE A' HAYMAN WHEN YA GET OUTTA HERE.
SO WHAT'S THE PLAN, SOLDIER?
TONIGHT, I INJECT A HARMLESS CHEMICAL IN YER ARM. YOU GIVE UP SOME BOGUS INFO, AN' THE ENEMY RUNS WITH IT.
ONCE COMMANDER HAUSSER SENDS THE INFORMATION TA BERLIN, I SIGNAL THE EXTRACTION TEAM.
WHAT'LL BE THE OUTCOME OF THIS LEAK?
IF ALL GOES ACCORDIN' TA PLAN...
THE DEATH A' HITLER AN' THE END A' THE WAR.
KEEP YER FINGERS AN' TOES CROSSED.

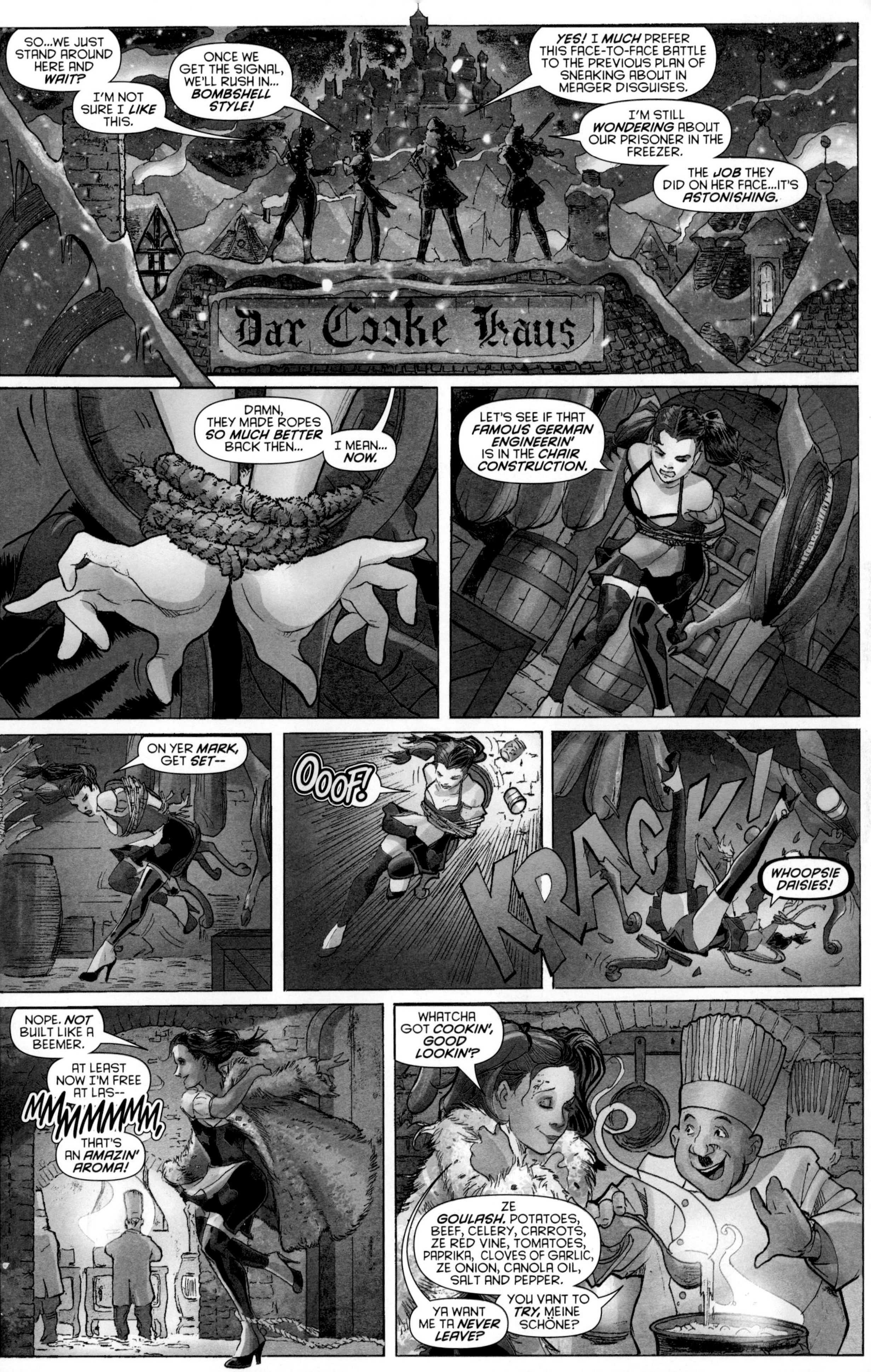
SO...WE JUST STAND AROUND HERE AND WAIT?
I'M NOT SURE I LIKE THIS.
ONCE WE GET THE SIGNAL, WE'LL RUSH IN... BOMBSHELL STYLE!
YES! I MUCH PREFER THIS FACE-TO-FACE BATTLE TO THE PREVIOUS PLAN OF SNEAKING ABOUT IN MEAGER DISGUISES.
I'M STILL WONDERING ABOUT OUR PRISONER IN THE FREEZER.
THE JOB THEY DID ON HER FACE...IT'S ASTONISHING.
Dar Cooke Haus
DAMN, THEY MADE ROPES SO MUCH BETTER BACK THEN...
I MEAN... NOW.
LET'S SEE IF THAT FAMOUS GERMAN ENGINEERIN' IS IN THE CHAIR CONSTRUCTION.
ON YER MARK, GET SET--
OOOF!
KRACK!
WHOOPSIE DAISIES!
NOPE. NOT BUILT LIKE A BEEMER.
AT LEAST NOW I'M FREE AT LAS--
MMMMMMM,
THAT'S AN AMAZIN' AROMA!
WHATCHA GOT COOKIN', GOOD LOOKIN'?
ZE GOULASH. POTATOES, BEEF, CELERY, CARROTS, ZE RED VINE, TOMATOES, PAPRIKA, CLOVES OF GARLIC, ZE ONION, CANOLA OIL, SALT AND PEPPER.
YOU VANT TO TRY, MEINE SCHÖNE?
YA WANT ME TA NEVER LEAVE?

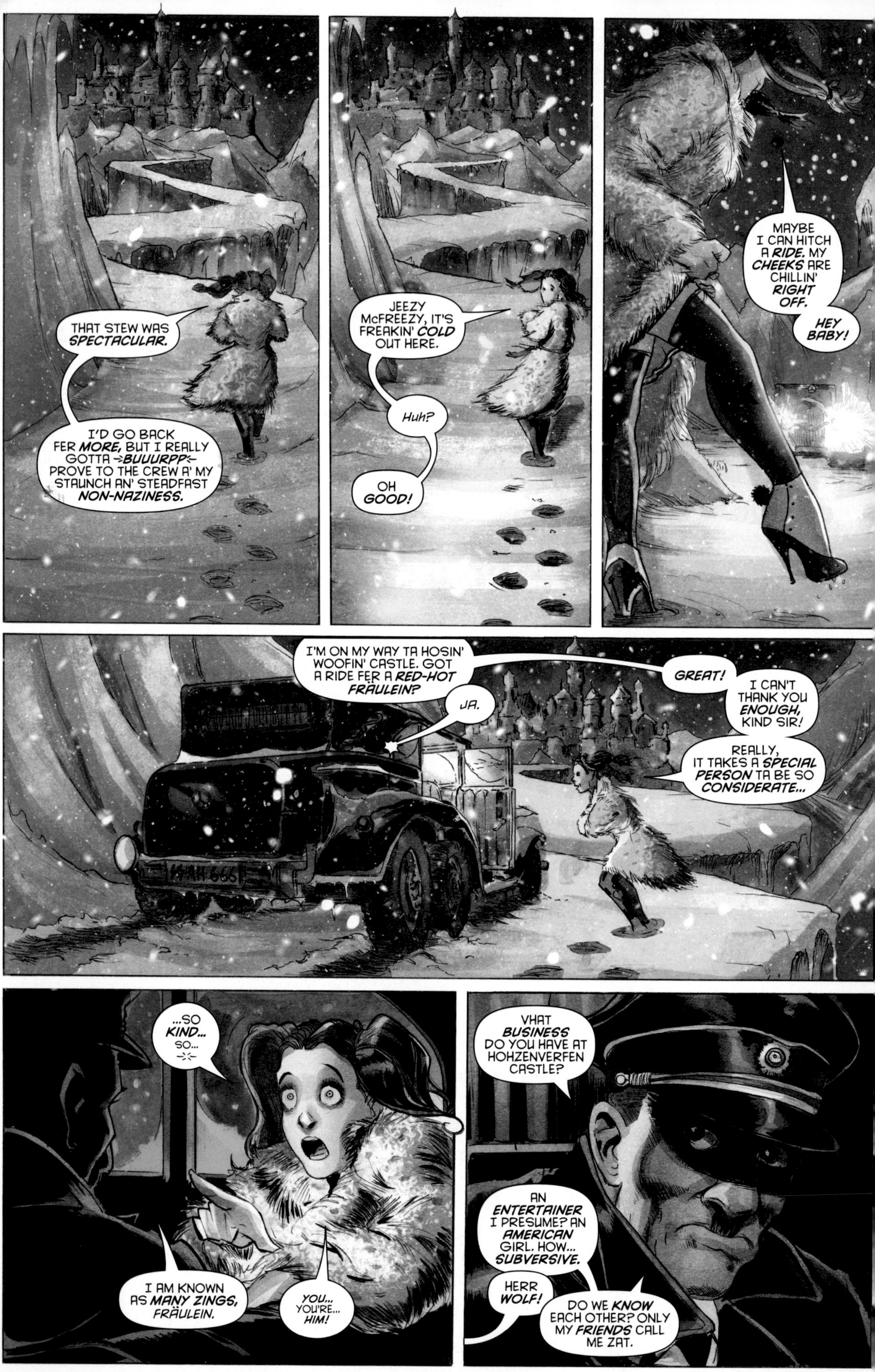

THAT STEW WAS SPECTACULAR.
I'D GO BACK FER MORE, BUT I REALLY GOTTA ⇒BUUURPP⇐ PROVE TO THE CREW A' MY STAUNCH AN' STEADFAST NON-NAZINESS.
JEEZY McFREEZY, IT'S FREAKIN' COLD OUT HERE.
Huh?
OH GOOD!
MAYBE I CAN HITCH A RIDE. MY CHEEKS ARE CHILLIN' RIGHT OFF.
HEY BABY!
I'M ON MY WAY TA HOSIN' WOOFIN' CASTLE. GOT A RIDE FER A RED-HOT FRÄULEIN?
JA.
GREAT!
I CAN'T THANK YOU ENOUGH, KIND SIR!
REALLY, IT TAKES A SPECIAL PERSON TA BE SO CONSIDERATE...
...SO KIND... SO...
I AM KNOWN AS MANY ZINGS, FRÄULEIN.
YOU... YOU'RE... HIM!
VHAT BUSINESS DO YOU HAVE AT HOHZENVERFEN CASTLE?
AN ENTERTAINER I PRESUME? AN AMERICAN GIRL. HOW... SUBVERSIVE.
HERR WOLF!
DO WE KNOW EACH OTHER? ONLY MY FRIENDS CALL ME ZAT.

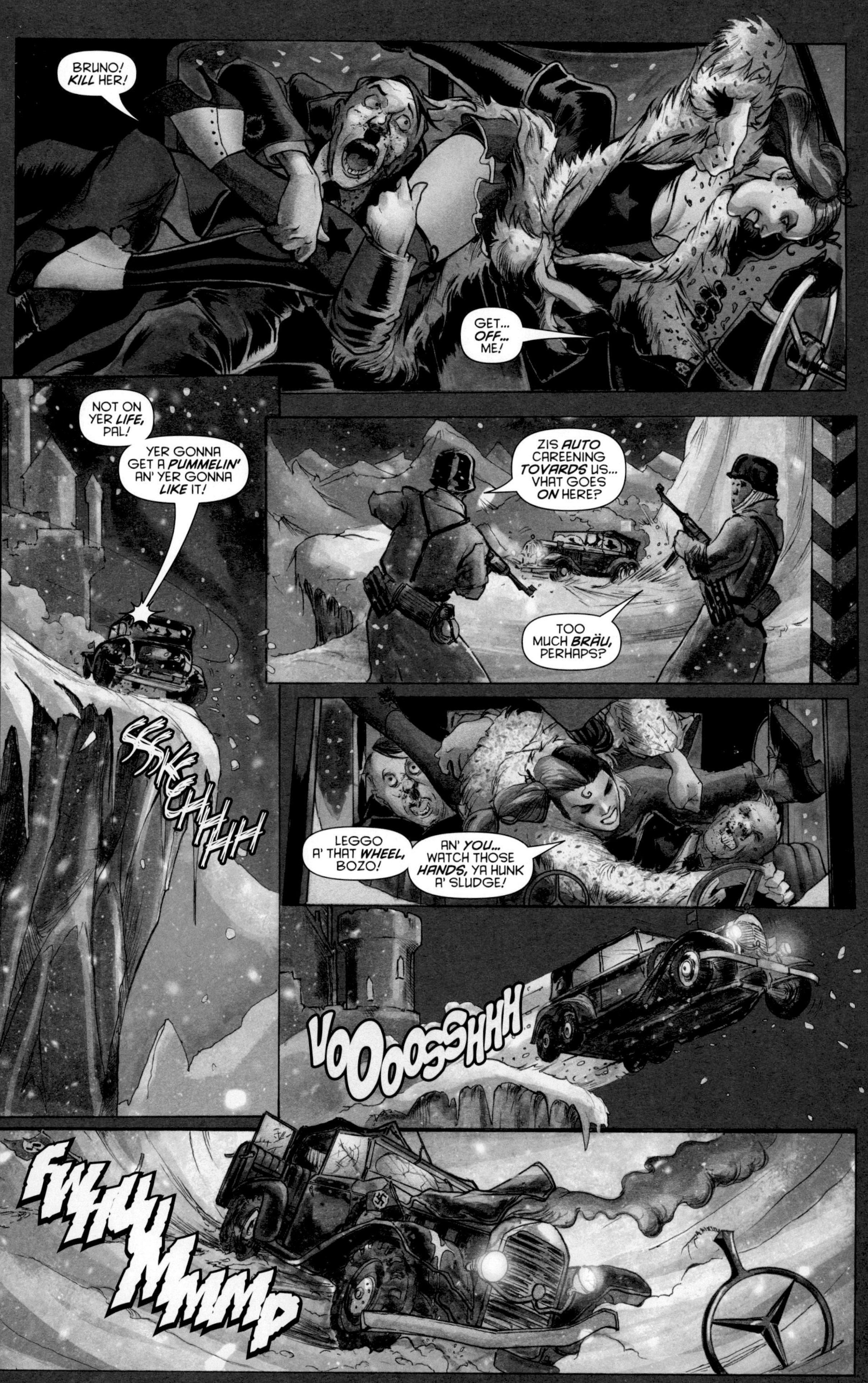
BRUNO! KILL HER!
GET... OFF... ME!
NOT ON YER LIFE, PAL!
YER GONNA GET A PUMMELIN' AN' YER GONNA LIKE IT!
ZIS AUTO CAREENING TOVARDS US... VHAT GOES ON HERE?
TOO MUCH BRÄU, PERHAPS?
LEGGO A' THAT WHEEL, BOZO!
AN' YOU... WATCH THOSE HANDS, YA HUNK A' SLUDGE!
VOOOOSSHHH
FWHUMMMP

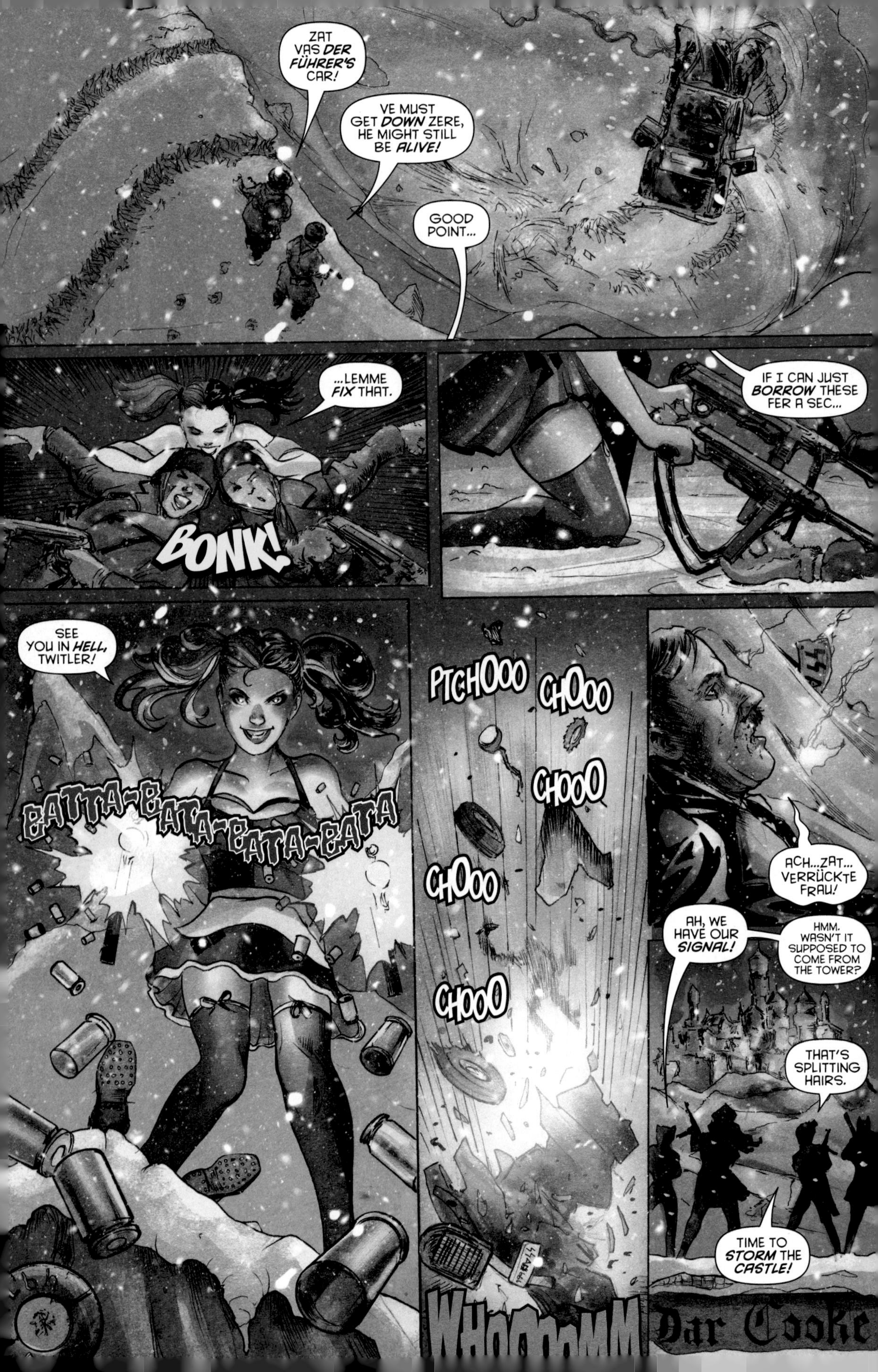
ZAT VAS DER FÜHRER'S CAR!
VE MUST GET DOWN ZERE, HE MIGHT STILL BE ALIVE!
GOOD POINT...
...LEMME FIX THAT.
BONK!
IF I CAN JUST BORROW THESE FER A SEC...
SEE YOU IN HELL, TWITLER!
BATTA-BATA-BATA-BATA
PTCHOOO
CHOOO
CHOOO
CHOOO
CHOOO
WHOOOOMM
ACH...ZAT... VERRÜCKTE FRAU!
AH, WE HAVE OUR SIGNAL!
HMM. WASN'T IT SUPPOSED TO COME FROM THE TOWER?
THAT'S SPLITTING HAIRS.
TIME TO STORM THE CASTLE!
Dar Cooke

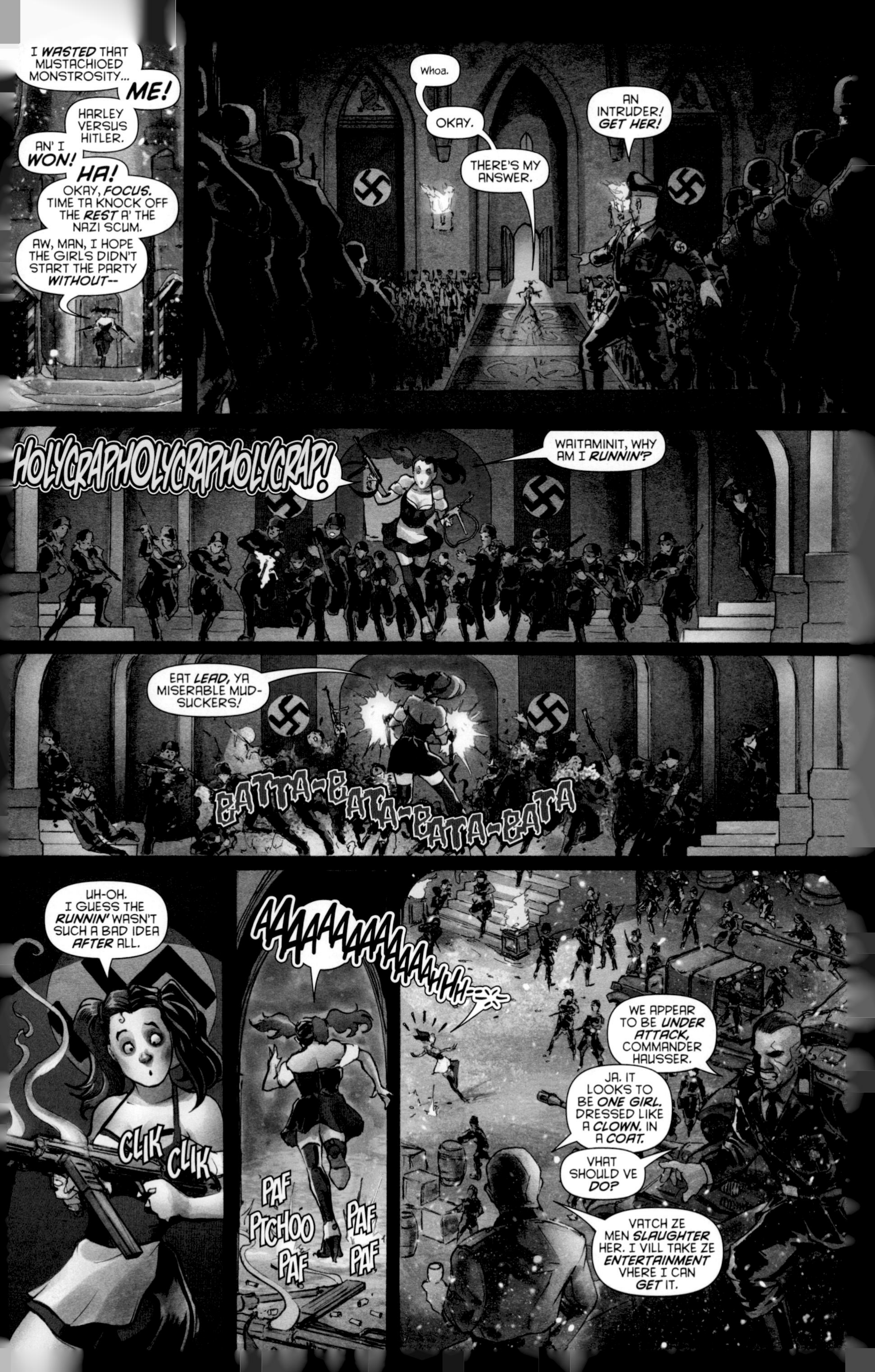
I WASTED THAT MUSTACHIOED MONSTROSITY... ME!
HARLEY VERSUS HITLER.
AN' I WON!
HA!
OKAY, FOCUS. TIME TA KNOCK OFF THE REST A' THE NAZI SCUM.
AW, MAN, I HOPE THE GIRL'S DIDN'T START THE PARTY WITHOUT--
Whoa.
OKAY.
THERE'S MY ANSWER.
AN INTRUDER! GET HER!
HOLYCRAPHOLYCRAPHOLYCRAP!
WAITAMINIT, WHY AM I RUNNIN'?
EAT LEAD, YA MISERABLE MUD-SUCKERS!
BATTA-BATA-BATA-BATA
UH-OH. I GUESS THE RUNNIN' WASN'T SUCH A BAD IDEA AFTER ALL.
CLIK
CLIK
AAAAAAAAAAAAAAHHH--
PAF
PICHOO
PAF
PAF
PAF
WE APPEAR TO BE UNDER ATTACK, COMMANDER HAUSSER.
JA. IT LOOKS TO BE ONE GIRL. DRESSED LIKE A CLOWN. IN A COAT.
VHAT SHOULD VE DO?
VATCH ZE MEN SLAUGHTER HER. I VILL TAKE ZE ENTERTAINMENT VHERE I CAN GET IT.

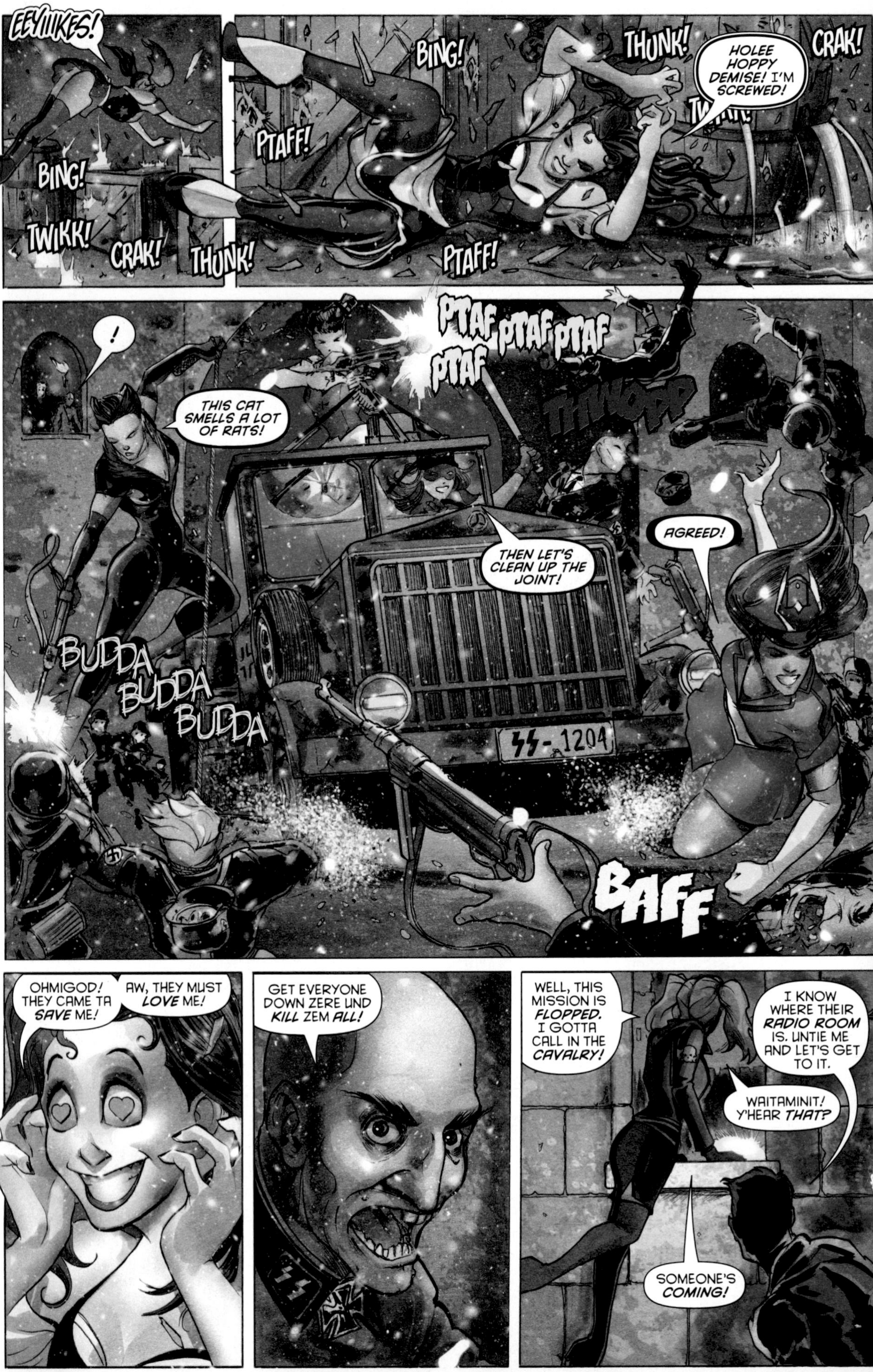
EEYIIIKES!
BING!
TWIKK!
CRAK!
THUNK!
BING!
PTAFF!
THUNK!
HOLEE HOPPY DEMISE! I'M SCREWED!
CRAK!
PTAFF!
!
THIS CAT SMELLS A LOT OF RATS!
PTAF PTAF PTAF PTAF
THWOPP
THEN LET'S CLEAN UP THE JOINT!
AGREED!
BUDDA BUDDA BUDDA
SS-1204
BAFF
OHMIGOD! THEY CAME TA *SAVE* ME!
AW, THEY MUST *LOVE* ME!
GET EVERYONE DOWN ZERE UND *KILL* ZEM *ALL*!
WELL, THIS MISSION IS *FLOPPED*. I GOTTA CALL IN THE *CAVALRY*!
I KNOW WHERE THEIR *RADIO ROOM* IS. UNTIE ME AND LET'S GET TO IT.
WAITAMINIT! Y'HEAR *THAT*?
SOMEONE'S *COMING*!

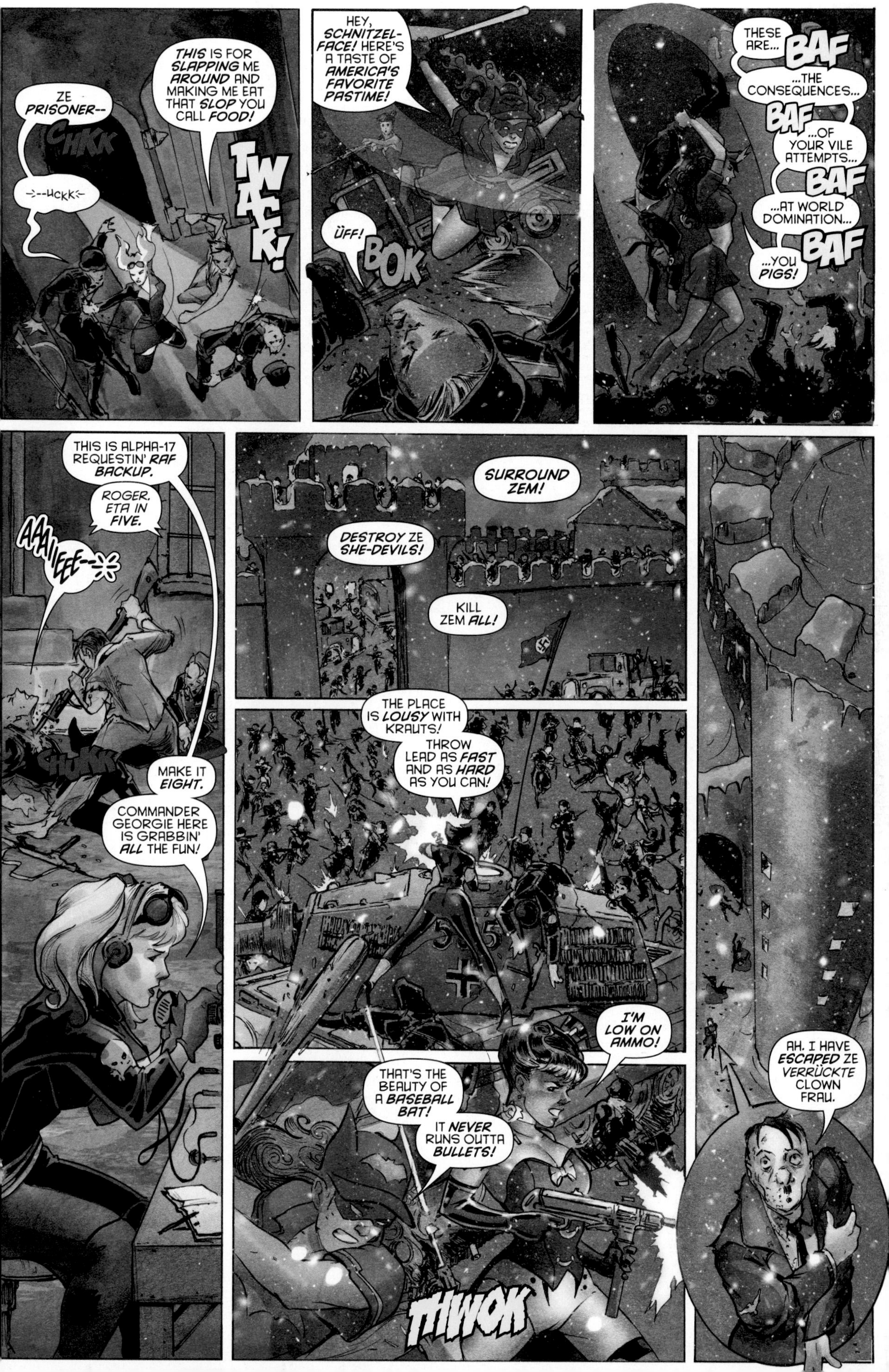

ZE PRISONER--
CHKK
--HCKK--
THIS IS FOR SLAPPING ME AROUND AND MAKING ME EAT THAT SLOP YOU CALL FOOD!
TWACK!
HEY, SCHNITZEL-FACE! HERE'S A TASTE OF AMERICA'S FAVORITE PASTIME!
ÜFF!
BOK
THESE ARE...
BAF
...THE CONSEQUENCES...
BAF
...OF YOUR VILE ATTEMPTS...
BAF
...AT WORLD DOMINATION...
BAF
...YOU PIGS!
THIS IS ALPHA-17 REQUESTIN' RAF BACKUP.
ROGER. ETA IN FIVE.
AAAIIEEE--
CHUKK
MAKE IT EIGHT.
COMMANDER GEORGIE HERE IS GRABBIN' ALL THE FUN!
SURROUND ZEM!
DESTROY ZE SHE-DEVILS!
KILL ZEM ALL!
THE PLACE IS LOUSY WITH KRAUTS!
THROW LEAD AS FAST AND AS HARD AS YOU CAN!
I'M LOW ON AMMO!
THAT'S THE BEAUTY OF A BASEBALL BAT!
IT NEVER RUNS OUTTA BULLETS!
THWOK
AH. I HAVE ESCAPED ZE VERRÜCKTE CLOWN FRAU.

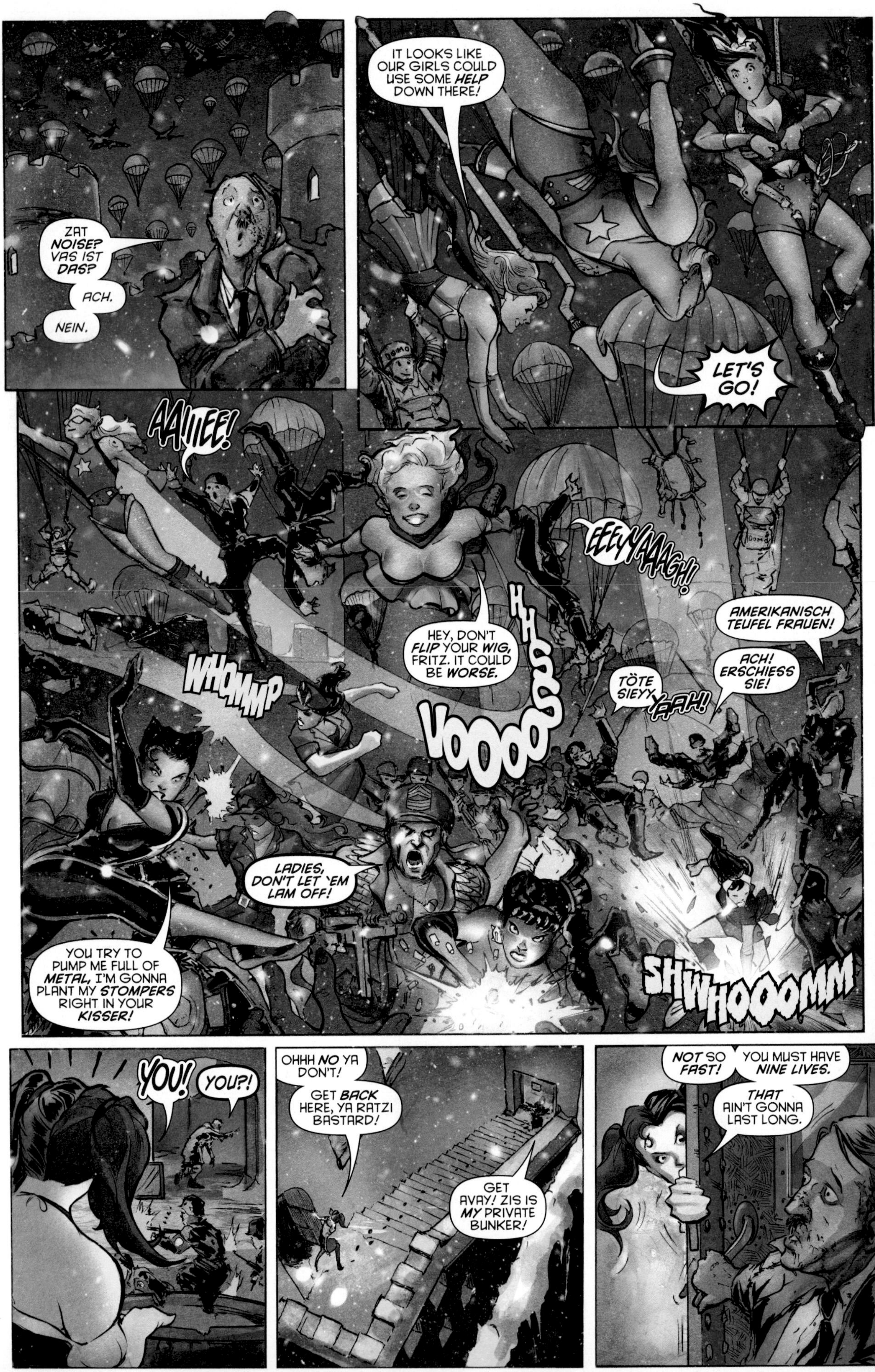
ZAT NOISE? VAS IST DAS?
ACH.
NEIN.
IT LOOKS LIKE OUR GIRLS COULD USE SOME HELP DOWN THERE!
LET'S GO!
AAIIIEE!
EEEYYAAAAGH!
HEY, DON'T FLIP YOUR WIG, FRITZ. IT COULD BE WORSE.
HHSS
AMERIKANISCH TEUFEL FRAUEN!
ACH! ERSCHIESS SIE!
TÖTE SIEYY YAAH!
WHOMMP
VOOOOSS
LADIES, DON'T LET 'EM LAM OFF!
YOU TRY TO PUMP ME FULL OF METAL, I'M GONNA PLANT MY STOMPERS RIGHT IN YOUR KISSER!
SHWHOOOMM
YOU!
YOU?!
OHHH NO YA DON'T!
GET BACK HERE, YA RATZI BASTARD!
GET AVAY! ZIS IS MY PRIVATE BUNKER!
NOT SO FAST!
YOU MUST HAVE NINE LIVES.
THAT AIN'T GONNA LAST LONG.

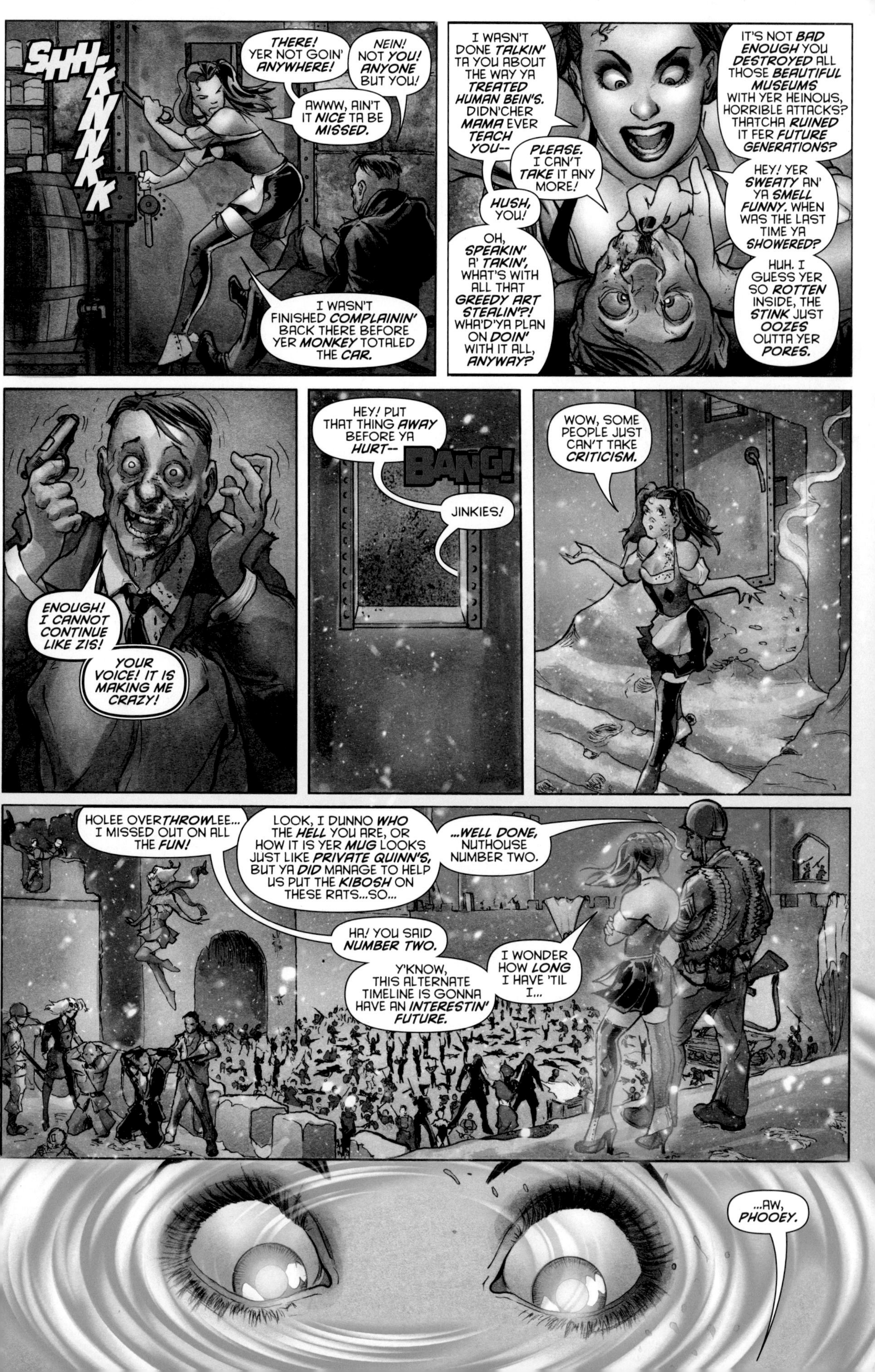
SHH-KNKK
THERE! YER NOT GOIN' ANYWHERE!
NEIN! NOT YOU! ANYONE BUT YOU!
AWWW, AIN'T IT NICE TA BE MISSED.
I WASN'T FINISHED COMPLAININ' BACK THERE BEFORE YER MONKEY TOTALED THE CAR.
I WASN'T DONE TALKIN' TA YOU ABOUT THE WAY YA TREATED HUMAN BEIN'S. DIDN'CHER MAMA EVER TEACH YOU--
PLEASE. I CAN'T TAKE IT ANY MORE!
HUSH, YOU!
OH, SPEAKIN' A' TAKIN', WHAT'S WITH ALL THAT GREEDY ART STEALIN'?! WHA'D'YA PLAN ON DOIN' WITH IT ALL, ANYWAY?
IT'S NOT BAD ENOUGH YOU DESTROYED ALL THOSE BEAUTIFUL MUSEUMS WITH YER HEINOUS, HORRIBLE ATTACKS? THATCHA RUINED IT FER FUTURE GENERATIONS?
HEY! YER SWEATY AN' YA SMELL FUNNY. WHEN WAS THE LAST TIME YA SHOWERED?
HUH. I GUESS YER SO ROTTEN INSIDE, THE STINK JUST OOZES OUTTA YER PORES.
ENOUGH! I CANNOT CONTINUE LIKE ZIS!
YOUR VOICE! IT IS MAKING ME CRAZY!
HEY! PUT THAT THING AWAY BEFORE YA HURT--
BANG!
JINKIES!
WOW, SOME PEOPLE JUST CAN'T TAKE CRITICISM.
HOLEE OVERTHROWLEE... I MISSED OUT ON ALL THE FUN!
LOOK, I DUNNO WHO THE HELL YOU ARE, OR HOW IT IS YER MUG LOOKS JUST LIKE PRIVATE QUINN'S, BUT YA DID MANAGE TO HELP US PUT THE KIBOSH ON THESE RATS...SO...
...WELL DONE, NUTHOUSE NUMBER TWO.
HA! YOU SAID NUMBER TWO.
Y'KNOW, THIS ALTERNATE TIMELINE IS GONNA HAVE AN INTERESTIN' FUTURE.
I WONDER HOW LONG I HAVE 'TIL I...
...AW, PHOOEY.

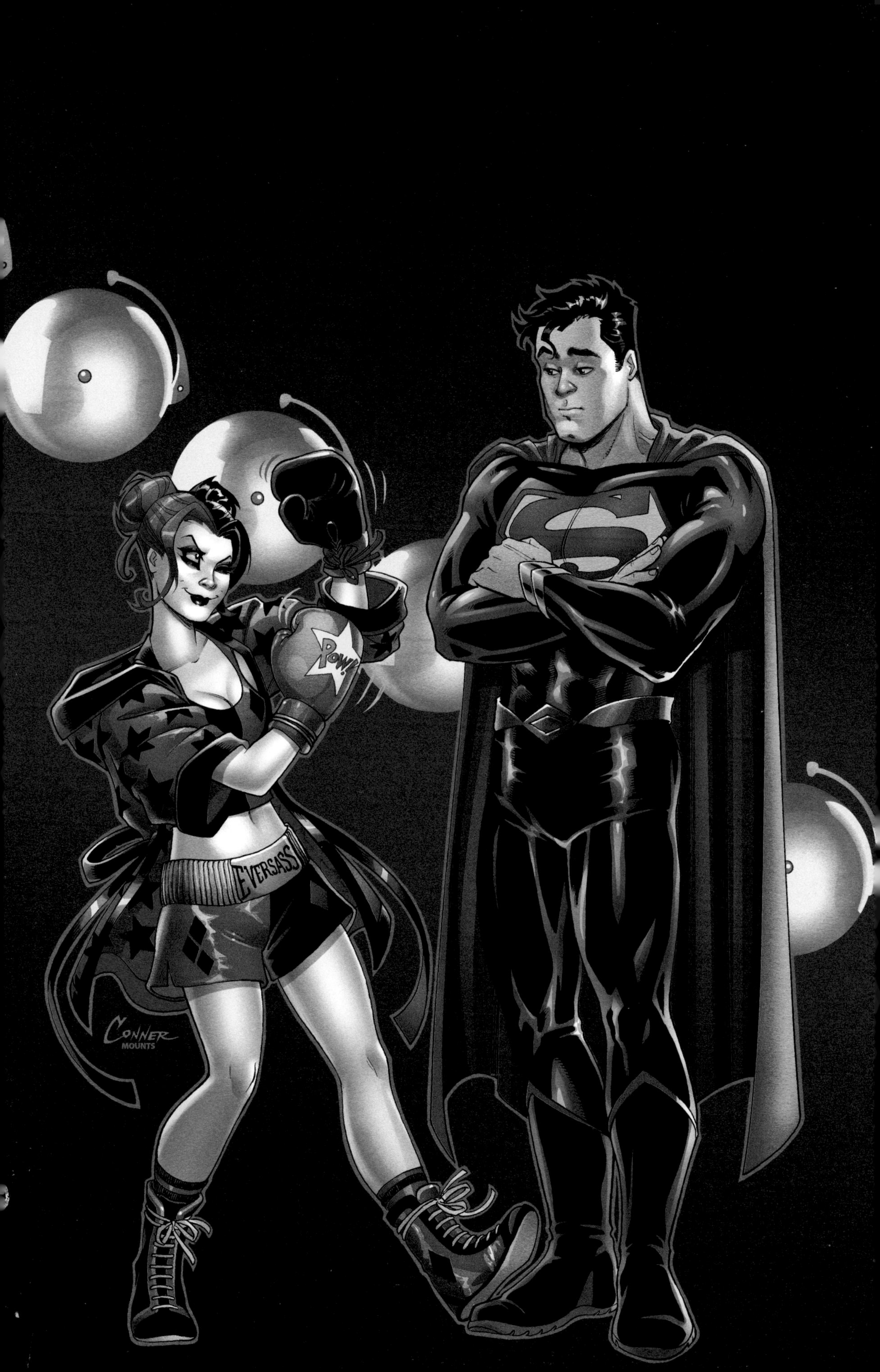
POW!
EVERSASS
CONNER
MOUNTS

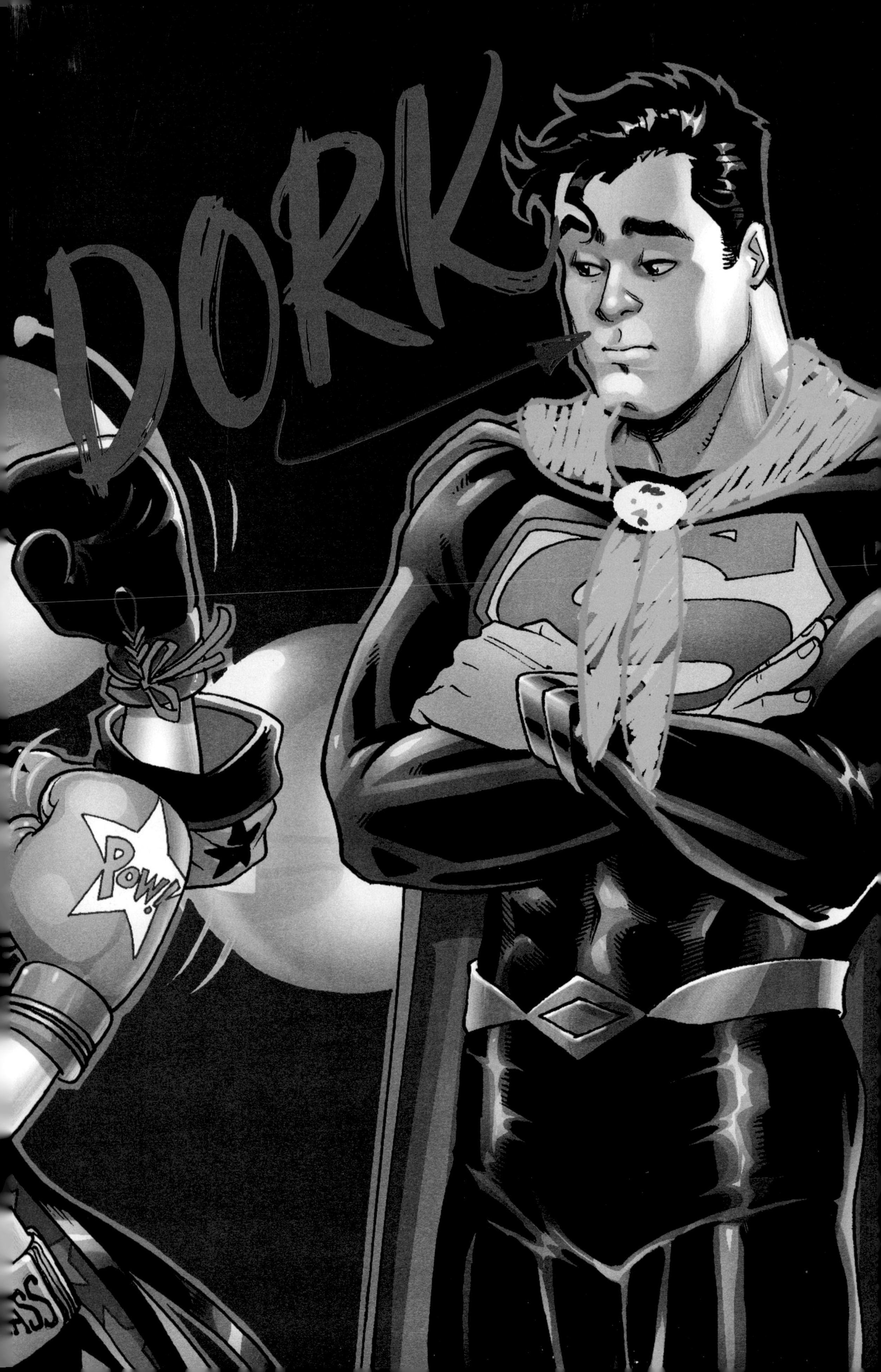
DORK
POW!

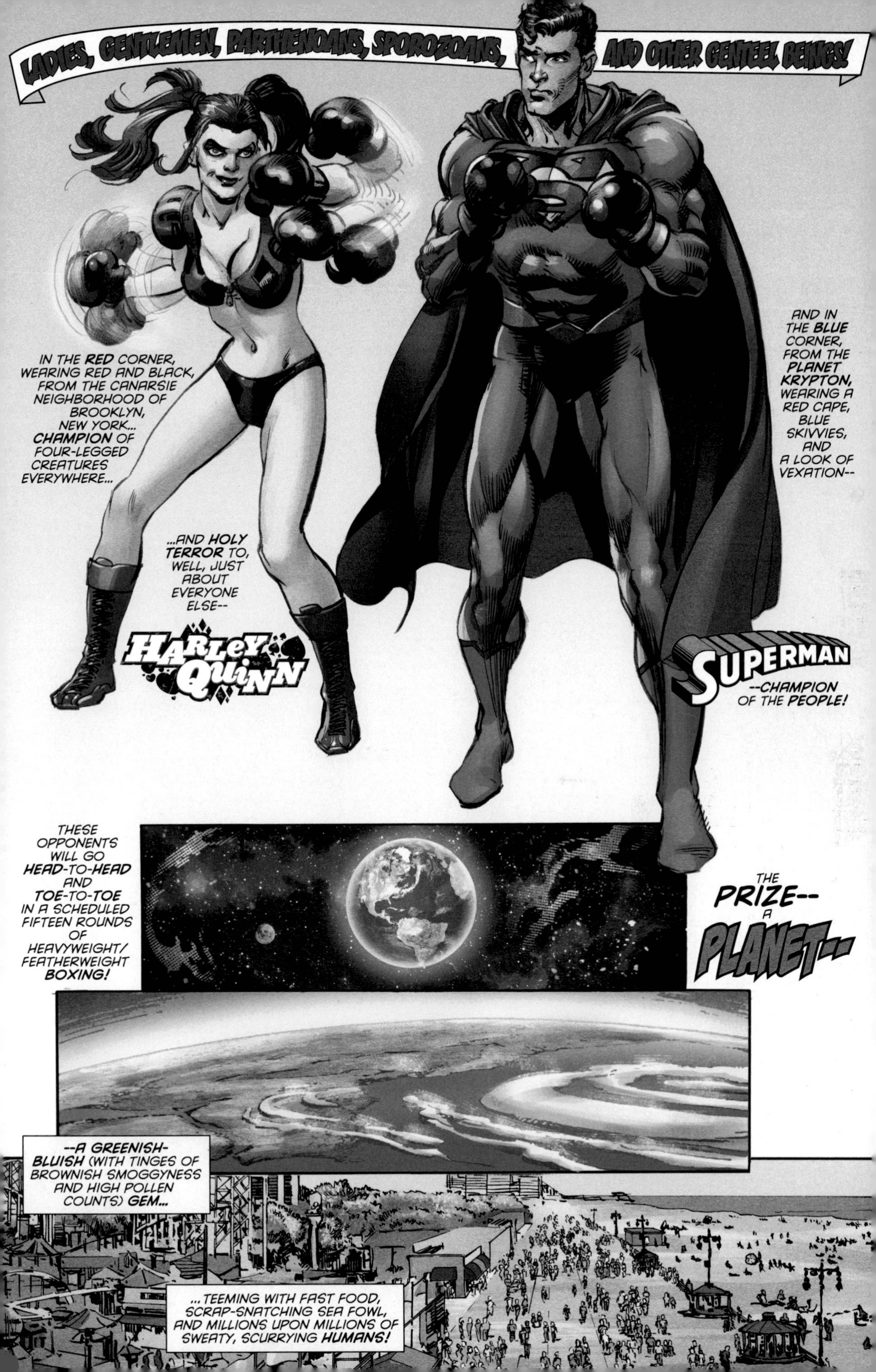

LADIES, GENTLEMEN, PARTHENOIDS, SPOROZOANS, AND OTHER GENTEEL BEINGS!
IN THE RED CORNER, WEARING RED AND BLACK, FROM THE CANARSIE NEIGHBORHOOD OF BROOKLYN, NEW YORK... CHAMPION OF FOUR-LEGGED CREATURES EVERYWHERE...
...AND HOLY TERROR TO, WELL, JUST ABOUT EVERYONE ELSE--
HARLEY QUINN
AND IN THE BLUE CORNER, FROM THE PLANET KRYPTON, WEARING A RED CAPE, BLUE SKIVVIES, AND A LOOK OF VEXATION--
SUPERMAN
--CHAMPION OF THE PEOPLE!
THESE OPPONENTS WILL GO HEAD-TO-HEAD AND TOE-TO-TOE IN A SCHEDULED FIFTEEN ROUNDS OF HEAVYWEIGHT/ FEATHERWEIGHT BOXING!
THE PRIZE-- A PLANET--
--A GREENISH-BLUISH (WITH TINGES OF BROWNISH SMOGGYNESS AND HIGH POLLEN COUNTS) GEM...
...TEEMING WITH FAST FOOD, SCRAP-SNATCHING SEA FOWL, AND MILLIONS UPON MILLIONS OF SWEATY, SCURRYING HUMANS!

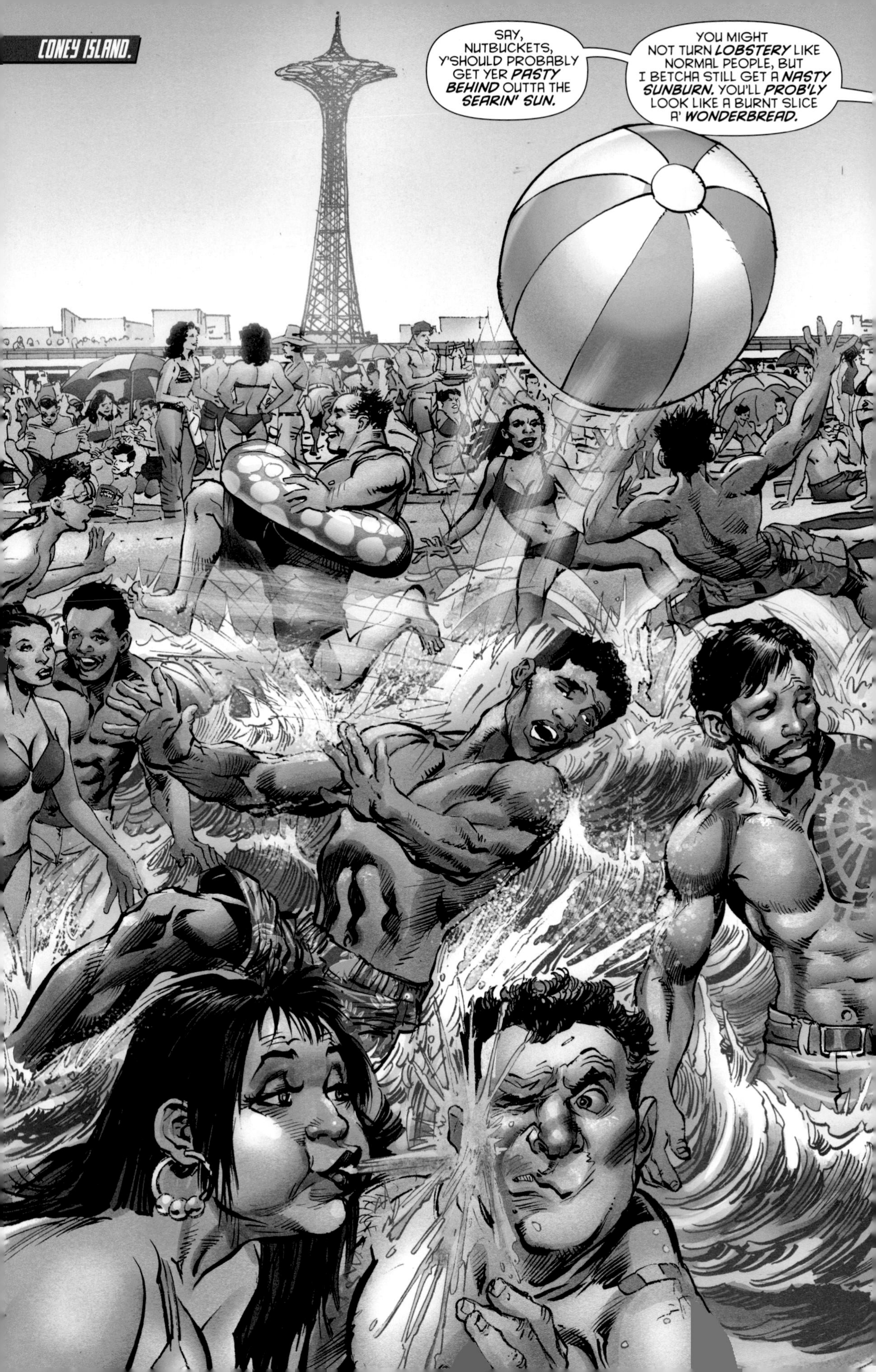
CONEY ISLAND.
SAY, NUTBUCKETS, Y'SHOULD PROBABLY GET YER PASTY BEHIND OUTTA THE SEARIN' SUN.
YOU MIGHT NOT TURN LOBSTERY LIKE NORMAL PEOPLE, BUT I BETCHA STILL GET A NASTY SUNBURN. YOU'LL PROB'LY LOOK LIKE A BURNT SLICE A' WONDERBREAD.

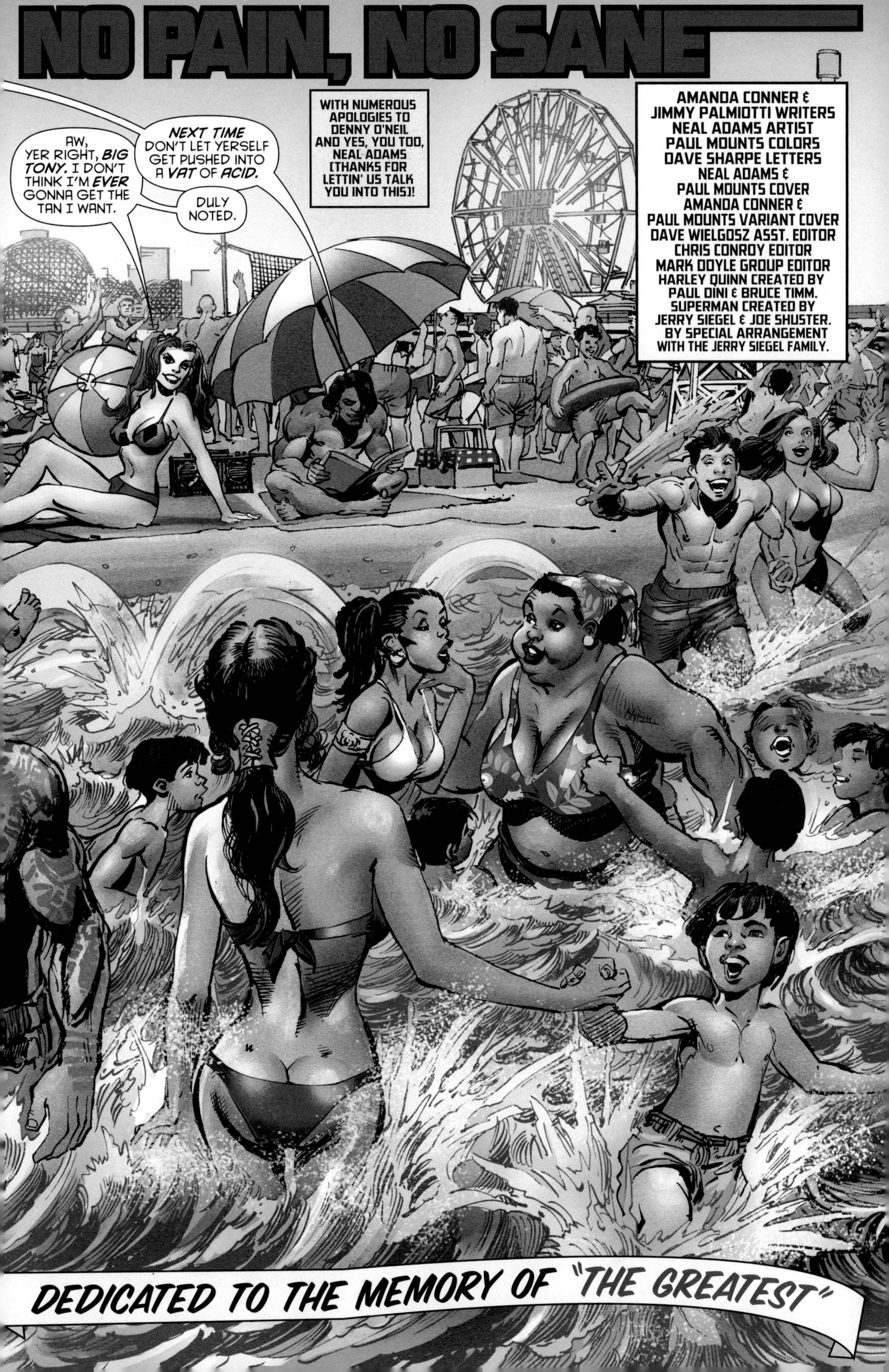
NO PAIN, NO SANE
AW, YER RIGHT, BIG TONY. I DON'T THINK I'M EVER GONNA GET THE TAN I WANT.
NEXT TIME DON'T LET YERSELF GET PUSHED INTO A VAT OF ACID.
DULY NOTED.
WITH NUMEROUS APOLOGIES TO DENNY O'NEIL AND YES, YOU TOO, NEAL ADAMS [THANKS FOR LETTIN' US TALK YOU INTO THIS]!
AMANDA CONNER & JIMMY PALMIOTTI WRITERS
NEAL ADAMS ARTIST
PAUL MOUNTS COLORS
DAVE SHARPE LETTERS
NEAL ADAMS & PAUL MOUNTS COVER
AMANDA CONNER & PAUL MOUNTS VARIANT COVER
DAVE WIELGOSZ ASST. EDITOR
CHRIS CONROY EDITOR
MARK DOYLE GROUP EDITOR
HARLEY QUINN CREATED BY PAUL DINI & BRUCE TIMM.
SUPERMAN CREATED BY JERRY SIEGEL & JOE SHUSTER.
BY SPECIAL ARRANGEMENT WITH THE JERRY SIEGEL FAMILY.
DEDICATED TO THE MEMORY OF "THE GREATEST"

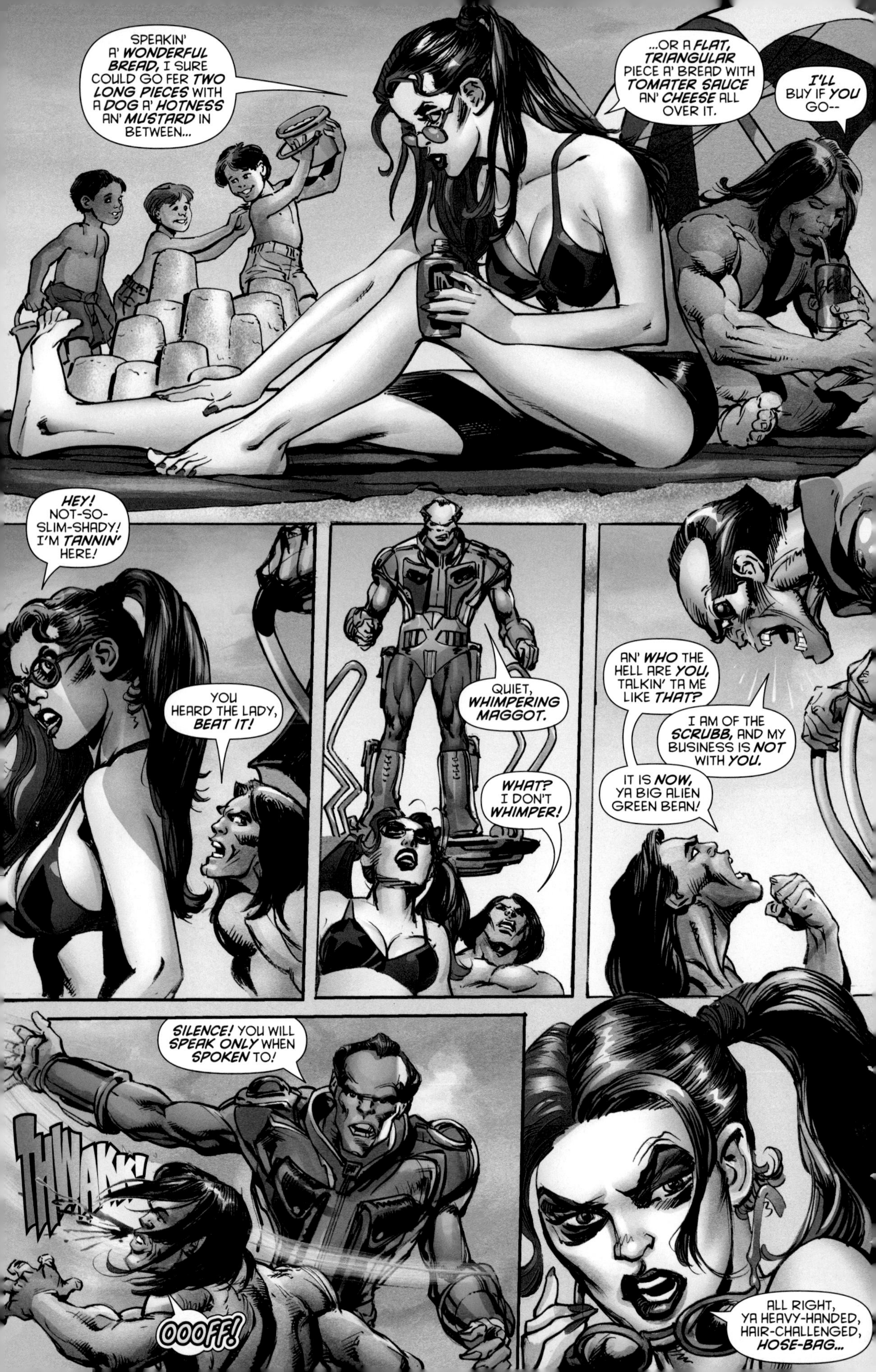
SPEAKIN' A' WONDERFUL BREAD, I SURE COULD GO FER TWO LONG PIECES WITH A DOG A' HOTNESS AN' MUSTARD IN BETWEEN...
...OR A FLAT, TRIANGULAR PIECE A' BREAD WITH TOMATER SAUCE AN' CHEESE ALL OVER IT.
I'LL BUY IF YOU GO--
HEY! NOT-SO-SLIM-SHADY! I'M TANNIN' HERE!
YOU HEARD THE LADY, BEAT IT!
QUIET, WHIMPERING MAGGOT.
WHAT? I DON'T WHIMPER!
AN' WHO THE HELL ARE YOU, TALKIN' TA ME LIKE THAT?
I AM OF THE SCRUBB, AND MY BUSINESS IS NOT WITH YOU.
IT IS NOW, YA BIG ALIEN GREEN BEAN!
SILENCE! YOU WILL SPEAK ONLY WHEN SPOKEN TO!
THWAKK!
OOOFF!
ALL RIGHT, YA HEAVY-HANDED, HAIR-CHALLENGED, HOSE-BAG...

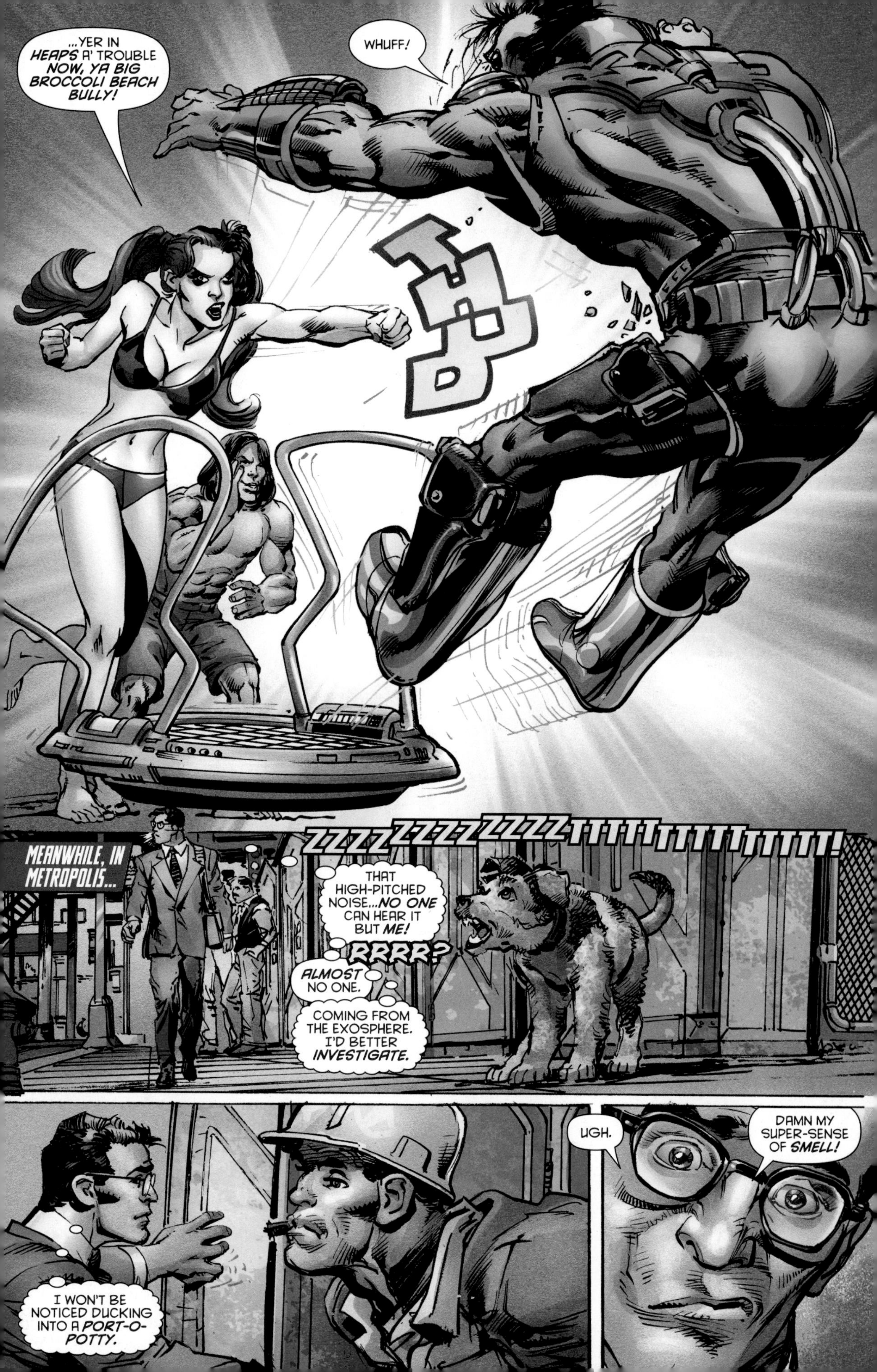

...YER IN HEAPS A' TROUBLE NOW, YA BIG BROCCOLI BEACH BULLY!
WHUFF!
MEANWHILE, IN METROPOLIS...
ZZZZZZZZZZZZTTTTTTTTTTTTTTTT!
THAT HIGH-PITCHED NOISE...NO ONE CAN HEAR IT BUT ME!
RRRR?
ALMOST NO ONE.
COMING FROM THE EXOSPHERE. I'D BETTER INVESTIGATE.
I WON'T BE NOTICED DUCKING INTO A PORT-O-POTTY.
UGH.
DAMN MY SUPER-SENSE OF SMELL!

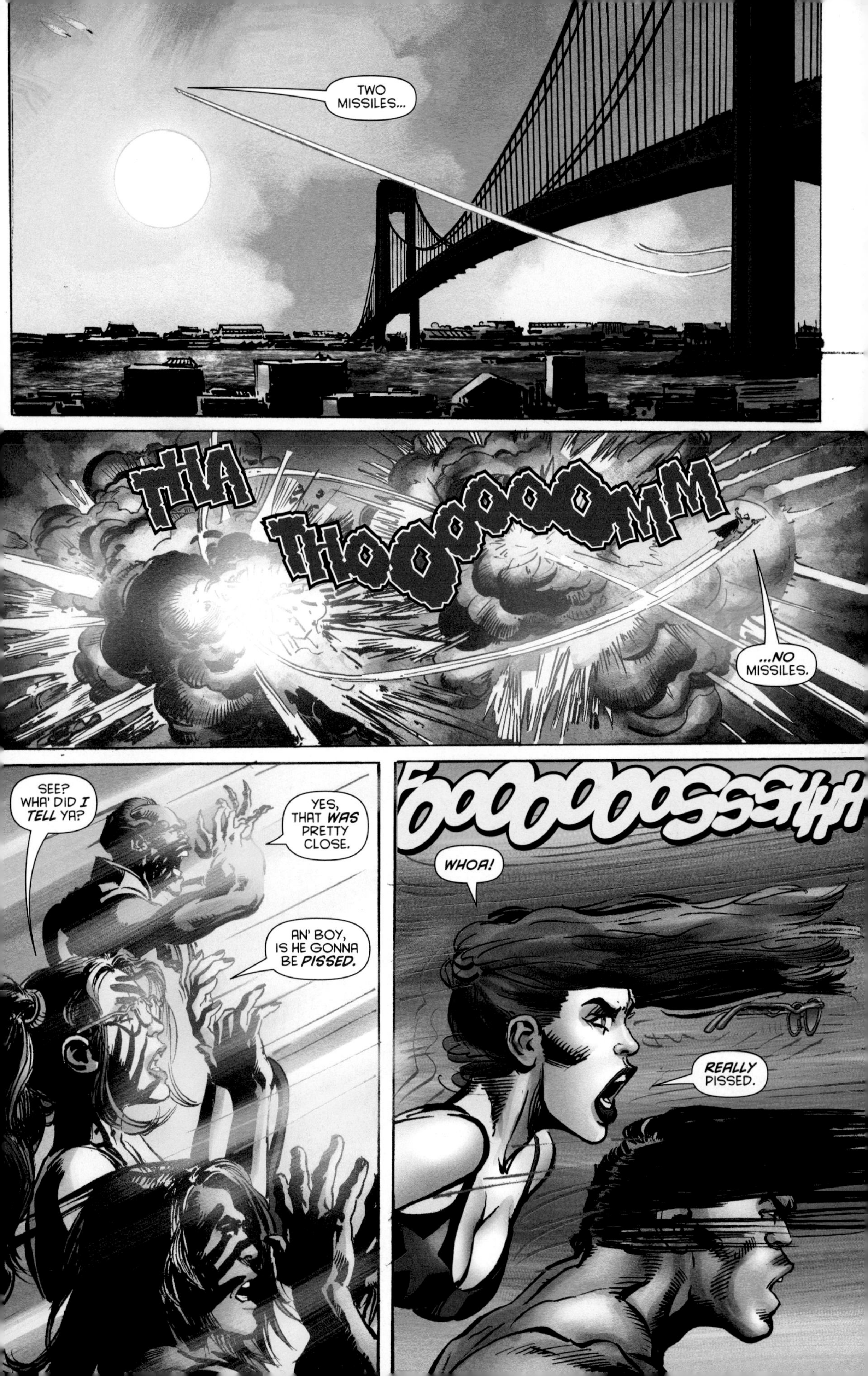
TWO MISSILES...
THA
THOOOOOOMM
...NO MISSILES.
SEE? WHA' DID I TELL YA?
YES, THAT WAS PRETTY CLOSE.
AN' BOY, IS HE GONNA BE PISSED.
FOOOOOOOSSSHH
WHOA!
REALLY PISSED.

Y'MEAN *MOI?*

I AM SO *FLATTERED!* OF *COURSE* I'LL FACE YER SPACE CHAMP IN BATTLE.

WHAT?

SHE MEANS *SUPERMAN.*

HARLEY, YOU MEAN *SUPERMAN,* RIGHT?

LOOK, I'M THE *LOGICAL CHOICE,* SO *I'LL* DO IT.

HOLD ON, MAN A' STEALIN' MY *LIMELIGHT.* I CAN HANDLE THIS *JUST FINE.*

SAVIN' EARTH IS MY *SECOND FAVORITE* THING TA *DO.*

HUH? WHAT'S YOUR *FIR--* WAIT. NEVER MIND.

AW, *C'MON!*

NOPE. *NOT* GOING TO HAPPEN, AND NEITHER IS YOU *FIGHTING* FOR THE FATE OF OUR *PLANET.*

HEY, I WAS *BORN* HERE! I FLY LIKE A BUTTERFLY AN' STING LIKE A BEE, LADIES FIRST, INNERNET OUTRAGE AN' *ANYTHING ELSE* THAT'LL GET ME THIS GIG.

HEY, IZZIS FIGHT GONNA BE *TELEVISED?*

YES. IT WILL BE TELECAST TO OVER THREE THOUSAND GALAXIES AND BILLED AS THE *GREATEST FIGHT* IN THE HISTORY OF *LIFE ITSELF.*

IN THAT CASE, *I ACCEPT.* SORRY, SUPIE. I'LL MAKE SURE YA GET A GOOD SEAT UP FRONT. IT'S THE *LEAST* I CAN DO.

HARLEY, YOU MAY BE A *TALENTED FIGHTER,* BUT YOU *DON'T KNOW* WHAT YOU'RE *UP* AGAINST. IT MAKES SENSE FOR SOMEONE LIKE *ME* TO HANDLE THIS.

LIKE *YOU?*

I HAVE *SUPER-POWERS!* I CAN CHANGE THE COURSE OF *MIGHTY RIVERS,* BEND *STEEL* WITH MY *BARE HANDS,* AND I...

YEAH, YEAH, SHOOT *LASER BEAMS* OUTTA YER *EYES, FLY,* BREATHE IN *SPACE,* FREEZE STUFF WITH YER *SUPER-BREATH,* TOSS YER *SUPERMAN LOGO* AN' MAKE IT A *SHRINK-WRAP THINGY,* HAVE *SUPER-HYPNOSIS,* HAVE *CLAWS* THAT COME OUTTA THE BACK A' YER *HAND,* CAN *DUPLICATE* YOURSELF, CAN TURN *INVISIBLE,* BLAH, BLAH...

SOME OF THAT IS *NOT* TRUE.

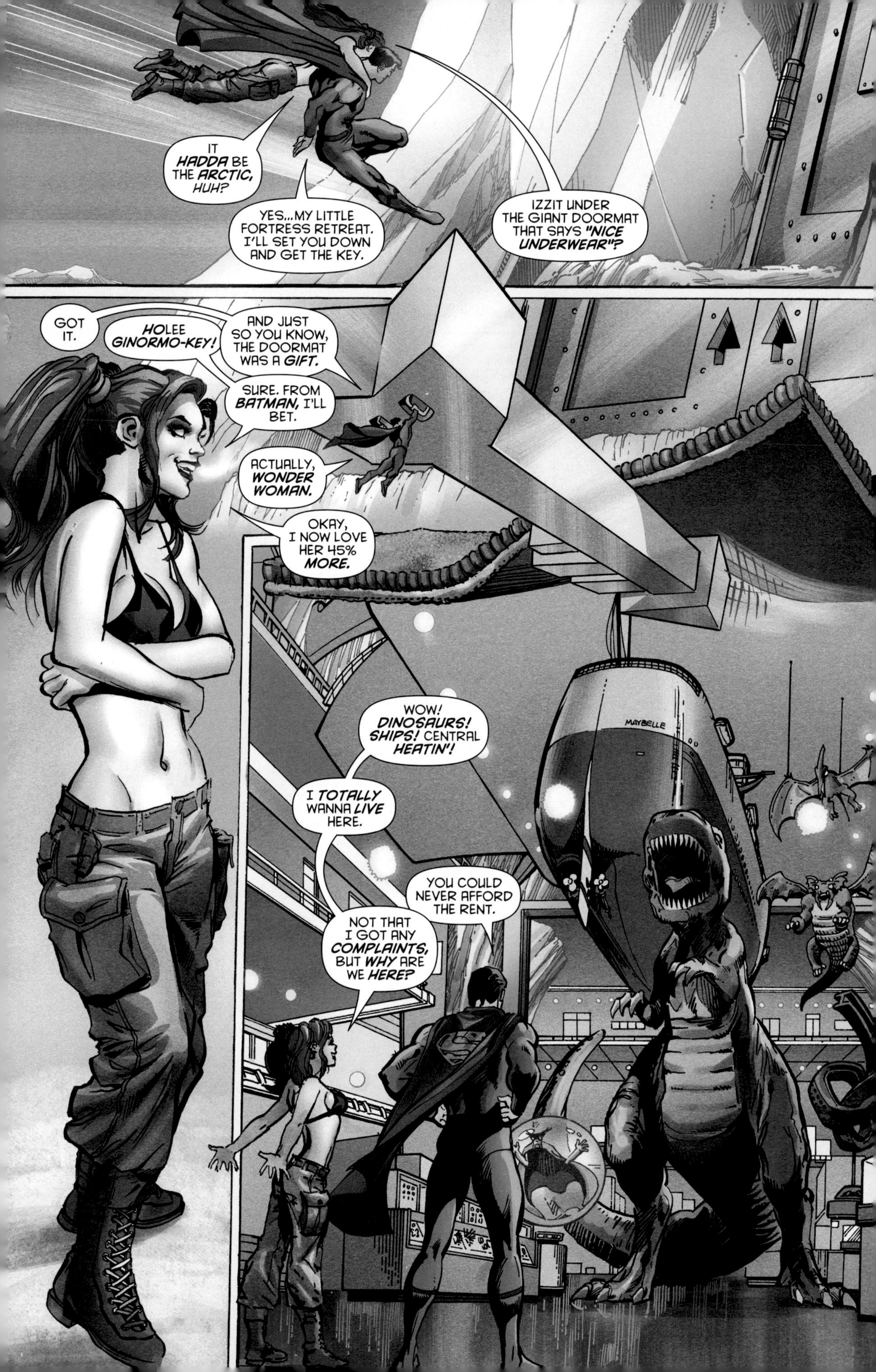

IT HADDA BE THE ARCTIC, HUH?
YES...MY LITTLE FORTRESS RETREAT. I'LL SET YOU DOWN AND GET THE KEY.
IZZIT UNDER THE GIANT DOORMAT THAT SAYS "NICE UNDERWEAR"?
GOT IT.
HOLEE GINORMO-KEY!
AND JUST SO YOU KNOW, THE DOORMAT WAS A GIFT.
SURE. FROM BATMAN, I'LL BET.
ACTUALLY, WONDER WOMAN.
OKAY, I NOW LOVE HER 45% MORE.
WOW! DINOSAURS! SHIPS! CENTRAL HEATIN'!
I TOTALLY WANNA LIVE HERE.
YOU COULD NEVER AFFORD THE RENT.
NOT THAT I GOT ANY COMPLAINTS, BUT WHY ARE WE HERE?
MAYBELLE

SO. DO YOU KNOW HOW TO BOX?

YEAH, I HAD THREE OBNOXIOUS *BROTHERS* AN' A SPORTS-OBSESSED *DAD*, SO I'M PRETTY *GOOD* AT IT.

YOU?

I HAD ONE OF THE *GREATEST FIGHTERS* IN THE *WORLD* TRAIN ME A WHILE BACK, SO, *YES*. WE NEED TO EVEN UP THE *FIGHT* A BIT, SO I FIGURE WE'LL TRAIN *HERE*.

I'M GUESSING THE PLACE WHERE THE MATCH WILL BE HAS A *RED SUN*, SO I'LL HAVE NO SUPERPOWERS AT ALL.

WAITAMINNIT, ARE YOU *SERIOUSLY* THINKIN' YA CAN BEAT ME IN A FAIR FIGHT *WITHOUT* YER POWERS?

I DON'T THINK WE CAN *FAKE* THE FIGHT, SO ONE OF US WILL HAVE TO *BEAT* THE OTHER, THEN GO ON TO FIGHT THEIR CHAMPION...

...WHO WILL PROBABLY BE A *BIT* OUT OF YOUR *LEAGUE*.

LISSEN, BUDDY...I HADDA LEARN HOW TA FIGHT MY ASS OFF OVER THE YEARS *WITHOUT* RELYIN' ON ANY *INDESTRUCTABILITIES*.

I'M THINKING *YOU'RE* THE ONE GOIN' DOWN AN' I'M GONNA HAVE TA WHUP THEIR CHAMPION'S INNERGALACTIC ASS TA SAVE OUR PLANET.

WELL, *WHATEVER* THE OUTCOME, WE'LL BE *BOXING*, AND I THINK WE NEED TO *SPAR* A BIT.

THIS PURPLE GLASS BALL IS A KRYPTONIAN CONTINUUM DISRUPTER.

ONCE I SHATTER IT, WE'LL BE TRANSPORTED TO THE *FRINGE* OF *CREATION*... WHERE TIME *CRAWLS*!

A *MINUTE HERE* IS AN *HOUR THERE*. IT'LL ONLY LAST *ONE EARTH HOUR*, BUT ONCE THERE, WE'LL HAVE OVER *TWO WHOLE DAYS*.

DID YOU SAY *FRIDGE*, 'CAUSE I'M *STARVIN'*.

FRINGE. I SAID *FRINGE*. STEP BACK.

HERE WE GO.

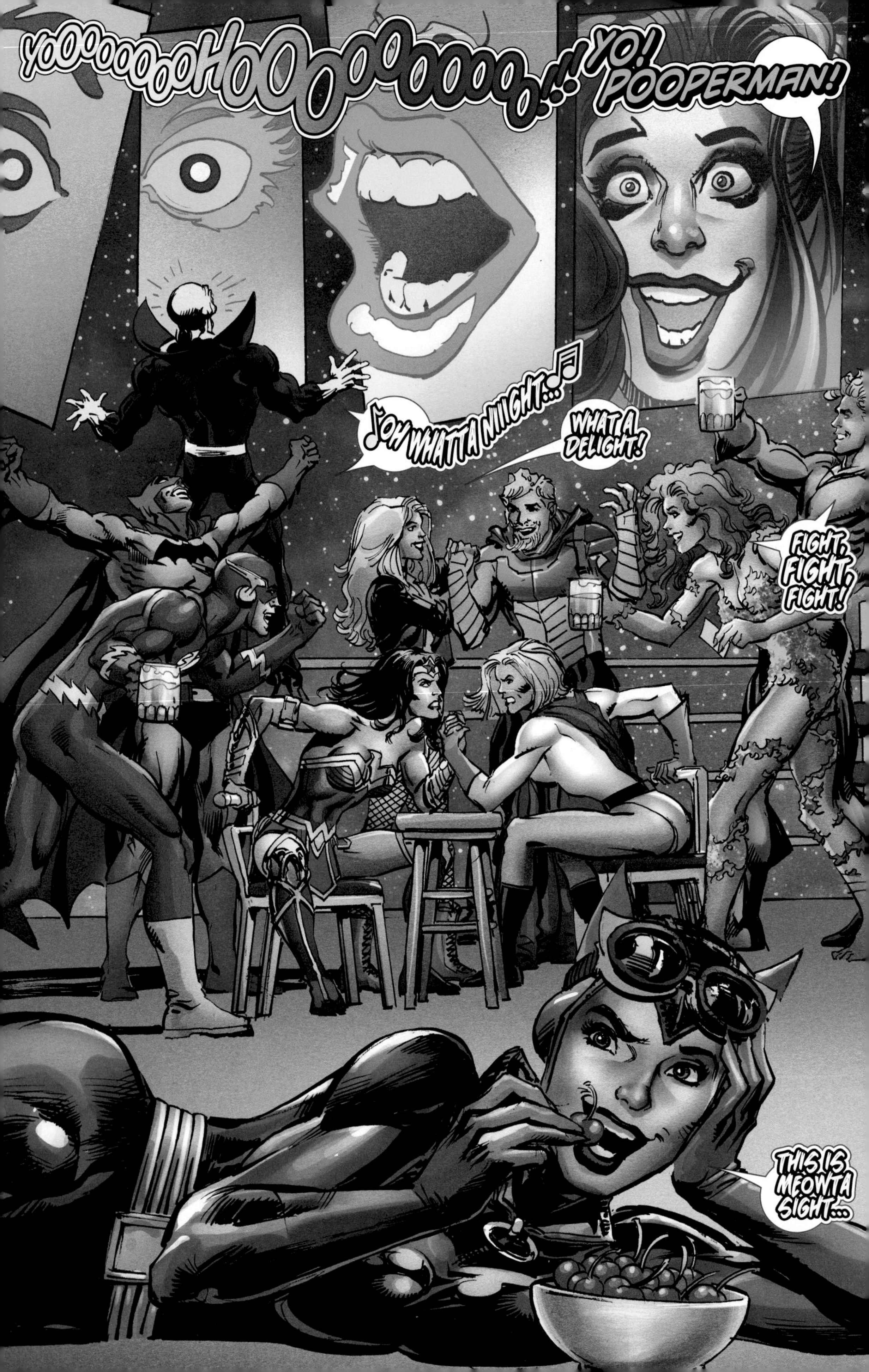
YOOOOOOOOHOOOOOOOOOOOO..!!
YO! POOPERMAN!
♪OH WHATTA NIIIGHT...♪♪
WHAT A DELIGHT!
FIGHT, FIGHT, FIGHT!
THIS IS MEOWTA SIGHT...

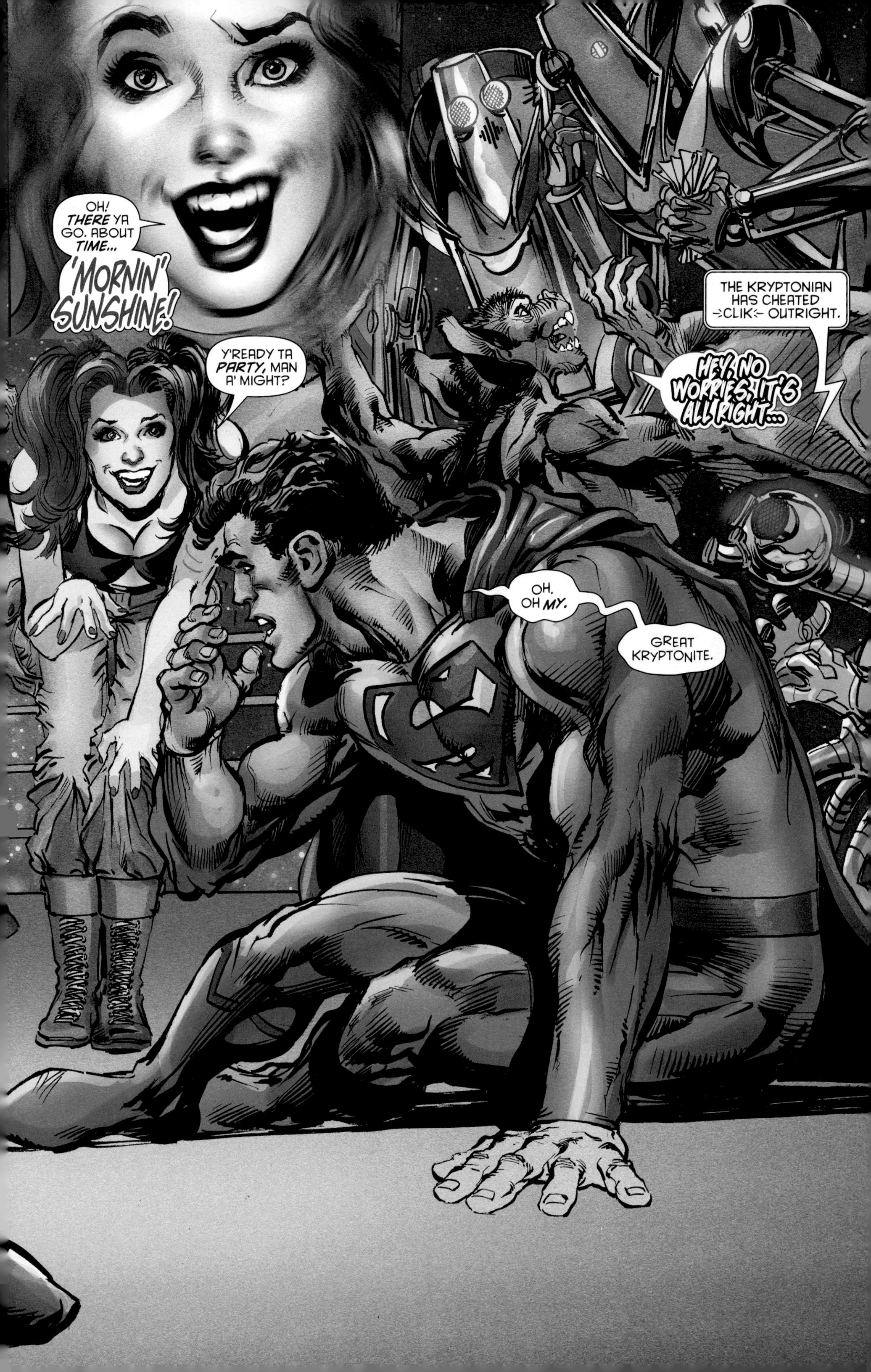
OH! THERE YA GO. ABOUT TIME...
'MORNIN' SUNSHINE!
THE KRYPTONIAN HAS CHEATED -CLIK- OUTRIGHT.
Y'READY TA PARTY, MAN A' MIGHT?
HEY, NO WORRIES, IT'S ALL RIGHT...
OH, OH MY.
GREAT KRYPTONITE.

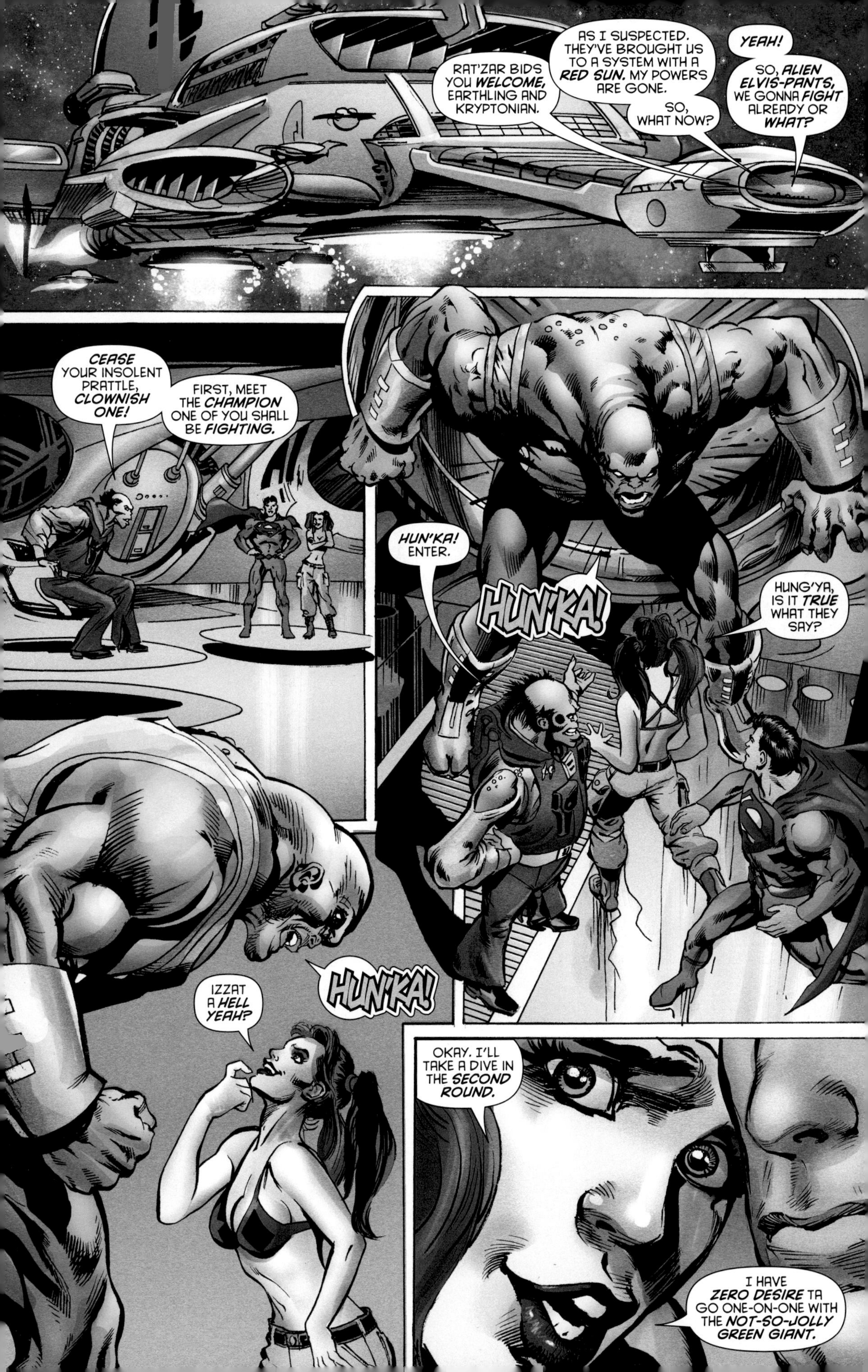

RAT'ZAR BIDS YOU WELCOME, EARTHLING AND KRYPTONIAN.
AS I SUSPECTED. THEY'VE BROUGHT US TO A SYSTEM WITH A RED SUN. MY POWERS ARE GONE.
SO, WHAT NOW?
YEAH!
SO, ALIEN ELVIS-PANTS, WE GONNA FIGHT ALREADY OR WHAT?
CEASE YOUR INSOLENT PRATTLE, CLOWNISH ONE!
FIRST, MEET THE CHAMPION ONE OF YOU SHALL BE FIGHTING.
HUN'KA! ENTER.
HUN'KA!
HUNG'YA, IS IT TRUE WHAT THEY SAY?
HUN'KA!
IZZAT A HELL YEAH?
OKAY. I'LL TAKE A DIVE IN THE SECOND ROUND.
I HAVE ZERO DESIRE TA GO ONE-ON-ONE WITH THE NOT-SO-JOLLY GREEN GIANT.

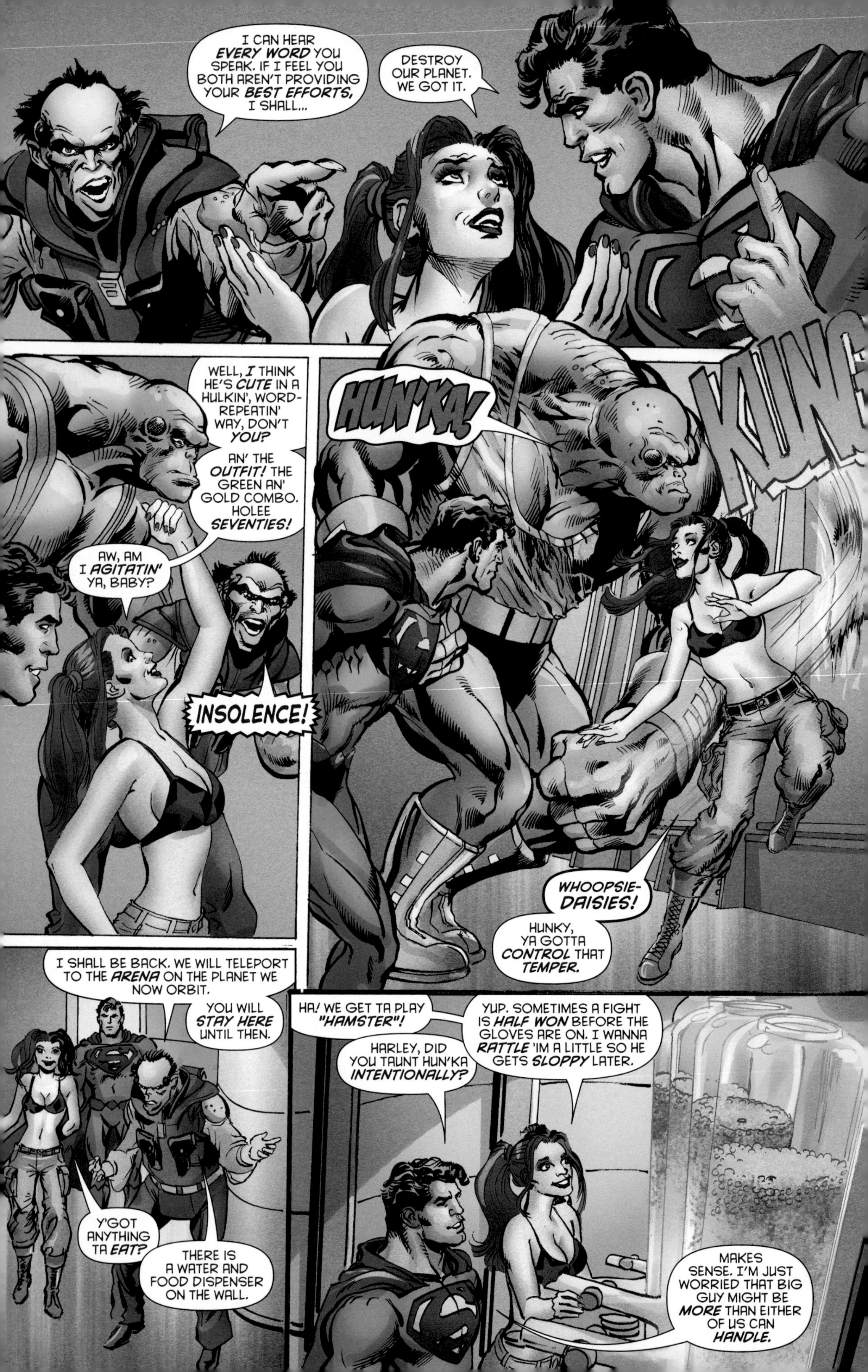
I CAN HEAR EVERY WORD YOU SPEAK. IF I FEEL YOU BOTH AREN'T PROVIDING YOUR BEST EFFORTS, I SHALL...
DESTROY OUR PLANET. WE GOT IT.
WELL, I THINK HE'S CUTE IN A HULKIN', WORD-REPEATIN' WAY, DON'T YOU?
AN' THE OUTFIT! THE GREEN AN' GOLD COMBO. HOLEE SEVENTIES!
AW, AM I AGITATIN' YA, BABY?
INSOLENCE!
HUN'KA!
KLUNG
WHOOPSIE-DAISIES!
HUNKY, YA GOTTA CONTROL THAT TEMPER.
I SHALL BE BACK. WE WILL TELEPORT TO THE ARENA ON THE PLANET WE NOW ORBIT.
YOU WILL STAY HERE UNTIL THEN.
Y'GOT ANYTHING TA EAT?
THERE IS A WATER AND FOOD DISPENSER ON THE WALL.
HA! WE GET TA PLAY "HAMSTER"!
HARLEY, DID YOU TAUNT HUN'KA INTENTIONALLY?
YUP. SOMETIMES A FIGHT IS HALF WON BEFORE THE GLOVES ARE ON. I WANNA RATTLE 'IM A LITTLE SO HE GETS SLOPPY LATER.
MAKES SENSE. I'M JUST WORRIED THAT BIG GUY MIGHT BE MORE THAN EITHER OF US CAN HANDLE.

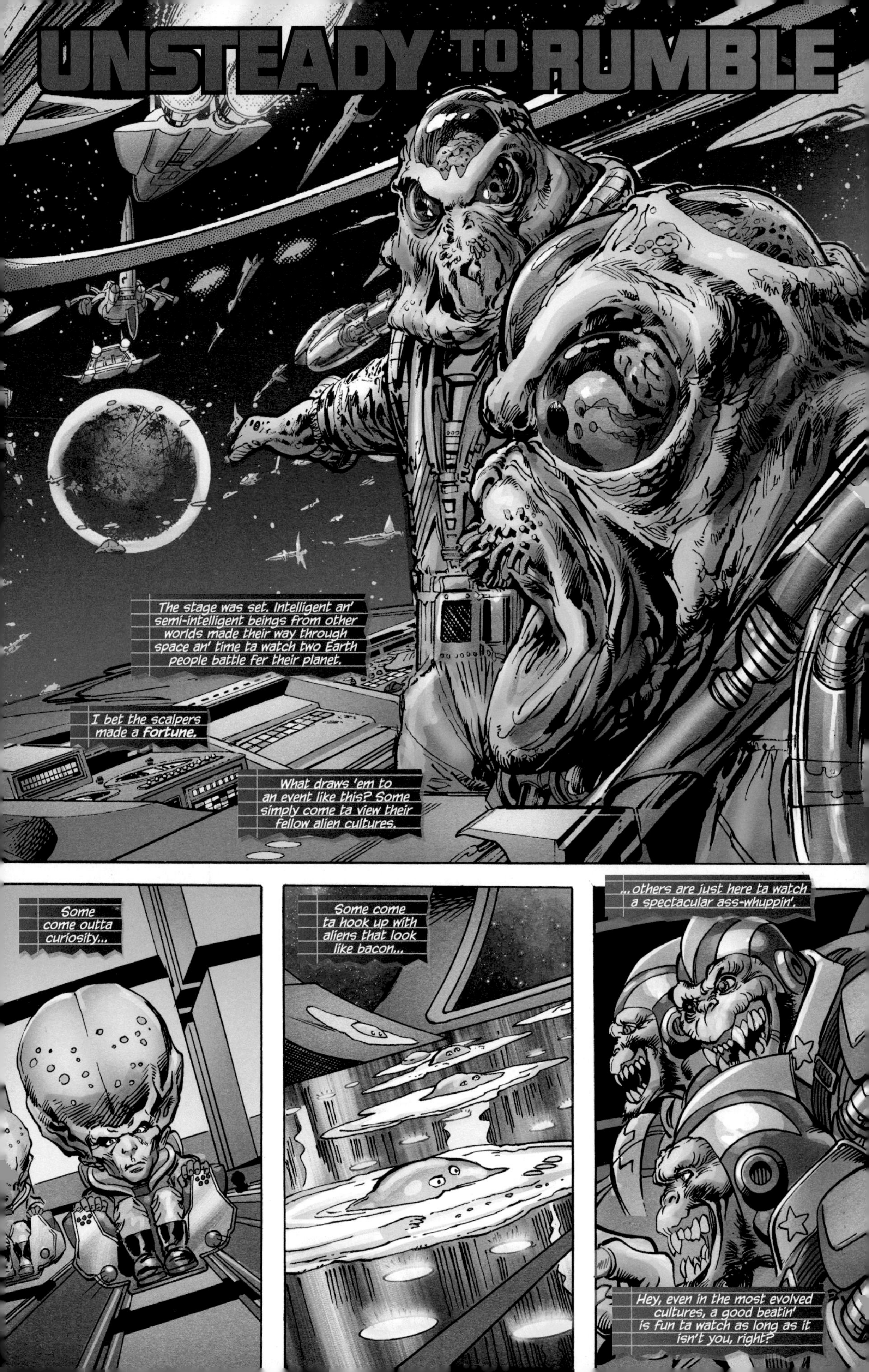
UNSTEADY TO RUMBLE
The stage was set. Intelligent an' semi-intelligent beings from other worlds made their way through space an' time ta watch two Earth people battle fer their planet.
I bet the scalpers made a fortune.
What draws 'em to an event like this? Some simply come ta view their fellow alien cultures.
Some come outta curiosity...
Some come ta hook up with aliens that look like bacon...
...others are just here ta watch a spectacular ass-whuppin'.
Hey, even in the most evolved cultures, a good beatin' is fun ta watch as long as it isn't you, right?

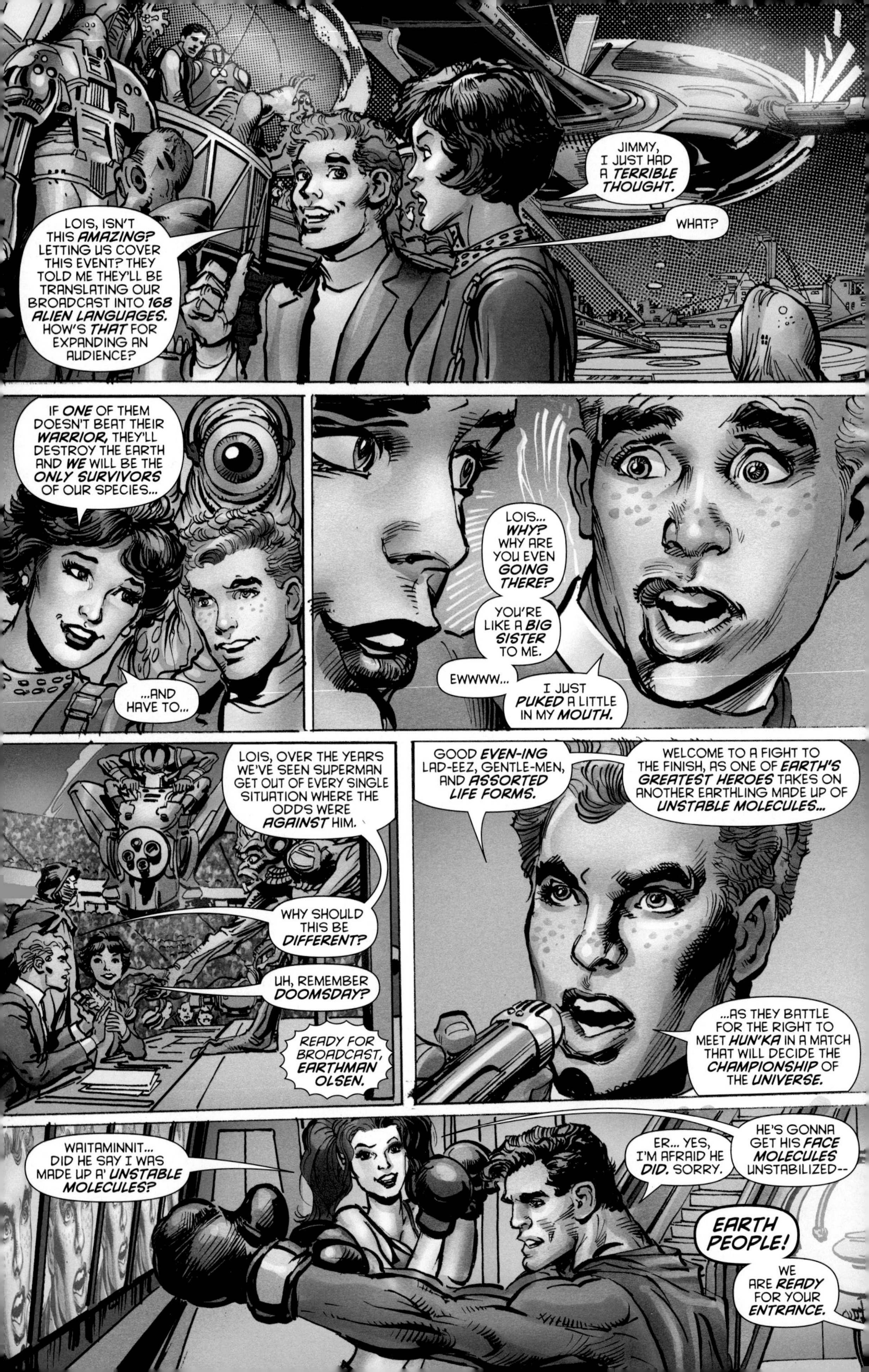
JIMMY, I JUST HAD A TERRIBLE THOUGHT.
LOIS, ISN'T THIS AMAZING? LETTING US COVER THIS EVENT? THEY TOLD ME THEY'LL BE TRANSLATING OUR BROADCAST INTO 168 ALIEN LANGUAGES. HOW'S THAT FOR EXPANDING AN AUDIENCE?
WHAT?
IF ONE OF THEM DOESN'T BEAT THEIR WARRIOR, THEY'LL DESTROY THE EARTH AND WE WILL BE THE ONLY SURVIVORS OF OUR SPECIES...
...AND HAVE TO...
LOIS... WHY? WHY ARE YOU EVEN GOING THERE?
YOU'RE LIKE A BIG SISTER TO ME.
EWWWW...
I JUST PUKED A LITTLE IN MY MOUTH.
LOIS, OVER THE YEARS WE'VE SEEN SUPERMAN GET OUT OF EVERY SINGLE SITUATION WHERE THE ODDS WERE AGAINST HIM.
WHY SHOULD THIS BE DIFFERENT?
UH, REMEMBER DOOMSDAY?
READY FOR BROADCAST, EARTHMAN OLSEN.
GOOD EVEN-ING LAD-EEZ, GENTLE-MEN, AND ASSORTED LIFE FORMS.
WELCOME TO A FIGHT TO THE FINISH, AS ONE OF EARTH'S GREATEST HEROES TAKES ON ANOTHER EARTHLING MADE UP OF UNSTABLE MOLECULES...
...AS THEY BATTLE FOR THE RIGHT TO MEET HUN'KA IN A MATCH THAT WILL DECIDE THE CHAMPIONSHIP OF THE UNIVERSE.
WAITAMINNIT... DID HE SAY I WAS MADE UP A' UNSTABLE MOLECULES?
ER... YES, I'M AFRAID HE DID. SORRY.
HE'S GONNA GET HIS FACE MOLECULES UNSTABILIZED--
EARTH PEOPLE!
WE ARE READY FOR YOUR ENTRANCE.

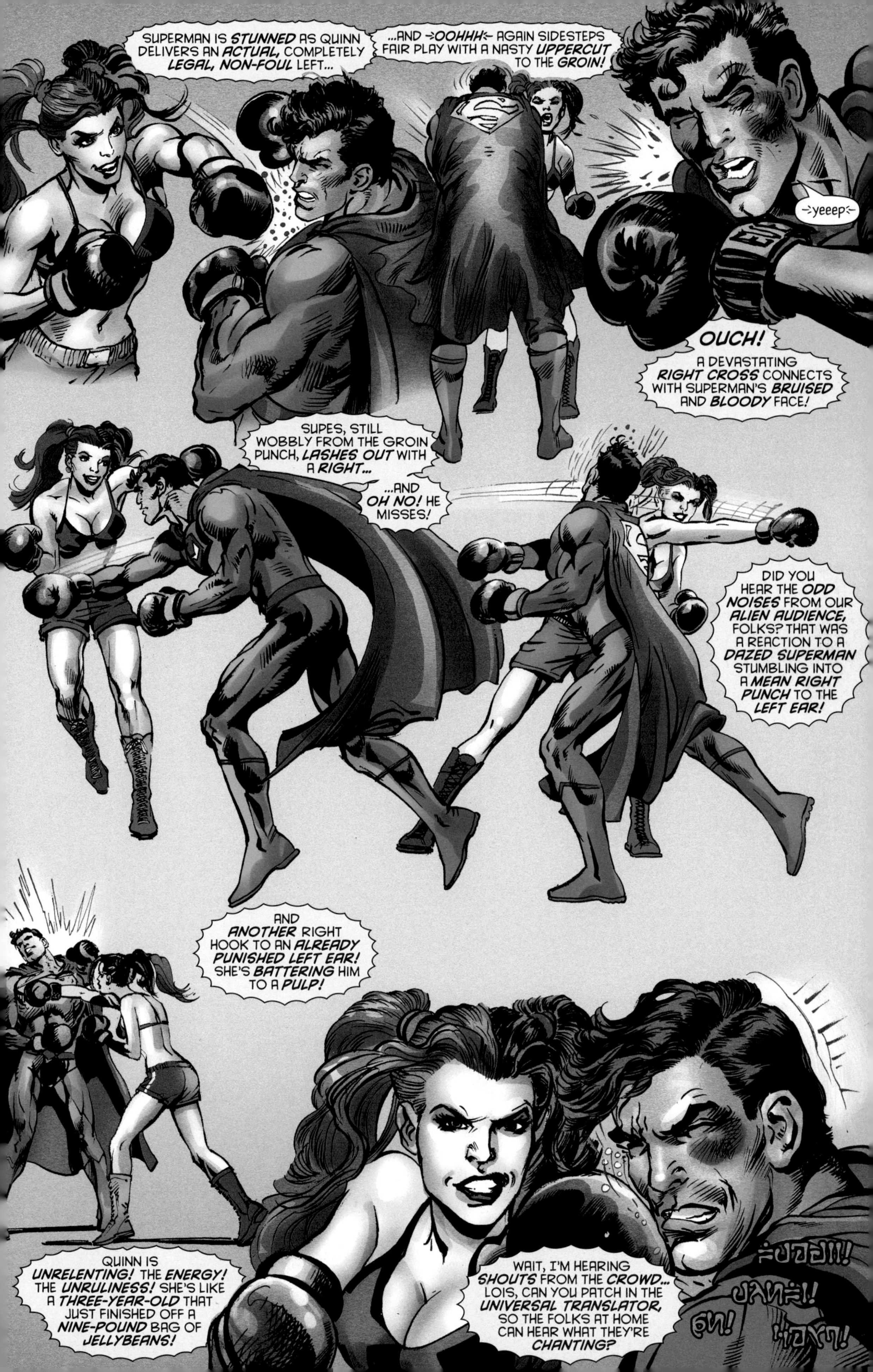
SUPERMAN IS STUNNED AS QUINN DELIVERS AN ACTUAL, COMPLETELY LEGAL, NON-FOUL LEFT...
...AND -OOHHH- AGAIN SIDESTEPS FAIR PLAY WITH A NASTY UPPERCUT TO THE GROIN!
-yeeep-
OUCH!
A DEVASTATING RIGHT CROSS CONNECTS WITH SUPERMAN'S BRUISED AND BLOODY FACE!
SUPES, STILL WOBBLY FROM THE GROIN PUNCH, LASHES OUT WITH A RIGHT...
...AND OH NO! HE MISSES!
DID YOU HEAR THE ODD NOISES FROM OUR ALIEN AUDIENCE, FOLKS? THAT WAS A REACTION TO A DAZED SUPERMAN STUMBLING INTO A MEAN RIGHT PUNCH TO THE LEFT EAR!
AND ANOTHER RIGHT HOOK TO AN ALREADY PUNISHED LEFT EAR! SHE'S BATTERING HIM TO A PULP!
QUINN IS UNRELENTING! THE ENERGY! THE UNRULINESS! SHE'S LIKE A THREE-YEAR-OLD THAT JUST FINISHED OFF A NINE-POUND BAG OF JELLYBEANS!
WAIT, I'M HEARING SHOUTS FROM THE CROWD... LOIS, CAN YOU PATCH IN THE UNIVERSAL TRANSLATOR, SO THE FOLKS AT HOME CAN HEAR WHAT THEY'RE CHANTING?

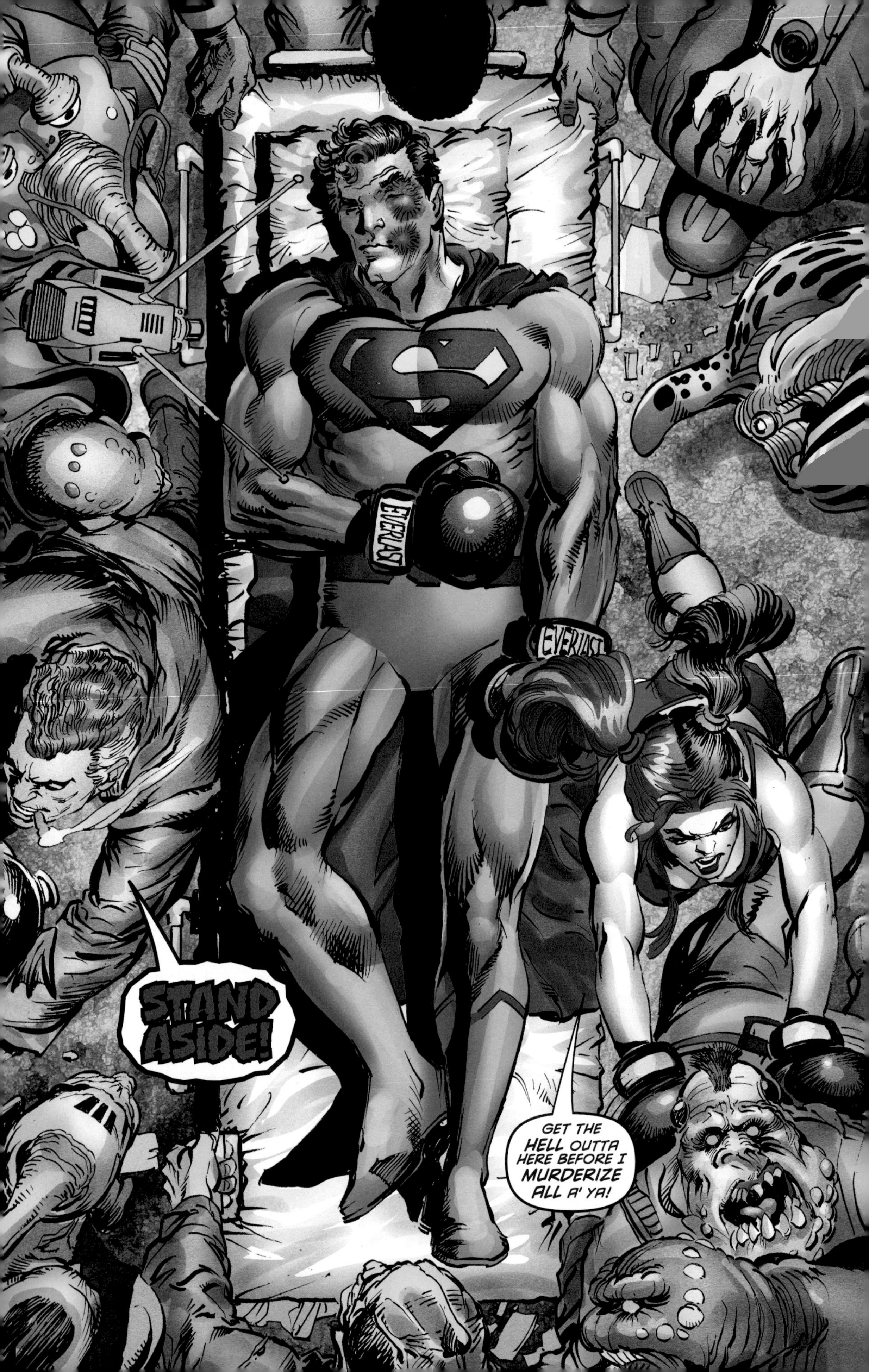
EVERLAST
EVERLAST
STAND ASIDE!
GET THE HELL OUTTA HERE BEFORE I MURDERIZE ALL A' YA!

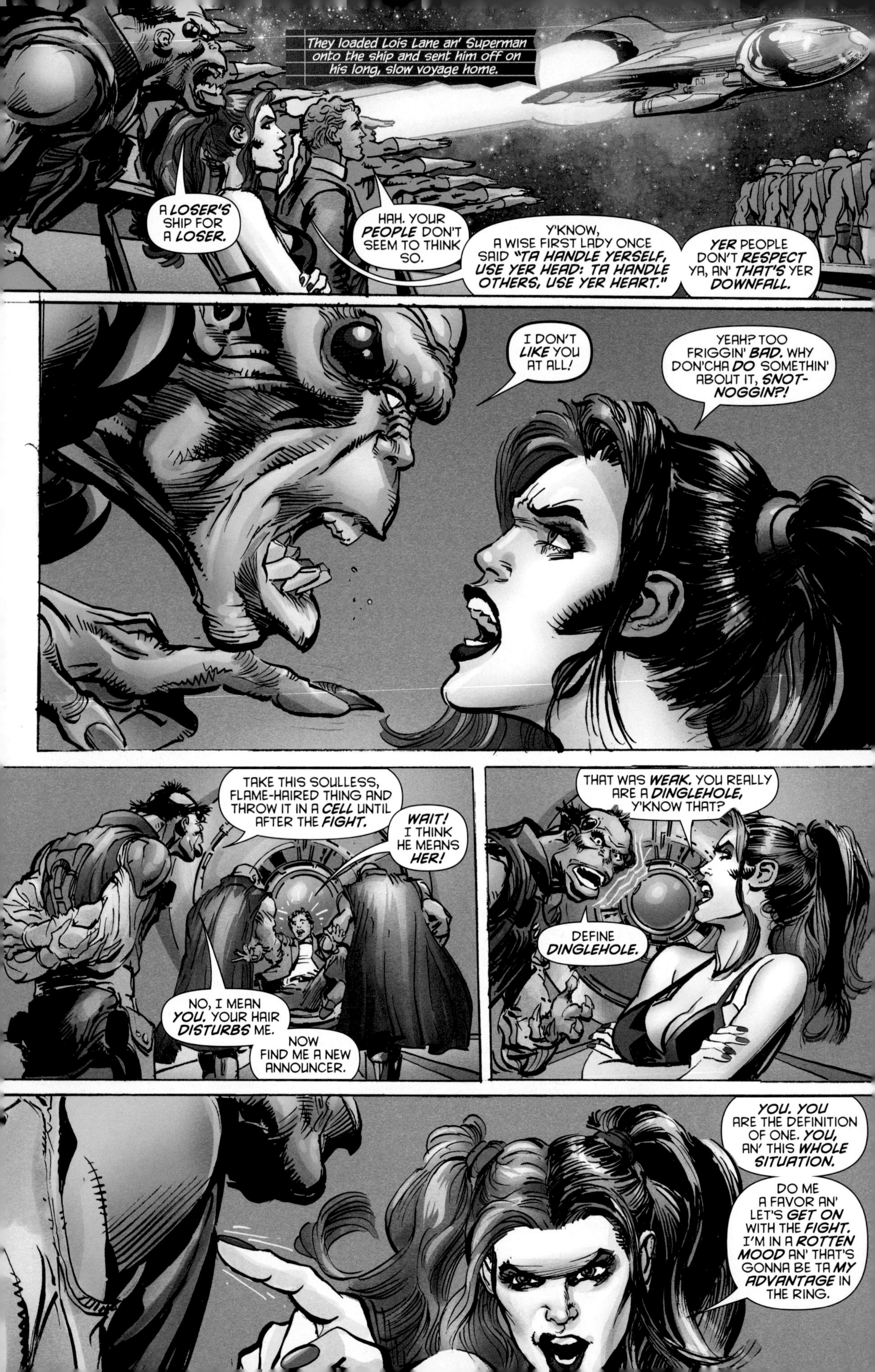
They loaded Lois Lane an' Superman onto the ship and sent him off on his long, slow voyage home.
A LOSER'S SHIP FOR A LOSER.
HAH. YOUR PEOPLE DON'T SEEM TO THINK SO.
Y'KNOW, A WISE FIRST LADY ONCE SAID "TA HANDLE YERSELF, USE YER HEAD: TA HANDLE OTHERS, USE YER HEART."
YER PEOPLE DON'T RESPECT YA, AN' THAT'S YER DOWNFALL.
I DON'T LIKE YOU AT ALL!
YEAH? TOO FRIGGIN' BAD. WHY DON'CHA DO SOMETHIN' ABOUT IT, SNOT-NOGGIN?!
TAKE THIS SOULLESS, FLAME-HAIRED THING AND THROW IT IN A CELL UNTIL AFTER THE FIGHT.
WAIT! I THINK HE MEANS HER!
NO, I MEAN YOU. YOUR HAIR DISTURBS ME.
NOW FIND ME A NEW ANNOUNCER.
THAT WAS WEAK. YOU REALLY ARE A DINGLEHOLE, Y'KNOW THAT?
DEFINE DINGLEHOLE.
YOU. YOU ARE THE DEFINITION OF ONE. YOU, AN' THIS WHOLE SITUATION.
DO ME A FAVOR AN' LET'S GET ON WITH THE FIGHT. I'M IN A ROTTEN MOOD AN' THAT'S GONNA BE TA MY ADVANTAGE IN THE RING.

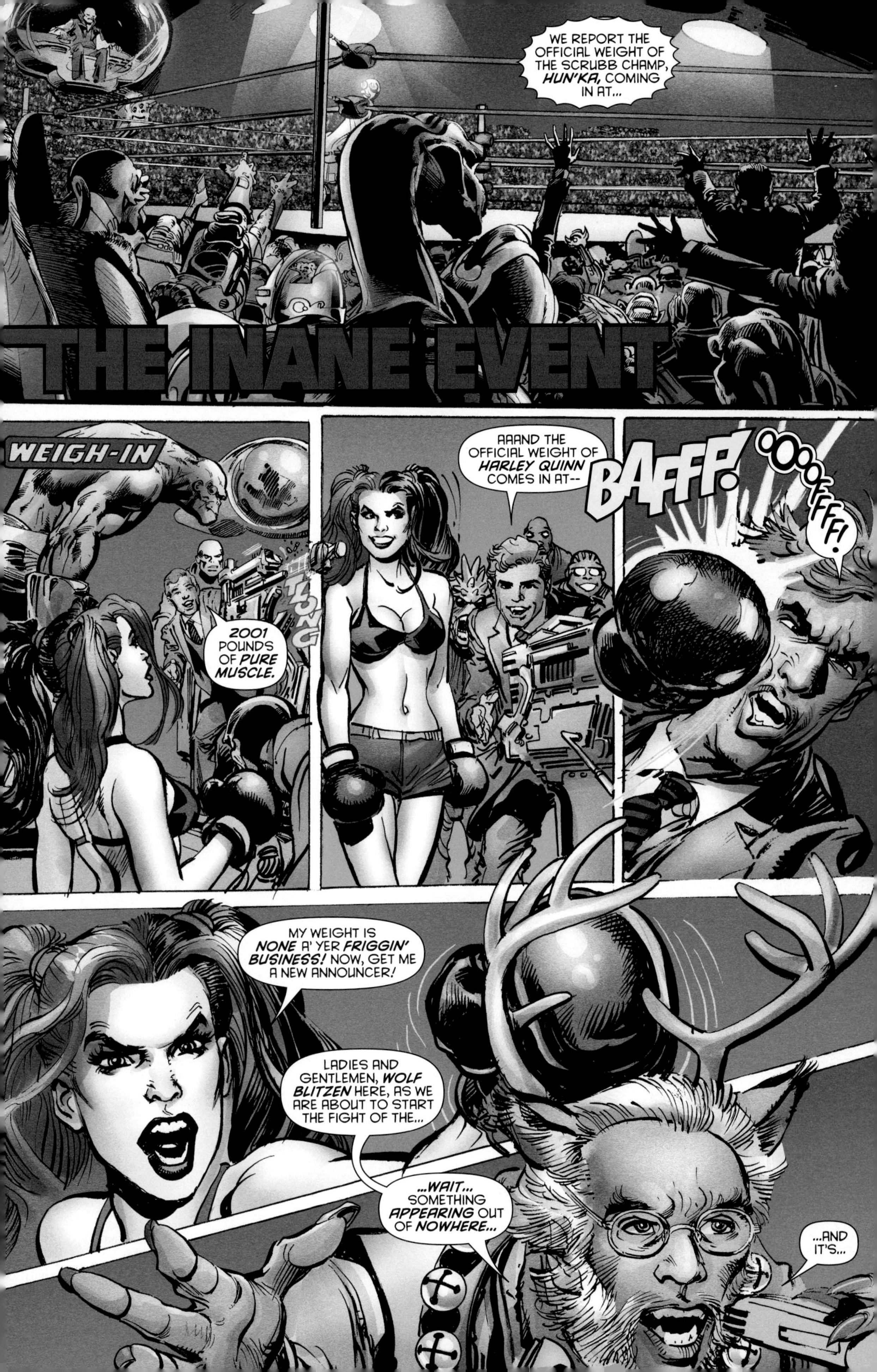
WE REPORT THE OFFICIAL WEIGHT OF THE SCRUBB CHAMP, HUN'KA, COMING IN AT...
THE INANE EVENT
WEIGH-IN
TLONG
2001 POUNDS OF PURE MUSCLE.
AAAND THE OFFICIAL WEIGHT OF HARLEY QUINN COMES IN AT--
BAFFP!
OOOOFFFF!
MY WEIGHT IS NONE A' YER FRIGGIN' BUSINESS! NOW, GET ME A NEW ANNOUNCER!
LADIES AND GENTLEMEN, WOLF BLITZEN HERE, AS WE ARE ABOUT TO START THE FIGHT OF THE...
...WAIT... SOMETHING APPEARING OUT OF NOWHERE...
...AND IT'S...

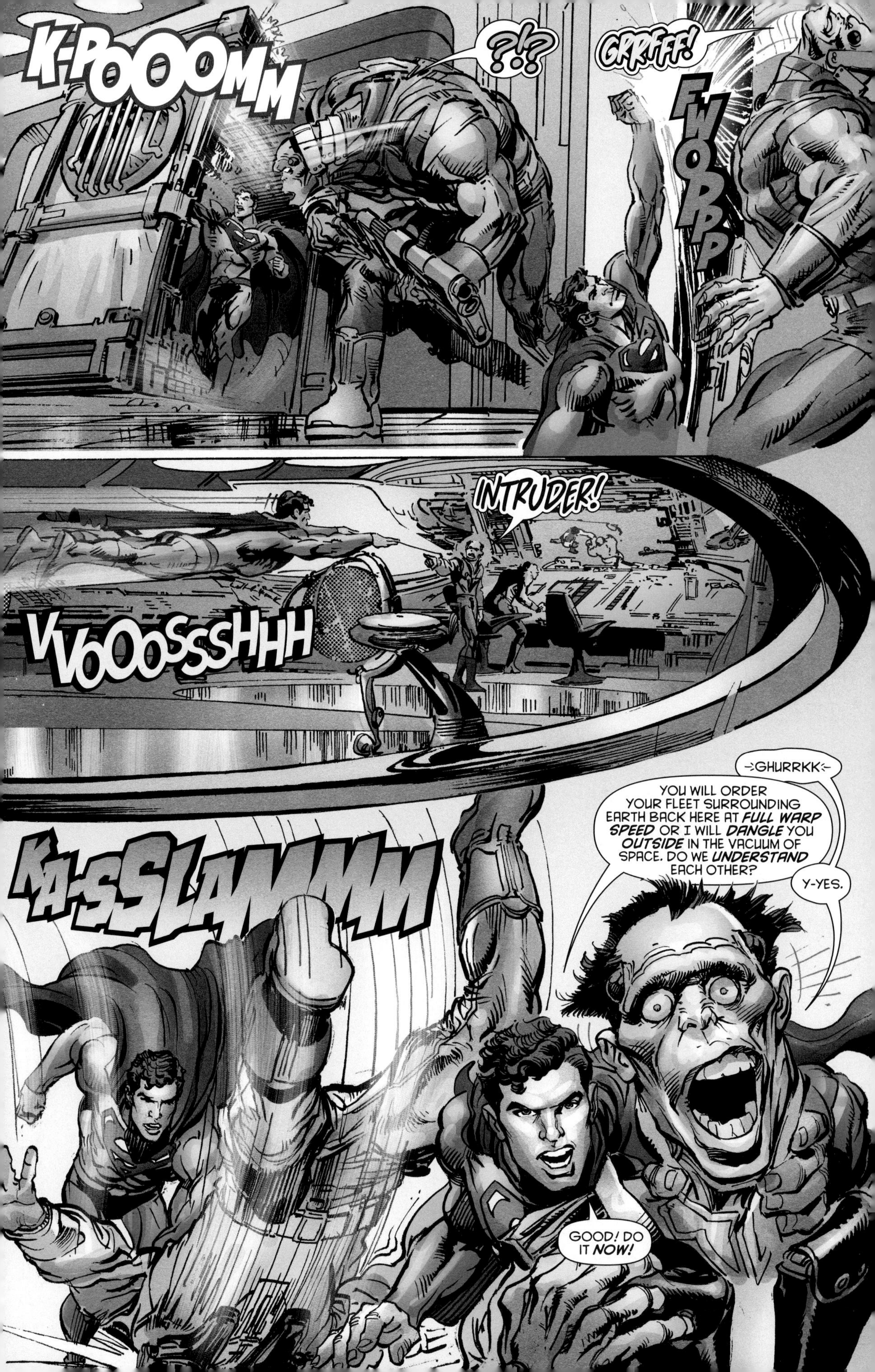
K-POOOOMMM
?!?
GRRFFF!
FWOPPP
INTRUDER!
VVOOOSSSHHH
KA-SSLAMMMM
-GHURRKK-
YOU WILL ORDER YOUR FLEET SURROUNDING EARTH BACK HERE AT *FULL WARP SPEED* OR I WILL *DANGLE* YOU *OUTSIDE* IN THE VACUUM OF SPACE. DO WE *UNDERSTAND* EACH OTHER?
Y-YES.
GOOD! DO IT *NOW!*

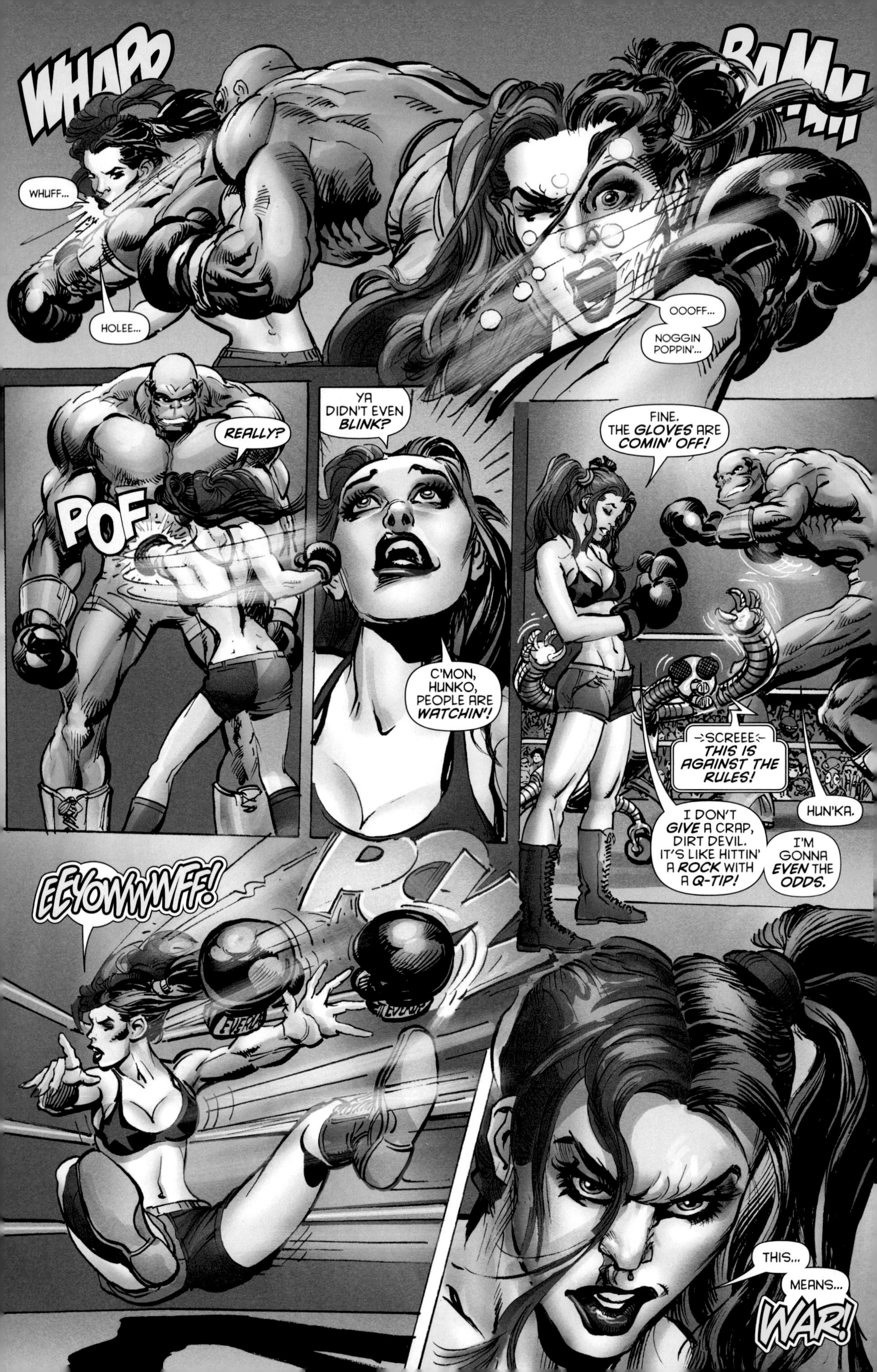
WHAPP
WHUFF...
HOLEE...
BAMM
OOOFF...
NOGGIN POPPIN'...
REALLY?
POF
YA DIDN'T EVEN BLINK?
C'MON, HUNKO, PEOPLE ARE WATCHIN'!
FINE. THE GLOVES ARE COMIN' OFF!
SCREEE THIS IS AGAINST THE RULES!
I DON'T GIVE A CRAP, DIRT DEVIL. IT'S LIKE HITTIN' A ROCK WITH A Q-TIP!
HUN'KA.
I'M GONNA EVEN THE ODDS.
EEYOWWWFF!
THIS...
MEANS...
WAR!

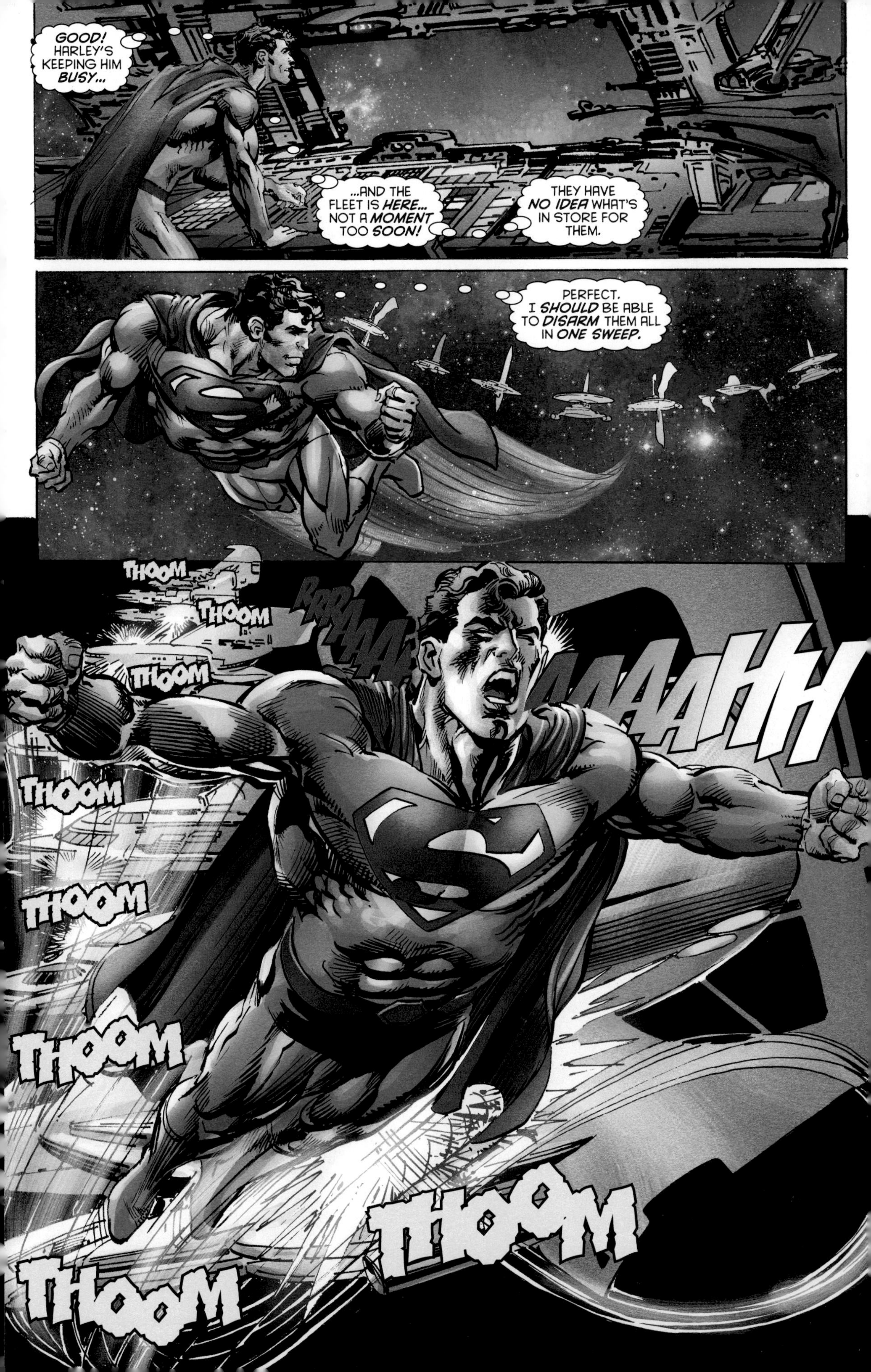
GOOD! HARLEY'S KEEPING HIM BUSY...
...AND THE FLEET IS HERE... NOT A MOMENT TOO SOON!
THEY HAVE NO IDEA WHAT'S IN STORE FOR THEM.
PERFECT. I SHOULD BE ABLE TO DISARM THEM ALL IN ONE SWEEP.
THOOM
THOOM
THOOM
RRRAAAAAAAAAHH
THOOM
THOOM
THOOM
THOOM
THOOM

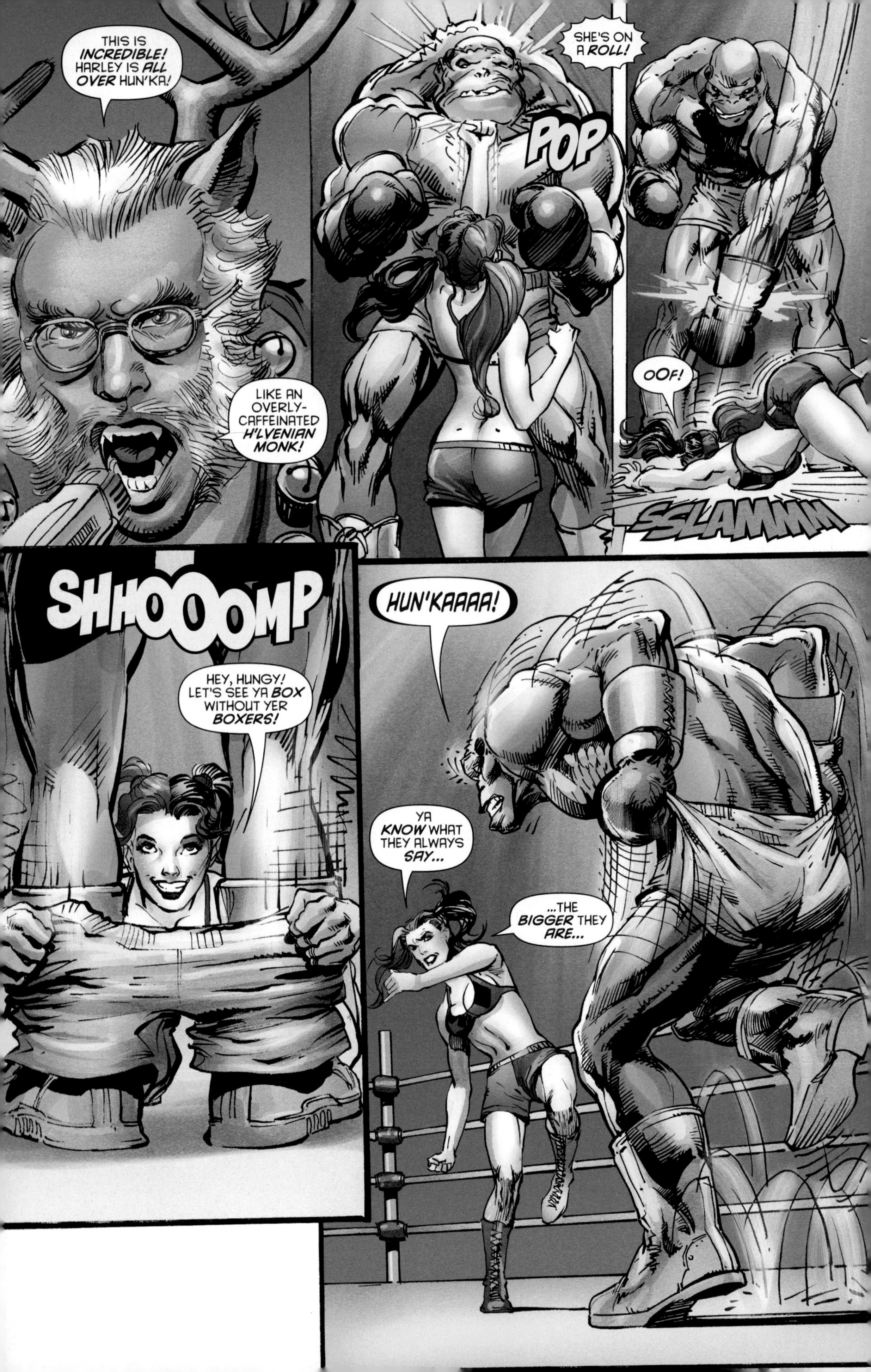
THIS IS INCREDIBLE! HARLEY IS ALL OVER HUN'KA!
LIKE AN OVERLY-CAFFEINATED H'LVENIAN MONK!
SHE'S ON A ROLL!
POP
OOF!
SSLAMMM
SHHOOOMP
HEY, HUNGY! LET'S SEE YA BOX WITHOUT YER BOXERS!
HUN'KAAAA!
YA KNOW WHAT THEY ALWAYS SAY...
...THE BIGGER THEY ARE...

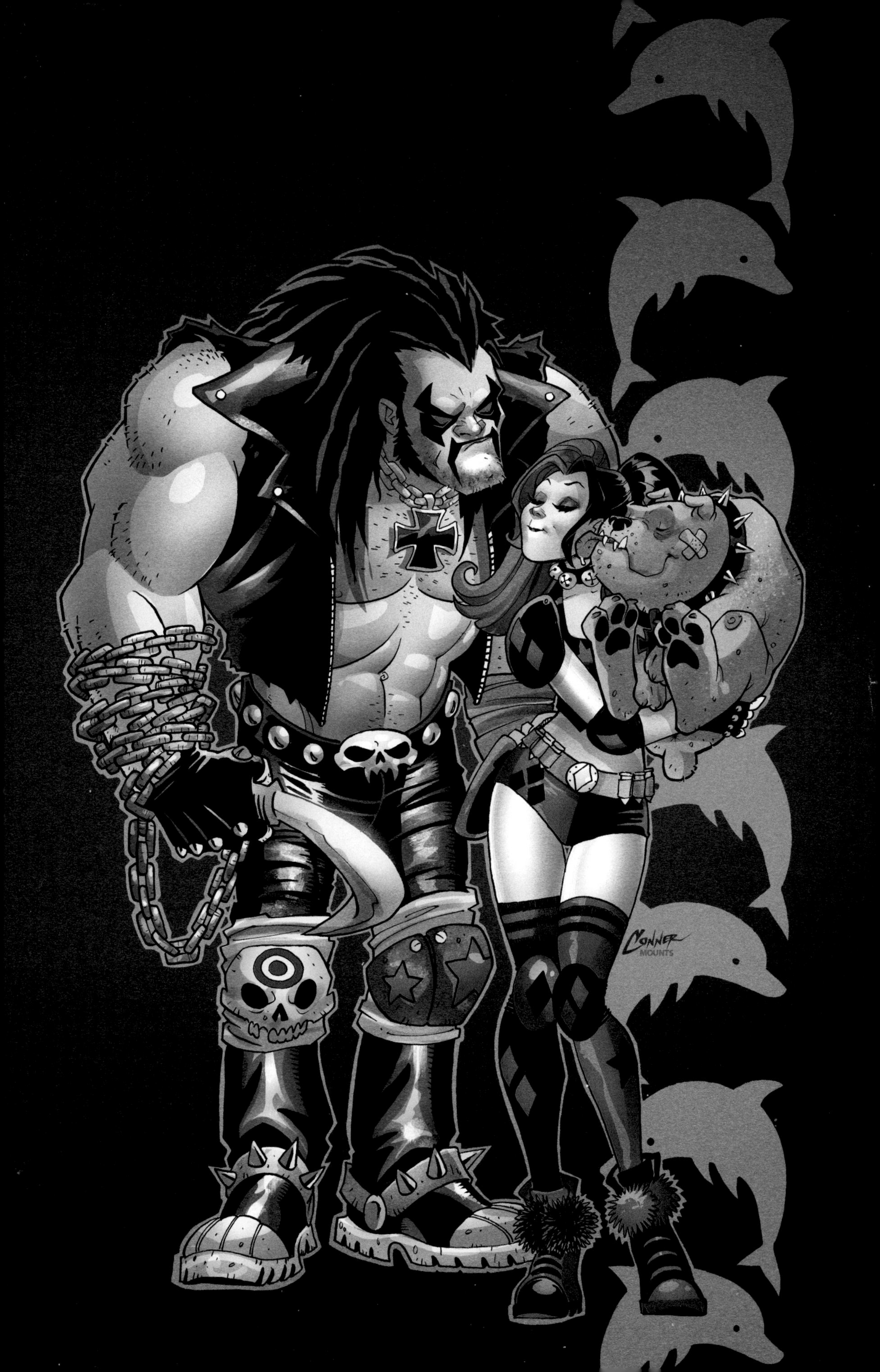
CONNER
MOUNTS

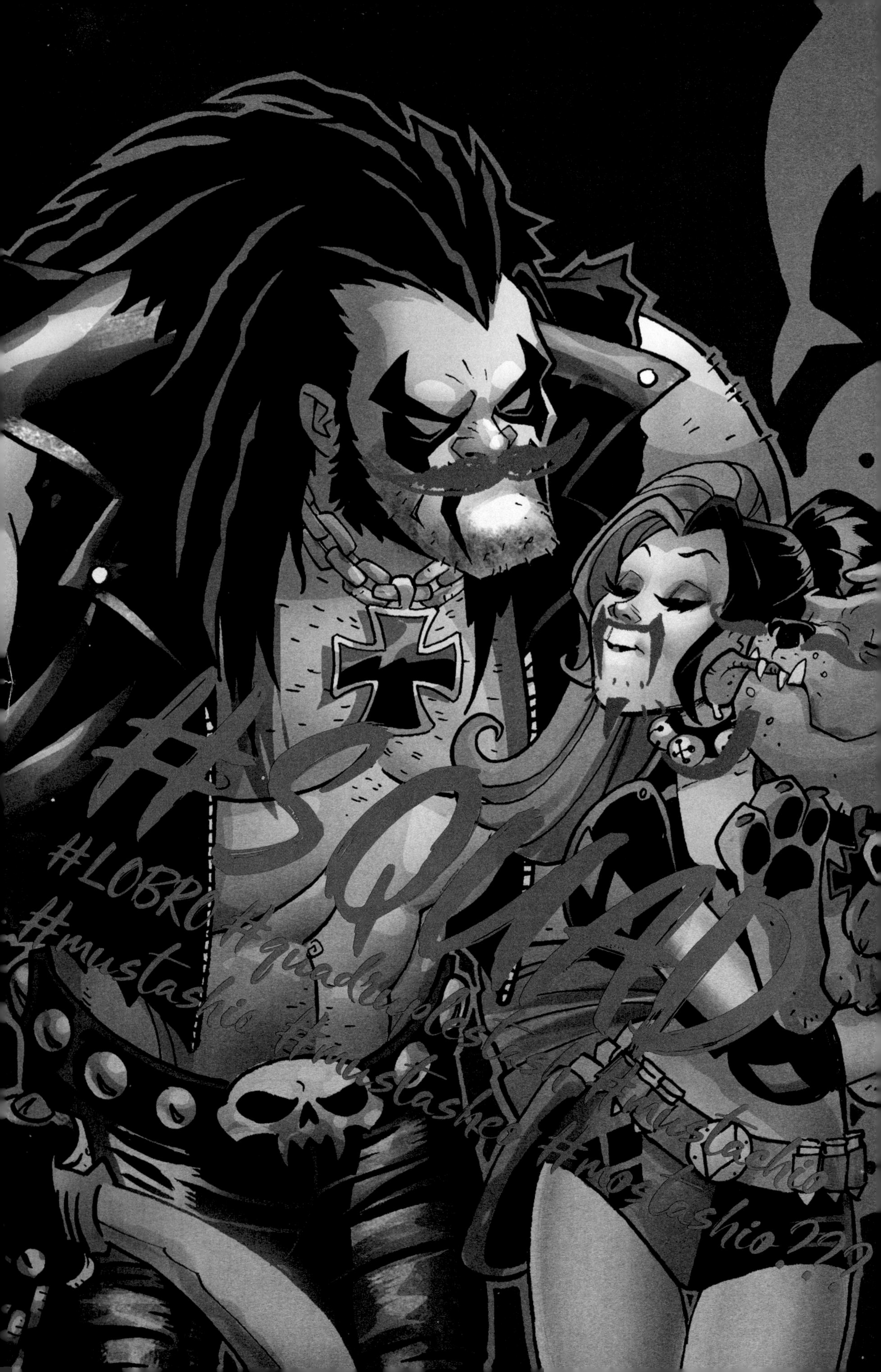
#SQUAD
#LOBRO #quadrupleslash
#mustashio #mustashed #mustachio #mostashio???

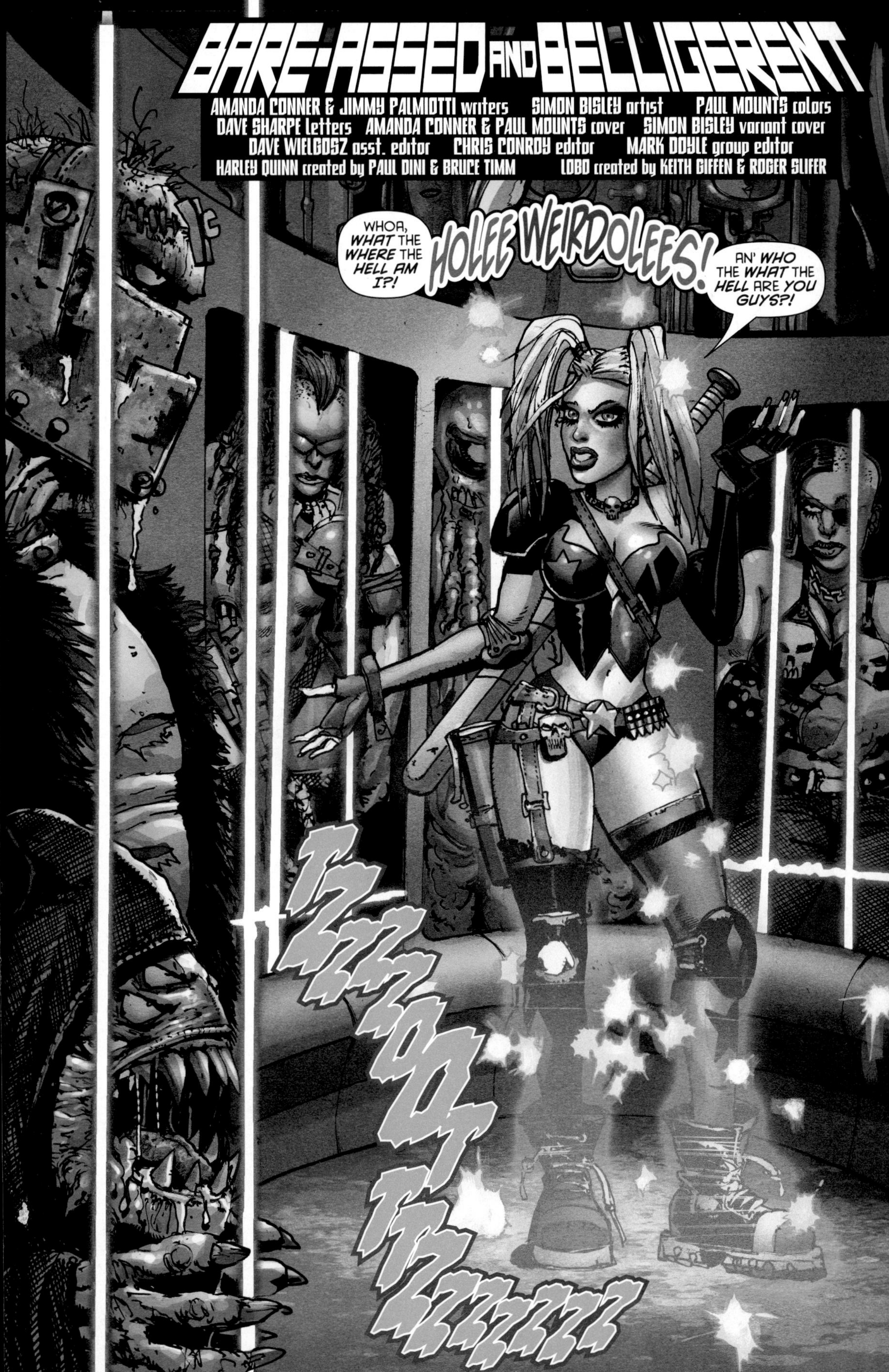
BARE-ASSED AND BELLIGERENT
AMANDA CONNER & JIMMY PALMIOTTI writers SIMON BISLEY artist PAUL MOUNTS colors
DAVE SHARPE letters AMANDA CONNER & PAUL MOUNTS cover SIMON BISLEY variant cover
DAVE WIELGOSZ asst. editor CHRIS CONROY editor MARK DOYLE group editor
HARLEY QUINN created by PAUL DINI & BRUCE TIMM LOBO created by KEITH GIFFEN & ROGER SLIFER
WHOA, WHAT THE WHERE THE HELL AM I?!
HOLEE WEIRDOLEES!
AN' WHO THE WHAT THE HELL ARE YOU GUYS?!
TZZZZOOOTTZZZZZZZZZZ

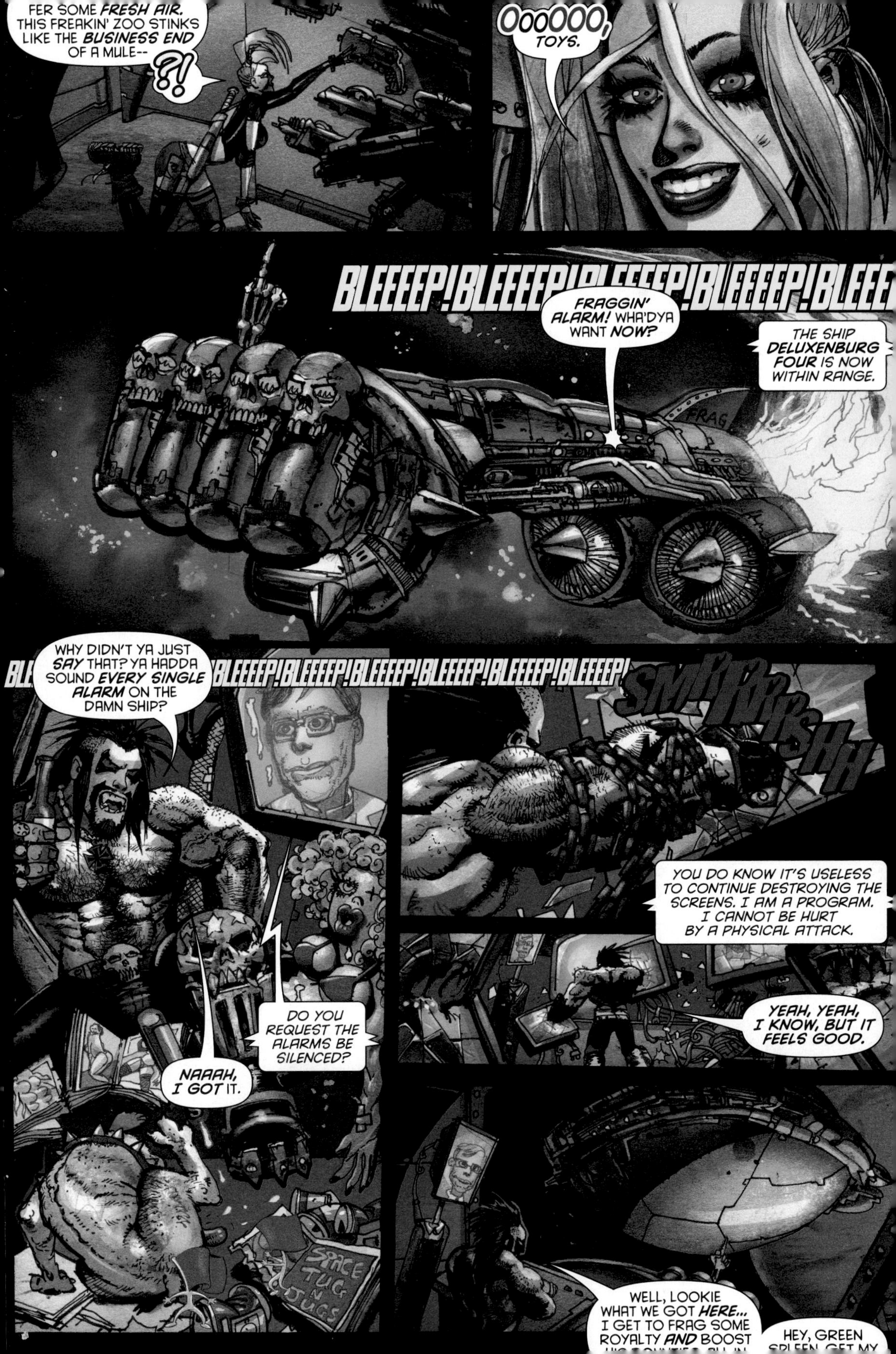
FER SOME FRESH AIR. THIS FREAKIN' ZOO STINKS LIKE THE BUSINESS END OF A MULE--
?!
OOOOOO, TOYS.
BLEEEEP! BLEEEEP! BLEEEEP! BLEEEEP! BLEEE
FRAGGIN' ALARM! WHA'DYA WANT NOW?
THE SHIP DELUXENBURG FOUR IS NOW WITHIN RANGE.
FRAG
BLEEEEP! BLEEEEP! BLEEEEP! BLEEEEP! BLEEEEP! BLEEEEP!
WHY DIDN'T YA JUST SAY THAT? YA HADDA SOUND EVERY SINGLE ALARM ON THE DAMN SHIP?
DO YOU REQUEST THE ALARMS BE SILENCED?
NAAAH, I GOT IT.
SPACE TUG N JUGS
SMKRRKRSHH
YOU DO KNOW IT'S USELESS TO CONTINUE DESTROYING THE SCREENS. I AM A PROGRAM. I CANNOT BE HURT BY A PHYSICAL ATTACK.
YEAH, YEAH, I KNOW, BUT IT FEELS GOOD.
WELL, LOOKIE WHAT WE GOT HERE... I GET TO FRAG SOME ROYALTY AND BOOST
HEY, GREEN

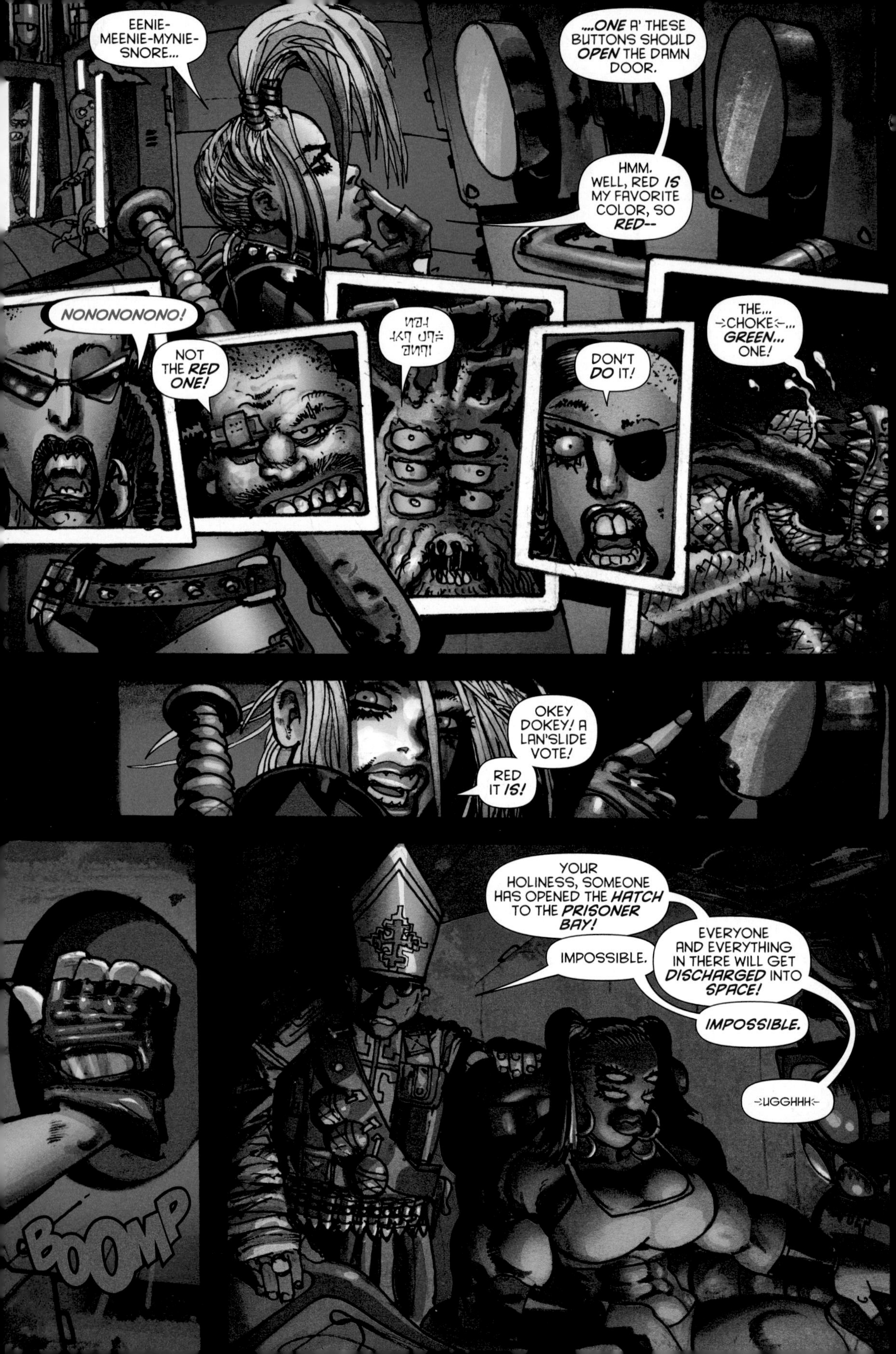
EENIE-MEENIE-MYNIE-SNORE...
...ONE A' THESE BUTTONS SHOULD OPEN THE DAMN DOOR.
HMM. WELL, RED IS MY FAVORITE COLOR, SO RED--
NONONONONO!
NOT THE RED ONE!
DON'T DO IT!
THE... -CHOKE-... GREEN... ONE!
OKEY DOKEY! A LAN'SLIDE VOTE!
RED IT IS!
BOOMP
YOUR HOLINESS, SOMEONE HAS OPENED THE HATCH TO THE PRISONER BAY!
IMPOSSIBLE.
EVERYONE AND EVERYTHING IN THERE WILL GET DISCHARGED INTO SPACE!
IMPOSSIBLE.
-UGGHHH-

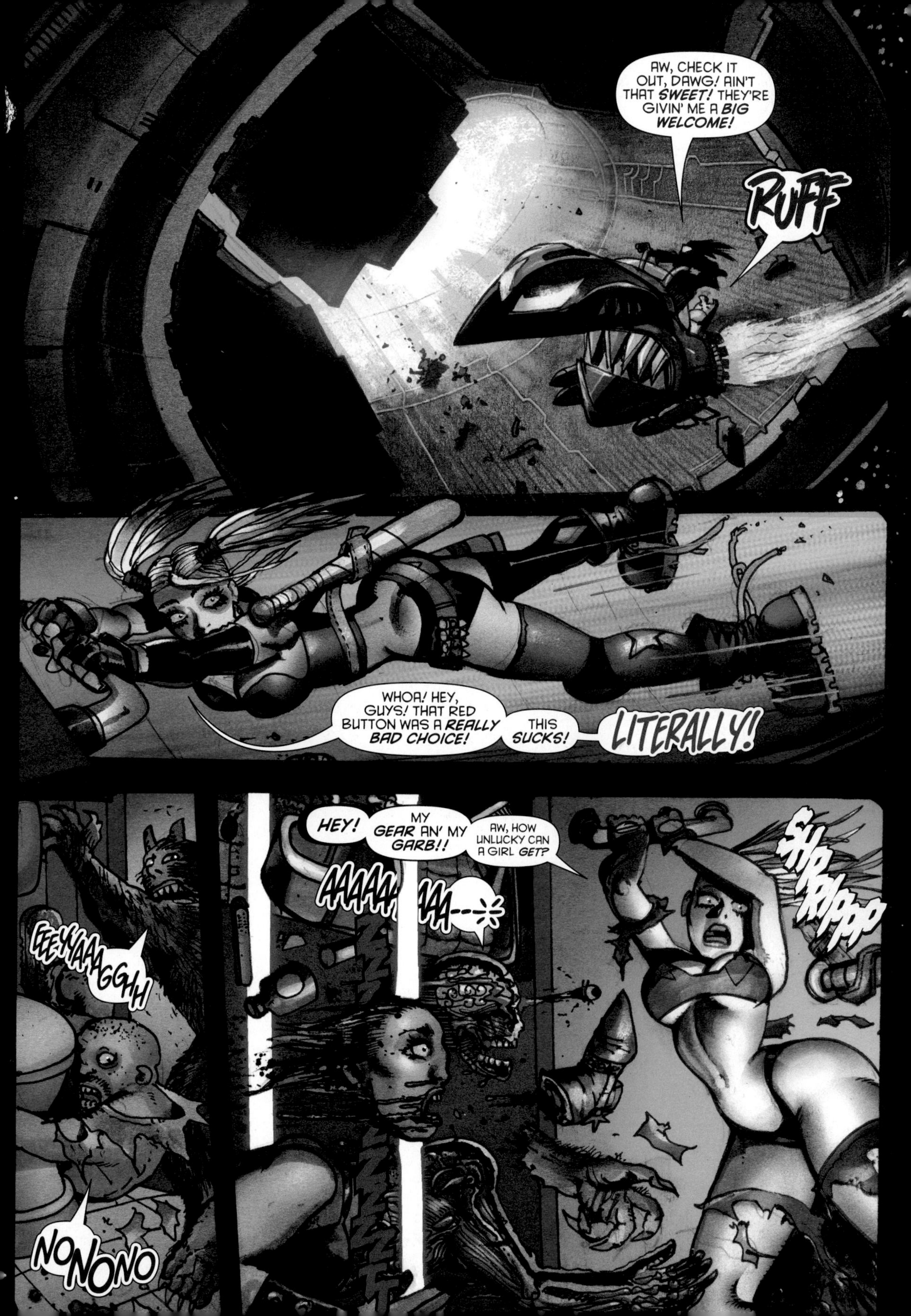

AW, CHECK IT OUT, DAWG! AIN'T THAT SWEET! THEY'RE GIVIN' ME A BIG WELCOME!
RUFF
WHOA! HEY, GUYS! THAT RED BUTTON WAS A REALLY BAD CHOICE!
THIS SUCKS!
LITERALLY!
EEEYAAAGGHH
NONONO
HEY!
MY GEAR AN' MY GARB!!
AW, HOW UNLUCKY CAN A GIRL GET?
SHRIPPP

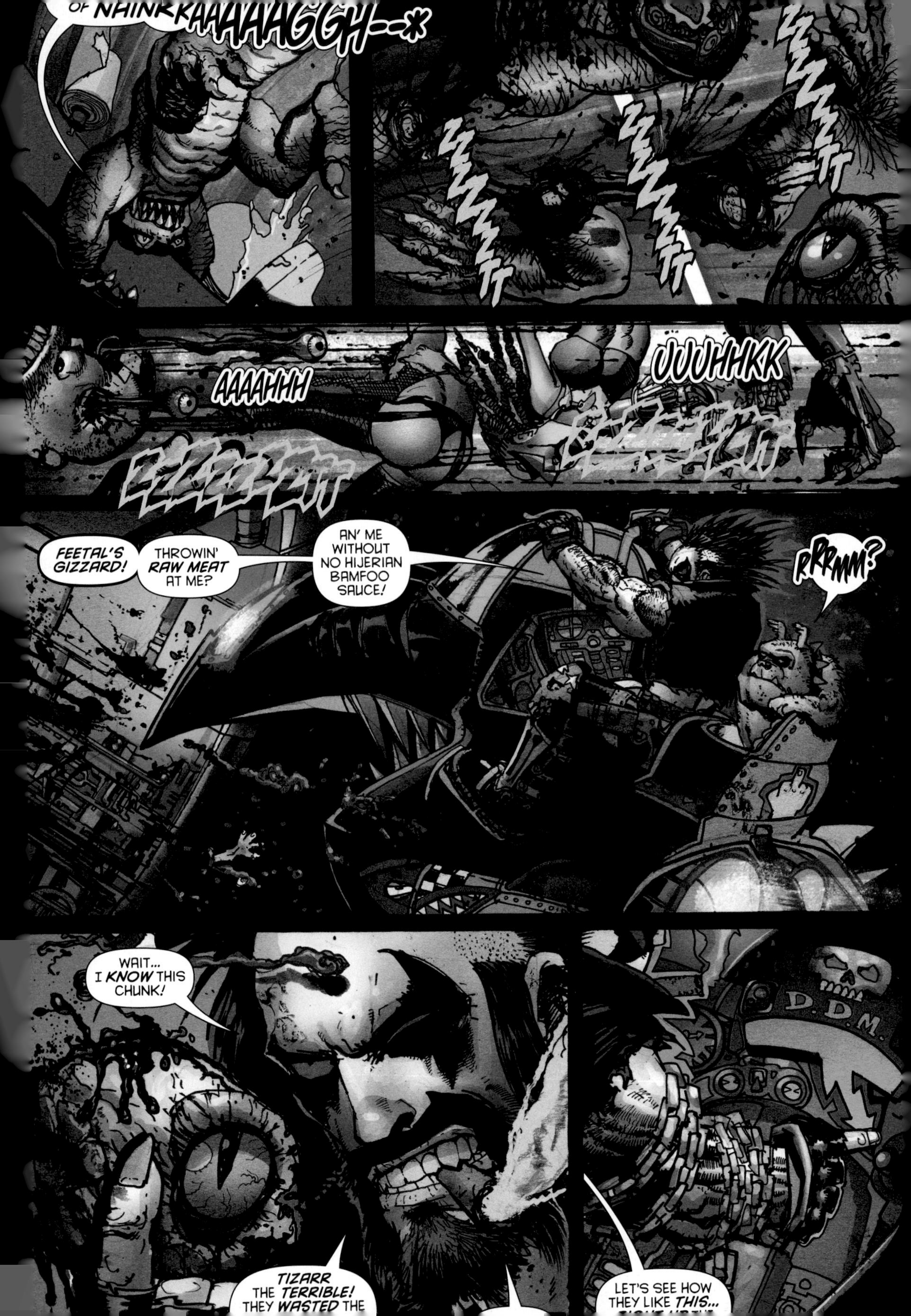
OF NHINKKAAAAAGGH--*
ZZZZZZZZTT
ZZZZZZZZTT
ZZZZZZZZTT
AAAAHHH
UUUHHKK
FEETAL'S GIZZARD!
THROWIN' RAW MEAT AT ME?
AN' ME WITHOUT NO HIJERIAN BAMFOO SAUCE!
RRRMM?
WAIT... I KNOW THIS CHUNK!
TIZARR THE TERRIBLE! THEY WASTED THE
D.D.M.
LET'S SEE HOW THEY LIKE THIS...

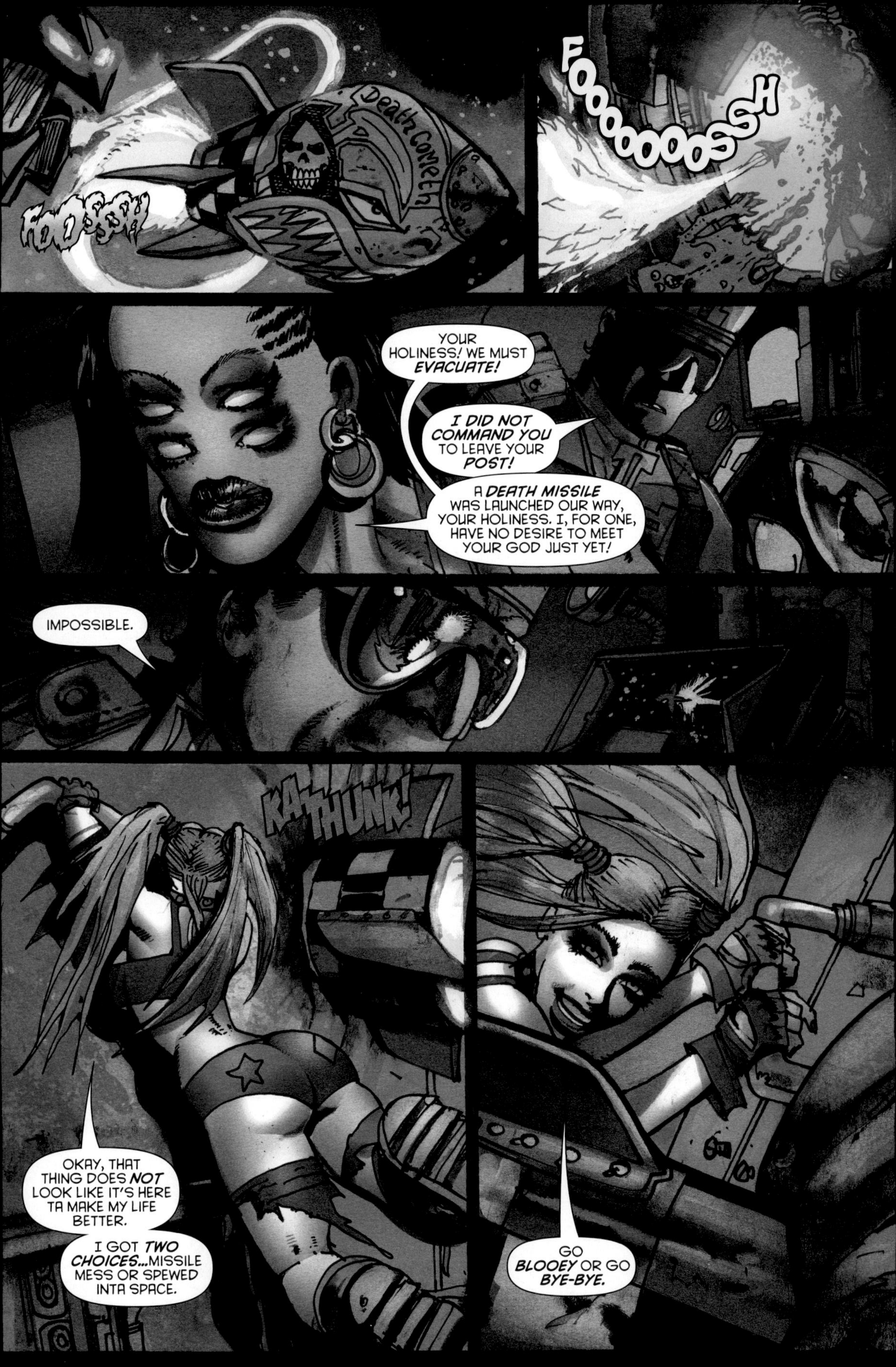
Death Cometh
FOOSSH
FOOOOOOOOSSH
YOUR HOLINESS! WE MUST EVACUATE!
I DID NOT COMMAND YOU TO LEAVE YOUR POST!
A DEATH MISSILE WAS LAUNCHED OUR WAY, YOUR HOLINESS. I, FOR ONE, HAVE NO DESIRE TO MEET YOUR GOD JUST YET!
IMPOSSIBLE.
KA-THUNK!
OKAY, THAT THING DOES NOT LOOK LIKE IT'S HERE TA MAKE MY LIFE BETTER.
I GOT TWO CHOICES...MISSILE MESS OR SPEWED INTA SPACE.
GO BLOOEY OR GO BYE-BYE.

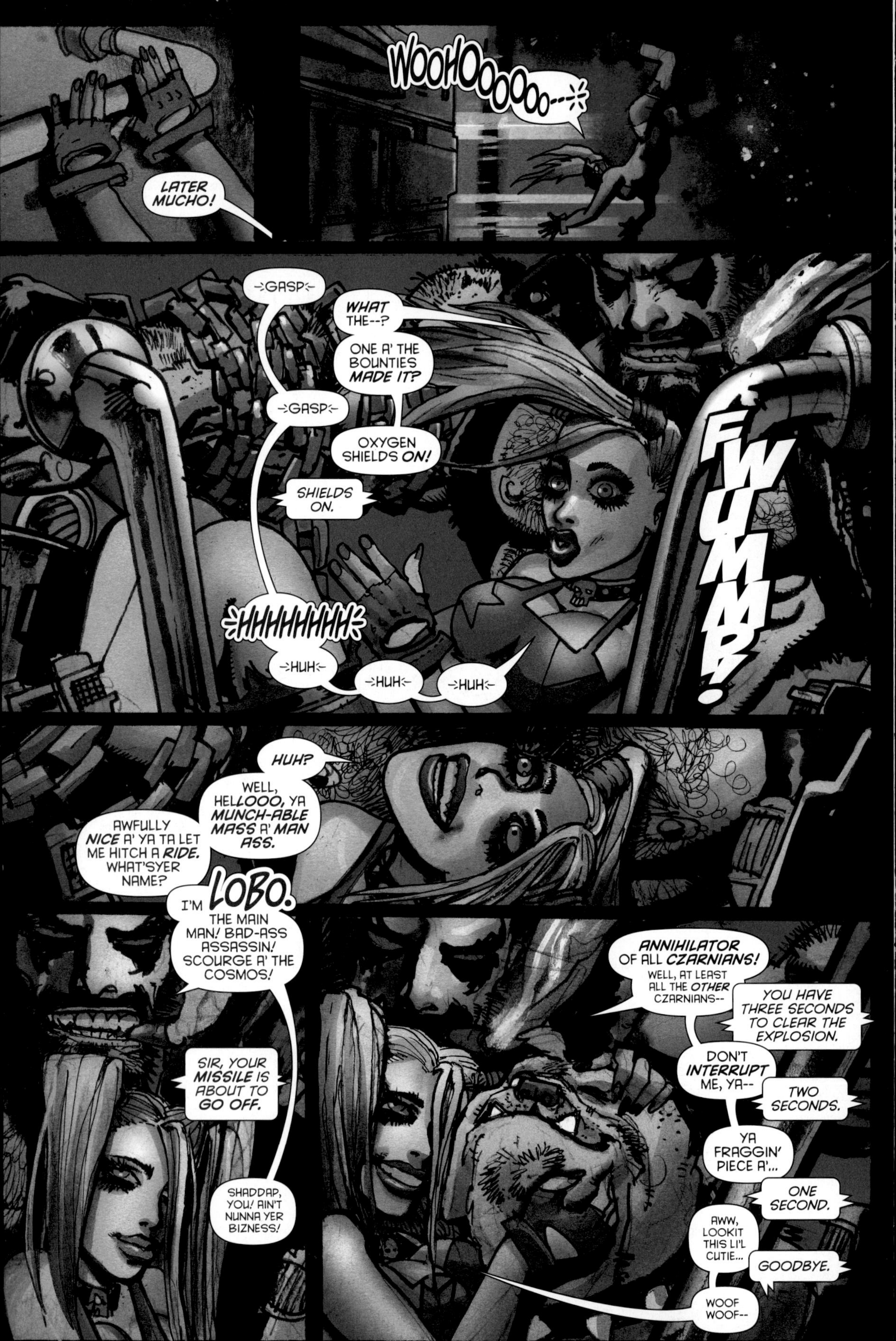
LATER MUCHO!
WOOHOOOOOO--!
-GASP-
WHAT THE--?
ONE A' THE BOUNTIES MADE IT?
-GASP-
OXYGEN SHIELDS ON!
SHIELDS ON.
HHHHHHHH
-HUH-
-HUH-
-HUH-
FWUMMB!
HUH?
WELL, HELLOOO, YA MUNCH-ABLE MASS A' MAN ASS.
AWFULLY NICE A' YA TA LET ME HITCH A RIDE. WHAT'SYER NAME?
I'M LOBO.
THE MAIN MAN! BAD-ASS ASSASSIN! SCOURGE A' THE COSMOS!
SIR, YOUR MISSILE IS ABOUT TO GO OFF.
SHADDAP, YOU! AIN'T NUNNA YER BIZNESS!
ANNIHILATOR OF ALL CZARNIANS!
WELL, AT LEAST ALL THE OTHER CZARNIANS--
YOU HAVE THREE SECONDS TO CLEAR THE EXPLOSION.
DON'T INTERRUPT ME, YA--
TWO SECONDS.
YA FRAGGIN' PIECE A'...
ONE SECOND.
AWW, LOOKIT THIS LI'L CUTIE...
GOODBYE.
WOOF WOOF--

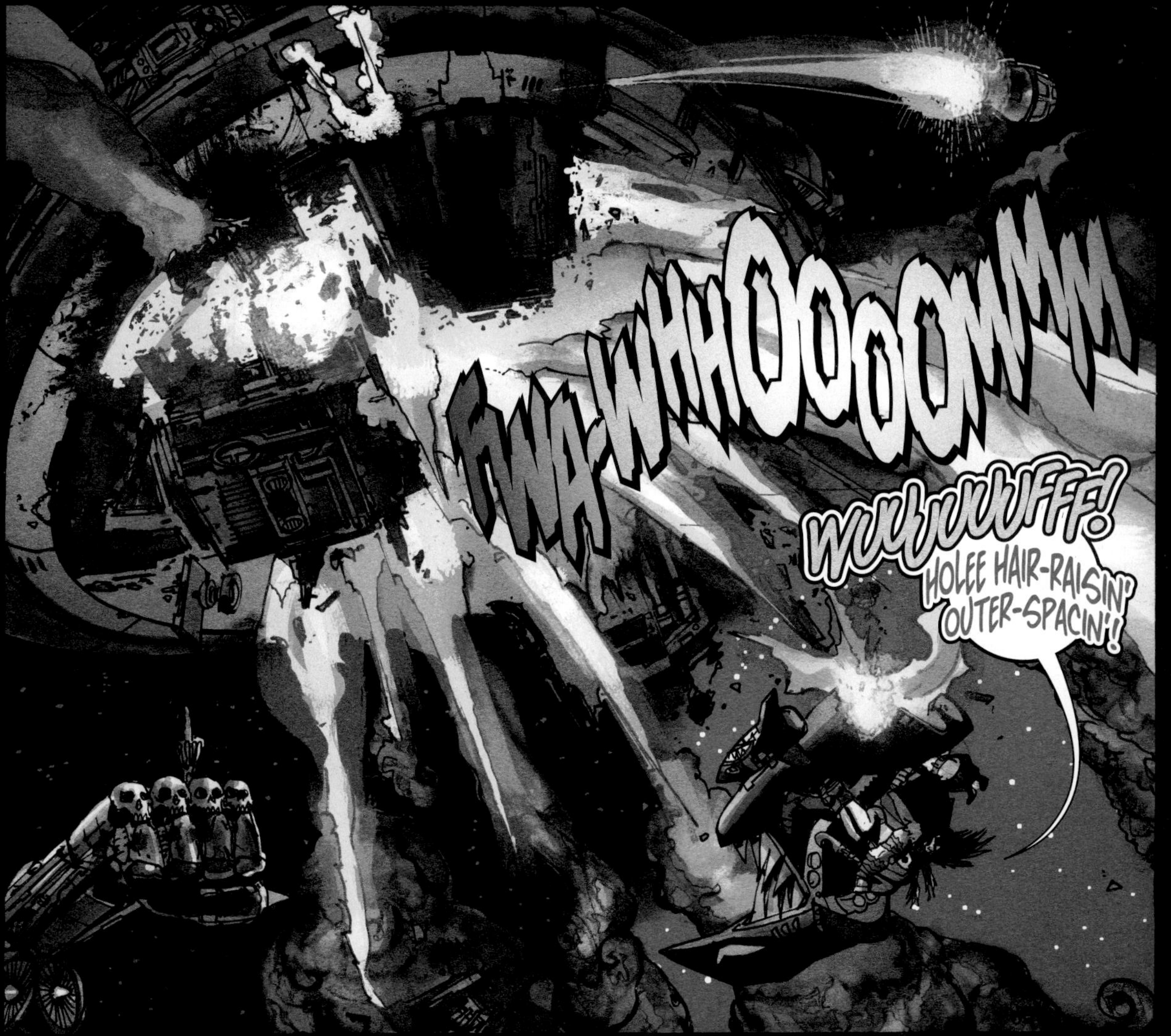
FWA-WHHOOOOOMM
WUUUUUFFF!
HOLEE HAIR-RAISIN' OUTER-SPACIN'!

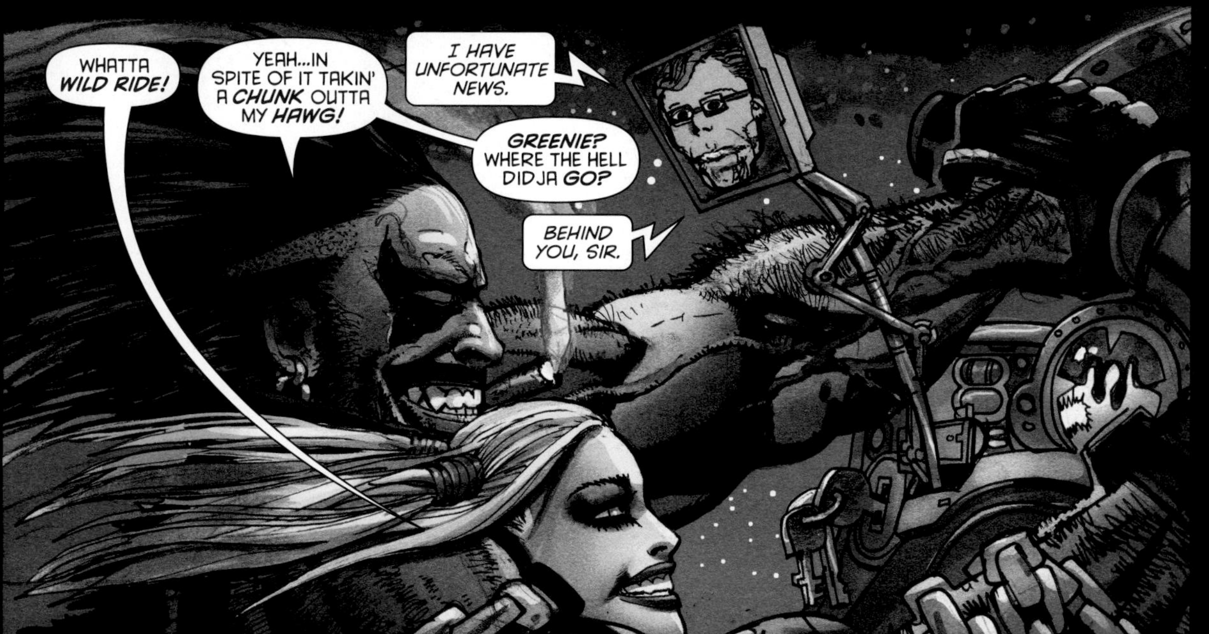
WHATTA WILD RIDE!
YEAH...IN SPITE OF IT TAKIN' A CHUNK OUTTA MY HAWG!
I HAVE UNFORTUNATE NEWS.
GREENIE? WHERE THE HELL DIDJA GO?
BEHIND YOU, SIR.

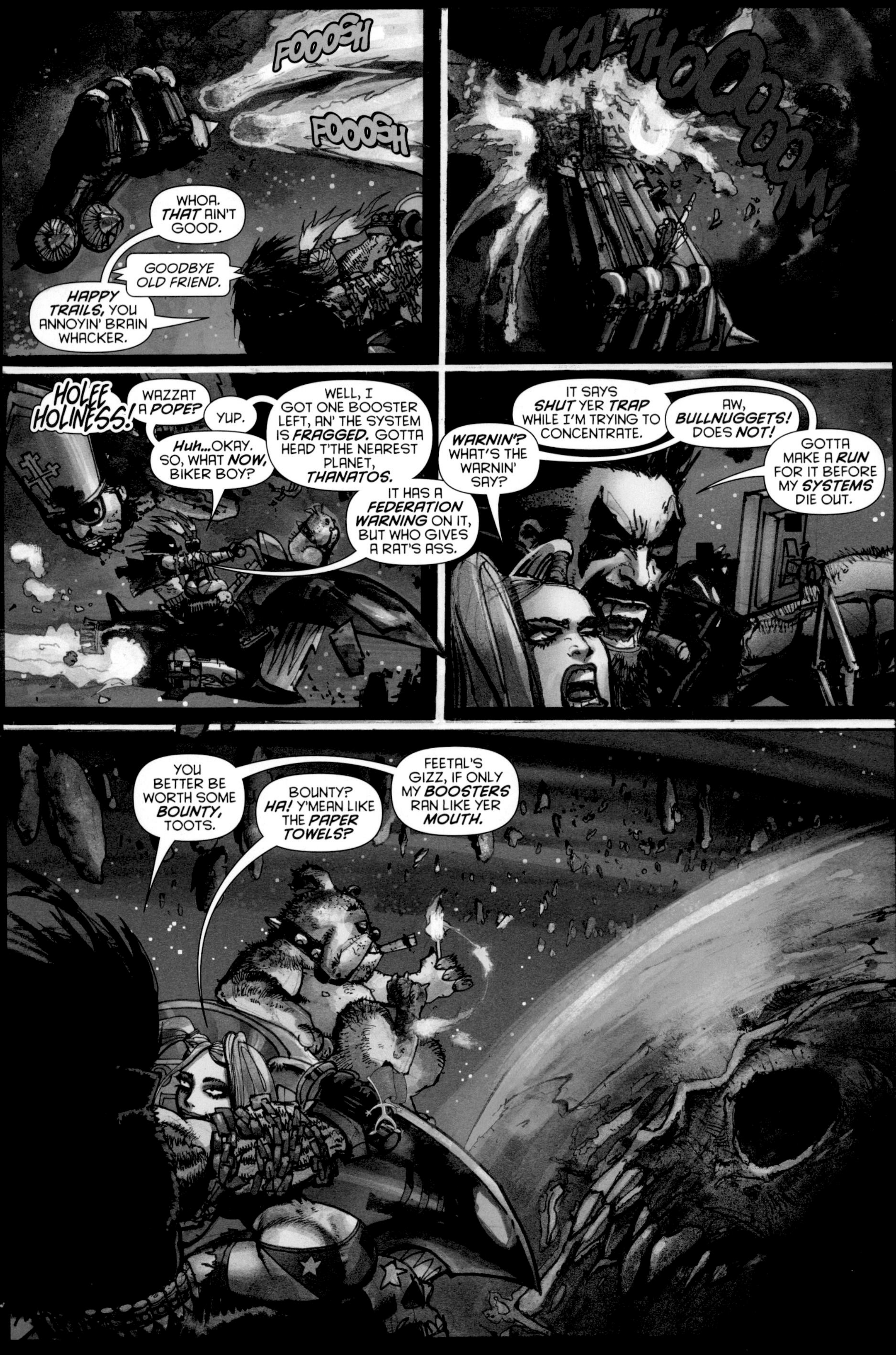
FOOOSH
FOOOSH
WHOA. THAT AIN'T GOOD.
GOODBYE OLD FRIEND.
HAPPY TRAILS, YOU ANNOYIN' BRAIN WHACKER.
KA-THOOOOOM!
HOLEE HOLINESS!
WAZZAT A POPE?
YUP.
Huh...OKAY. SO, WHAT NOW, BIKER BOY?
WELL, I GOT ONE BOOSTER LEFT, AN' THE SYSTEM IS FRAGGED. GOTTA HEAD T'THE NEAREST PLANET, THANATOS.
IT HAS A FEDERATION WARNING ON IT, BUT WHO GIVES A RAT'S ASS.
WARNIN'? WHAT'S THE WARNIN' SAY?
IT SAYS SHUT YER TRAP WHILE I'M TRYING TO CONCENTRATE.
AW, BULLNUGGETS! DOES NOT!
GOTTA MAKE A RUN FOR IT BEFORE MY SYSTEMS DIE OUT.
YOU BETTER BE WORTH SOME BOUNTY, TOOTS.
BOUNTY? HA! Y'MEAN LIKE THE PAPER TOWELS?
FEETAL'S GIZZ, IF ONLY MY BOOSTERS RAN LIKE YER MOUTH.

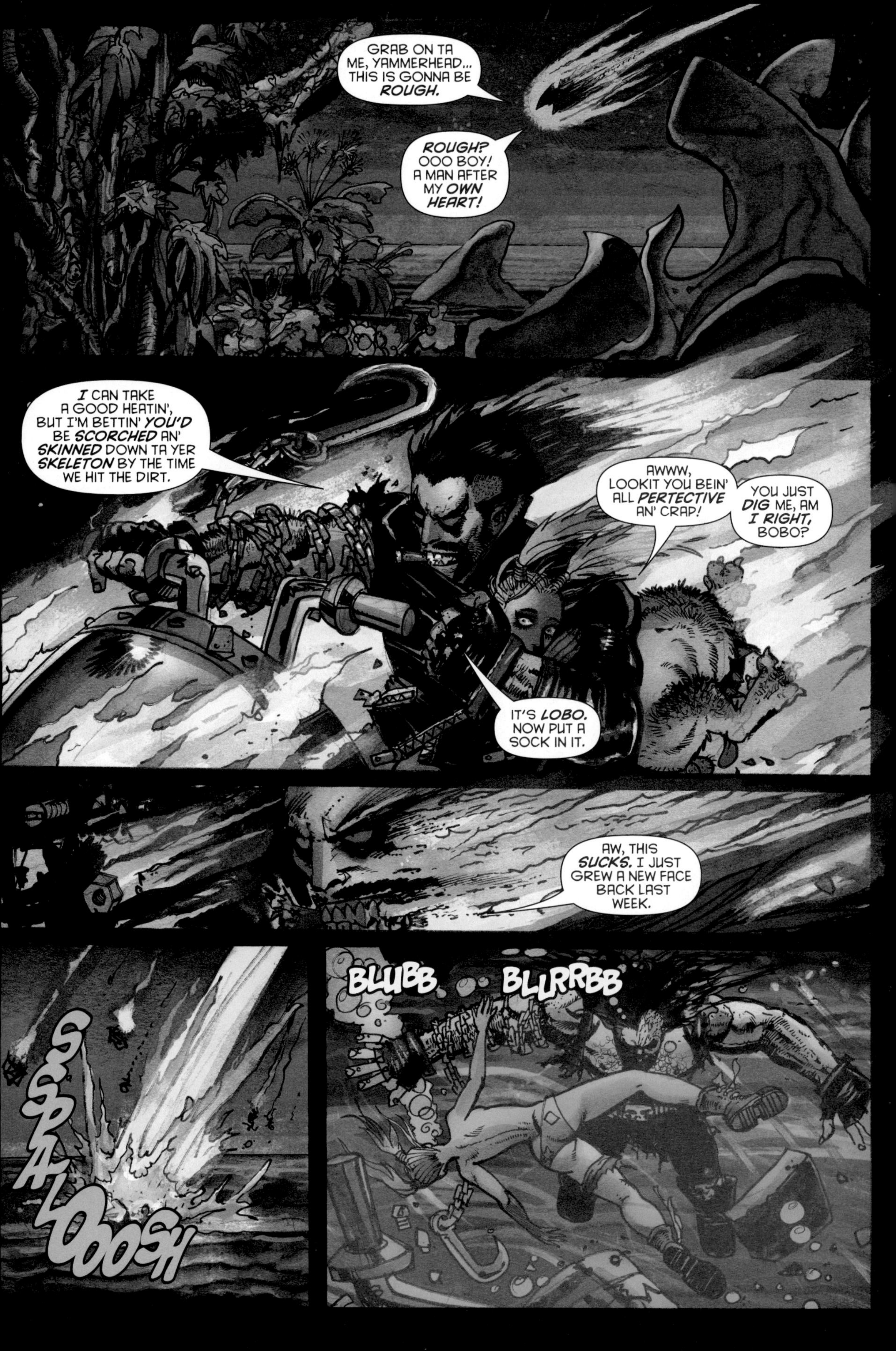
GRAB ON TA ME, YAMMERHEAD... THIS IS GONNA BE ROUGH.
ROUGH? OOO BOY! A MAN AFTER MY OWN HEART!
I CAN TAKE A GOOD HEATIN', BUT I'M BETTIN' YOU'D BE SCORCHED AN' SKINNED DOWN TA YER SKELETON BY THE TIME WE HIT THE DIRT.
AWWW, LOOKIT YOU BEIN' ALL PERTECTIVE AN' CRAP!
YOU JUST DIG ME, AM I RIGHT, BOBO?
IT'S LOBO. NOW PUT A SOCK IN IT.
AW, THIS SUCKS. I JUST GREW A NEW FACE BACK LAST WEEK.
SSPLALOOOSH
BLUBB
BLURRBB

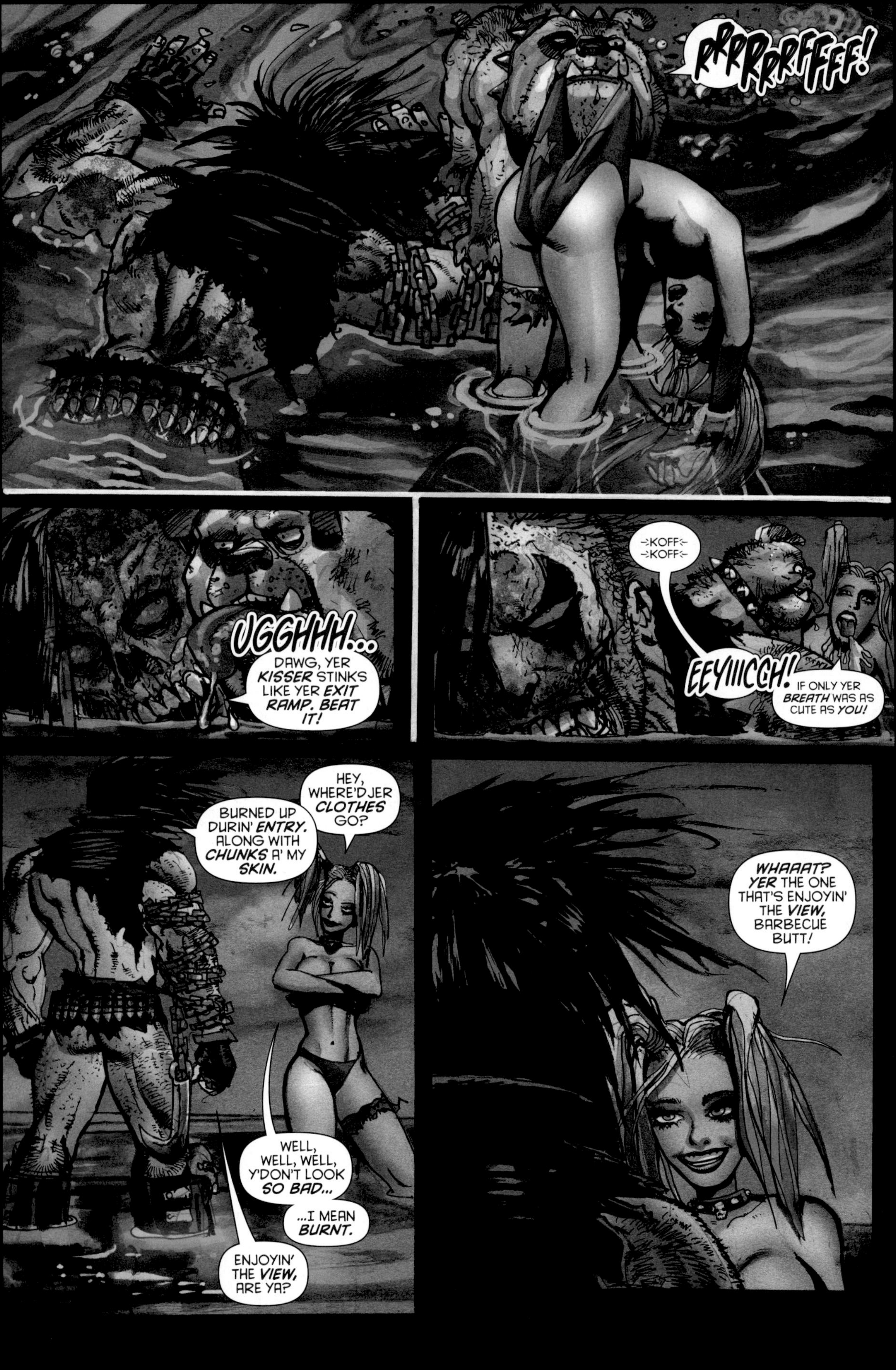
RRRRRRFFFFF!
UGGHHH...
DAWG, YER KISSER STINKS LIKE YER EXIT RAMP. BEAT IT!
-KOFF-
-KOFF-
EEYIIICGH!
IF ONLY YER BREATH WAS AS CUTE AS YOU!
HEY, WHERE'DJER CLOTHES GO?
BURNED UP DURIN' ENTRY. ALONG WITH CHUNKS A' MY SKIN.
WELL, WELL, WELL, Y'DON'T LOOK SO BAD...
...I MEAN BURNT.
ENJOYIN' THE VIEW, ARE YA?
WHAAAT? YER THE ONE THAT'S ENJOYIN' THE VIEW, BARBECUE BUTT!

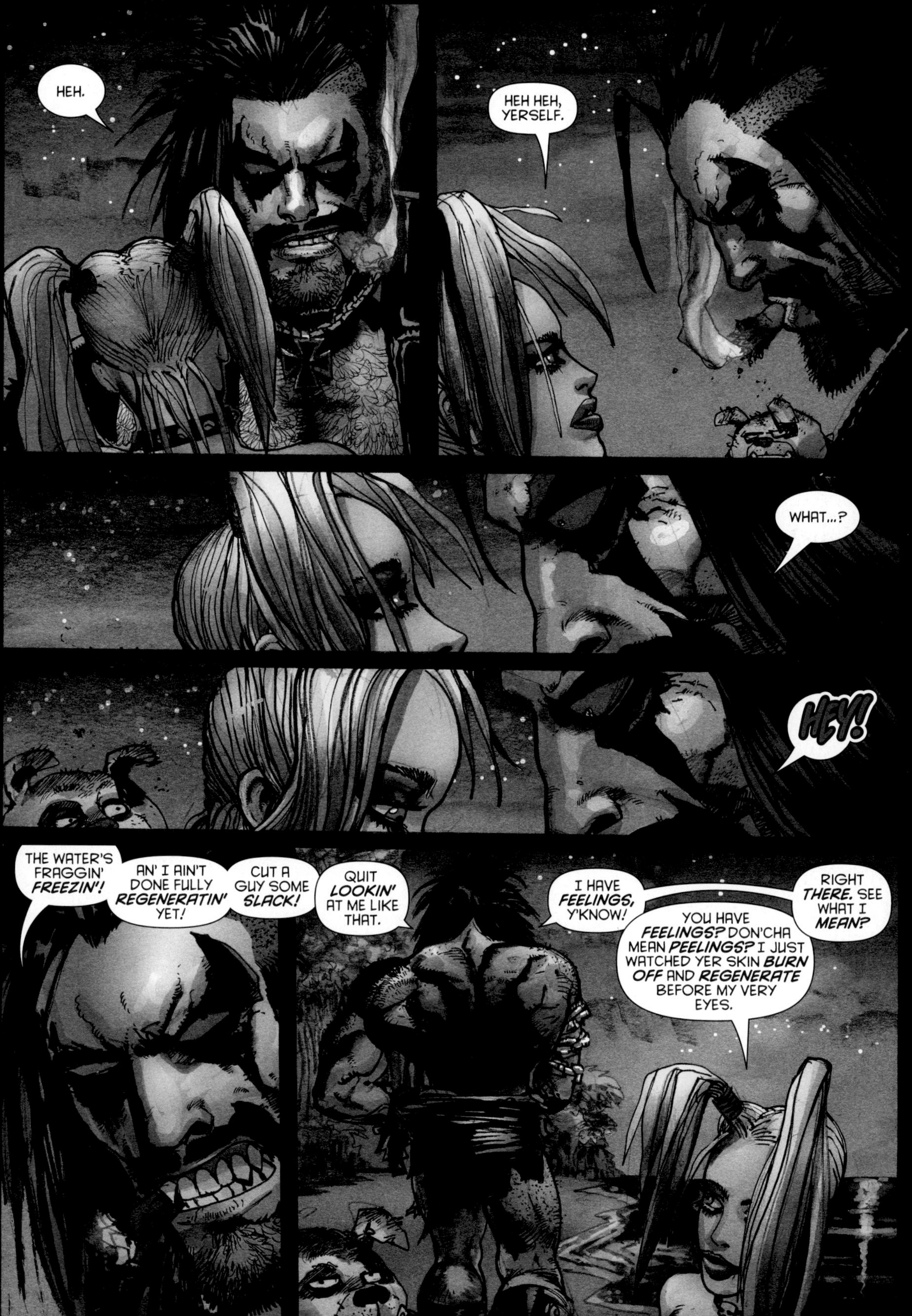
HEH.
HEH HEH, YERSELF.
WHAT...?
HEY!
THE WATER'S FRAGGIN' FREEZIN'!
AN' I AIN'T DONE FULLY REGENERATIN' YET!
CUT A GUY SOME SLACK!
QUIT LOOKIN' AT ME LIKE THAT.
I HAVE FEELINGS, Y'KNOW!
YOU HAVE FEELINGS? DON'CHA MEAN PEELINGS? I JUST WATCHED YER SKIN BURN OFF AND REGENERATE BEFORE MY VERY EYES.
RIGHT THERE. SEE WHAT I MEAN?

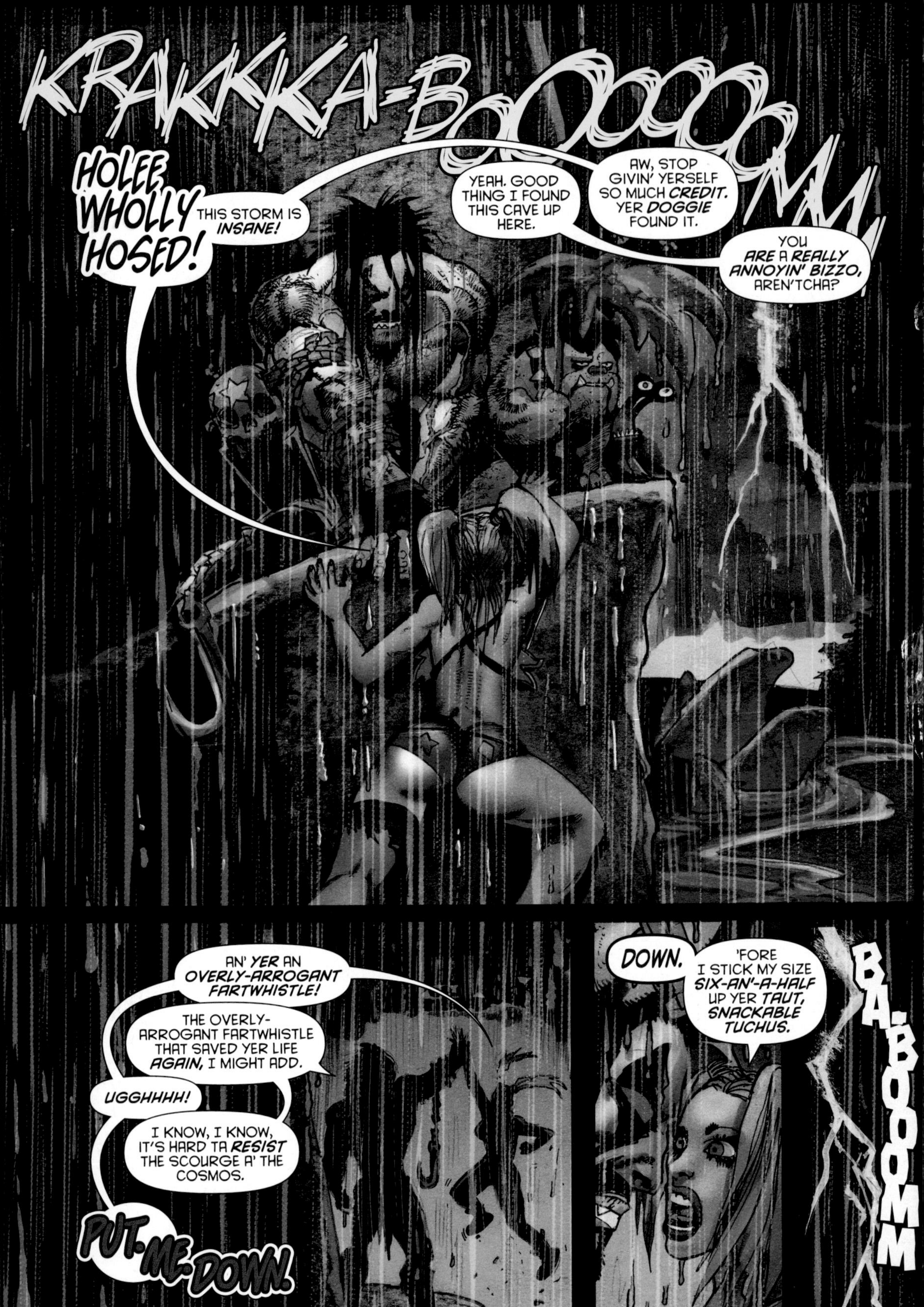
KRAKKA-BOOOOOOMM!
HOLEE WHOLLY HOSED!
THIS STORM IS INSANE!
YEAH. GOOD THING I FOUND THIS CAVE UP HERE.
AW, STOP GIVIN' YERSELF SO MUCH CREDIT. YER DOGGIE FOUND IT.
YOU ARE A REALLY ANNOYIN' BIZZO, AREN'TCHA?
AN' YER AN OVERLY-ARROGANT FARTWHISTLE!
THE OVERLY-ARROGANT FARTWHISTLE THAT SAVED YER LIFE AGAIN, I MIGHT ADD.
UGGHHHH!
I KNOW, I KNOW, IT'S HARD TA RESIST THE SCOURGE A' THE COSMOS.
PUT. ME. DOWN.
DOWN.
'FORE I STICK MY SIZE SIX-AN'-A-HALF UP YER TAUT, SNACKABLE TUCHUS.
BA-BOOOMM

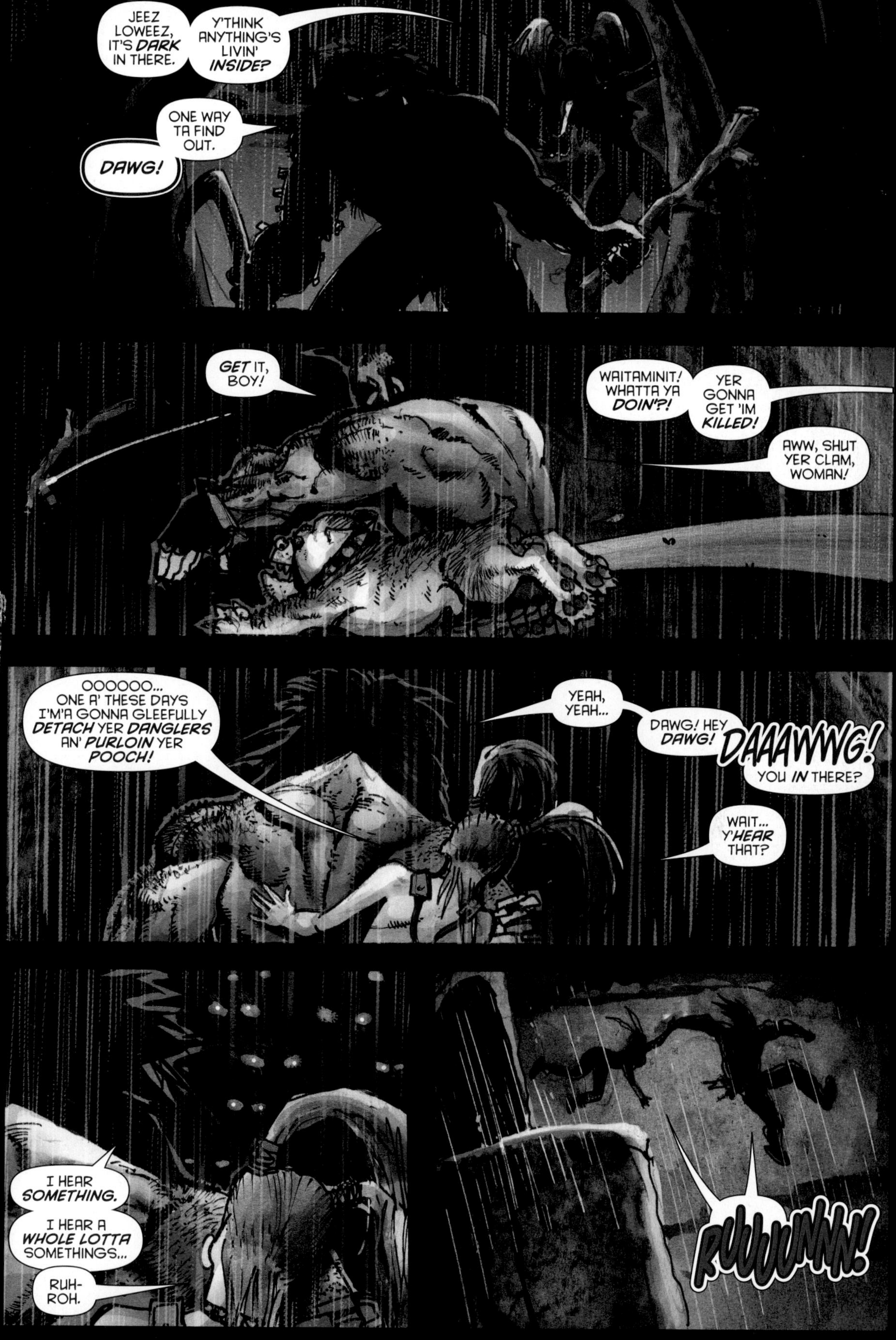
JEEZ LOWEEZ, IT'S DARK IN THERE.
Y'THINK ANYTHING'S LIVIN' INSIDE?
ONE WAY TA FIND OUT.
DAWG!
GET IT, BOY!
WAITAMINIT! WHATTA YA DOIN'?!
YER GONNA GET 'IM KILLED!
AWW, SHUT YER CLAM, WOMAN!
OOOOOO... ONE A' THESE DAYS I'M'A GONNA GLEEFULLY DETACH YER DANGLERS AN' PURLOIN YER POOCH!
YEAH, YEAH...
DAWG! HEY DAWG! DAAAWWG! YOU IN THERE?
WAIT... Y'HEAR THAT?
I HEAR SOMETHING.
I HEAR A WHOLE LOTTA SOMETHINGS...
RUH-ROH.
RUUUUNNN!

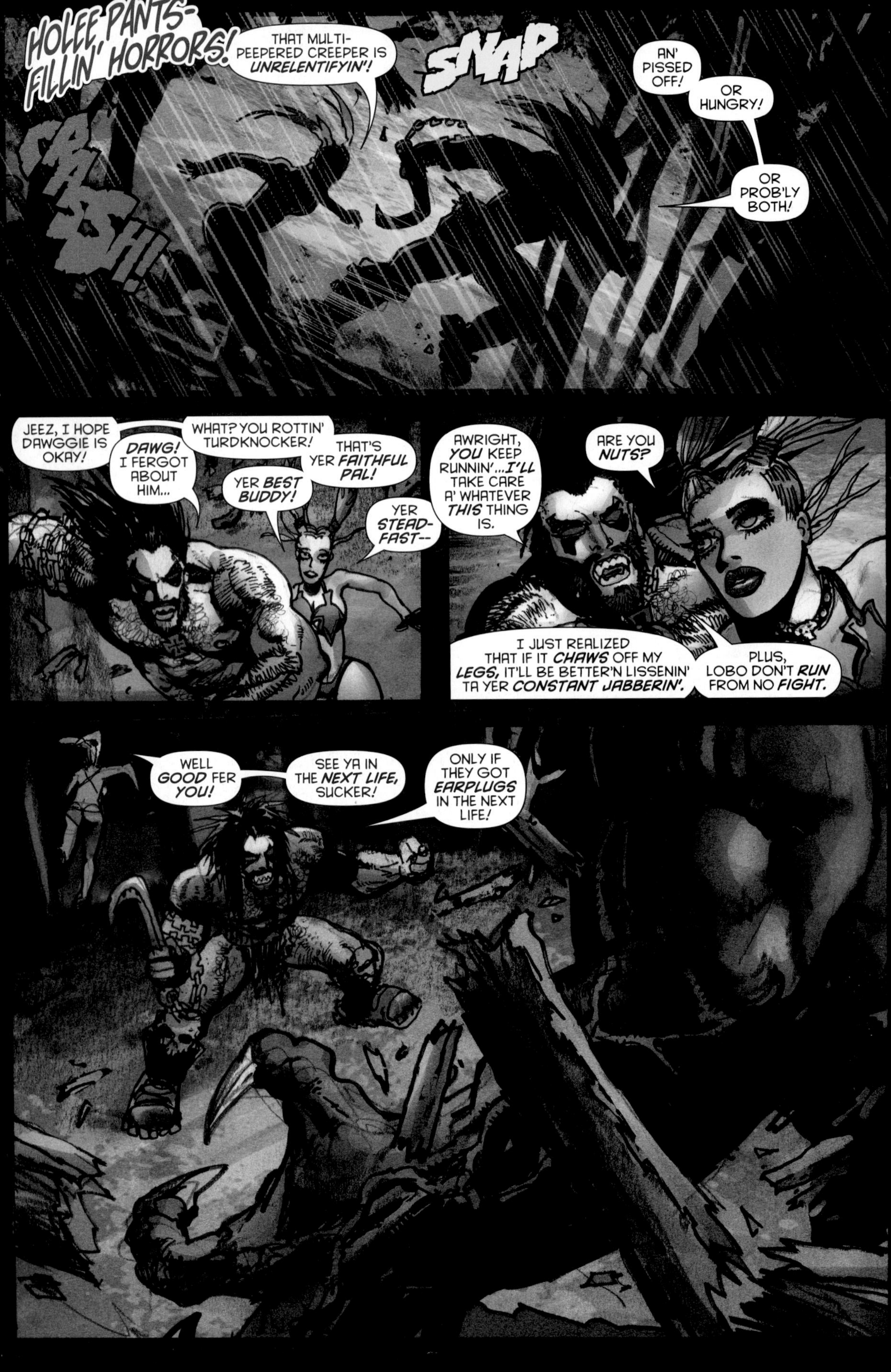
HOLEE PANTS-FILLIN' HORRORS!
THAT MULTI-PEEPERED CREEPER IS UNRELENTIFYIN'!
SNAP
CRASH!
AN' PISSED OFF!
OR HUNGRY!
OR PROB'LY BOTH!
JEEZ, I HOPE DAWGGIE IS OKAY!
WHAT? YOU ROTTIN' TURDKNOCKER!
DAWG! I FERGOT ABOUT HIM...
THAT'S YER FAITHFUL PAL!
YER BEST BUDDY!
YER STEADFAST--
AWRIGHT, YOU KEEP RUNNIN'...I'LL TAKE CARE A' WHATEVER THIS THING IS.
ARE YOU NUTS?
I JUST REALIZED THAT IF IT CHAWS OFF MY LEGS, IT'LL BE BETTER'N LISSENIN' TA YER CONSTANT JABBERIN'.
PLUS, LOBO DON'T RUN FROM NO FIGHT.
WELL GOOD FER YOU!
SEE YA IN THE NEXT LIFE, SUCKER!
ONLY IF THEY GOT EARPLUGS IN THE NEXT LIFE!

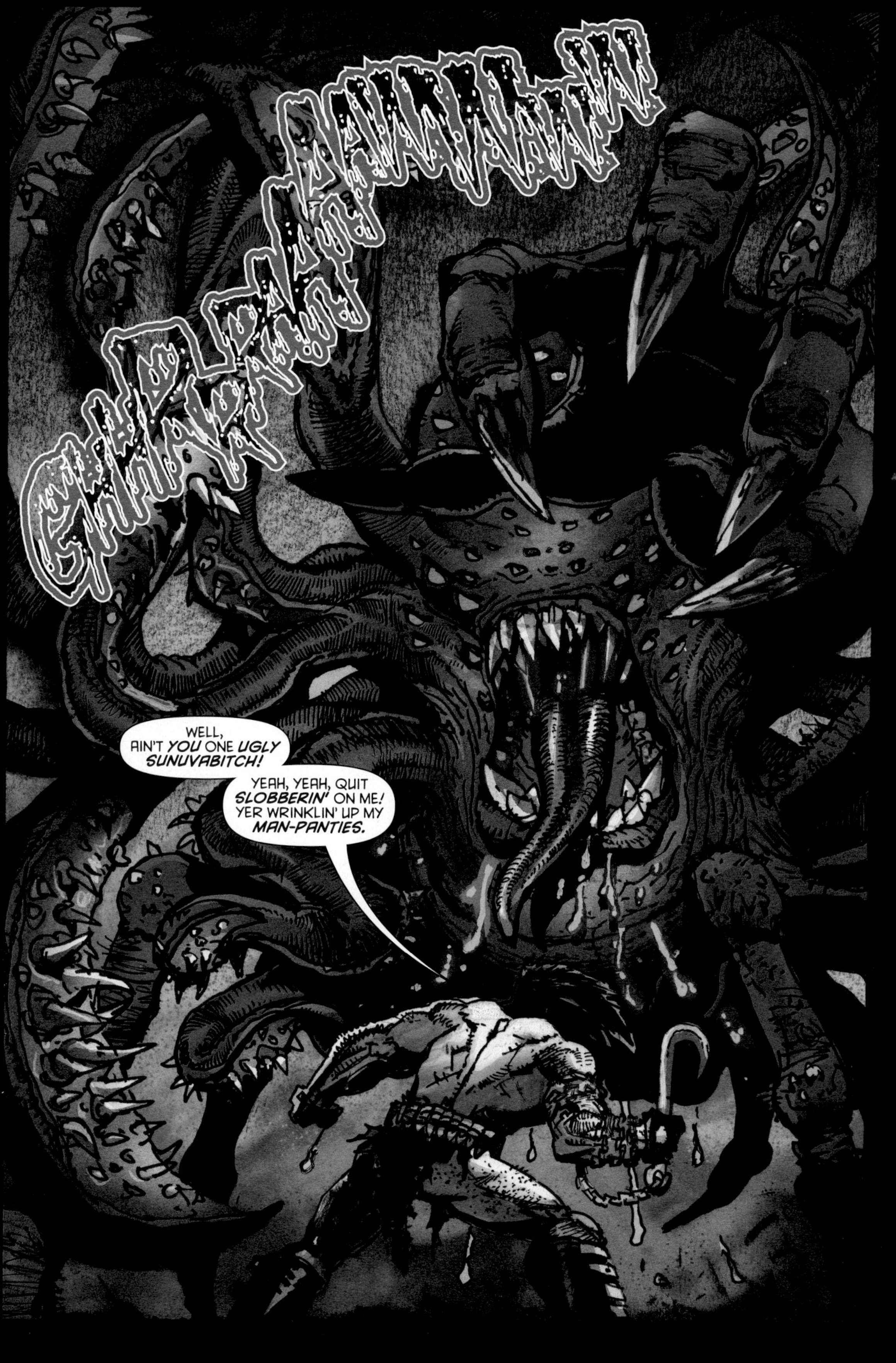
WELL, AIN'T YOU ONE UGLY SUNUVABITCH!
YEAH, YEAH, QUIT SLOBBERIN' ON ME! YER WRINKLIN' UP MY MAN-PANTIES.

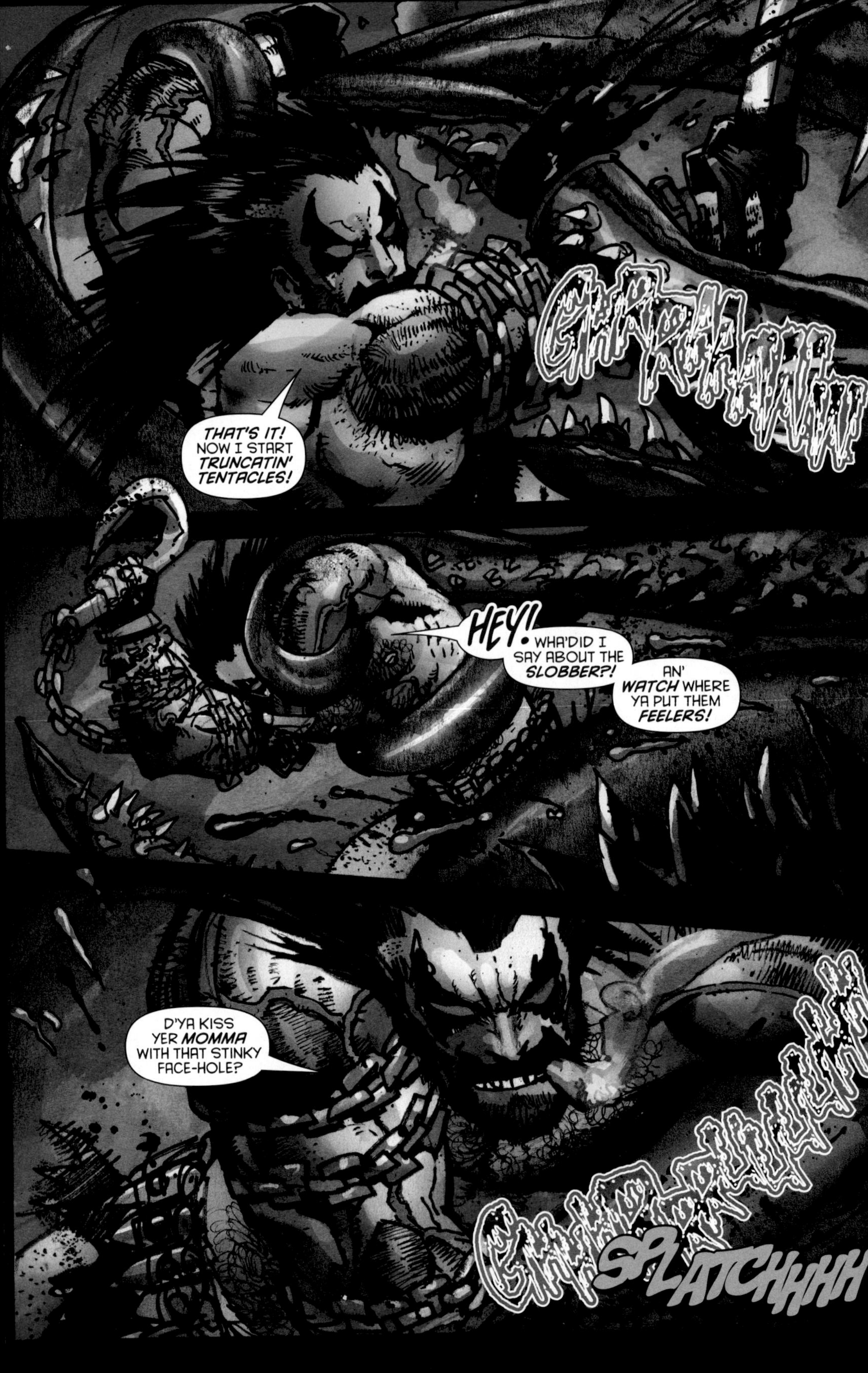
THAT'S IT! NOW I START TRUNCATIN' TENTACLES!
HEY!
WHA'DID I SAY ABOUT THE SLOBBER?!
AN' WATCH WHERE YA PUT THEM FEELERS!
D'YA KISS YER MOMMA WITH THAT STINKY FACE-HOLE?
SPLATCHHHH

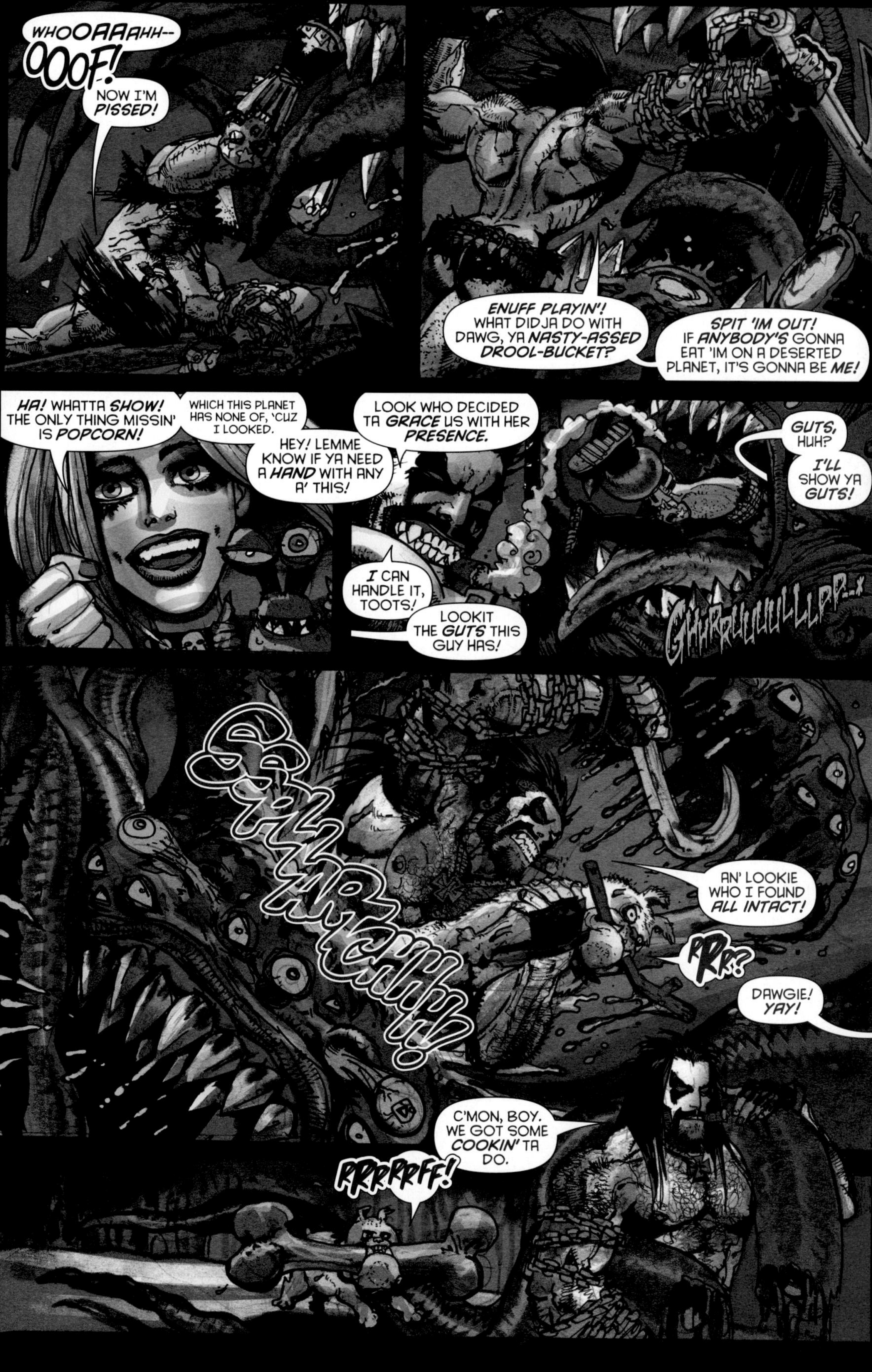
WHOOAAAHH--
OOOF!
NOW I'M PISSED!
ENUFF PLAYIN'! WHAT DIDJA DO WITH DAWG, YA NASTY-ASSED DROOL-BUCKET?
SPIT 'IM OUT! IF ANYBODY'S GONNA EAT 'IM ON A DESERTED PLANET, IT'S GONNA BE ME!
HA! WHATTA SHOW! THE ONLY THING MISSIN' IS POPCORN!
WHICH THIS PLANET HAS NONE OF, 'CUZ I LOOKED.
HEY! LEMME KNOW IF YA NEED A HAND WITH ANY A' THIS!
LOOK WHO DECIDED TA GRACE US WITH HER PRESENCE.
I CAN HANDLE IT, TOOTS!
LOOKIT THE GUTS THIS GUY HAS!
GUTS, HUH?
I'LL SHOW YA GUTS!
AN' LOOKIE WHO I FOUND ALL INTACT!
RRR?
DAWGIE! YAY!
C'MON, BOY. WE GOT SOME COOKIN' TA DO.
RRRRRFF!

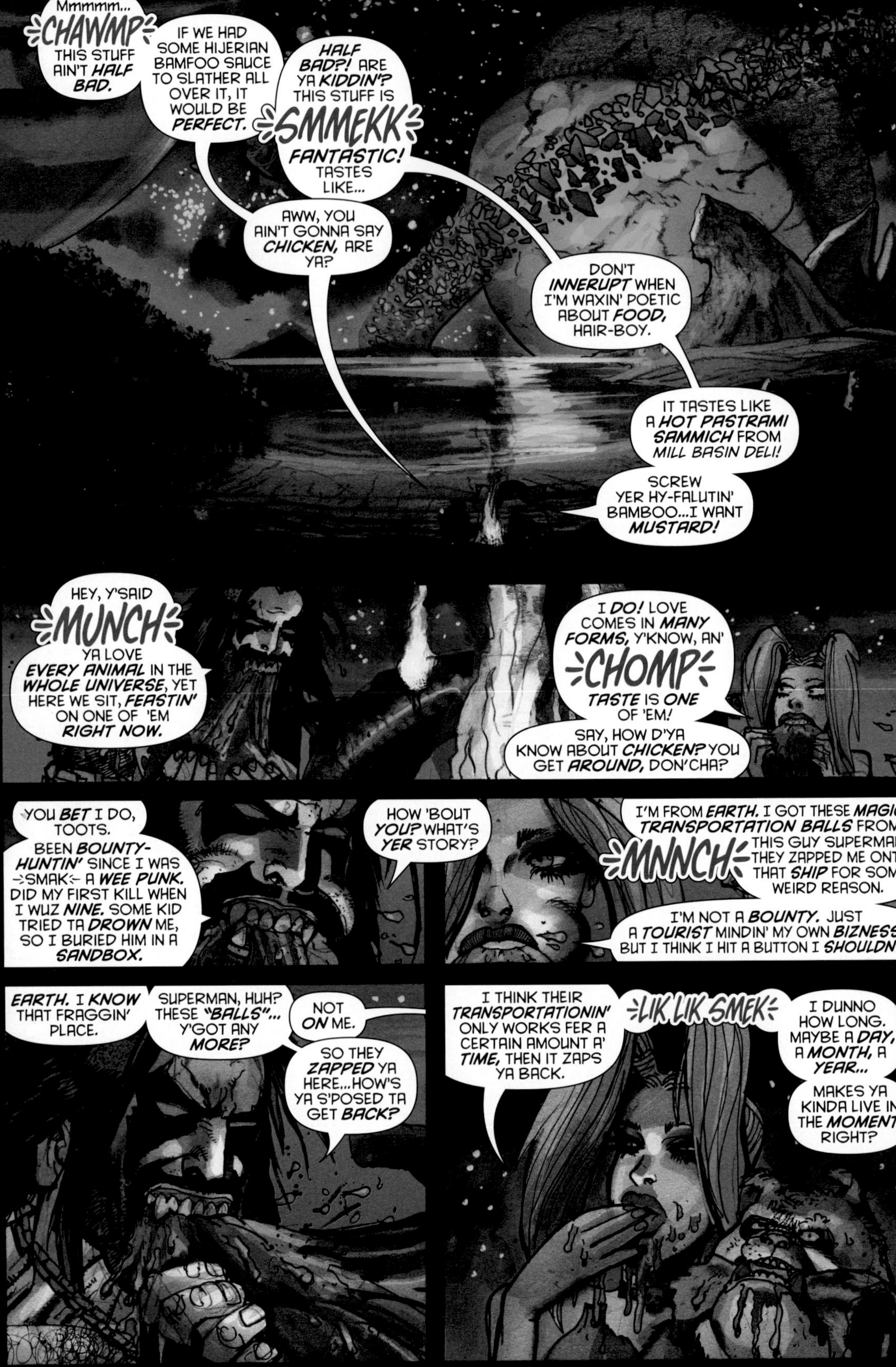

Mmmmm... CHAWMP THIS STUFF AIN'T HALF BAD.
IF WE HAD SOME HIJERIAN BAMFOO SAUCE TO SLATHER ALL OVER IT, IT WOULD BE PERFECT.
HALF BAD?! ARE YA KIDDIN'? THIS STUFF IS SMMEKK FANTASTIC! TASTES LIKE...
AWW, YOU AIN'T GONNA SAY CHICKEN, ARE YA?
DON'T INNERUPT WHEN I'M WAXIN' POETIC ABOUT FOOD, HAIR-BOY.
IT TASTES LIKE A HOT PASTRAMI SAMMICH FROM MILL BASIN DELI!
SCREW YER HY-FALUTIN' BAMBOO...I WANT MUSTARD!
HEY, Y'SAID MUNCH YA LOVE EVERY ANIMAL IN THE WHOLE UNIVERSE, YET HERE WE SIT, FEASTIN' ON ONE OF 'EM RIGHT NOW.
I DO! LOVE COMES IN MANY FORMS, Y'KNOW, AN' CHOMP TASTE IS ONE OF 'EM!
SAY, HOW D'YA KNOW ABOUT CHICKEN? YOU GET AROUND, DON'CHA?
YOU BET I DO, TOOTS.
BEEN BOUNTY-HUNTIN' SINCE I WAS ⇒SMAK⇐ A WEE PUNK. DID MY FIRST KILL WHEN I WUZ NINE. SOME KID TRIED TA DROWN ME, SO I BURIED HIM IN A SANDBOX.
HOW 'BOUT YOU? WHAT'S YER STORY?
I'M FROM EARTH. I GOT THESE MAGIC TRANSPORTATION BALLS FROM MNNCH THIS GUY SUPERMAN. THEY ZAPPED ME ONTA THAT SHIP FOR SOME WEIRD REASON.
I'M NOT A BOUNTY. JUST A TOURIST MINDIN' MY OWN BIZNESS. BUT I THINK I HIT A BUTTON I SHOULDN'A.
EARTH. I KNOW THAT FRAGGIN' PLACE.
SUPERMAN, HUH? THESE "BALLS"... Y'GOT ANY MORE?
NOT ON ME.
SO THEY ZAPPED YA HERE...HOW'S YA S'POSED TA GET BACK?
I THINK THEIR TRANSPORTATIONIN' ONLY WORKS FER A CERTAIN AMOUNT A' TIME, THEN IT ZAPS YA BACK.
LIK LIK SMEK
I DUNNO HOW LONG. MAYBE A DAY, A MONTH, A YEAR...
MAKES YA KINDA LIVE IN THE MOMENT, RIGHT?

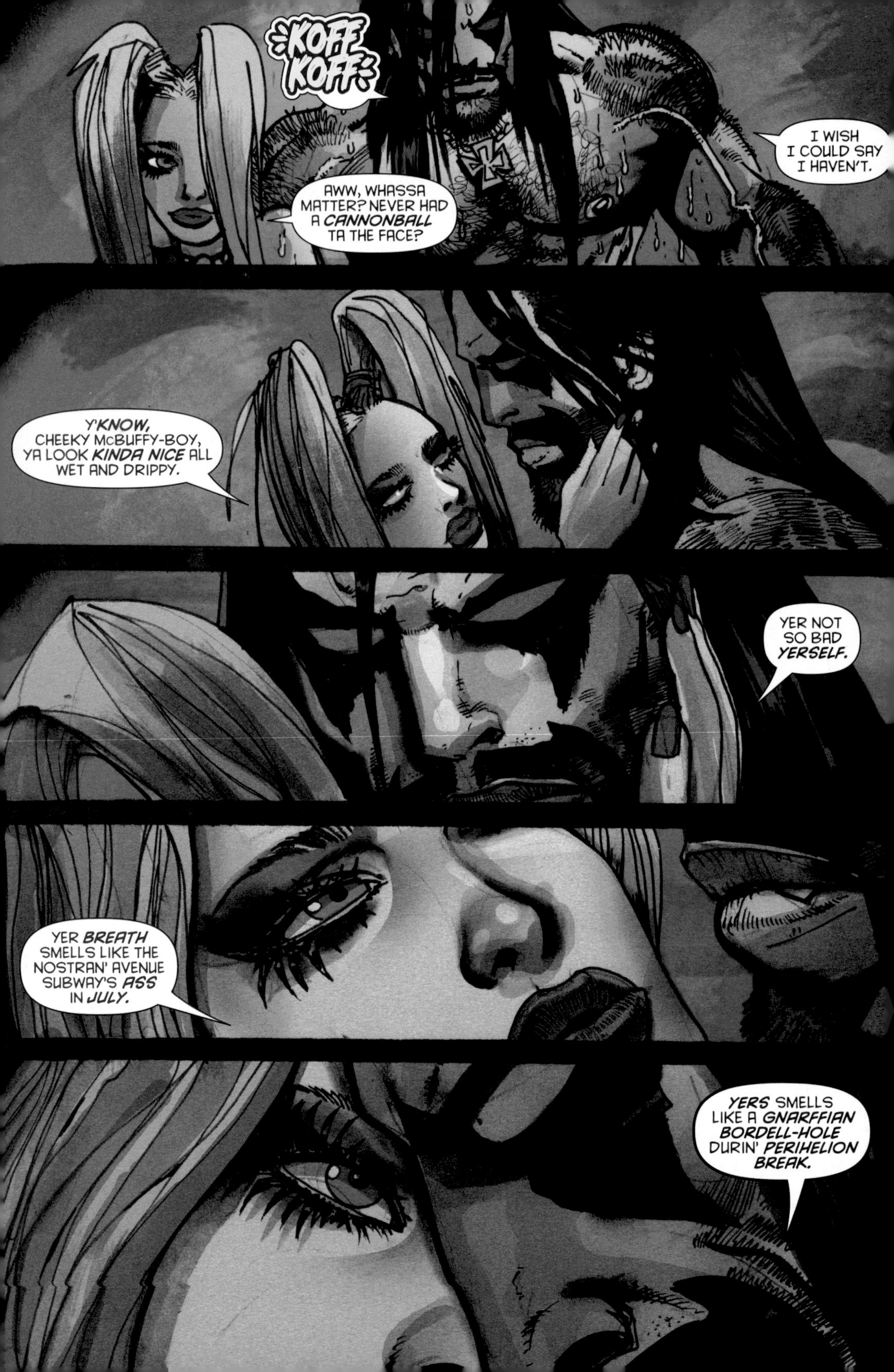
KOFF KOFF
I WISH I COULD SAY I HAVEN'T.
AWW, WHASSA MATTER? NEVER HAD A CANNONBALL TA THE FACE?
Y'KNOW, CHEEKY McBUFFY-BOY, YA LOOK KINDA NICE ALL WET AND DRIPPY.
YER NOT SO BAD YERSELF.
YER BREATH SMELLS LIKE THE NOSTRAN' AVENUE SUBWAY'S ASS IN JULY.
YERS SMELLS LIKE A GNARFFIAN BORDELL-HOLE DURIN' PERIHELION BREAK.

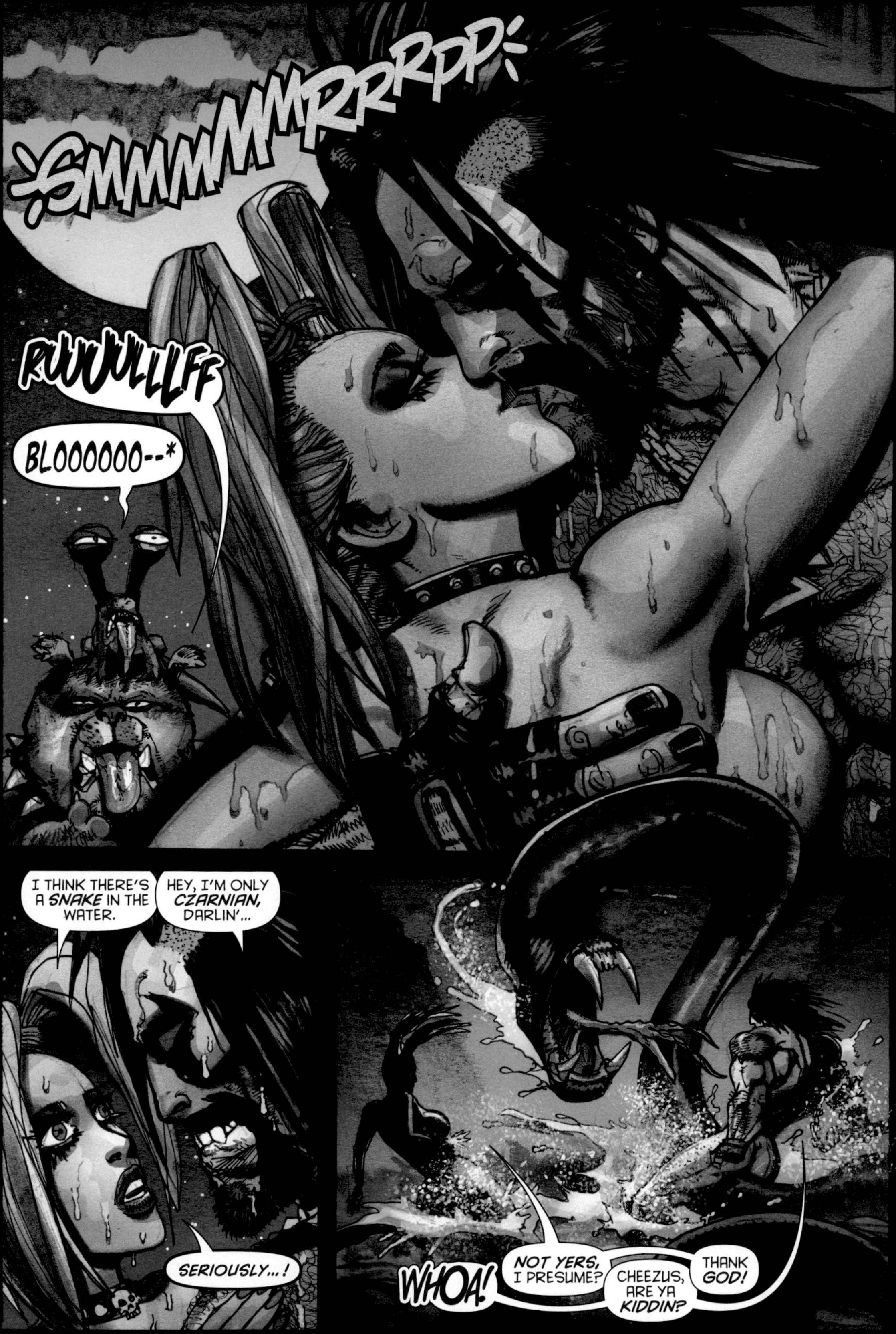
SMMMMMMRRRPP
RUUUULLLFF
BLOOOOOO--*
I THINK THERE'S A *SNAKE* IN THE WATER.
HEY, I'M ONLY *CZARNIAN,* DARLIN'...
SERIOUSLY...!
WHOA!
NOT YERS, I PRESUME?
CHEEZUS, ARE YA *KIDDIN?*
THANK *GOD!*

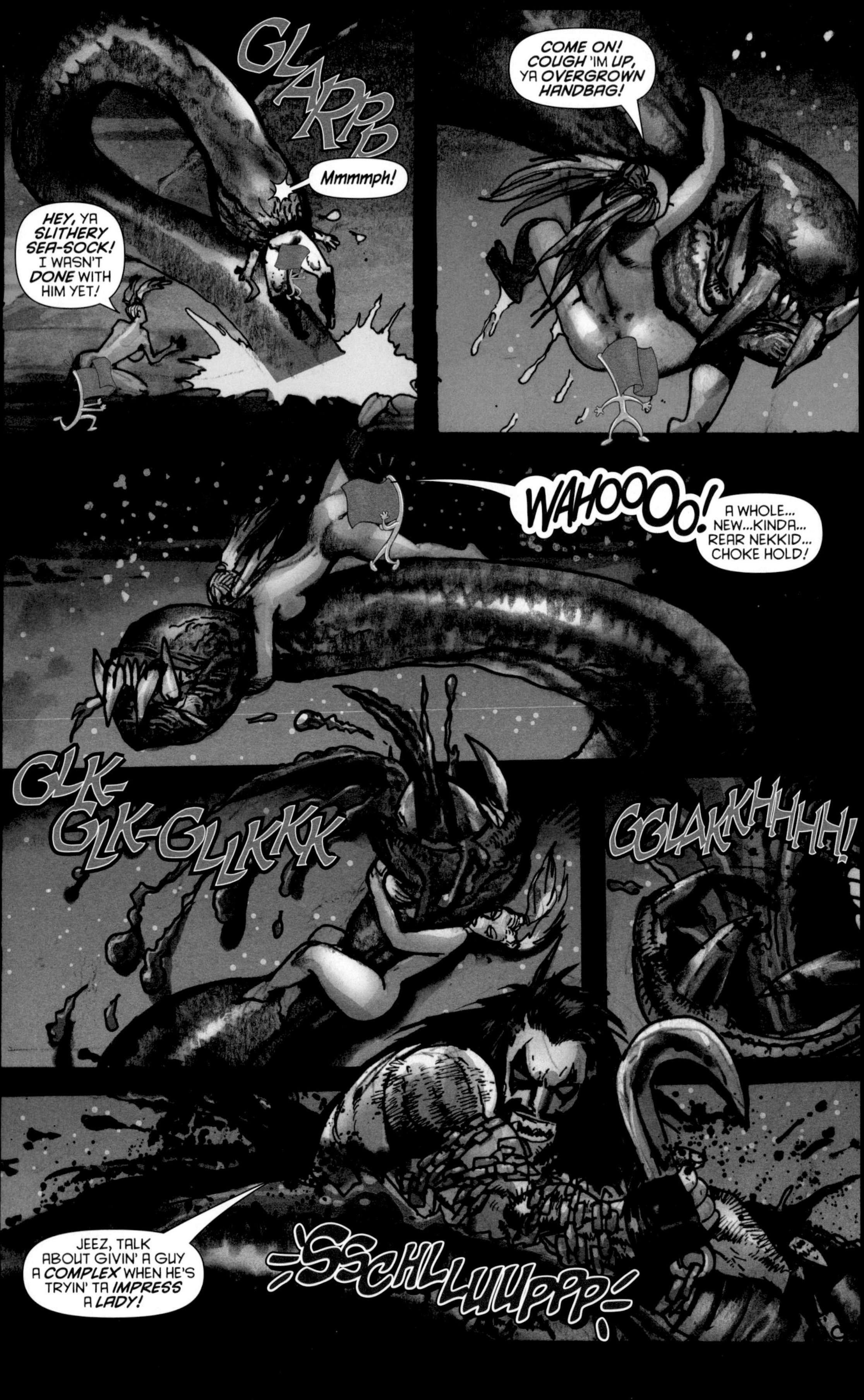
GLARPP
Mmmmph!
HEY, YA SLITHERY SEA-SOCK! I WASN'T DONE WITH HIM YET!
COME ON! COUGH 'IM UP, YA OVERGROWN HANDBAG!
WAHOOOOO!
A WHOLE... NEW...KINDA... REAR NEKKID... CHOKE HOLD!
GLK-GLK-GLKKK
GGLAKKHHHH!
JEEZ, TALK ABOUT GIVIN' A GUY A COMPLEX WHEN HE'S TRYIN' TA IMPRESS A LADY!
SSCHLLUUPPP!

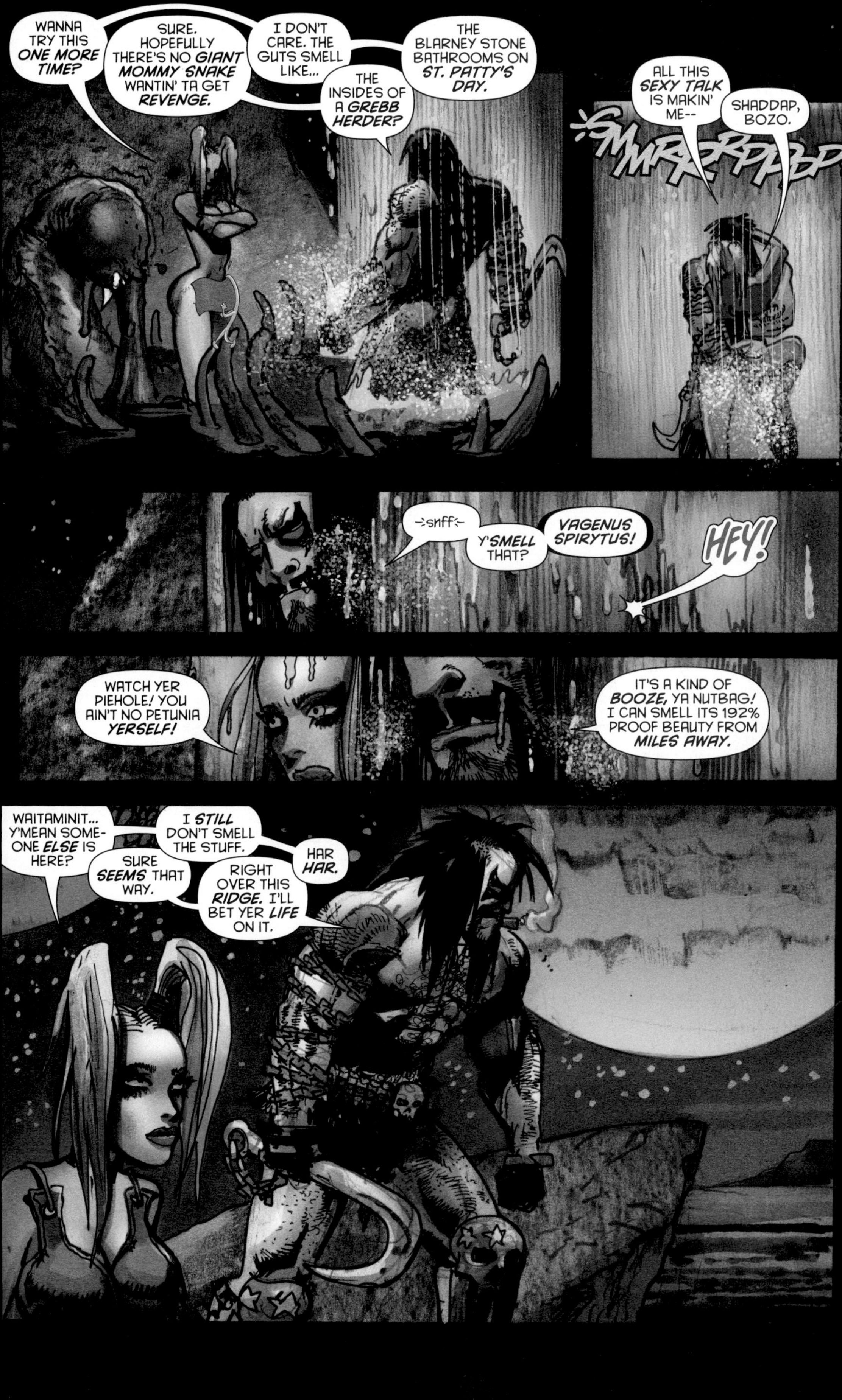
WANNA TRY THIS ONE MORE TIME?
SURE. HOPEFULLY THERE'S NO GIANT MOMMY SNAKE WANTIN' TA GET REVENGE.
I DON'T CARE. THE GUTS SMELL LIKE...
THE BLARNEY STONE BATHROOMS ON ST. PATTY'S DAY.
THE INSIDES OF A GREBB HERDER?
ALL THIS SEXY TALK IS MAKIN' ME--
SHADDAP, BOZO.
-snff-
Y'SMELL THAT?
VAGENUS SPIRYTUS!
HEY!
WATCH YER PIEHOLE! YOU AIN'T NO PETUNIA YERSELF!
IT'S A KIND OF BOOZE, YA NUTBAG! I CAN SMELL ITS 192% PROOF BEAUTY FROM MILES AWAY.
WAITAMINIT... Y'MEAN SOME-ONE ELSE IS HERE?
I STILL DON'T SMELL THE STUFF.
HAR HAR.
SURE SEEMS THAT WAY.
RIGHT OVER THIS RIDGE. I'LL BET YER LIFE ON IT.

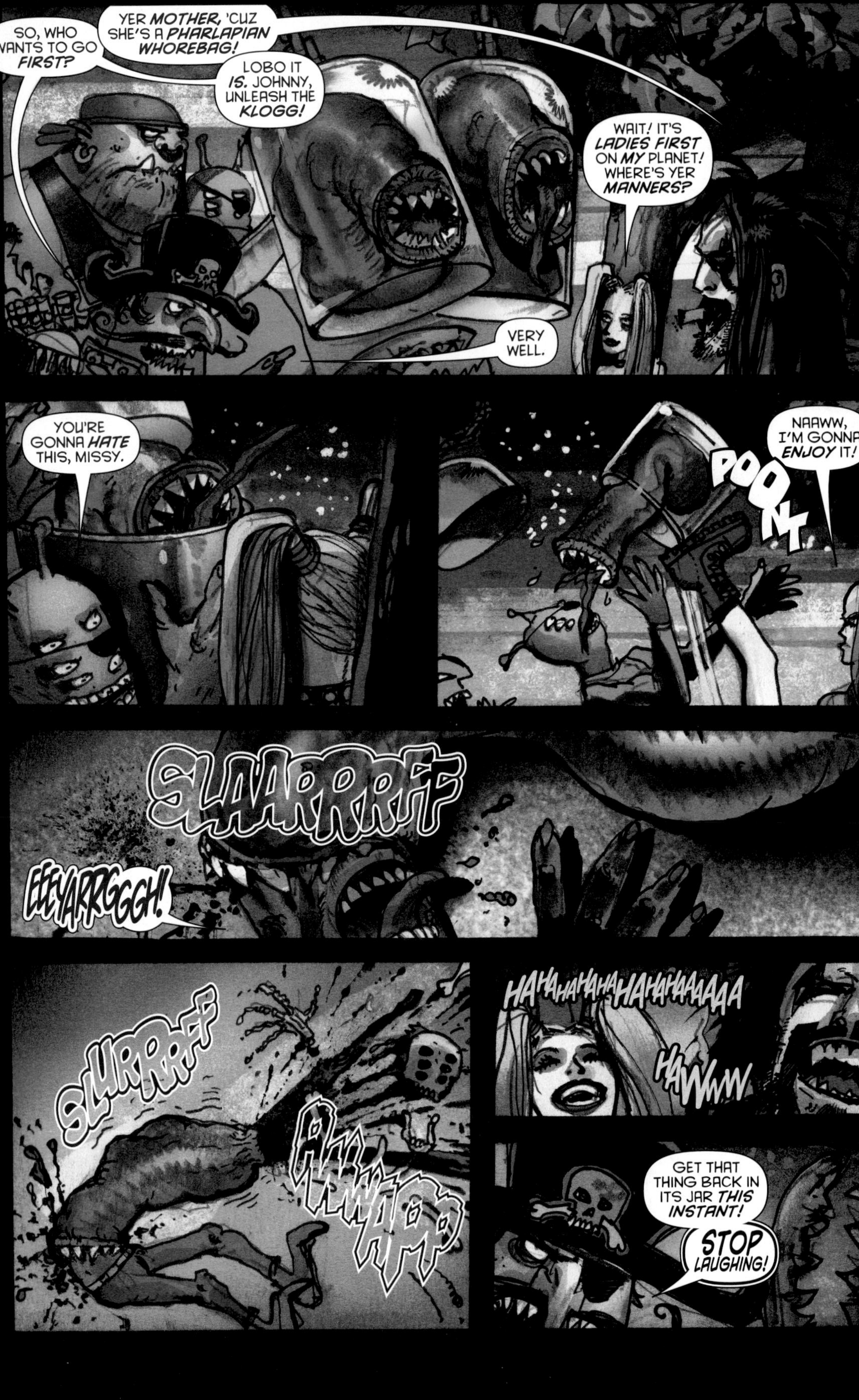
SO, WHO WANTS TO GO FIRST?
YER MOTHER, 'CUZ SHE'S A PHARLAPIAN WHOREBAG!
LOBO IT IS. JOHNNY, UNLEASH THE KLOGG!
WAIT! IT'S LADIES FIRST ON MY PLANET! WHERE'S YER MANNERS?
VERY WELL.
YOU'RE GONNA HATE THIS, MISSY.
POOONK
NAAWW, I'M GONNA ENJOY IT!
SLAARRRRFF
EEEYARRGGGH!
SLURRRFF
HAHAHAHAHAHAHAHAAAAAAA
HAWWW
GET THAT THING BACK IN ITS JAR THIS INSTANT!
STOP LAUGHING!

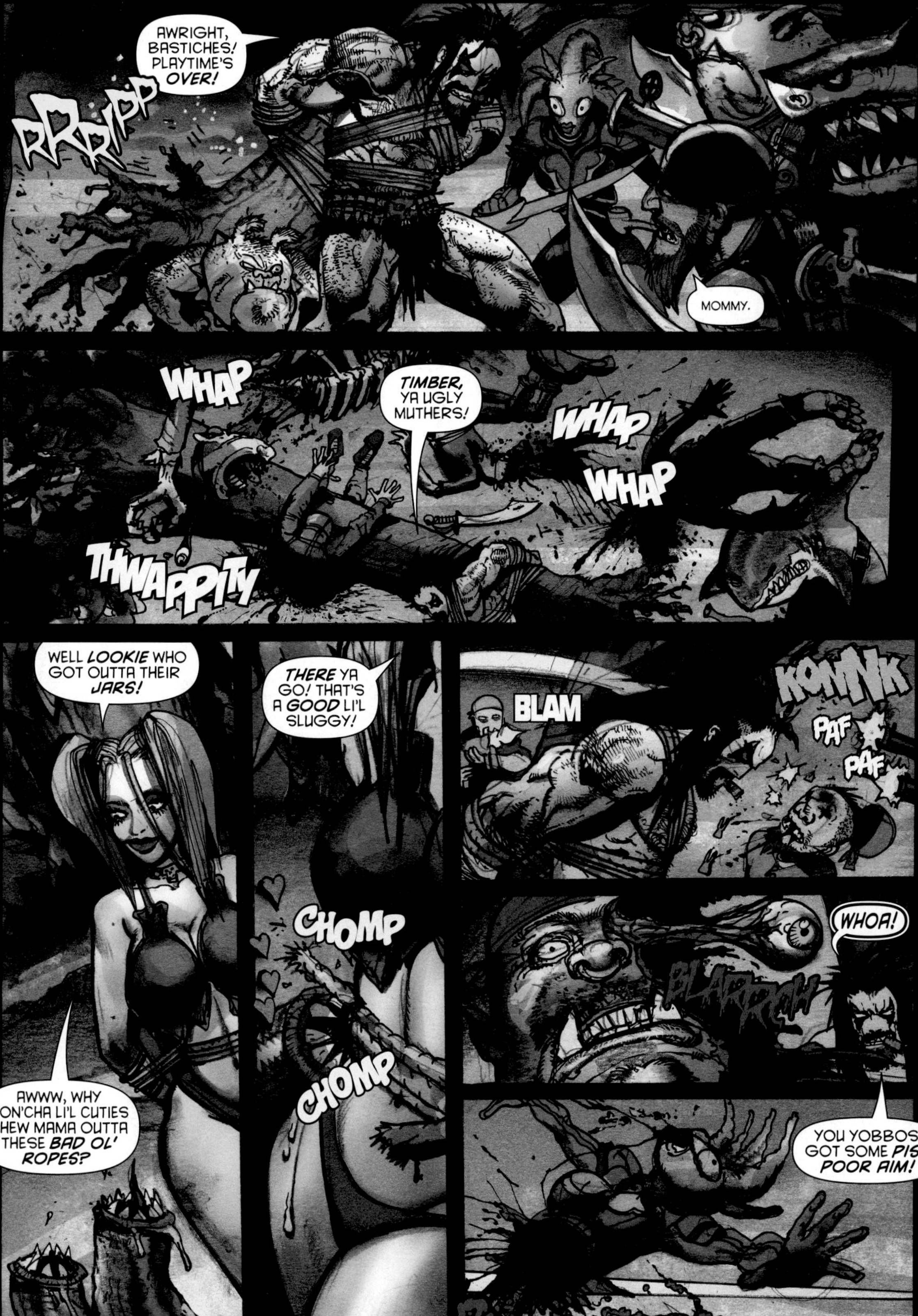
AWRIGHT, BASTICHES! PLAYTIME'S OVER!
RRRIPP
MOMMY.
WHAP
TIMBER, YA UGLY MUTHERS!
WHAP
WHAP
THWAPPITY
WELL LOOKIE WHO GOT OUTTA THEIR JARS!
AWWW, WHY DON'CHA LI'L CUTIES CHEW MAMA OUTTA THESE BAD OL' ROPES?
THERE YA GO! THAT'S A GOOD LI'L SLUGGY!
CHOMP
CHOMP
BLAM
KONNK
PAF
PAF
WHOA!
YOU YOBBOS GOT SOME PISS POOR AIM!

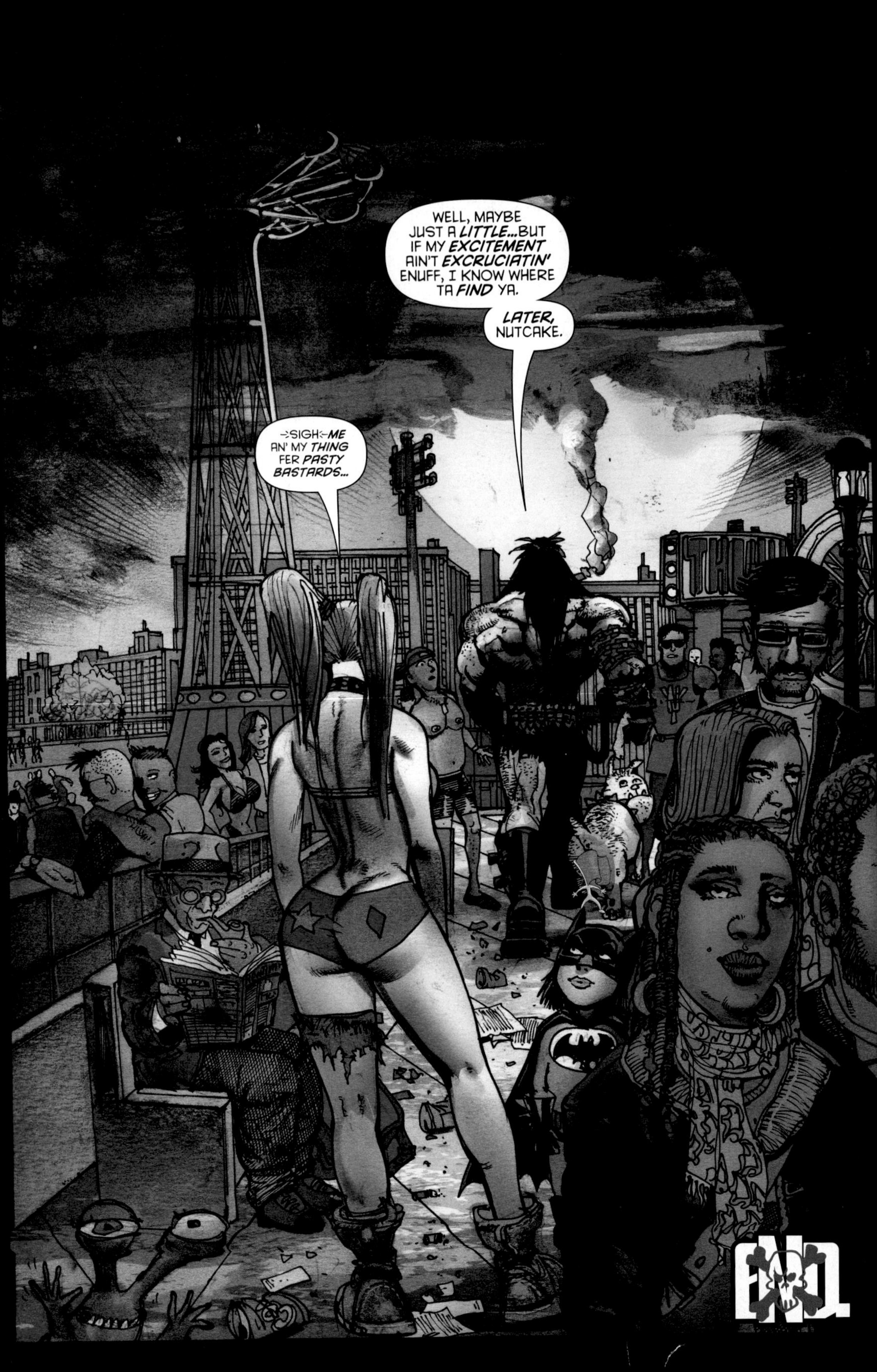
WELL, MAYBE JUST A LITTLE...BUT IF MY EXCITEMENT AIN'T EXCRUCIATIN' ENUFF, I KNOW WHERE TA FIND YA.
LATER, NUTCAKE.
-SIGH- ME AN' MY THING FER PASTY BASTARDS...
END

VARIANT COVER GALLERY

HARLEY'S LITTLE BLACK BOOK
polybag art by Amanda Conner

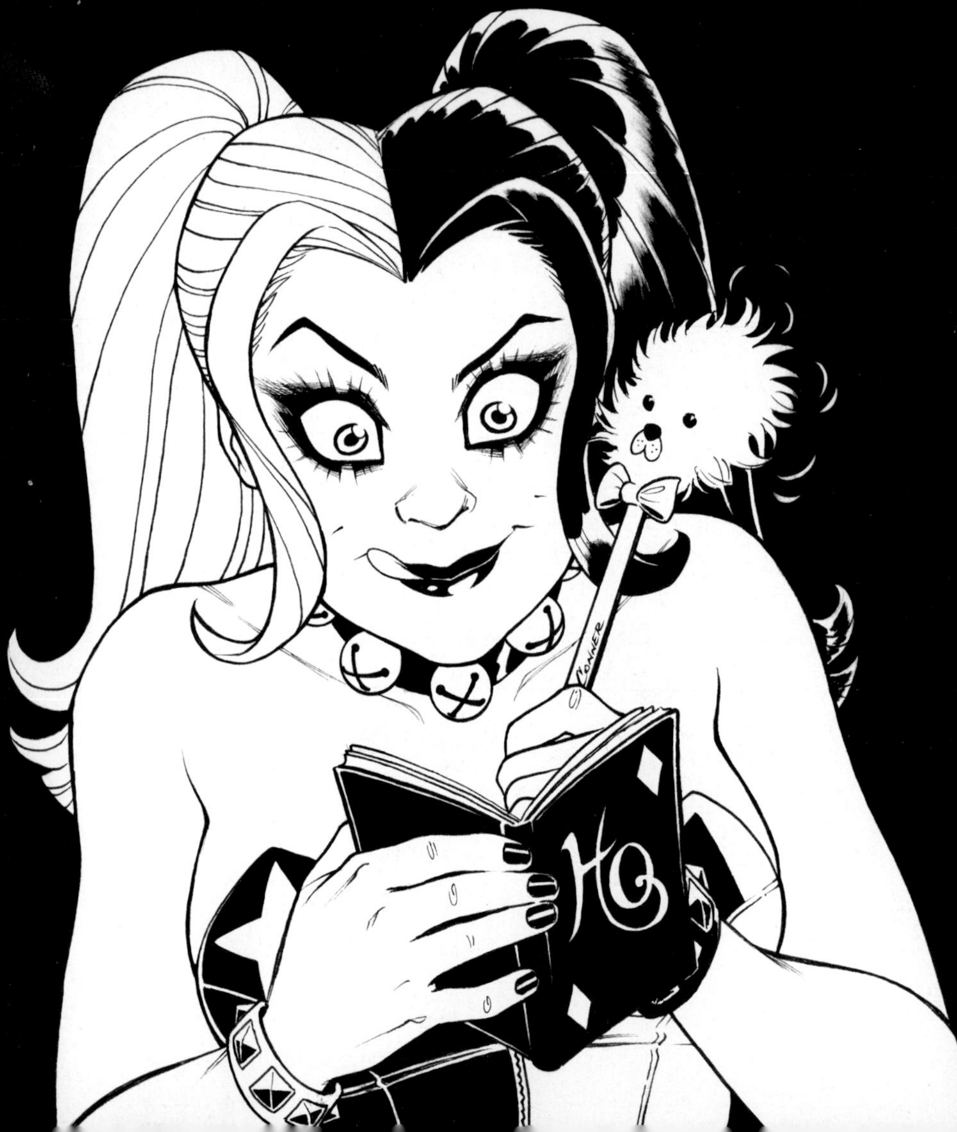

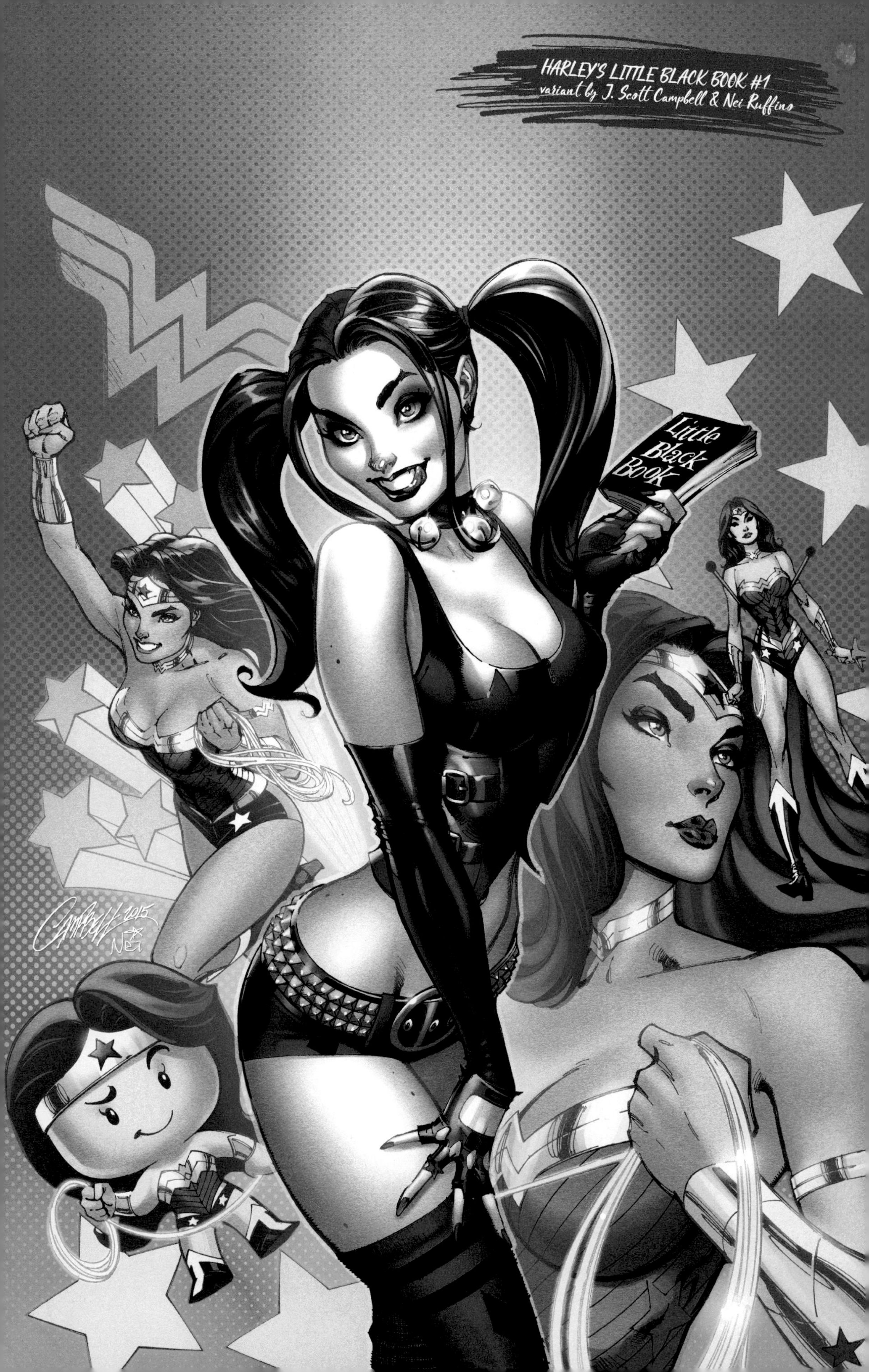
Little Black Book

HARLEY'S LITTLE BLACK BOOK #1
variant by J. Scott Campbell & Nei Ruffino

HARLEY'S LITTLE BLACK BOOK #1
ink variant by J. Scott Campbell

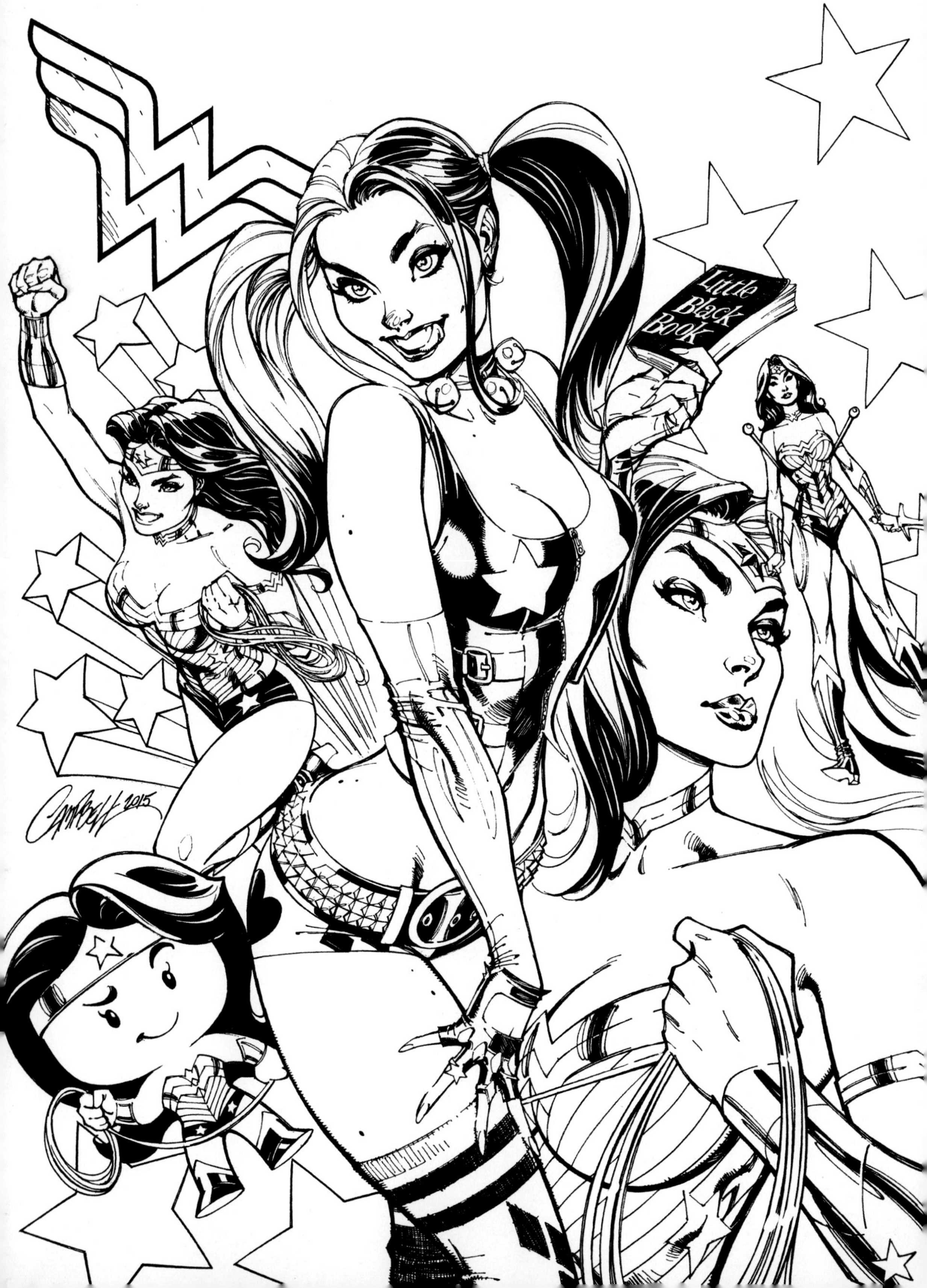

Little Black Book
Campbell 2015

HARLEY'S LITTLE BLACK BOOK #1
pencil variant by J. Scott Campbell

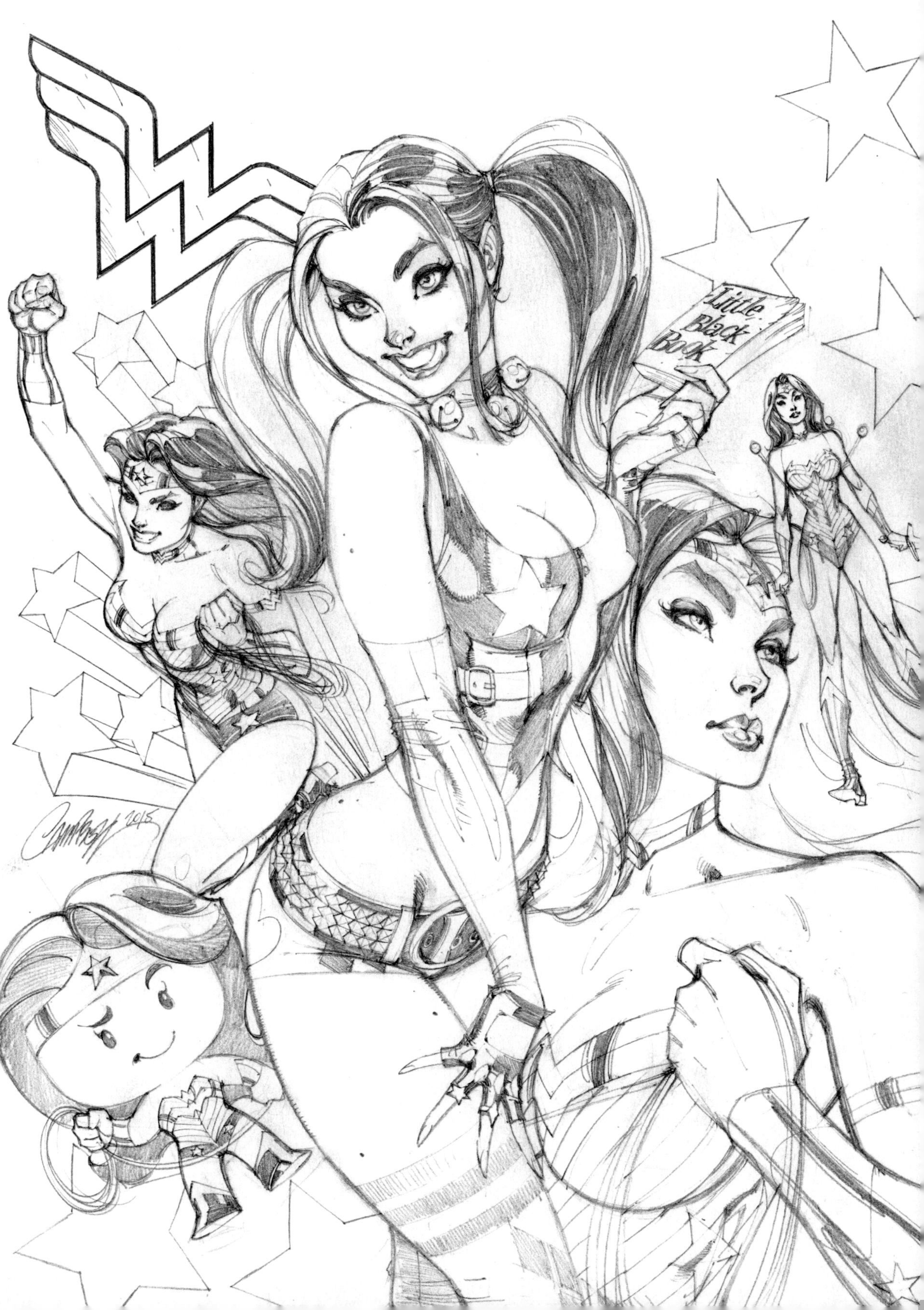
Little Black Book

HARLEY'S LITTLE BLACK BOOK #2
variant by John Timms

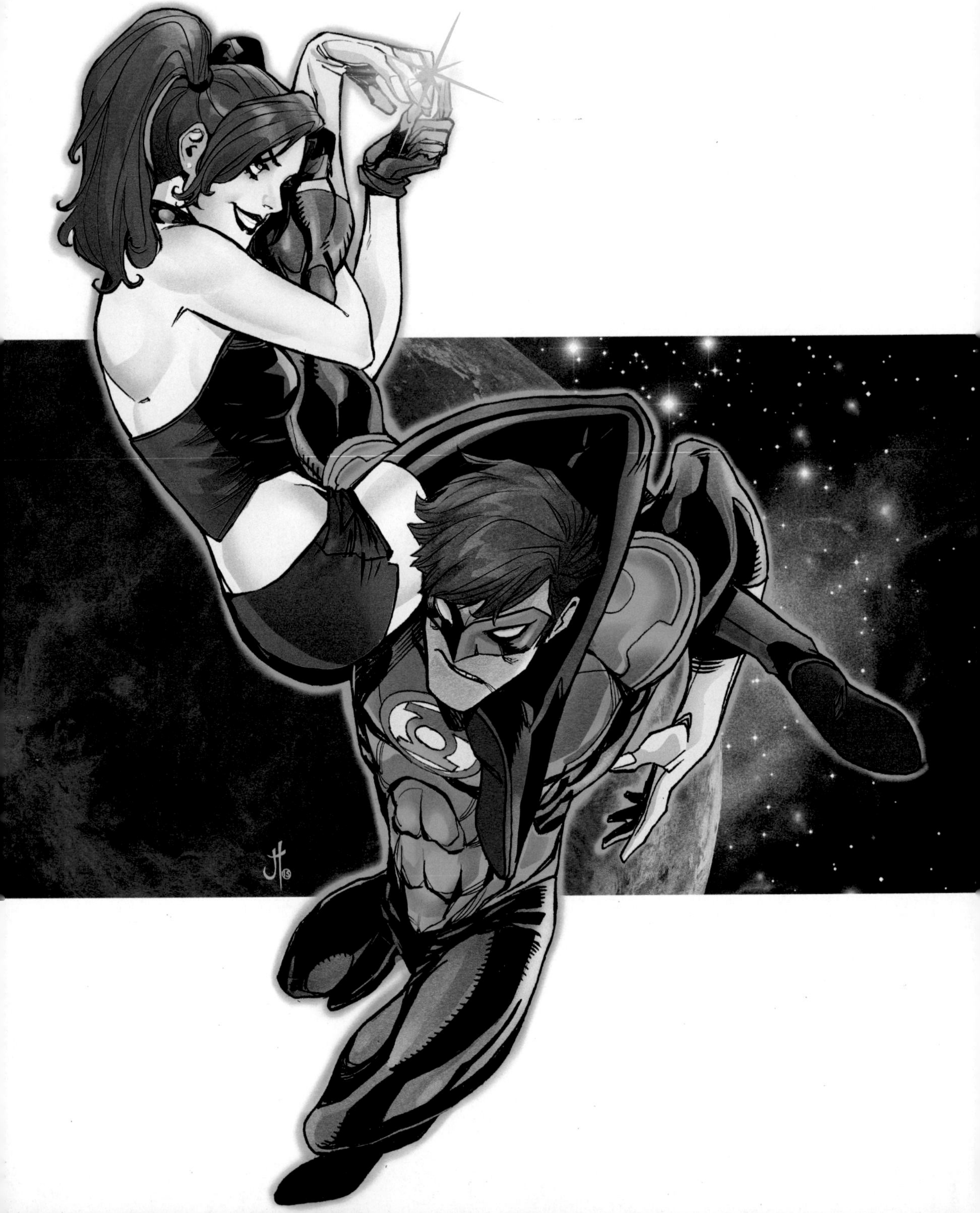

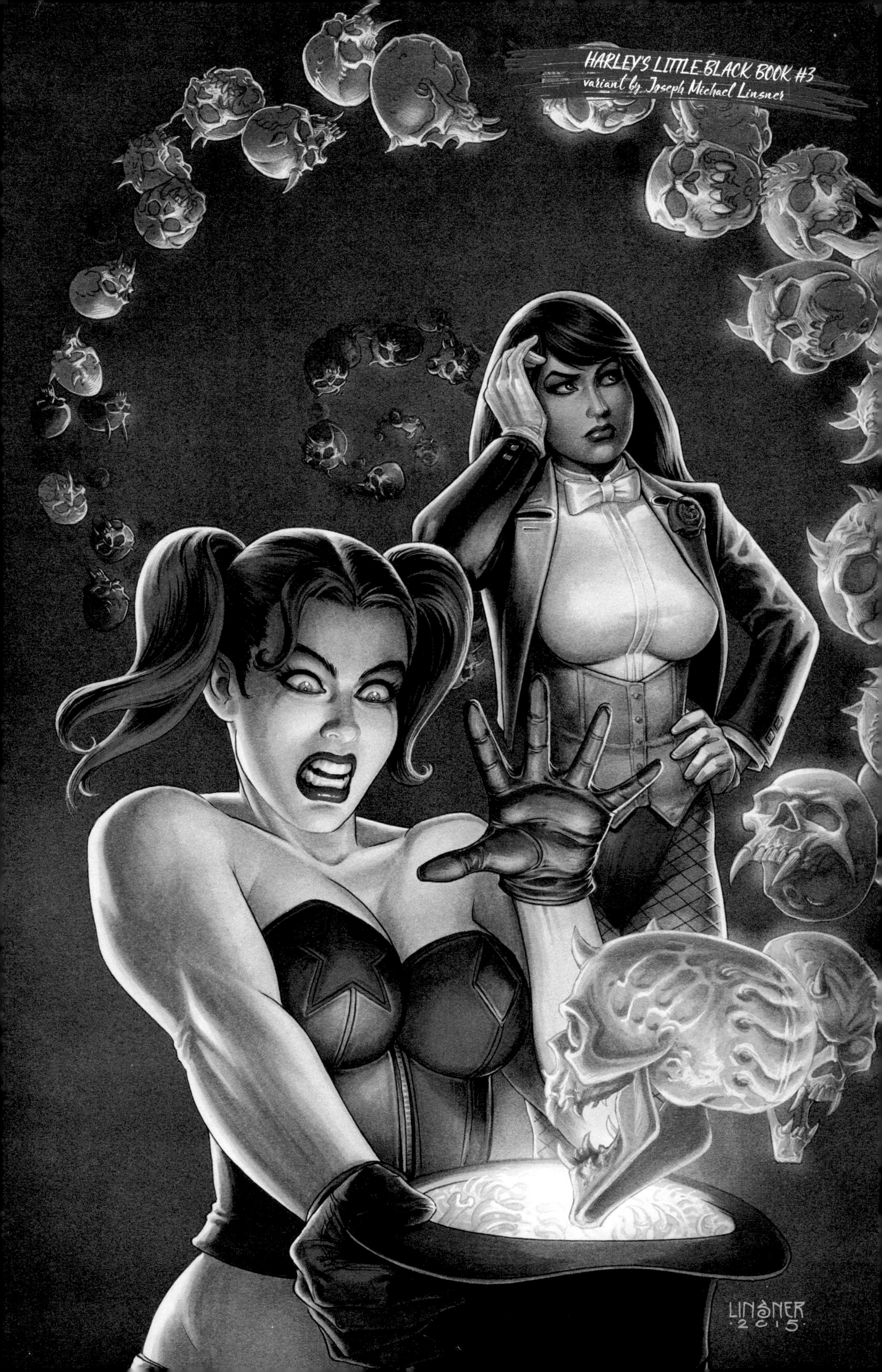

HARLEY'S LITTLE BLACK BOOK #3
variant by Joseph Michael Linsner

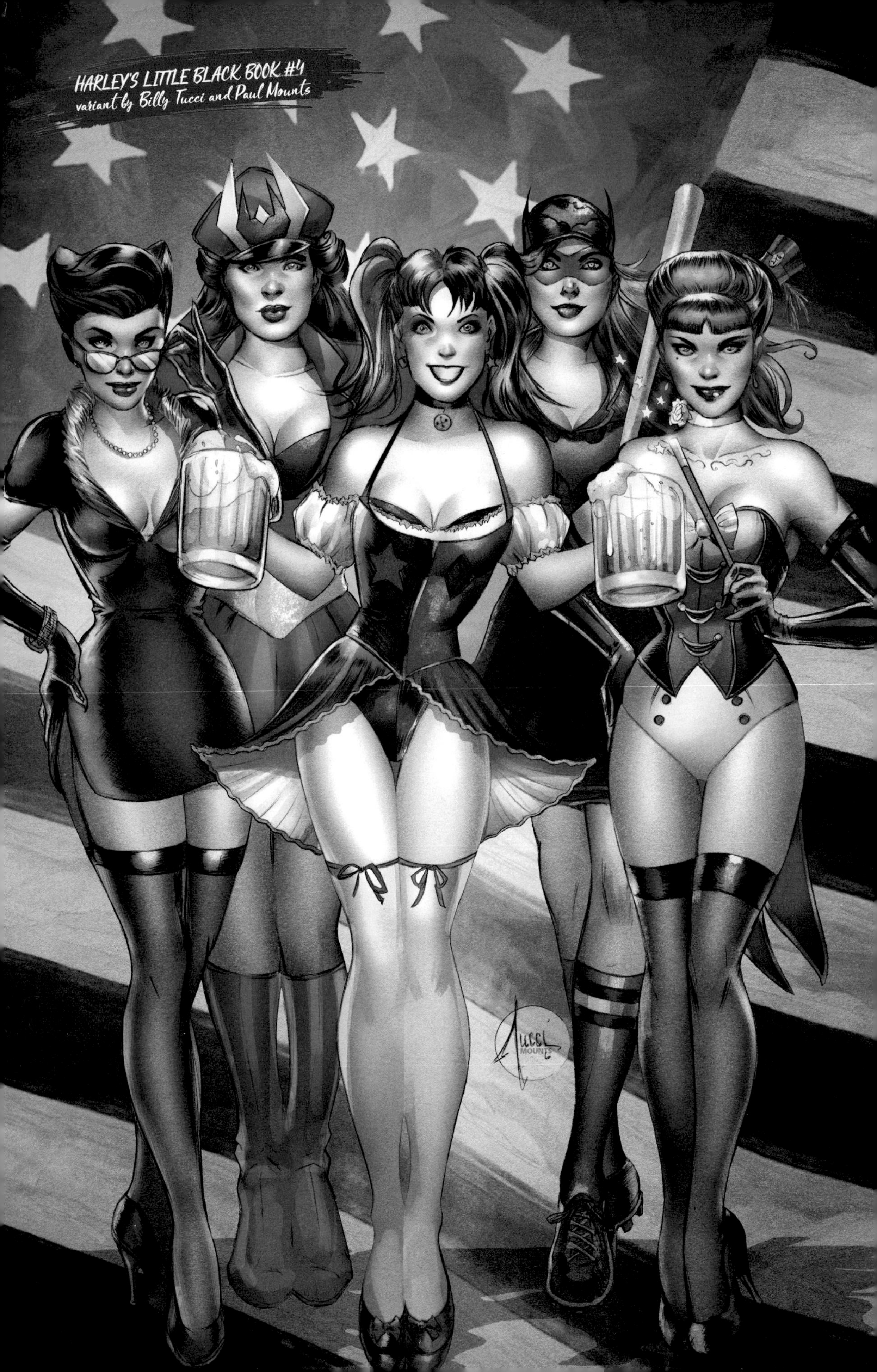

HARLEY'S LITTLE BLACK BOOK #4
variant by Billy Tucci and Paul Mounts

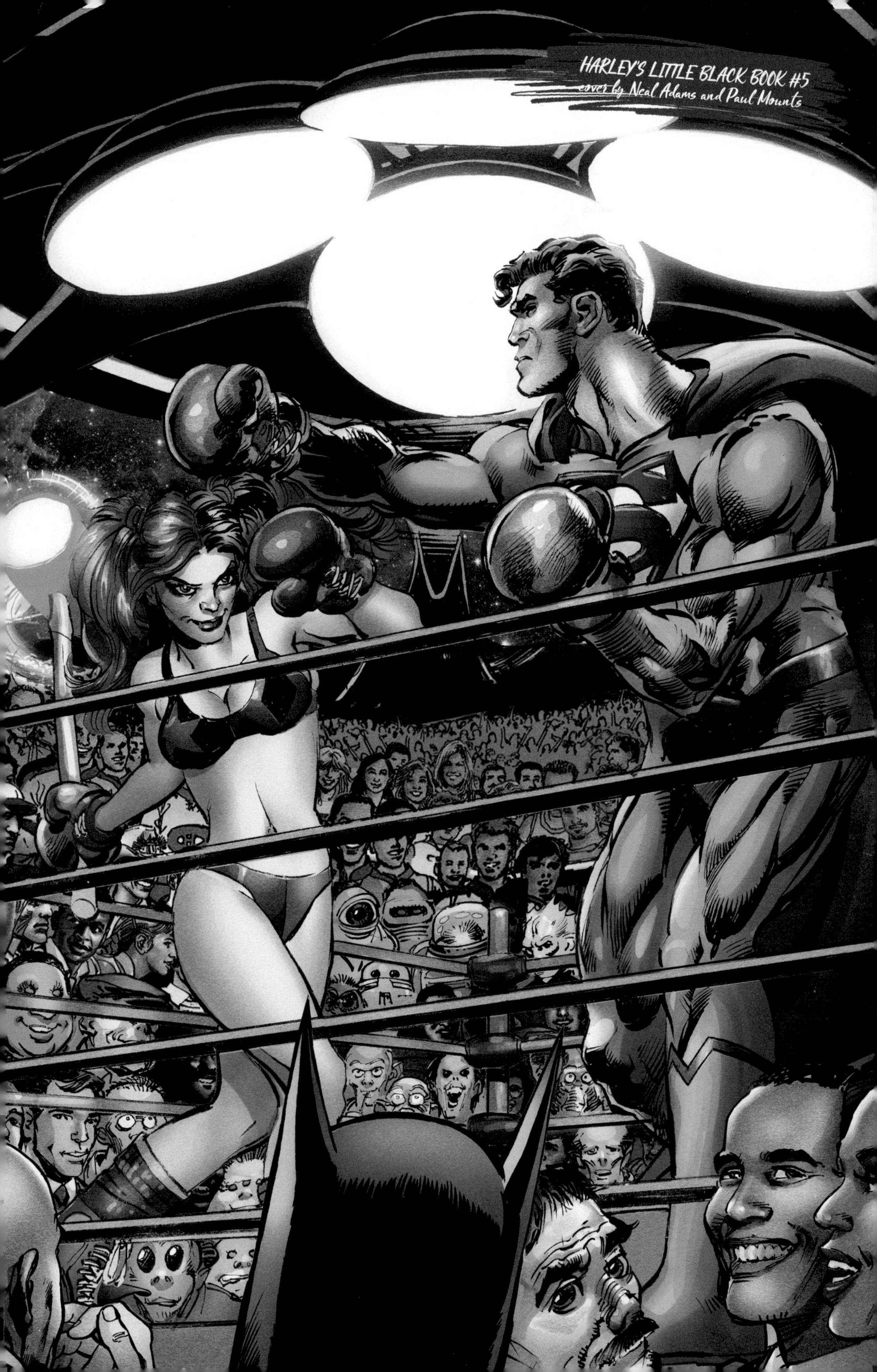
HARLEY'S LITTLE BLACK BOOK #5
cover by Neal Adams and Paul Mounts

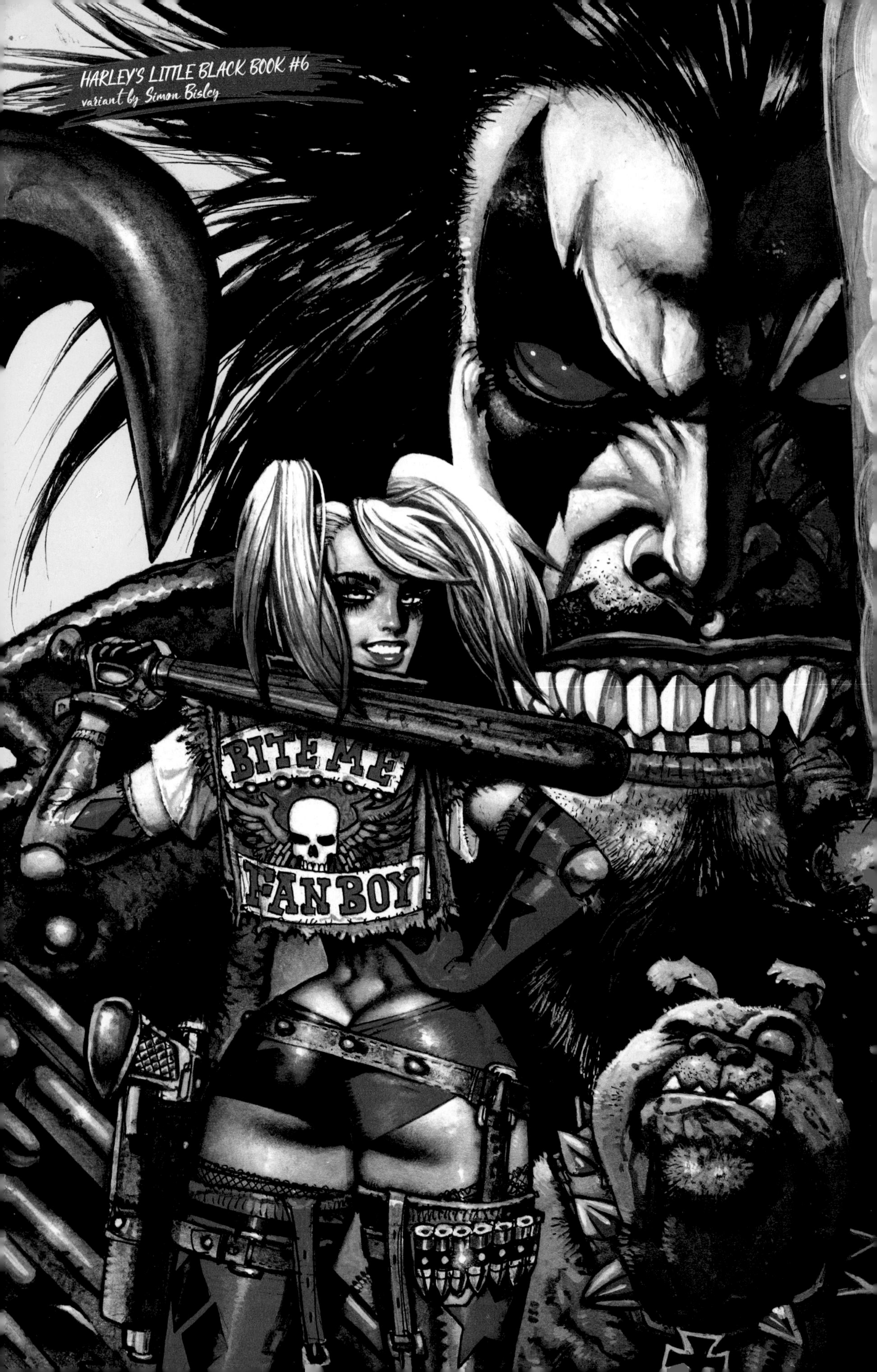
BITE ME
FANBOY
HARLEY'S LITTLE BLACK BOOK #6
variant by Simon Bisley

Amanda Conner's cover line art for

HARLEY'S LITTLE BLACK BOOK #1-6

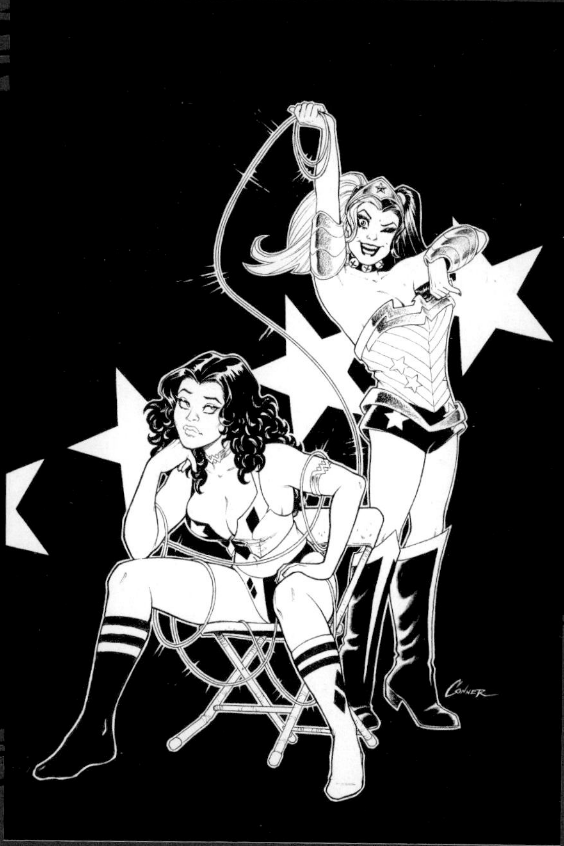
CONNER

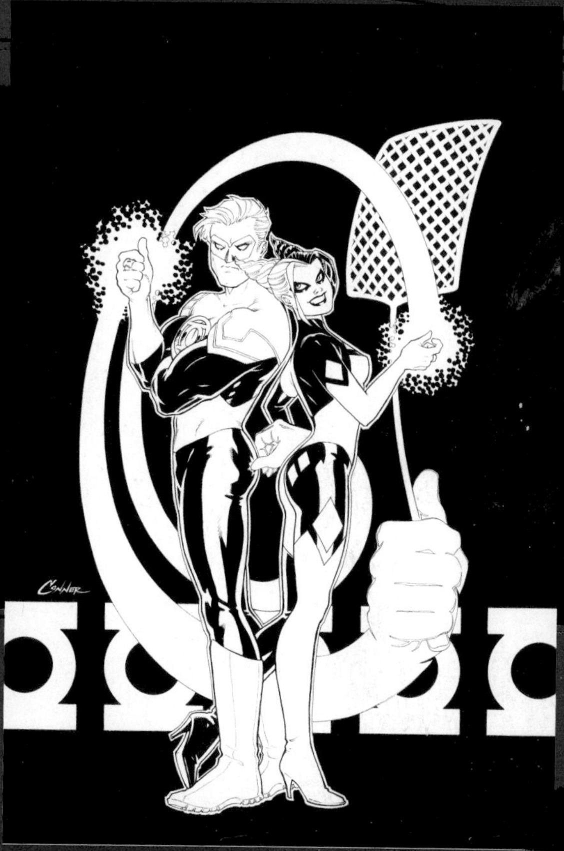
CONNER

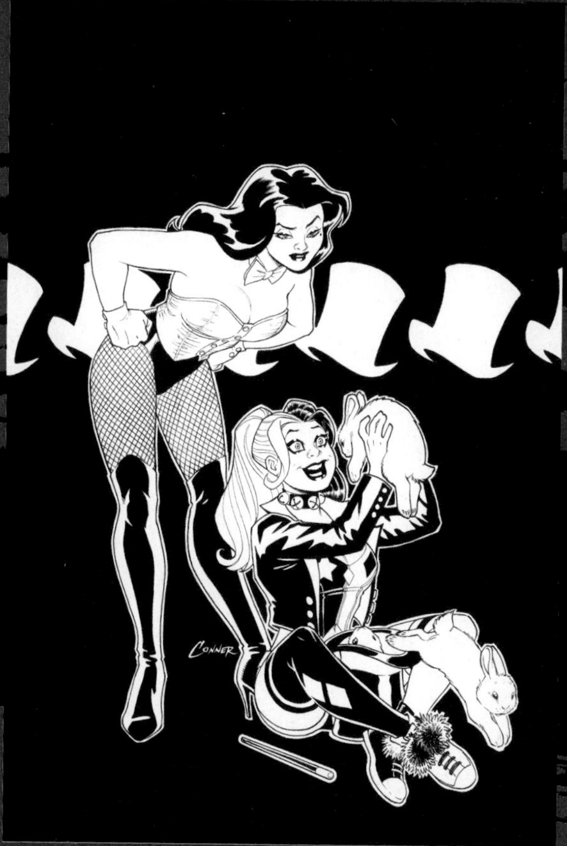
CONNER

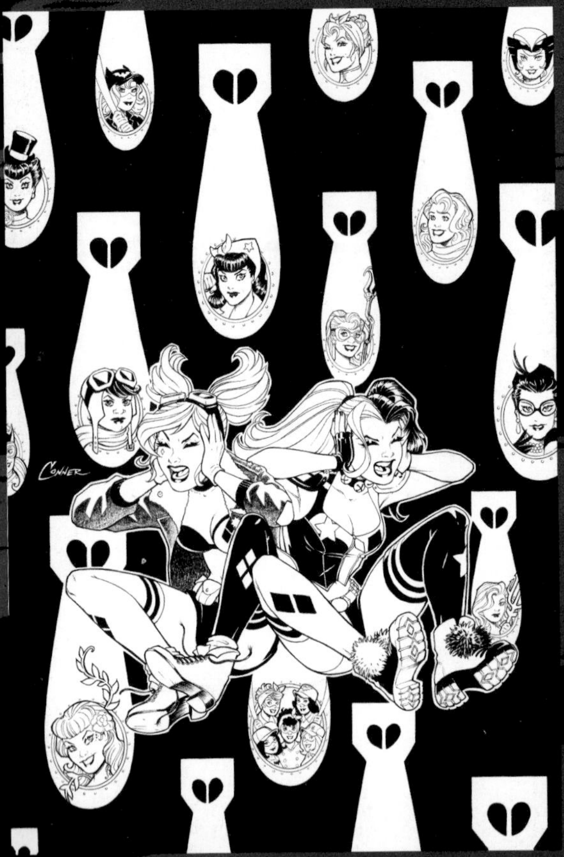
CONNER

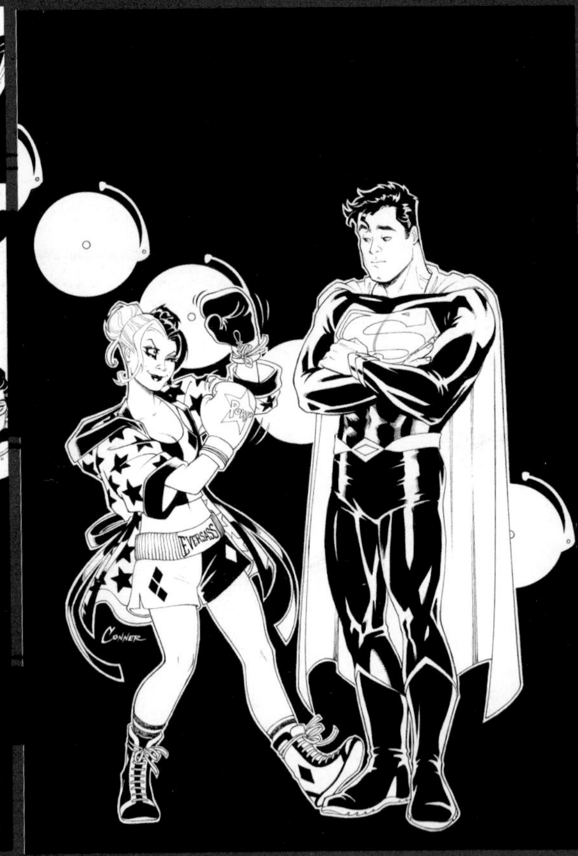
CONNER

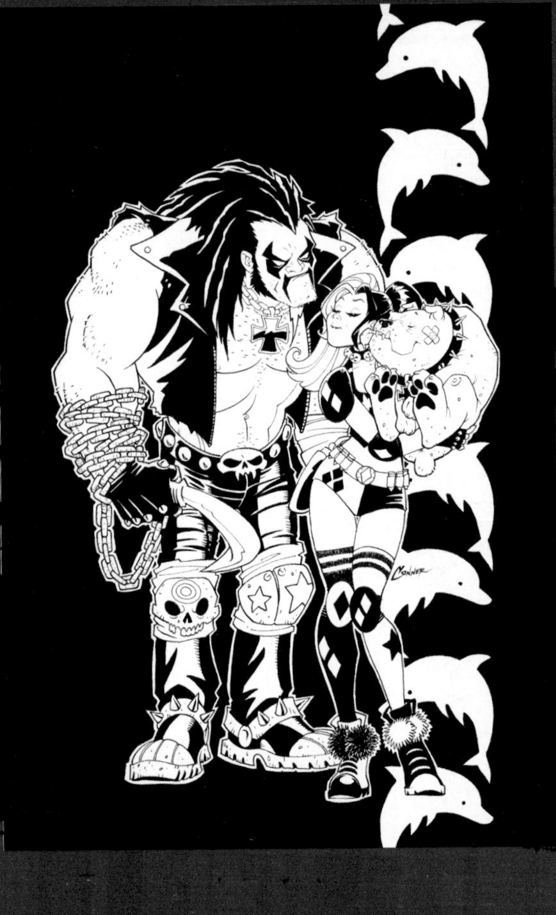
CONNER